WeightWatchers®
ONE POT
COOKBOOK

WeightWatchers®
ONE POT
COOKBOOK

WILEY

John Wiley & Sons, Inc.

Library of Congress Cataloging-in-Publication Data
Weight watchers one pot cookbook. -- 1st ed.
p. cm.
Includes index.
ISBN 978-1-118-03812-3 (hardback); ISBN 978-1-118-19853-7 (ebk); ISBN 978-1-118-19854-4 (ebk); ISBN 978-1-118-19855-1 (ebk)
1. Casserole cooking. 2. One-dish meals. 3. Quick and easy cooking. I. Weight Watchers International.
TX693.W45 2011
641.82'1--dc23
2011028956

Manufactured in China

10 9 8 7 6 5 4 3 2 1

About Weight Watchers

Weight Watchers International, Inc., is the world's leading provider of weight-management services, operating globally through a network of company-owned and franchise operations. Weight Watchers holds nearly 50,000 weekly meetings worldwide, at which members receive group support and education about healthful eating patterns, behavior modification, and physical activity. Weight-loss and weight-management results vary by individual. We recommend that you attend Weight Watchers meetings to benefit from the supportive environment you find there and follow the comprehensive Weight Watchers program, which includes a food plan, an activity plan, and a behavioral component. In addition, Weight Watchers offers a wide range of products, publications, and programs for people interested in weight loss and weight control. For the Weight Watchers meeting nearest you, call **1-800-651-6000** and visit us at our Web site, **WeightWatchers.com**. For information about bringing Weight Watchers to your workplace, call **1-800-8AT-WORK** and look for *Weight Watchers Magazine* at your newsstand or in your meeting room.

Weight Watchers Publishing Group

VP, Editorial Director Nancy Gagliardi

Creative Director Ed Melnitsky

Photo Director Deborah Hardt

Managing Editor Diane Davia

Food Editor Eileen Runyan

Editor Deborah Mintcheff

Nutrition Consultant Jacqueline Kroon

Photographer Con Poulos

Food Stylist Maggie Ruggiero

Prop Stylist Theo Vamvounakis

Wiley Publishing, Inc.

Publisher Natalie Chapman

Associate Publisher Jessica Goodman

Executive Editor Anne Ficklen

Editorial Assistant Heather Dabah

Production Manager Michael Olivo

Senior Production Editor Amy Zarkos

Interior and Cover Designer Hana Nakamura for Mucca Design

Manufacturing Manager Kevin Watt

**Succulent Braised Pork
Loin Asian-Style, page 132**

CONTENTS

About Our Recipes

While losing weight isn't only about what you eat, Weight Watchers realizes the critical role it plays in your success and overall good health. That's why our philosophy is to offer great-tasting, easy recipes that are nutritious as well as delicious. We make every attempt to use wholesome ingredients and to ensure that our recipes fall within the recommendations of the U.S. Dietary Guidelines for Americans for a diet that promotes health and reduces the risk for disease. In accordance with the guidelines, Weight Watchers encourages consuming fruits and vegetables and whole grains, choosing fat-free and low-fat dairy products, selecting lean meats, and limiting sodium, saturated fat, cholesterol, trans fats, added sugars, refined grains, and alcohol. If you have special dietary needs, consult with your health-care professional for advice on a diet that is best for you, then adapt these recipes to meet your specific nutritional needs.

To achieve these good-health goals and get the maximum satisfaction from the foods you eat, we suggest you keep the following information in mind while preparing our recipes:

The *PointsPlus*® program and Good Nutrition

• Recipes in this book have been developed for Weight Watchers members who are following the *PointsPlus* program. *PointsPlus* values are given for each recipe. They're assigned based on the amount of protein (grams), carbohydrates (grams), fat (grams), and fiber (grams) contained in a single serving of a recipe.

• Recipes include approximate nutritional information; they are analyzed for Calories (Cal), Total Fat, Saturated Fat (Sat Fat), Trans Fat, Cholesterol (Chol), Sodium (Sod), Carbohydrates (Carb), Sugar, Dietary Fiber (Fib), Protein (Prot), and Calcium (Calc). The nutritional values are calculated by dietitians, using nutrition analysis software.

• Substitutions made to the ingredients will alter the per-serving nutritional information and may affect the *PointsPlus* value.

• Our recipes meet Weight Watchers Good Health Guidelines for eating lean proteins and fiber-rich whole grains, and having at least five servings of vegetables and fruits and two servings of low-fat or fat-free dairy products a day, while limiting your intake of saturated fat, sugar, and sodium.

• Health agencies recommend limiting sodium intake. To stay in line with this recommendation we keep sodium levels in our recipes reasonably low; to boost flavor, we often include fresh herbs or a squeeze of citrus instead of salt. If you don't have to restrict your sodium, feel free to add a touch more salt as desired.

• Healthy Extra suggestions have a *PointsPlus* value of 0 unless otherwise stated.

• (20 min) indicates recipes that can be made in 20 minutes or less from start to finish.

For information about the science behind lasting weight loss and more, please visit **WeightWatchers. com/science**.

PointsPlus® value Not What You Expected?

• You might expect some of the *PointsPlus* values in this book to be lower when some of the foods they're made from, such as fruits and vegetables, have no *PointsPlus* values. All fruits and most veggies have no *PointsPlus* values when served as a snack or part of a meal, like a cup of berries with a sandwich. But if these foods are part of a recipe, their fiber and nutrient content are incorporated into the recipe calculations. These nutrients can affect the *PointsPlus* values.

• Alcohol is included in our *PointsPlus* calculations. Because alcohol information is generally not included on nutrition labels, it's not an option to include when using the hand calculator or the online calculator. But since we include alcohol information that we get from our nutritionists you might notice discrepancies between the *PointsPlus* values you see in our recipes, and the values you get using the calculator. The *PointsPlus* values listed for our recipes are the most accurate values.

Shopping for Ingredients

As you learn to eat healthier and add more Power Foods to your meals, remember these tips for choosing foods wisely:

Lean Meats and Poultry Purchase lean meats and poultry, and trim them of all visible fat before cooking. When poultry is cooked with the skin on, we recommend removing the skin before eating. Nutritional information for recipes that include meat, poultry, and fish is based on cooked, skinless boneless portions (unless otherwise stated), with the fat trimmed.

Seafood Whenever possible, our recipes call for seafood that is sustainable and deemed the most healthful for human consumption so that your choice of seafood is not only good for the oceans but also good for you. For more information about the best seafood choices and to download a pocket guide, go to **environmentaldefensefund.org** or **montereybayaquarium.org**. For information about mercury and seafood go to **weightwatchers.com**.

Produce For best flavor, maximum nutrient content, and the lowest prices, buy fresh, local produce, such as vegetables, leafy greens, and fruits in season. Rinse them thoroughly before using and keep a supply of cut-up vegetables and fruits in your refrigerator for convenient, healthy snacks.

Whole Grains Explore your market for whole grain products such as whole wheat and whole grain breads and pastas, brown rice, bulgur, barley, cornmeal, whole wheat couscous, oats, and quinoa to enjoy with your meals.

Preparation and Measuring

Read the Recipe Take a couple of minutes to read through the ingredients and directions before you start to prepare a recipe. This will prevent you from discovering midway through that you don't have an important ingredient or that a recipe requires several hours of marinating. And it's also a good idea to assemble all ingredients and utensils within easy reach before you begin a recipe.

Weighing and Measuring The success of any recipe depends on accurate weighing and measuring. The effectiveness of the Weight Watchers program and the accuracy of the nutritional analysis depend on correct measuring as well. Use the following techniques:

• Weigh food such as meat, poultry, and fish on a food scale.

• To measure liquids, use a standard glass or plastic measuring cup placed on a level surface. For amounts less than ¼ cup, use standard measuring spoons.

• To measure dry ingredients, use metal or plastic measuring cups that come in ¼-, ⅓-, ½-, and 1-cup sizes. Fill the appropriate cup and level it with the flat edge of a knife or spatula. For amounts less than ¼ cup, use standard measuring spoons.

IN A
BOWL

CHAPTER 1

IN A BOWL

TOSS-IT-TOGETHER SALADS & SANDWICHES

Bowls are one of the most basic—and frequently used—pieces of kitchen equipment. They are good for tossing, mixing, stirring, whisking, blending, folding, and beating. A flat bottom keeps them steady, while their round shape makes it easy to thoroughly combine ingredients. Most mixing bowls are made of stainless steel or glass, although some are made of melamine (a hard plastic), enamel-coated steel, or earthenware.

Types

Stainless Steel Mixing Bowls—A good-quality set of stainless steel mixing bowls will last a lifetime. A set of three to five nesting bowls ranging in size from about 1 quart to 5 quarts will handle most cooking needs. The best bowls are heavy-gauge steel and have a brushed satin finish so scratches don't show. Some bowls come with nonskid bottoms so they stay put during mixing, while a plastic exterior protects your hands if the bowls are very hot or very cold. Stainless steel bowls can be washed by hand with hot, soapy water and a sponge or nylon scrub soap pad or in the dishwasher.

Glass Mixing Bowls—There are also chip- and break-resistant glass bowls that come in nesting sets of nine or more bowls, ranging in size from about ¼ cup to 6 quarts. The glass is tempered, so the bowls can be set over simmering water—especially handy for melting chocolate. They are also microwave- and freezer-safe. Glass bowls can be washed by hand with hot, soapy water and a sponge or nylon scrub pad or in the dishwasher.

Enamel-Coated Steel Mixing Bowls—These bowls come in graduated sets of three or more. They often come in inviting colors, making them decorative as well as useful. These bowls can be washed by hand with hot, soapy water and a sponge or nylon scrub pad or in the dishwasher.

Useful Extra—It is often necessary to cover a bowl to keep food fresh. This can be done using plastic wrap or foil but there is another alternative: reusable, graduated-size bowl covers that resemble shower caps and come in packages of about 50.

Roast Beef Salad with Red Onion, Mâche & Blue Cheese

5
PointsPlus®
value
PER SERVING

serves
4

2 tablespoons red wine vinegar

1 tablespoon extra-virgin olive oil

1 garlic clove mashed to paste with ¼ teaspoon salt

¾ teaspoon Dijon mustard

¼ teaspoon black pepper

½ pound (¼-inch) slices lean sirloin roast beef, trimmed and cut into thin strips

5 cups lightly packed mâche and/or other baby lettuce

1 cup halved cooked small beets

1 small red onion, thinly sliced

2 tablespoons crumbled blue cheese

1   To make dressing, whisk together vinegar, oil, garlic paste, mustard, and pepper in large bowl.

2   Add roast beef, mâche, tomatoes, onion, and parsley to dressing; toss until mixed well. Serve sprinkled with blue cheese.

PER SERVING (1½ cups salad and ½ tablespoon cheese): 192 Cal, 9 g Total Fat, 3 g Sat Fat, 0 g Trans Fat, 62 mg Chol, 269 mg Sod, 5 g Carb, 2 g Sugar, 1 g Fib, 21 g Prot, 57 mg Calc

FYI   Mâche, also known as corn salad, lamb's lettuce, field salad, and nut lettuce, has been cultivated since the 16th century. It is comprised of very tender, spoon-shaped leaves that grow in clusters. When purchasing mâche, look for bright green leaves without any yellowing or wilting. Store it in a plastic bag in the crisper drawer of the refrigerator for up to 2 days.

Spicy Beef Salad with Chipotle-Lime Dressing

 serves **4** | **20** min

PER SERVING

1 tablespoon lime juice

½ teaspoon minced chipotles en adobo

1 teaspoon ground cumin

¼ teaspoon salt

⅛ teaspoon black pepper

1½ cups fresh corn kernels (about 3 ears of corn)

1 large tomato, seeded and cut into ½-inch dice

1 Hass avocado, halved pitted, peeled, and cut into ½-inch dice

½ cup lightly packed fresh cilantro leaves

1 pound thinly sliced lean sirloin roast beef, trimmed

1 To make dressing, whisk together lime juice, chipotles en adobo, cumin, salt, and pepper in large bowl.

2 Add all ingredients except roast beef to dressing; toss until mixed well. Divide slices of roast beef evenly among 4 plates; top evenly with corn mixture.

PER SERVING (1 salad): 326 Cal, 13 g Total Fat, 3 g Sat Fat, 0 g Trans Fat, 66 mg Chol, 239 mg Sod, 16 g Carb, 3 g Sugar, 5 g Fib, 38 g Prot, 38 mg Calc.

FYI Here's how to remove the kernels from corn on the cob: Strip off the husk and remove the silk. Stand an ear of corn on a cutting board. With a long serrated knife, cut down along the cob to cut off the kernels as close to the cob as possible. Repeat until all the kernels are removed.

Roast Beef Salad with Grapefruit, Basil & Shallots

 serves **4** | **20** min

PER SERVING

2 teaspoons red wine vinegar

2 teaspoons extra-virgin olive oil

2 teaspoons coarse-grained Dijon mustard

⅛ teaspoon black pepper

1 pound (¼-inch) slices lean sirloin roast beef, trimmed and cut into thin strips

2 small pink grapefruit, peeled and sectioned

1 shallot, minced

8 fresh basil leaves, thinly sliced

8 small butter lettuce leaves

1 To make dressing, whisk together vinegar, oil, mustard, and pepper in large bowl.

2 Add all remaining ingredients except lettuce to dressing; toss until mixed well. Place 2 lettuce leaves on each of 4 plates; place equal amount of beef salad on each lettuce leaf.

PER SERVING (2 filled lettuce leaves): 270 Cal, 9 g Total Fat, 3 g Sat Fat, 0 g Trans Fat, 66 mg Chol, 134 mg Sod, 10 g Carb, 7 g Sugar, 1 g Fib, 36 g Prot, 43 mg Calc.

Healthy Extra Thinly sliced fennel would lend a tempting licorice note to this unusual salad. Cut off the top of a small fennel bulb and trim the root end. Cut the fennel lengthwise in half, then slice crosswise as thinly as possible—use a vegetable slicer for the best results—and add to the salad in step 2.

Creamy Chicken & Cantaloupe Salad

6 PointsPlus value — serves 4 — 20 min
PER SERVING

2 cups (¾-inch) diced cooked skinless chicken breast

1 small cantaloupe, peeled, halved, seeded, and cut into ¾-inch pieces (about 2 cups)

1 cup seedless green grapes, halved

1 cup diced celery

½ cup chopped red onion

2 tablespoons chopped fresh basil

½ cup fat-free mayonnaise

¼ teaspoon salt

¼ teaspoon black pepper

12 small romaine lettuce leaves

Toss together all ingredients except romaine in large bowl. Place 3 lettuce leaves on each of 4 plates; top each serving with about 1½ cups of chicken salad.

PER SERVING (1 salad): 222 Cal, 4 g Total Fat, 1 g Sat Fat, 0 g Trans Fat, 62 mg Chol, 492 mg Sod, 24 g Carb, 19 g Sugar, 3 g Fib, 24 g Prot, 50 mg Calc.

Healthy Extra   Serve with reduced-calorie bread topped with sliced fat-free cheese. Two slices of reduced-calorie bread sandwiched with 1 (¾-ounce) slice of fat-free Cheddar cheese per serving will increase the *PointsPlus* value by 4.

All-Tossed-Together Cobb Salad

7 PointsPlus value — serves 4 — 20 min
PER SERVING

2 tablespoons red wine vinegar

1 tablespoon extra-virgin olive oil

¼ teaspoon salt

⅛ teaspoon black pepper

1 small head romaine lettuce, thinly sliced

2 cups shredded cooked skinless chicken breast

1 large tomato, seeded and chopped

1 small Hass avocado, halved, pitted, peeled, and cut into ½-inch dice

2 scallions, thinly sliced

2 hard-cooked large egg whites, chopped

¼ cup crumbled reduced-fat blue cheese

2 tablespoons chopped fresh flat-leaf parsley

1   To make dressing, whisk together vinegar, oil, salt, and pepper in serving bowl.

2   Add all ingredients except blue cheese and parsley to dressing; toss until mixed well. Serve sprinkled with cheese and parsley.

PER SERVING (2 cups): 260 Cal, 13 g Total Fat, 3 g Sat Fat, 0 g Trans Fat, 62 mg Chol, 277 mg Sod, 11 g Carb, 3 g Sugar, 6 g Fib, 28 g Prot, 106 mg Calc.

FYI   One night in 1937 at Hollywood's Brown Derby restaurant, owner Bob Cobb was looking for a snack. He found a head of lettuce, an avocado, watercress, tomatoes, cooked chicken breast, hard-cooked egg, and cheese. He chopped it up, added some crispy bacon, and served it with French dressing. It was so good that Sid Grauman of Grauman's Chinese Theatre, who was with Bob at the time, returned the next day and asked for a Cobb Salad.

Mexican Gazpacho Chicken Salad

Mexican Gazpacho Chicken Salad

serves
6

20
min

PointsPlus value
7
PER SERVING

Grated zest and juice of 1 lime

1 large garlic clove, minced

1 tablespoon extra-virgin olive oil

¾ teaspoon salt

¼ teaspoon black pepper

2 pounds tomatoes, coarsely chopped

6 tomatillos, husked, rinsed, and chopped

1 large red bell pepper, cut into ½-inch dice

½ English (seedless) cucumber, cut into ½-inch dice

¼ red onion, sliced

1 jalapeño pepper, seeded and minced

3 cups sliced cooked skinless chicken breast

3 tablespoons chopped fresh cilantro

1   To make dressing, whisk together lime zest and juice, garlic, oil, salt, and black pepper in large bowl.

2   Add all remaining ingredients except chicken and cilantro to dressing; toss until mixed well. Divide vegetable mixture evenly among 6 plates or large shallow bowls. Top each serving with ½ cup of chicken; sprinkle with cilantro.

PER SERVING (1 salad): 286 Cal, 8 g Total Fat, 2 g Sat Fat, 0 g Trans Fat, 89 mg Chol, 529 mg Sod, 18 g Carb, 11 g Sugar, 6 g Fib, 36 g Prot, 62 mg Calc.

FYI   The easiest way to husk a tomatillo is to hold it under cool running water while peeling off the husk. Be sure to rub the outside of the tomatillo until any residual stickiness is washed away.

BBQ-Sauced Turkey & Slaw Salad

 serves 4 | 20 min

PER SERVING

3 tablespoons lime juice

1 tablespoon Asian (dark) sesame oil

2 teaspoons honey

½ teaspoon salt

1 (14-ounce) bag coleslaw mix

½ red bell pepper, chopped

3 scallions, cut on diagonal into thin slices

1 jalapeño pepper, seeded and minced

1 (1-pound) piece cooked skinless turkey breast, cut into strips

3 tablespoons barbecue sauce, warmed

¼ cup lightly packed fresh cilantro leaves, torn

1 To make dressing, whisk together lime juice, oil, honey, and salt in large bowl. Add coleslaw mix, bell pepper, scallions, and jalapeño; toss to coat evenly.

2 Combine turkey and barbecue sauce in large zip-close plastic bag. Press out air and seal bag; shake bag to coat turkey. Divide slaw evenly among 4 plates and top evenly with turkey; sprinkle with cilantro.

PER SERVING (about 1½ cups slaw and ½ cup turkey): 248 Cal, 5 g Total Fat, 1 g Sat Fat, 0 g Trans Fat, 94 mg Chol, 483 mg Sod, 15 g Carb, 7 g Sugar, 3 g Fib, 36 g Prot, 72 mg Calc.

FYI The coleslaw can be prepared up to 4 hours ahead and refrigerated, keeping in mind that the longer the slaw sits, the softer it will become. You can also make the slaw and dressing, then store them separately until ready to serve.

Tex-Mex Turkey Salad with Cilantro-Lime Dressing

 serves 4 | 20 min

PER SERVING

3 tablespoons lime juice

2 tablespoons taco sauce

1 tablespoon olive oil

1 teaspoon ground cumin

1 teaspoon chili powder

½ teaspoon salt

4 cups lightly packed baby romaine lettuce

1 large tomato, cut into small dice

½ red onion, thinly sliced

¼ cup canned chopped mild green chiles, drained

½ cup chopped fresh cilantro

1 pound thinly sliced cooked skinless turkey breast

1 To make dressing, whisk together lime juice, taco sauce, oil, cumin, chili powder, and salt in serving bowl.

2 Add romaine, tomato, onion, chiles, and cilantro to dressing; toss until mixed well. Divide turkey evenly among 4 plates; top evenly with salad.

PER SERVING (1 salad): 218 Cal, 5 g Total Fat, 1 g Sat Fat, 0 g Trans Fat, 94 mg Chol, 422 mg Sod, 7 g Carb, 3 g Sugar, 2 g Fib, 35 g Prot, 47 mg Calc.

FYI If you like, a fresh jalapeño pepper, seeded and minced, can be substituted for the canned chiles.

Apple, Endive & Smoked Turkey Salad

serves **4** | **20** min

PER SERVING

2 tablespoons champagne vinegar

1 tablespoon olive oil

2 shallots, minced

2 teaspoons Dijon mustard

¼ teaspoon black pepper

1 Gala or Braeburn apple, unpeeled, cored, and thinly sliced

2 heads Belgian endive, thinly sliced lengthwise

1 bunch watercress, trimmed

1 (¾-pound) piece skinless smoked turkey breast, cut into ¼-inch strips

To make dressing, whisk together vinegar, oil, shallots, mustard, and pepper in serving bowl. Add all remaining ingredients; toss until mixed well.

PER SERVING (1 salad): 212 Cal, 7 g Total Fat, 1 g Sat Fat, 0 g Trans Fat, 39 mg Chol, 882 mg Sod, 23 g Carb, 8 g Sugar, 9 g Fib, 21 g Prot, 210 mg Calc.

FYI You can use just about any favorite apple in this tasty salad, including Golden Delicious, Granny Smith, and Red Delicious.

Turkey Salad with Chutney, Cashews & Cranberries

serves **4** | **20** min

PER SERVING

¼ cup reduced-fat mayonnaise

¼ cup plain fat-free yogurt

2 tablespoons mango chutney

1 tablespoon curry powder, preferably Madras

¼ teaspoon black pepper

2 cups diced cooked skinless turkey breast

1 mango, peeled, pitted, and diced

2 celery stalks, thinly sliced

4 scallions, thinly sliced

4 cups lightly packed mixed baby salad greens

4 tablespoons unsalted cashews, chopped

4 tablespoons dried cranberries

1 To make dressing, whisk together mayonnaise, yogurt, chutney, curry powder, and pepper in large bowl. Add turkey, mango, celery, and scallions; toss until mixed well.

2 Line 4 plates evenly with salad greens. Top evenly with turkey mixture and sprinkle each with 1 tablespoon cashews and 1 tablespoon cranberries.

PER SERVING (1 salad): 371 Cal, 12 g Total Fat, 2 g Sat Fat, 0 g Trans Fat, 94 mg Chol, 295 mg Sod, 30 g Carb, 17 g Sugar, 4 g Fib, 39 g Prot, 85 mg Calc.

Healthy Extra Use 4 celery stalks instead of 2.

Dilled Salmon Salad with Lemon-Buttermilk Dressing

PER SERVING

serves
4

20
min

¾ cup low-fat buttermilk

2 scallions, finely chopped

Grated zest and juice of 1 lemon

2 teaspoons Dijon mustard

¼ teaspoon black pepper

1 (7½-ounce) can no-salt-added salmon, drained

1 (1-pound) package cooked diced potatoes

1 large zucchini, quartered lengthwise and sliced

½ red onion, thinly sliced

¼ cup chopped fresh dill

2 bunches arugula, trimmed

2 tomatoes, cut into wedges

12 Kalamata olives

1 To make dressing, whisk together buttermilk, scallions, lemon zest and juice, mustard, and pepper in large bowl.

2 Flake salmon into same bowl. Add potatoes, zucchini, onion, and dill; gently toss until mixed well.

3 Divide arugula evenly among 4 plates; top evenly with salmon mixture. Place one-fourth of tomato wedges and 3 olives on each plate.

PER SERVING (1 salad): 303 Cal, 8 g Total Fat, 2 g Sat Fat, 0 g Trans Fat, 25 mg Chol, 533 mg Sod, 39 g Carb, 10 g Sugar, 6 g Fib, 21 g Prot, 399 mg Calc.

FYI To store any leftover dill sprigs, place them in a glass filled with 1 inch of water, then loosely cover the glass with a plastic bag. Refrigerated, the dill will keep for about 5 days. Be sure to change the water every 2 days.

**Dilled Salmon Salad with
Lemon-Buttermilk Dressing**

Halibut Seviche with Corn & Avocado

9 PointsPlus value
PER SERVING

serves 4

1 pound halibut, cut into ¼- to ½-inch dice

½ cup lime juice, or more if needed

2 tomatoes, cut into ¼-inch dice

1 Hass avocado, halved, pitted, peeled, and diced

1½ cups thawed frozen or fresh corn kernels (about 3 ears of corn)

¼ small red onion, finely chopped

¼ cup chopped fresh cilantro

1 jalapeño pepper, seeded and minced

½ teaspoon salt

4 cups lightly packed mixed baby salad greens

2 ounces low-fat tortilla chips (about 40)

1   Put halibut in medium bowl and add lime juice, adding more if fish is not covered completely. Cover bowl with plastic wrap and refrigerate, stirring once or twice, until fish looks cooked, at least 1 hour or up to 2 hours.

2   Add all remaining ingredients except salad greens and tortilla chips to halibut; toss until mixed well.

3   Divide salad greens evenly among 4 plates. With slotted spoon, top each serving of greens with one-fourth of seviche. Serve with tortilla chips.

PER SERVING (1 cup salad greens, about 1 cup seviche, and 10 chips): 329 Cal, 11 g Total Fat, 2 g Sat Fat, 0 g Trans Fat, 37 mg Chol, 529 mg Sod, 33 g Carb, 6 g Sugar, 7 g Fib, 29 g Prot, 93 mg Calc.

FYI   The amount of time the halibut needs to marinate until "cooked" will depend upon the size of the dice. If the fish is cut into ¼-inch dice, it will take about 1 hour; if the fish is cut into ½-inch dice it will take about 2 hours.

Rustic Tuna Panzanella

5 PointsPlus value
PER SERVING

serves 6

2 tablespoons extra-virgin olive oil

2 tablespoons red wine vinegar

1 large garlic clove, minced

¼ teaspoon salt

¼ teaspoon black pepper

8 ounces day-old country-style whole wheat Italian bread, thickly sliced, toasted, and cut into 1-inch cubes

1½ pounds tomatoes, coarsely chopped

½ English (seedless) cucumber, unpeeled, quartered lengthwise, and sliced

1 yellow bell pepper, cut into ¾-inch pieces

½ red onion, thinly sliced

10 fresh basil leaves, coarsely chopped

2 tablespoons nonpareil (tiny) capers, drained and rinsed

2 (5-ounce) cans chunk light tuna in water, drained

1   To make dressing, whisk together oil, vinegar, garlic, salt, and black pepper in salad bowl.

2   Add all remaining ingredients except tuna to dressing; toss until mixed well. Coarsely flake tuna into salad; gently toss to combine. Let stand at least 20 minutes or up to 30 minutes before serving.

PER SERVING (about 2 cups): 218 Cal, 6 g Total Fat, 1 g Sat Fat, 0 g Trans Fat, 25 mg Chol, 531 mg Sod, 24 g Carb, 6 g Sugar, 4 g Fib, 13 g Prot, 48 mg Calc.

FYI   We like chunk light tuna for its more pronounced tuna flavor and also because it is lower in mercury than white albacore tuna.

Tuna Salad–Stuffed Tomatoes

serves
4

2 (5-ounce) cans light tuna packed in water, drained

½ cup chopped fennel

1 scallion, chopped

2 tablespoons chopped fresh flat-leaf parsley

1 tablespoon nonpareil (tiny) capers, drained and rinsed

⅓ cup reduced-fat mayonnaise

¼ teaspoon black pepper

4 large tomatoes

1   Flake tuna in medium bowl. Add all remaining ingredients except tomatoes, stirring to combine.

2   Cut off tops of tomatoes; chop and stir into tuna salad. Scoop out seeds and membranes from tomatoes; discard. Fill each tomato with one-fourth of tuna mixture.

PER SERVING (1 stuffed tomato): 154 Cal, 4 g Total Fat, 1 g Sat Fat, 0 g Trans Fat, 21 mg Chol, 508 mg Sod, 11 g Carb, 6 g Sugar, 3 g Fib, 20 g Prot, 39 mg Calc.

Healthy Extra   Serve each stuffed tomato on a bed of baby spinach.

Saigon Shrimp & Cellophane Noodle Salad

8 PointsPlus® value
PER SERVING

serves **4**

1 (6.35-ounce) package rice stick noodles (vermicelli)

1 pound cooked peeled and deveined small shrimp

1 cup cooked small broccoli florets

½ cup thinly sliced shallots

3 scallions, thinly sliced

2 tablespoons seasoned rice vinegar

1 tablespoon reduced-sodium soy sauce

1 tablespoon Asian fish sauce

⅛ teaspoon black pepper

½ cup lightly packed fresh cilantro leaves

1   Put noodles in serving bowl and add enough hot water to cover. Cover bowl with plastic wrap and soak until noodles are softened, about 10 minutes. Drain well.

2   Add all remaining ingredients except cilantro to noodles; toss until mixed well. Serve sprinkled with cilantro.

PER SERVING (about 2 cups): 322 Cal, 1 g Total Fat, 0 g Sat Fat, 0 g Trans Fat, 221 mg Chol, 889 mg Sod, 44 g Carb, 4 g Sugar, 1 g Fib, 29 g Prot, 70 mg Calc.

FYI   Fish sauce is a staple in Thai cooking. It has a rich reddish brown color, a pronounced aroma, and an exotic flavor that is unmistakable. Good-quality fish sauce is made from a mixture of fish (usually anchovies) and salt that has fermented for at least 1 year or up to 18 months. The best brands contain only these two ingredients.

Saigon Shrimp
& Cellophane Noodle Salad

Shrimp with Creamy Red Cabbage Slaw

serves
6

20
min

PER SERVING

1 cup low-fat buttermilk

3 tablespoons fat-free mayonnaise

1 tablespoon prepared horseradish

½ teaspoon salt

½ teaspoon black pepper

3 cups lightly packed thinly sliced red cabbage

½ English (seedless) cucumber, quartered lengthwise and thinly sliced

1 Granny Smith apple, unpeeled, cored, and diced

½ cup matchstick-cut carrot

3 scallions, thinly sliced

⅓ cup chopped fresh parsley

1 pound cooked peeled and deveined large shrimp

1　To make dressing, whisk together buttermilk, mayonnaise, horseradish, salt, and pepper in large bowl. Reserve ¼ cup.

2　Add cabbage, cucumber, apple, carrot, scallions, and parsley to dressing; toss until mixed well. Divide slaw evenly among 6 plates. Arrange one-fourth of shrimp around each serving of slaw; drizzle evenly with reserved dressing.

PER SERVING (about 1 cup slaw and 8 shrimp): 117 Cal, 1 g Total Fat, 0 g Sat Fat, 0 g Trans Fat, 114 mg Chol, 559 mg Sod, 12 g Carb, 8 g Sugar, 2 g Fib, 14 g Prot, 105 mg Calc.

FYI　The slaw can be prepared up to several hours ahead and stored in the refrigerator. Top it with the shrimp just before serving. The slaw—without the shrimp—is excellent served as a side dish.

Tropical Papaya-Shrimp Salad

serves **4**

20 min

PER SERVING

Grated zest of ½ orange

¼ cup orange juice

2 tablespoons lemon juice

1 small jalapeño pepper, seeded and minced

2 teaspoons honey

1 teaspoon olive oil

½ teaspoon salt

1 pound cooked peeled and deveined large shrimp

2 papayas, seeded, peeled, and cut into ¾-inch chunks

¼ cup thinly sliced fresh mint

4 cups lightly packed mixed baby salad greens

¼ cup freshly grated coconut

1 To make dressing, whisk together orange zest and juice, lemon juice, jalapeño, honey, oil, and salt in large bowl. Add shrimp, papayas, and mint; toss until coated evenly.

2 Divide salad greens evenly among 4 plates; top evenly with salad. Sprinkle with coconut.

PER SERVING (generous 1 cup shrimp salad, 1 cup greens, and 1 tablespoon coconut): 202 Cal, 4 g Total Fat, 2 g Sat Fat, 0 g Trans Fat, 221 mg Chol, 568 mg Sod, 17 g Carb, 9 g Sugar, 4 g Fib, 25 g Prot, 70 mg Calc.

FYI You can substitute packaged flaked unsweetened coconut for the fresh, if you like.

Chunky Lobster & Cantaloupe Salad

serves **4**

20 min

PER SERVING

¼ cup seasoned rice vinegar

1 tablespoon canola oil

2 teaspoons minced crystallized ginger

¼ teaspoon black pepper

1 small cantaloupe, peeled, halved, seeded, and cut into ¾-inch cubes (about 2 cups)

1 pound cooked lobster meat, cut into ¾-inch chunks

8 cups lightly packed herb salad mix or other baby salad greens

2 large shallots, thinly sliced into rings and separated

1 To make dressing, whisk together vinegar, oil, ginger, and pepper in serving bowl. Add cantaloupe and toss to coat evenly. Let stand 10 minutes.

2 Add lobster, salad mix, and shallots to cantaloupe; toss until mixed well.

PER SERVING (about 2 cups): 282 Cal, 6 g Total Fat, 1 g Sat Fat, 0 g Trans Fat, 102 mg Chol, 617 mg Sod, 26 g Carb, 15 g Sugar, 4 g Fib, 33 g Prot, 91 mg Calc.

FYI You can use other melons in this wonderful summertime salad, including Crenshaw, Persian, and casaba. To pick a melon, use your thumb to gently press the blossom end (which is opposite the stem end). If it yields, the melon is ripe. Melons should also be heavy for their size and smell sweet.

Perfect Summer Lobster Salad

¼ cup reduced-fat sour cream

1½ teaspoons chopped fresh tarragon

¼ teaspoon salt

¼ teaspoon black pepper

1 pound cooked lobster meat, cut into ½-inch pieces

1½ cups fresh corn kernels (about 3 ears of corn)

1 cup halved grape or cherry tomatoes

1 small Hass avocado, halved, pitted, peeled, and cut into ½-inch dice

1 kirby cucumber, cut on diagonal into ¼-inch slices and then into thin strips

12 thick tomato slices

1 To make dressing, whisk together sour cream, tarragon, salt, and pepper in large bowl.

2 Add lobster, corn, tomatoes, avocado, and cucumber to dressing; toss until mixed well. Place 3 tomato slices on each of 4 plates; top evenly with lobster mixture.

PER SERVING (3 tomato slices and about 1 cup lobster salad): 323 Cal, 11 g Total Fat, 3 g Sat Fat, 0 g Trans Fat, 107 mg Chol, 435 mg Sod, 24 g Carb, 6 g Sugar, 6 g Fib, 35 g Prot, 118 mg Calc.

Healthy Extra Serve the salad on a bed of your favorite greens. Consider using a combination to make it interesting both to the eyes and to the palate.

Frisée with Smoked Salmon, Oranges & Radishes

2 large oranges, peeled and sectioned, juice reserved

1 tablespoon red wine vinegar

1 tablespoon olive oil

1 garlic clove mashed to paste with ½ teaspoon salt

¼ teaspoon ground coriander

¼ teaspoon black pepper

2 small heads frisée (about ½ pound), trimmed and separated into leaves

3 large radishes, thinly sliced

1 (4-ounce) package thinly sliced smoked salmon, cut into thin strips

1 To make dressing, whisk together 2 tablespoons of reserved orange juice, the vinegar, oil, garlic paste, coriander, and pepper in serving bowl.

2 Add frisée, orange sections, radishes, and salmon to dressing; toss until mixed well.

PER SERVING (generous 2 cups): 114 Cal, 5 g Total Fat, 1 g Sat Fat, 0 g Trans Fat, 7 mg Chol, 371 mg Sod, 12 g Carb, 9 g Sugar, 3 g Fib, 6 g Prot, 49 mg Calc.

FYI The oranges can be sectioned up to several hours ahead and refrigerated, while the dressing can be prepared and set aside.

Feta-Topped Pasta, Tomato & Pea Salad

serves 4

20 min

1 teaspoon grated lemon zest

2 tablespoons lemon juice

1 tablespoon extra-virgin olive oil

½ teaspoon salt

¼ teaspoon black pepper

8 ounces whole wheat rotini or elbow macaroni, cooked according to package directions

2 small kirby cucumbers, cut on diagonal into ¼-inch slices and then into matchsticks

1 cup halved grape or cherry tomatoes

1 cup frozen baby peas, thawed

1 large shallot, minced

2 tablespoons snipped fresh dill

2 tablespoons crumbled reduced-fat feta cheese

1   To make dressing, whisk together lemon zest and juice, oil, salt, and pepper in serving bowl.

2   Rinse pasta under cold running water; drain. Add to dressing in bowl. Add all remaining ingredients except feta; toss until mixed well. Serve sprinkled with feta.

PER SERVING (1½ cups): 286 Cal, 5 g Total Fat, 1 g Sat Fat, 0 g Trans Fat, 1 mg Chol, 388 mg Sod, 52 g Carb, 6 g Sugar, 8 g Fib, 12 g Prot, 65 mg Calc.

FYI   We like using kirby cucumbers in this salad, as they don't have to be peeled and their flesh is meaty and flavorful. But if you happen to have English (seedless) cucumbers, Persian (mini) cucumbers, or regular cucumbers, on hand, use them instead.

Greek-Style Pasta Salad

serves 4

1 teaspoon grated lemon zest

2 tablespoons lemon juice

1 tablespoon extra-virgin olive oil

½ teaspoon salt

¼ teaspoon black pepper

8 ounces whole grain medium shells, cooked according to package directions

1 pint cherry tomatoes, halved

1 bunch arugula, trimmed and cut into 1-inch pieces

¼ cup chopped fresh flat-leaf parsley

2 tablespoons chopped pitted Kalamata olives

1 To make dressing, whisk together lemon zest and juice, oil, salt, and pepper in serving bowl.

2 Rinse pasta under cold running water; drain. Add to dressing along with remaining ingredients; toss until mixed well.

PER SERVING (about 2 cups): 262 Cal, 6 g Total Fat, 1 g Sat Fat, 0 g Trans Fat, 0 mg Chol, 372 mg Sod, 47 g Carb, 5 g Sugar, 6 g Fib, 10 g Prot, 125 mg Calc.

Healthy Extra Add ½ cup diced red onion to the salad along with the other ingredients in step 2 for a bit of zesty flavor.

Lemony Brown Rice & Spinach Salad

serves 4

2 tablespoons cider vinegar

1 tablespoon extra-virgin olive oil

Grated zest of ½ orange

1 large garlic clove mashed to paste with ¾ teaspoon salt

¼ teaspoon ground allspice

¼ teaspoon black pepper

2 cups lightly packed baby spinach

1 cup brown basmati rice, cooked according to package directions and cooled (makes about 3 cups cooked)

1 cup canned chickpeas, rinsed and drained

½ cup roasted peppers (not packed in oil), diced

12 fresh basil leaves, thinly sliced

1 To make dressing, whisk together vinegar, oil, orange zest, garlic paste, allspice, and black pepper in serving bowl.

2 Add all remaining ingredients except basil to dressing; toss until mixed well. Add basil and gently toss.

PER SERVING (about 1⅓ cups): 251 Cal, 6 g Total Fat, 1 g Sat Fat, 0 g Trans Fat, 0 mg Chol, 599 mg Sod, 46 g Carb, 2 g Sugar, 5 g Fib, 7 g Prot, 32 mg Calc.

Healthy Extra Add 1 cup sliced celery to the salad in step 2.

Tabbouleh-Style Barley Salad

 5 PointsPlus value PER SERVING | serves **4**

1 teaspoon grated lemon zest

3 tablespoons lemon juice

2 tablespoons thinly sliced fresh mint

1 garlic clove, minced

⅛ teaspoon black pepper

1 pound tomatoes, seeded and cut into ½-inch dice

1 cup pearl barley (not quick-cooking) or brown rice, cooked according to package directions and cooled

½ cup chopped fresh flat-leaf parsley

2 scallions, thinly sliced

Whisk together lemon zest and juice, mint, garlic, and pepper in serving bowl. Add remaining ingredients; toss until mixed well.

PER SERVING (1½ cups): 206 Cal, 1 g Total Fat, 0 g Sat Fat, 0 g Trans Fat, 0 mg Chol, 313 mg Sod, 46 g Carb, 4 g Sugar, 10 g Fib, 6 g Prot, 51 mg Calc.

FYI To cut a tomato into small dice, cut out the core, then cut the tomato into ½-inch slices. Stack half of the slices and cut into ½-inch-wide strips, then cut the strips crosswise into ½-inch dice. Repeat with the remaining slices of tomato.

Bulgur Salad with Citrus & Mint

 6 PointsPlus value PER SERVING | serves **4**

2 large oranges, peeled and sectioned, juice reserved

2 small pink grapefruit, peeled and sectioned, juice reserved

1 tablespoon extra-virgin olive oil

½ teaspoon salt

¼ teaspoon black pepper

1 cup bulgur, prepared according to package directions and cooled

1 small red onion, thinly sliced

3 tablespoons thinly sliced fresh mint

1 To make dressing, whisk together 1 tablespoon each of reserved orange and grapefruit juices, the oil, salt, and pepper in serving bowl.

2 Cut orange and grapefruit sections crosswise into thirds. Add to dressing along with remaining ingredients; toss until mixed well.

PER SERVING (1½ cups): 233 Cal, 4 g Total Fat, 1g Sat Fat, 0 g Trans Fat, 0 mg Chol, 298 mg Sod, 47 g Carb, 16 g Sugar, 10 g Fib, 6 g Prot, Alcohol, 69 mg Calc.

FYI Bulgur wheat, a staple in Middle Eastern cooking, is made of wheat kernels that have been steamed, dried, and crushed. It has a pleasantly chewy texture and nutty flavor. Best of all, bulgur needs only to be rehydrated—not cooked. It comes in coarse, medium, and fine grinds. Look for it in the supermarket and health food stores.

Black-Eyed Pea & Peach Salad

serves
6

3 tablespoons lemon juice

1 tablespoon olive oil

2 teaspoons ground cumin

¾ teaspoon salt

½ teaspoon black pepper

Pinch cayenne

2 (15½-ounce) cans black-eyed peas, rinsed and drained

2 large peaches, halved, pitted, and cut into wedges

1 red bell pepper, chopped

1 yellow bell pepper, chopped

1 bunch watercress, trimmed

6 scallions, thinly sliced

3 celery stalks, chopped

To make dressing, whisk together lemon juice, oil, cumin, salt, and black pepper in serving bowl. Add all remaining ingredients; toss until mixed well.

PER SERVING (about 2 cups): 192 Cal, 4 g Total Fat, 0 g Sat Fat, 0 g Trans Fat, 0 mg Chol, 368 mg Sod, 30 g Carb, 9 g Sugar, 7 g Fib, 9 g Prot, 115 mg Calc.

Healthy Extra   Peaches and tomatoes make a surprisingly delicious combination. During the summer and early fall, go to the farmers' market and pick up green zebra tomatoes or other heirloom varieties. Add 2 tomatoes, coarsely chopped, to the salad.

Black-Eyed Pea & Peach Salad

Turkey–Mango Chutney Sandwiches

PER SERVING

1 (¾-pound) piece cooked skinless turkey breast, cut into ¼-inch matchsticks

⅓ cup lightly packed fresh cilantro leaves

¼ cup reduced-fat sour cream

3 tablespoons mango chutney

⅛ teaspoon black pepper

1⅓ cups lightly packed mixed baby salad greens

4 (2-ounce) whole grain sandwich rolls, split

12 small tomato slices

1 Toss together turkey, cilantro, sour cream, chutney, and pepper in medium bowl.

2 Divide salad greens evenly among bottom halves of rolls; top each with 3 tomato slices and one-fourth of turkey mixture. Cover with tops of rolls.

PER SERVING (1 sandwich): 337 Cal, 7 g Total Fat, 2 g Sat Fat, 0 g Trans Fat, 76 mg Chol, 458 mg Sod, 38 g Carb, 6 g Sugar, 5 g Fib, 32 g Prot, 100 mg Calc.

Healthy Extra Make this tasty sandwich even better by layering each sandwich with thinly sliced cucumber and red onion.

Salmon Sandwiches with Dill Mayo

PER SERVING

1 (15-ounce) can no-salt-added salmon, drained

2 hard-cooked large egg whites

3 tablespoons reduced-fat mayonnaise

3 tablespoons snipped fresh dill

Grated zest and juice of 1 lemon

2 teaspoons Dijon mustard

½ teaspoon salt

¼ teaspoon black pepper

1 cup alfalfa or broccoli sprouts

8 thin slices dark bread

1 large tomato, thinly sliced

16 thin slices unpeeled cucumber

1 Flake salmon into medium bowl. Grate egg whites over salmon. Add mayonnaise, dill, lemon zest and juice, mustard, salt, and pepper, stirring until mixed well.

2 Place ¼ cup of sprouts on each of 4 slices of bread and top evenly with tomato and cucumber slices. Spread one-fourth of salmon mixture on each sandwich and cover with remaining slices of bread. Cut each sandwich in half.

PER SERVING (½ sandwich): 216 Cal, 6 g Total Fat, 1 g Sat Fat, 0 g Trans Fat, 24 mg Chol, 450 mg Sod, 25 g Carb, 7 g Sugar, 3 g Fib, 16 g Prot, 177 mg Calc.

Healthy Extra A leaf or two of crisp romaine lettuce is an enticing addition to these sandwiches. Serve some unsweetened pickles alongside.

Asian Flavors Shrimp Salad Sandwiches

serves 4

20 min

1 pound cooked peeled and deveined small shrimp

1 cup halved cherry tomatoes

6 scallions, thinly sliced

¼ cup reduced-fat mayonnaise

2 tablespoons chopped fresh cilantro

2 teaspoons seasoned rice vinegar

½ teaspoon Asian (dark) sesame oil

¼ teaspoon salt

⅛ teaspoon black pepper

12 small inner romaine lettuce leaves

4 (2-ounce) whole grain rolls, split

1   Mix together shrimp, tomatoes, scallions, mayonnaise, cilantro, vinegar, oil, salt, and pepper in medium bowl.

2   Place 3 lettuce leaves on bottom half of each roll. Top each with about ¾ cup shrimp salad; cover with tops of rolls.

PER SERVING (1 sandwich): 312 Cal, 7 g Total Fat, 1 g Sat Fat, 0 g Trans Fat, 221 mg Chol, 857 mg Sod, 35 g Carb, 8 g Sugar, 6 g Fib, 30 g Prot, 131 mg Calc.

FYI   In supermarkets and fish stores, shrimp is labeled small, medium, large, and so on. Although these names help a bit, they are not used consistently. When shrimp is purchased for retail, it is bought according to the number of shrimp per pound. Knowing the number of shrimp per pound can help you figure how much you need. Here's how shrimp is graded: colossal is 15 to the pound, jumbo is 21–25 to the pound, extra-large is 26–30 to the pound, large is 31–35 to the pound, and medium is 35–40 to the pound.

Maine-Style Crab Rolls

Maine-Style Crab Rolls

serves 4

20 min

1 pound lump crabmeat, picked over

6 tablespoons fat-free mayonnaise

¼ cup chopped fresh flat-leaf parsley

½ teaspoon grated lemon zest

⅛ teaspoon black pepper

1 cup lightly packed thinly sliced romaine lettuce

4 split top whole wheat hot dog rolls, split, doughy centers removed, and toasted

1   Stir together crabmeat, mayonnaise, parsley, lemon zest, and pepper in medium bowl.

2   Divide lettuce among rolls, top each with generous ½ cup of crab salad.

PER SERVING (1 sandwich): 247 Cal, 4 g Total Fat, 1 g Sat Fat, 0 g Trans Fat, 82 mg Chol, 813 mg Sod, 27 g Carb, 7 g Sugar, 4 g Fib, 28 g Prot, 135 mg Calc.

Healthy Extra   Serve the crab rolls with sliced tomatoes dressed with fresh lemon juice, a sprinkling of snipped fresh chives, and a touch of salt and pepper.

Curried Tofu Salad Sandwiches

serves 4

20 min

1 (1-pound) package reduced-fat firm tofu, drained

2 scallions, finely sliced

2 tablespoons reduced-fat mayonnaise

¾ teaspoon curry powder

½ teaspoon salt

¼ teaspoon black pepper

8 thin slices whole grain bread, toasted

12 thin tomato slices

1 cup lightly packed alfalfa sprouts

1   With fork, mash tofu in medium bowl. Add scallions, mayonnaise, curry powder, salt, and pepper, stirring until mixed well.

2   Spread ½ cup of tofu mixture on each of 4 slices of bread. Top each with 3 tomato slices and ¼ cup of sprouts; cover with remaining slices of bread.

PER SERVING (1 sandwich): 225 Cal, 5 g Total Fat, 1 g Sat Fat, 0 g Trans Fat, 0 mg Chol, 617 mg Sod, 28 g Carb, 5 g Sugar, 6 g Fib, 17 g Prot, 277 mg Calc.

Healthy Extra   Enjoy these good-for-you sandwiches with a red onion and cucumber salad dressed with unseasoned rice vinegar and topped with torn fresh mint.

IN A
SKILLE

CHAPTER 2

IN A SKILLET

QUICK & EASY BREAKFASTS, LUNCHES & DINNERS

The skillet, also known as a frying pan, is a flat-bottomed pan with low sides that flare outward. It has one long handle and usually no lid. These handy pans are great for browning and sautéing meat, chicken, fish, eggs, vegetables, and potatoes, especially because their low sides make it easy to turn food.

Types

Early skillets were made of **iron, copper, and cast iron.** In the U.S. in the mid-1800s, manufacturers, such as the Griswold and Wagner Companies, began producing lighter, easier-to-handle cast-iron skillets, which remain popular to this day. These almost indestructible pans—which become nonstick through years of use—are often passed down from generation to generation. Other companies, such as Lodge, manufacture cast-iron skillets today. They can be found in department stores, big box stores, and kitchenware stores.

Nonstick skillets were first produced by DuPont in 1956 under the Teflon brand name. Since then, improvements have been made, including the development of nonstick surfaces that either are more resistant to or impervious to scratches, such as the high-end brand GreenPan™, which can be heated to 450°F and is also ovenproof. When purchasing a nonstick skillet, choose one that has more than one layer of nonstick coating and feels heavy, which means it will retain heat well and brown foods better. Look for oven-safe handles so the pan can go from stovetop to oven with ease.

Appreciated for their sleek look, **stainless steel skillets** have the ability to hold heat well and cook food evenly. They are also extremely durable. High-end brands, such as All-Clad, boast a hand-polished, mirror-finish exterior. These skillets are produced using a three-ply bond core that incorporates an aluminum center, which helps conduct heat better.

Enamel cast-iron skillets, such as Le Creuset, have been produced in France since 1925 and are meant to last a lifetime. These skillets have either a stone-colored enamel interior or a matte black enamel finish that is practically nonstick. Enamel cast iron distributes heat evenly, which prevents hot spots and also retains heat longer than some other cookware, which is especially useful when serving directly from the pan.

The first **electric skillet** was manufactured by Sunbeam in 1953 and was called a "controlled heat automatic fry pan." The square-shaped cast-aluminum pan had a built-in cooking element and a heat control in the handle. The brochure featured an aproned homemaker happily cooking up nine fried eggs at one time. Electric skillets range in size from 12 to 16 inches and often come with lids. They are available round and square, and some are nonstick. Electric skillets are appreciated for their ability to maintain constant heat.

Sizes and Shapes

Skillets range in size from about 6 inches to 14 inches. For most kitchens, it is recommended to have a small skillet (6 to 8 inches), a medium skillet (8 to 10 inches), and a large skillet (11 to 12 inches). Skillets are measured across the diameter at the top.

Basics for Care

These days, **cast-iron skillets** often come already seasoned (nonstick). If you buy one that isn't, here's how to do it: Wipe the inside of the skillet with a light coating of flavorless vegetable oil. Place the pan in a 350°F oven for 1 hour. Remove it from the oven and let it cool completely, then wipe the skillet dry with a paper towel. To clean a cast-iron skillet, rinse it under hot water as soon as it is cool enough to be handled to prevent any food from sticking, then use a nonabrasive powder cleaner or kosher salt and a stiff brush to remove any food particles. Dry the pan immediately to prevent rusting.

To ensure that the coating of a **nonstick skillet** lasts, clean it gently and avoid scratching the surface. Wash the skillet using hot, soapy water and a sponge or nylon scrub pad. The nonstick surface should prevent any food from sticking.

To clean a **stainless steel skillet,** immerse it in warm water once it has cooled down slightly. Apply a paste of nonabrasive powder cleanser mixed with water and rub in a circular motion from the center outward using a sponge or nylon scrub pad. Wash the pan with hot, soapy water, rinse it well, and dry it thoroughly. Avoid using a steel wool pad, which would scratch the surface. These pans can also be washed in the dishwasher.

Enamel cast-iron skillets are easy to care for. Let them cool down completely before washing them to avoid shocking the enamel due to the change in temperature. Hand-wash the pan with hot, soapy water, then rinse under warm water and dry it thoroughly. If any food remains stuck, soak the pan for about 15 minutes, then use a nylon scrub pad to remove the residue. Enamel-coated skillets are dishwasher safe, but it is not recommended, as the detergent will dull the enamel surface over time.

The lid of an **electric skillet** is dishwasher safe. The skillet itself should be washed by hand using hot, soapy water, taking care not to get the heating element or electric plug wet. Refer to the manufacturer's instruction booklet for details.

Zucchini & Mint Frittata

 serves 4

PER SERVING

1 tablespoon olive oil

1 large red onion, thinly sliced

2 garlic cloves, minced

2 zucchini, cut into matchsticks

1 orange bell pepper, cut into thin strips

½ teaspoon salt

¼ teaspoon black pepper

1 (16-ounce) container fat-free egg substitute

2 tablespoons thinly sliced fresh mint

1 teaspoon balsamic vinegar

1 Preheat oven to 350°F.

2 Heat oil in 10-inch ovenproof nonstick skillet over medium heat. Add onion and cook, stirring, until softened, about 5 minutes. Stir in garlic and cook, stirring, until fragrant, about 30 seconds. Increase heat to medium-high; add zucchini, bell pepper, salt, and black pepper. Cook, stirring frequently, until vegetables are softened, about 8 minutes. Remove skillet from heat.

3 Stir egg substitute, mint, and vinegar into vegetables until combined well. Cook, without stirring, until eggs begin to set, about 3 minutes. Place skillet in oven and bake until eggs are set, about 12 minutes longer. Slide frittata onto plate and cut into 4 wedges.

PER SERVING (1 wedge): 102 Cal, 4 g Total Fat, 1 g Sat Fat, 0 g Trans Fat, 0 mg Chol, 473 mg Sod, 7 g Carb, 3 g Sugar, 1 g Fib, 11 g Prot, 59 mg Calc.

FYI Here's the easiest way to quickly and neatly slice fresh mint—or basil—leaves. Stack the leaves (it's best to use leaves of equal size) and roll them up jelly-roll style, starting with a long side. With a very sharp large knife, thinly slice the mint crosswise.

Goat Cheese–Chive Frittata

 serves 4

PER SERVING

1 tablespoon olive oil

1 red onion, thinly sliced

¼ teaspoon salt

⅛ teaspoon black pepper

1 red bell pepper, cut into matchsticks

1 garlic clove, minced

1 (16-ounce) container fat-free egg substitute

2 tablespoons reduced-fat (2%) milk

2 tablespoons snipped fresh chives

¼ cup crumbled soft goat cheese

1 Preheat oven to 350°F.

2 Heat oil in 10-inch ovenproof nonstick skillet over medium heat. Add onion, salt, and black pepper; cook, stirring, until softened, about 5 minutes. Stir in bell pepper and cook, stirring, until softened, about 5 minutes. Stir in garlic and cook, stirring, until fragrant, about 30 seconds longer.

3 Stir egg substitute, milk, and 1 tablespoon of chives into vegetables until combined well. Cook, without stirring, until eggs begin to set, about 3 minutes. Sprinkle goat cheese and remaining 1 tablespoon chives evenly over eggs. Place skillet in oven and bake until eggs are set, about 12 minutes longer. Slide frittata onto plate and cut into 4 wedges.

PER SERVING (1 wedge): 115 Cal, 5 g Total Fat, 2 g Sat Fat, 0 g Trans Fat, 4 mg Chol, 356 mg Sod, 5 g Carb, 3 g Sugar, 1 g Fib, 12 g Prot, 70 mg Calc.

FYI It's easier than you might think to cut a bell pepper into uniform matchstick strips, otherwise known as julienne. Here's how: With a sharp knife, cut off the stem end and base of the pepper, then cut the pepper in half. Remove the seeds and membranes and discard. Place one pepper half, skin side down, on the cutting board and cut into ¼-inch-thick strips.

Diner Turkey Hash Patties with Scrambled Eggs

4 PointsPlus value

PER SERVING

serves **6**

3 teaspoons canola oil

1 onion, finely chopped

2 celery stalks, chopped

1 (7-ounce) baking potato, peeled and chopped

½ pound ground skinless turkey breast

1 large egg white

1 tablespoon Worcestershire sauce

½ teaspoon ground sage

½ teaspoon salt

½ teaspoon black pepper

3 cups fat-free egg substitute

2 tablespoons chopped fresh parsley

2 tablespoons snipped fresh chives

1   Heat 2 teaspoons of oil in large nonstick skillet over medium heat. Add onion and celery; cook, stirring, until softened, about 5 minutes. Add potato and cook, stirring until almost cooked through, about 10 minutes. Transfer to plate and let cool. Wipe skillet clean.

2   Mix together cooled onion mixture, the turkey, egg white, Worcestershire sauce, sage, salt, and pepper in bowl until combined well. With damp hands, shape mixture into 12 (½-inch-thick) patties.

3   Heat remaining 1 teaspoon oil in skillet over medium heat. Add patties, in batches if needed, and cook until browned and cooked through, about 6 minutes per side. Transfer to platter and keep warm. Wipe skillet clean.

4   Spray skillet with nonstick spray and set over medium heat. Pour egg substitute into skillet; add parsley and chives. Cook until eggs begin to set, about 1½ minutes, pushing egg mixture toward center of skillet to form large soft curds, cooking eggs until set, about 3 minutes longer. Serve with hash patties.

PER SERVING (2 patties and ⅙ of eggs): 142 Cal, 3 g Total Fat, 0 g Sat Fat, 0 g Trans Fat, 15 mg Chol, 410 mg Sod, 9 g Carb, 2 g Sugar, 2 g Fib, 21 g Prot, 61 mg Calc.

Healthy Extra   Serve sliced navel oranges alongside the patties and eggs.

Fresh Corn & Blueberry Pancakes

9 PointsPlus® value
PER SERVING

serves
6

2 cups all-purpose flour

½ cup yellow cornmeal

2 tablespoons sugar

1 tablespoon + 1 teaspoon baking powder

¼ teaspoon salt

1¾ cups low-fat (1%) milk

½ cup fat-free egg substitute

1 tablespoon canola oil

¾ cup fresh or frozen blueberries

¾ cup fresh corn kernels (about 2 ears of corn) or frozen corn kernels

6 teaspoons pure maple syrup, warmed

1   Whisk together flour, cornmeal, sugar, baking powder, and salt in medium bowl. Make a well in middle of flour mixture. Combine milk, egg substitute, and oil in well; with fork stir until mixed thoroughly. With rubber spatula, stir flour mixture into milk mixture just until flour mixture is moistened (batter will be lumpy). Gently stir in blueberries and corn.

2   Spray nonstick griddle with nonstick spray and set over medium heat. Pour scant ¼ cupfuls of batter onto griddle. Cook until bubbles appear and edges of pancakes look dry, about 3 minutes. Turn pancakes over and cook until golden brown on second side, about 3 minutes longer. Transfer to platter and keep warm. Repeat with remaining batter, spraying griddle between batches, making total of 24 pancakes. Serve with maple syrup.

PER SERVING (4 pancakes and 1 teaspoon maple syrup): 324 Cal, 4 g Total Fat, 1 g Sat Fat, 0 g Trans Fat, 4 mg Chol, 482 mg Sod, 62 g Carb, 13 g Sugar, 2 g Fib, 10 g Prot, 169 mg Calc.

FYI   Making a well is a classic cooking technique used when combining wet and dry ingredients for pasta dough, gnocchi dough, pancakes, and quick breads. Whisk together the dry ingredients in a bowl, then push the mixture to the sides of the bowl to create an empty space in the middle of the bowl, known as a "well." The wet ingredients are poured into the well and the dry ingredients are then gradually mixed in.

Yogurt Pancakes with Any Berry Sauce

PER SERVING

1½ cups fresh blueberries, raspberries, blackberries, or a combination

1 tablespoon granulated sugar

1 tablespoon lemon juice

¼ teaspoon ground nutmeg

1⅓ cups white whole wheat flour

1 teaspoon baking powder

¼ teaspoon baking soda

¼ teaspoon salt

1¼ cups plain fat-free yogurt

1 large egg

1 tablespoon canola oil

1 tablespoon confectioners' sugar

1 To make sauce, combine berries, granulated sugar, lemon juice, and nutmeg in small saucepan; bring to boil over medium-high heat. Reduce heat and simmer, stirring occasionally, until berries soften, about 8 minutes; transfer to serving bowl.

2 Meanwhile, whisk together flour, baking powder, baking soda, and salt in medium bowl. Make a well in center of flour mixture. Combine yogurt, egg, and oil in well; with fork, stir until mixed thoroughly. With rubber spatula, stir flour mixture into yogurt mixture just until flour mixture is moistened (batter will be lumpy).

3 Generously spray nonstick griddle with nonstick spray and set over medium heat. Pour scant ¼ cupfuls of batter onto griddle. Cook until bubbles appear and edges of pancakes look dry, about 3 minutes. Turn pancakes over and cook until golden brown on second side, about 3 minutes longer. Transfer to platter and keep warm. Repeat with remaining batter, making total of 12 pancakes. Dust pancakes with confectioners' sugar and serve with berry sauce.

PER SERVING (3 pancakes and about 3 tablespoons sauce): 299 Cal, 6 g Total Fat, 1 g Sat Fat, 0 g Trans Fat, 55 mg Chol, 438 mg Sod, 52 g Carb, 17 g Sugar, 2 g Fib, 11 g Prot, 192 mg Calc.

Heavenly Hots

serves
4

PER SERVING

½ cup cake flour (not self-rising)

3 tablespoons sugar

½ teaspoon baking soda

1 (16-ounce) container fat-free sour cream

¾ cup fat-free egg substitute

1 (6-ounce) container fresh raspberries

1   Whisk together flour, sugar, and baking soda in small bowl. Whisk in sour cream and egg substitute until smooth.

2   Spray nonstick griddle with nonstick spray and set over medium heat. Drop ⅛ cupfuls of batter onto griddle. Cook until bubbles appear and edges of pancakes look dry, about 2 minutes. Gently turn pancakes over and cook until golden brown on second side, about 2 minutes longer. Transfer to platter and keep warm. Repeat with remaining batter, spraying griddle between batches, making total of 24 pancakes. Serve topped with raspberries.

PER SERVING (6 pancakes and about 8 raspberries): 213 Cal, 1 g Total Fat, 0 g Sat Fat, 0 g Trans Fat, 10 mg Chol, 388 mg Sod, 43 g Carb, 9 g Sugar, 3 g Fib, 9 g Prot, 170 mg Calc.

FYI   Heavenly hots are mini pancakes that are creamy, feather light, and irresistibly tangy. Their proportion of 4 parts sour cream to 1 part flour is unlike any other pancake batter, but that is what makes them so light. Take care when flipping them, as they are very delicate.

Open-Face Gruyère-Vegetable Melts

Eggs in Purgatory

serves
4

PER SERVING

4 cups water

1 teaspoon cider vinegar

4 large eggs

2 (14½-ounce) cans reduced-sodium petite diced tomatoes

¼ teaspoon salt

¼ teaspoon red pepper flakes

1½ tablespoons very thinly sliced fresh basil + 4 small sprigs

4 slices whole grain country-style bread, toasted

2 tablespoons grated Parmesan cheese

1   To poach eggs, combine water and vinegar in 10-inch nonstick skillet and bring to boil over medium-high heat. Reduce heat to bare simmer. Break 1 egg into cup. Holding cup close to water, slip in egg. Repeat with remaining eggs. Cook until whites are firm but yolks are still soft, about 5 minutes. With slotted spoon, transfer eggs, one at a time, to paper towel–lined plate. Keep warm. Pour out water from skillet; wipe skillet dry.

2   Combine tomatoes, salt, and pepper flakes in same skillet; bring to boil over medium-high heat. Reduce heat and simmer, stirring occasionally, until liquid is almost evaporated, about 6 minutes. Remove skillet from heat and stir in sliced basil.

3   Place 1 slice of toast in each of 4 shallow bowls. Spoon about ½ cup of tomato sauce over each slice of toast; place poached egg on top of each slice of toast and sprinkle evenly with Parmesan. Garnish each serving with basil sprig.

PER SERVING (1 dish): 249 Cal, 7 g Total Fat, 3 g Sat Fat, 0 g Trans Fat, 220 mg Chol, 638 mg Sod, 33 g Carb, 11 g Sugar, 3 g Fib, 12 g Prot, 380 mg Calc.

Healthy Extra   Round out this meal by starting off with a classic Italian salad of arugula, sliced radicchio, and sliced endive.

Open-Face Gruyère-Vegetable Melts

serves
4

PER SERVING

1 teaspoon olive oil

1 onion, thinly sliced

2 zucchini, thinly sliced

1 red bell pepper, diced

1 garlic clove, minced

½ teaspoon dried oregano

¼ teaspoon salt

¼ teaspoon black pepper

4 thin slices whole wheat bread, toasted

2 tomatoes, sliced

12 large basil leaves

1 cup shredded Gruyère cheese

1 cup lightly packed baby arugula

1   Preheat broiler.

2   Heat oil in large nonstick skillet over medium-high heat. Add onion, zucchini, bell pepper, garlic, oregano, salt, and black pepper; cook, stirring, until vegetables are softened, about 5 minutes.

3   Arrange slices of toast on rack of broiler pan. Top each slice with one-fourth each of tomatoes and basil. Top each with one-fourth of vegetable mixture and sprinkle evenly with Gruyère. Broil until cheese is melted, about 1 minute. Top evenly with arugula.

PER SERVING (1 open-face sandwich): 241 Cal, 11 g Total Fat, 6 g Sat Fat, 0 g Trans Fat, 30 mg Chol, 386 mg Sod, 23 g Carb, 9 g Sugar, 5 g Fib, 14 g Prot, 351 mg Calc.

Healthy Extra   To help keep you on target, serve a bowl of fresh berries of your choice for dessert. Enjoy up to 1 cup for each serving.

Red Curry Tofu-Noodle Bowl

PER SERVING

serves
6

1 (15-ounce) package low-fat firm tofu

3 teaspoons canola oil

1 tablespoon grated peeled fresh ginger

3 garlic cloves, minced

1½ teaspoons Thai red curry paste

1 red onion, chopped

1 (14½-ounce) can diced tomatoes

1 cup light (reduced-fat) coconut milk

2 teaspoons sugar

12 ounces small broccoli florets

½ teaspoon salt

3 cups hot cooked whole wheat capellini

1 Wrap tofu in paper towels and place on plate. Place small skillet on top and weight with large can of food. Let stand until excess liquid is pressed out, about 20 minutes. Discard liquid; cut tofu into ½-inch cubes.

2 Heat 1½ teaspoons of oil in large nonstick skillet over medium-high heat. Add tofu and cook, turning, until golden, about 3 minutes; transfer to plate. Add remaining 1½ teaspoons oil to skillet. Add ginger, garlic, and curry paste; cook, stirring, until fragrant, about 30 seconds. Reduce heat to medium; add onion and cook, stirring, until softened, about 5 minutes.

3 Add tomatoes, coconut milk, and sugar to skillet; bring to boil. Reduce heat and simmer, stirring, until mixture is slightly thickened, about 5 minutes. Add broccoli, tofu, and salt; cook, covered, until broccoli is tender, about 10 minutes longer. Serve in bowls over capellini.

PER SERVING (1⅓ cups tofu mixture and ½ cup capellini): 219 Cal, 7 g Total Fat, 1 g Sat Fat, 0 g Trans Fat, 0 mg Chol, 437 mg Sod, 31 g Carb, 5 g Sugar, 5 g Fib, 13 g Prot, 187 mg Calc.

Healthy Extra   Straw mushrooms, ready to use right from the can, make a tasty addition to this spicy noodle bowl. Add about ½ cup of drained mushrooms to the skillet along with the tomatoes in step 3.

Red Curry Tofu-Noodle Bowl

Filet Mignon & Mushroom Stroganoff

serves
4

PER SERVING

2 tablespoons all-purpose flour

¼ + ⅛ teaspoon salt

⅛ teaspoon black pepper

10 ounces filet mignon, trimmed and cut into ½-inch pieces

1 tablespoon olive oil

1 large red onion, thinly sliced

½ pound cremini mushrooms, sliced

1 cup reduced-sodium beef broth

¼ cup reduced-fat sour cream

¼ cup chopped fresh flat-leaf parsley

3 cups hot cooked yolk-free whole wheat noodles

1 Combine flour, ¼ teaspoon of salt, and the pepper in large zip-close plastic bag. Add beef and seal bag; toss until coated evenly, shaking off excess flour.

2 Heat oil in large nonstick skillet over medium heat. Add beef and cook, stirring frequently, until lightly browned, about 4 minutes; transfer to plate.

3 Add onion to skillet and cook, stirring, until softened, about 5 minutes. Add to beef on plate. Add mushrooms and remaining ⅛ teaspoon salt to skillet; cook, stirring frequently, until softened, about 6 minutes. Add broth; reduce heat and simmer until juices are slightly reduced, about 3 minutes.

4 Return beef and onion to skillet along with any accumulated juices; cook, stirring, until heated through, about 2 minutes longer. Remove skillet from heat; stir in sour cream and parsley. Serve with noodles.

PER SERVING (½ cup stroganoff and ¾ cup noodles): 333 Cal, 11 g Total Fat, 4 g Sat Fat, 0 g Trans Fat, 47 mg Chol, 299 mg Sod, 33 g Carb, 4 g Sugar, 4 g Fib, 25 g Prot, 66 mg Calc.

FYI While food historians agree that this dish gets its name from Count Stroganoff, a 19th century Russian noble, there are differing accounts regarding the true origins of the dish. It is believed that while the dish had been prepared long before the count gained recognition for it, the dish did not gain in popularity until the count, a great home entertainer, made it famous.

Sunday Supper Braciole

serves
8

PER SERVING

1 cup coarse whole wheat bread crumbs (about 2 slices bread)

¼ cup grated Parmesan cheese

¼ cup sliced fresh basil

3 large garlic cloves, minced

Pinch red pepper flakes

8 (2-ounce) thin slices beef top round, trimmed

¾ teaspoon salt

¼ teaspoon black pepper

1 tablespoon olive oil

1 pound cremini mushrooms, sliced

1 (14½-ounce) can diced tomatoes

1 teaspoon dried oregano

4 cups hot cooked whole wheat penne or rigatoni

1 Stir together bread crumbs, Parmesan, basil, half of garlic, and the pepper flakes on sheet of wax paper.

2 Place slices of beef between two pieces of plastic wrap; pound with meat mallet or bottom of small heavy saucepan to ⅛-inch thickness. Sprinkle beef with ½ teaspoon of salt and ⅛ teaspoon of black pepper. Sprinkle bread crumb mixture evenly over beef, pressing lightly so it adheres. Roll up each slice of beef beginning with short side. Secure each roll with toothpick.

3 Heat oil in large nonstick skillet over medium-high heat. Add beef rolls and cook until browned on all sides, about 4 minutes. Transfer to large plate.

4 Add mushrooms and remaining garlic, ¼ teaspoon salt, and ⅛ teaspoon black pepper to skillet. Cook, stirring, until mushrooms are softened, about 5 minutes. Return beef with any accumulated juices to skillet; stir in tomatoes with their juice and the oregano; bring to simmer. Cook, covered, until beef is very tender when pierced with fork, about 30 minutes. Transfer braciole to platter; remove toothpicks. Spoon some tomato sauce over braciole. Toss remaining sauce with pasta and serve alongside.

PER SERVING (1 braciole, about ½ cup sauce, and ½ cup pasta): 283 Cal, 6 g Total Fat, 2 g Sat Fat, 0 g Trans Fat, 30 mg Chol, 569 mg Sod, 33 g Carb, 5 g Sugar, 4 g Fib, 22 g Prot, 106 mg Calc.

FYI When freezing food in plastic containers, be sure to look for the snowflake icon, an indication that the containers are recommended for freezer use.

Charred Beef Salad with Noodles & Mixed Greens

8 PointsPlus® value
PER SERVING

serves **6**

⅓ cup lime juice

2 tablespoons Asian fish sauce

1 tablespoon reduced-sodium soy sauce

1 tablespoon packed brown sugar

1 tablespoon canola oil

3 garlic cloves, minced

⅛ teaspoon black pepper

1 pound beef top round, trimmed and cut into thin strips

1 (7-ounce) package rice stick noodles (vermicelli)

1 bunch watercress, trimmed

1 large red bell pepper, cut into thin strips

1 large tomato, seeded and diced

1 cup bean sprouts

⅓ cup lightly packed fresh cilantro leaves

¼ cup thinly sliced fresh mint

¼ cup unsalted peanuts, finely chopped

1 To make dressing, whisk together lime juice, fish sauce, soy sauce, brown sugar, oil, garlic, and black pepper in serving bowl. Transfer 2 tablespoons of dressing to large zip-close plastic bag; add beef. Squeeze out air and seal bag; turn to coat beef. Refrigerate, turning bag occasionally, at least 30 minutes or up to 3 hours.

2 Meanwhile, put noodles in large bowl and add enough hot water to cover. Cover bowl with plastic wrap and soak until noodles are softened, about 10 minutes. Drain.

3 Heat large heavy nonstick or cast-iron skillet over high heat. Remove beef from marinade; discard marinade. Lightly pat beef dry with paper towels. Cook beef, in batches, turning once, until cooked through and lightly charred along edges, about 3 minutes per batch; transfer to dressing in bowl.

4 Add noodles, watercress, bell pepper, tomato, bean sprouts, cilantro, and mint to dressing in bowl; toss until mixed well. Top with beef mixture and sprinkle with peanuts.

PER SERVING (about 2 cups): 324 Cal, 9 g Total Fat, 2 g Sat Fat, 0 g Trans Fat, 37 mg Chol, 595 mg Sod, 34 g Carb, 5 g Sugar, 2 g Fib, 24 g Prot, 69 mg Calc.

FYI The easiest way to thinly slice a piece of beef is to first put it on a plate or sheet of foil and freeze until very firm, which will take about 30 minutes. When slicing, be sure to use a long thin-bladed knife for the best results.

Bolognese Sauce with Bacon & Fennel

 serves **6**

PER SERVING

¾ pound ground lean beef (7% fat or less)

4 slices turkey bacon, chopped

1 onion, chopped

1 carrot, chopped

1 celery stalk, chopped

2 garlic cloves, minced

½ teaspoon ground fennel

½ teaspoon ground cumin

1 (28-ounce) can crushed tomatoes

½ cup dry red wine

¼ teaspoon black pepper

6 cups hot cooked whole wheat spaghetti

¾ cup fat-free ricotta cheese

¼ cup chopped fresh mint

1   Heat large nonstick skillet over medium heat. Add beef and bacon; cook, breaking beef up with side of spoon, until beef and bacon are browned, about 5 minutes. Add onion, carrot, celery, garlic, fennel, and cumin; cook, stirring, until vegetables are softened, about 5 minutes.

2   Add tomatoes, wine, and pepper to skillet; bring to boil. Reduce heat and simmer, stirring occasionally, until slightly thickened, about 15 minutes.

3   Divide spaghetti equally among 6 large shallow bowls; top evenly with Bolognese sauce and ricotta. Sprinkle with mint.

PER SERVING (about ⅔ cup sauce, 1 cup pasta, and 2 tablespoons ricotta): 381 Cal, 7 g Total Fat, 2 g Sat Fat, 0 g Trans Fat, 46 mg Chol, 484 mg Sod, 53 g Carb, 4 g Sugar, 10 g Fib, 28 g Prot, 191 mg Calc.

Cuban-Style Picadillo

 serves **6**

PER SERVING

1 tablespoon olive oil

1 large green bell pepper, chopped

1 red onion, chopped

3 garlic cloves, minced

1 pound ground lean beef (7% fat or less)

1 (14½-ounce) can diced tomatoes

2 teaspoons ground cumin

1 teaspoon hot pepper sauce

½ teaspoon salt

¼ teaspoon black pepper

1 cup frozen baby peas

¼ cup dark raisins

¼ cup pitted green olives, coarsely chopped

3 cups hot cooked brown rice

1   Heat oil in large nonstick skillet over medium heat. Add bell pepper, onion, and garlic; cook, stirring, until onion is golden, about 8 minutes. Add beef and cook, breaking it apart with side of spoon, until browned, about 6 minutes.

2   Add tomatoes, cumin, pepper sauce, salt, and black pepper to skillet; bring to boil. Reduce heat and simmer, covered, until flavors are blended, about 10 minutes. Stir in peas, raisins, and olives; cook, stirring, about 5 minutes longer. Serve with rice.

PER SERVING (scant 1 cup picadillo and ½ cup rice): 310 Cal, 8 g Total Fat, 2 g Sat Fat, 0 g Trans Fat, 16 mg Chol, 104 mg Sod, 39 g Carb, 10 g Sugar, 5 g Fib, 20 g Prot, 50 mg Calc.

FYI   Picadillo is a very versatile dish. It can be used as a stuffing for lightly cooked vegetables, including zucchini, tomato, and baby eggplant. It's also delicious served over whole wheat pasta or as a burrito filling using whole wheat tortillas.

Pork Tenderloin in Sour Cream–Paprika Sauce

8 PointsPlus® value
PER SERVING

serves **4**

1 tablespoon all-purpose flour

½ teaspoon salt

¼ teaspoon black pepper

1 pound pork tenderloin, trimmed and cut into 1-inch chunks

2 teaspoons olive oil

1 onion, thinly sliced

1 large green bell pepper, cut into thin strips

1 tablespoon paprika, preferably Hungarian

¾ cup reduced-sodium chicken broth

½ cup fat-free sour cream

2 tablespoons chopped fresh parsley

3 cups hot cooked wide whole wheat egg noodles

1 Combine flour, salt, and black pepper in large zip-close plastic bag. Add pork; seal bag and shake until pork is coated evenly.

2 Heat oil in large nonstick skillet over medium-high heat. Cook pork, in batches, until lightly browned, about 3 minutes per batch; transfer to plate.

3 Add onion and bell pepper to skillet. Cook, stirring, until onion is softened, about 5 minutes; stir in paprika. Return pork with any accumulated juices to skillet. Stir in broth and bring to boil. Reduce heat and simmer, covered, until pork is tender, about 25 minutes. Remove skillet from heat; stir in sour cream until blended. Sprinkle with parsley and serve with noodles.

PER SERVING (about 1 cup pork with sauce and ¾ cup noodles): 320 Cal, 6 g Total Fat, 1 g Sat Fat, 0 g Trans Fat, 77 mg Chol, 518 mg Sod, 36 g Carb, 5 g Sugar, 5 g Fib, 31 g Prot, 78 mg Calc.

FYI Paprika, made by finely grinding dried sweet or hot red peppers, is made in California, Spain, South America, and Hungary, which some consider the best in the world. For most dishes, sweet paprika is the way to go. For a touch of heat, reach for hot paprika. And to add deep smoky flavor to a dish, try Spanish smoked paprika, *pimentón*, which is made by slowly smoking peppers over an oak fire.

Fragrant Indian-Spiced Lamb Stew

serves
6

PER SERVING

2 tablespoons minced peeled fresh ginger

2 teaspoons ground cumin

¾ teaspoon salt

½ teaspoon ground turmeric

¼ teaspoon ground cinnamon

⅛ teaspoon cayenne

1 pound boneless leg of lamb, trimmed and cut into ¾-inch chunks

⅓ cup plain fat-free yogurt

2 teaspoons canola oil

1 large onion, chopped

1 cup basmati rice

1½ cups reduced-sodium chicken broth

3 tablespoons chopped unsalted cashews

3 tablespoons golden raisins

1 Combine ginger, cumin, salt, turmeric, cinnamon, and cayenne on sheet of wax paper. Put lamb in large zip-close plastic bag. Add yogurt and half of spice mixture. Squeeze out air and seal bag; toss until coated evenly. Refrigerate at least 2 hours or up to 5 hours.

2 Heat oil in large nonstick skillet over medium heat. Add onion and cook, stirring, until softened, about 5 minutes. Add remaining spice mixture and cook, stirring constantly, until fragrant, about 2 minutes. Add lamb and cook, stirring, about 3 minutes longer.

3 Add rice to skillet and cook, stirring, 2 minutes. Stir in broth and bring to boil. Reduce heat and simmer, covered, until lamb is fork-tender, rice is tender, and liquid is absorbed, about 30 minutes. Remove skillet from heat; let stand 5 minutes. Serve sprinkled with cashews and raisins.

PER SERVING (scant 1 cup lamb mixture, ½ tablespoon cashews, and ½ tablespoon raisins): 358 Cal, 12 g Total Fat, 4 g Sat Fat, 0 g Trans Fat, 80 mg Chol, 507 mg Sod, 36 g Carb, 6 g Sugar, 2 g Fib, 26 g Prot, 73 mg Calc.

Healthy Extra Serve the stew with a side of steamed whole green beans and a bowl of fragrant brown basmati rice (⅔ cup cooked brown basmati rice per serving will increase the *PointsPlus* value by **3**.)

Lamb-Bulgur Meatballs in Quick Tomato Sauce

PER SERVING

serves
6

1 pound ground lean lamb

½ cup bulgur

½ cup chopped fresh parsley

1 large onion, chopped

2 large garlic cloves, minced

¼ cup fat-free egg substitute

1 teaspoon ground cumin

¾ teaspoon salt

¼ teaspoon black pepper

4 teaspoons olive oil

1 (14½-ounce) can whole peeled tomatoes

1 cup fat-free tomato sauce

1 cup water

3 cups hot cooked brown rice

1 Mix together lamb, bulgur, parsley, half of onion, half of garlic, the egg substitute, cumin, ½ teaspoon of salt, and ⅛ teaspoon of pepper in medium bowl. Knead mixture until mixed well and smooth; cover and refrigerate at least 30 minutes or up to 4 hours. Shape lamb mixture into 24 walnut-size meatballs.

2 Heat oil in large nonstick skillet over medium heat. Add remaining onion and garlic; cook, stirring, until onion is golden, about 8 minutes. Add tomatoes with their juice, breaking them up with side of spoon.

3 Add meatballs, tomato sauce, water, and remaining ¼ teaspoon salt and ⅛ teaspoon pepper to skillet; bring to boil. Reduce heat and simmer, covered, turning meatballs occasionally, until cooked through and sauce is slightly thickened, about 20 minutes. Serve with rice.

PER SERVING (4 meatballs, about 1 cup sauce, and ½ cup rice): 266 Cal, 8 g Total Fat, 2 g Sat Fat, 0 g Trans Fat, 48 mg Chol, 699 mg Sod, 32 g Carb, 4 g Sugar, 5 g Fib, 18 g Prot, 59 mg Calc.

Healthy Extra   Round out this meal by serving it with zucchini sprinkled with chopped fresh mint. Slice the zucchini and put into a microwavable dish with a few tablespoons of water. Cover and cook on High until crisp-tender, about 5 minutes. Drain and serve sprinkled with a pinch of salt, pepper, and some mint.

Lamb-Bulgur Meatballs
in Quick Tomato Sauce

Smoky Chicken-Seafood Paella

9 PointsPlus® value

PER SERVING

serves **4**

3 slices turkey bacon, chopped

1 onion, chopped

3 garlic cloves, minced

2 different color bell peppers, diced

2 teaspoons smoked paprika

½ pound skinless boneless chicken breasts, cut into 1-inch chunks

¾ cup long-grain white rice

¾ cup frozen baby peas

1½ cups reduced-sodium chicken broth, warmed

¼ teaspoon saffron threads, crushed

16 littleneck clams, scrubbed

½ pound large shrimp, peeled and deveined

1   Heat large cast-iron or heavy nonstick skillet over medium-high heat. Add bacon and cook until beginning to brown, about 3 minutes. Add onion and garlic; cook, stirring, until onion is softened, about 5 minutes. Add bell peppers and paprika; cook, stirring, until peppers are crisp-tender, about 3 minutes.

2   Add chicken to skillet and cook, stirring occasionally, until golden, about 4 minutes. Stir in rice, peas, broth, and saffron; bring to boil. Reduce heat and simmer, covered, until liquid is almost absorbed and rice is tender, about 25 minutes longer.

3   Scatter clams and shrimp over rice mixture. Increase heat to medium and cook, covered, until clams open and shrimp are just opaque in center, about 5 minutes. Discard any clams that do not open.

PER SERVING (2 cups): 371 Cal, 6 g Total Fat, 1 g Sat Fat, 0 g Trans Fat, 151 mg Chol, 433 mg Sod, 40 g Carb, 6 g Sugar, 4 g Fib, 38 g Prot, 87 mg Calc.

FYI   Saffron is the world's most expensive spice—and for good reason. It takes over 14,000 of the small purple crocus's stigmas (each flower produces only three) to produce one ounce of saffron. Luckily the spice is so aromatic that it takes only a pinch to flavor dishes.

Weeknight Skillet Chicken & Rice

10 PointsPlus® value
PER SERVING

serves **4**

1 pound skinless boneless chicken breasts, cut into 1½-inch chunks

¼ teaspoon salt

¼ teaspoon black pepper

2 teaspoons olive oil

½ pound cremini mushrooms, sliced

1 onion, chopped

1 green bell pepper, chopped

2 celery stalks, thinly sliced

2 carrots, chopped

2 large garlic cloves, minced

½ cup dry white wine or dry vermouth

1 (6-ounce) box long-grain and wild rice mix

2 cups reduced-sodium chicken broth

1 cup canned diced tomatoes, drained

1 teaspoon dried thyme

1 Sprinkle chicken with salt and black pepper. Heat 1 teaspoon of oil in large nonstick skillet over medium-high heat. Add chicken and cook until browned on all sides, 6 minutes; transfer to plate.

2 Reduce heat to medium and add remaining 1 teaspoon oil to skillet. Add mushrooms, onion, bell pepper, celery, carrots, and garlic; cook, stirring, until onion is softened, about 5 minutes. Stir in wine and cook until it is evaporated, about 4 minutes.

3 Add rice mix to skillet, stirring until grains are coated. Return chicken to skillet along with broth, tomatoes, and thyme; bring to boil. Reduce heat and simmer, covered, until broth is absorbed, rice is tender, and chicken is cooked through, about 25 minutes. Remove skillet from heat; let stand 5 minutes before serving.

PER SERVING (about 1½ cups): 374 Cal, 6 g Total Fat, 2 g Sat Fat, 0 g Trans Fat, 63 mg Chol, 685 mg Sod, 49 g Carb, 8 g Sugar, 6 g Fib, 31 g Prot, 82 mg Calc.

Zesty Arugula & Tomato Salad–Topped Turkey Cutlets

5 PointsPlus® value
PER SERVING

serves **4**

8 (2-ounce) turkey cutlets

1 teaspoon salt

¼ teaspoon black pepper

1 tablespoon + 2 teaspoons olive oil

1 bunch arugula, trimmed

½ cup lightly packed fresh basil leaves, torn

½ small red onion, thinly sliced

1 large tomato, chopped

1 small carrot, grated

Juice of 1 lemon

1 Place cutlets between two pieces of plastic wrap and pound to ⅛-inch thickness with meat mallet or bottom of small heavy saucepan. Sprinkle turkey with ½ teaspoon of salt and ⅛ teaspoon of pepper.

2 Heat 1 tablespoon of oil in large nonstick skillet over medium-high heat. Add 4 cutlets and cook until cooked through, about 3 minutes per side. Transfer to plate and keep warm. Repeat with remaining cutlets.

3 To make salad, combine arugula, basil, onion, tomato, and carrot in bowl. Drizzle with lemon juice and remaining 2 teaspoons oil; sprinkle with remaining ½ teaspoon salt and ⅛ teaspoon pepper. Toss. Serve cutlets topped with salad.

PER SERVING (2 turkey cutlets and about 1 cup salad): 205 Cal, 7 g Total Fat, 1 g Sat Fat, 0 g Trans Fat, 45 mg Chol, 708 mg Sod, 7 g Carb, 4 g Sugar, 2 g Fib, 30 g Prot, 113 mg Calc.

FYI During the warmer months, grill the turkey cutlets on a medium-high grill until cooked through, about 3 minutes per side.

Basque-Style Cutlets with Peppers, Tomato & Bacon

serves
4

PER SERVING

3 teaspoons olive oil

4 (¼-pound) turkey cutlets

1 large onion, sliced

1 green bell pepper, cut into strips

1 red bell pepper, cut into strips

1 tomato, cut into thin wedges

2 ounces Canadian bacon, chopped

2 large garlic cloves, minced

¾ cup reduced-sodium
chicken broth

1 teaspoon dried oregano

½ teaspoon salt

¼ teaspoon black pepper

1   Heat 2 teaspoons of oil in large nonstick skillet over medium-high heat. Add turkey cutlets and cook until browned, about 3 minutes per side; transfer to plate.

2   Reduce heat to medium and add remaining 1 teaspoon oil to skillet. Add onion and bell peppers; cook, stirring, until softened, about 5 minutes. Add tomato, Canadian bacon, and garlic; cook, stirring, until tomato is softened, about 5 minutes longer.

3   Add broth, oregano, salt, and black pepper to skillet; bring to boil. Reduce heat and simmer, covered, until flavors are blended, about 10 minutes. Return turkey to skillet and cook until heated through, about 2 minutes longer.

PER SERVING (1 turkey cutlet and ¾ cup vegetable mixture): 209 Cal, 5 g Total Fat, 1 g Sat Fat, 0 g Trans Fat, 50 mg Chol, 638 mg Sod, 9 g Carb, 4 g Sugar, 2 g Fib, 32 g Prot, 29 mg Calc.

Healthy Extra   Enjoy this Basque dish with a side dish of mashed sweet potatoes — 2 large sweet potatoes, cooked and mashed for 4 servings will increase the per-serving *PointsPlus* value by *2*.

Basque-Style Cutlets with
Peppers, Tomato & Bacon

Spinach & Provolone–Stuffed Chicken

serves
4

PER SERVING

4 (¼-pound) chicken cutlets

¼ teaspoon black pepper

4 very thin slices prosciutto

1 (10-ounce) package frozen
chopped spinach, thawed and
squeezed dry

¼ cup grated Parmesan cheese

2 slices reduced-fat provolone
cheese, each cut in half

1 tablespoon olive oil

1 (14½-ounce) can reduced-sodium
chicken broth

1 tablespoon finely
chopped fresh parsley

1   Place chicken cutlets between two pieces of plastic wrap and pound to even thickness with meat mallet or bottom of small heavy saucepan.

2   Sprinkle chicken with pepper. Place 1 slice of prosciutto on top of each cutlet. Spread spinach evenly over prosciutto and sprinkle evenly with Parmesan. Top each cutlet with ½ slice of provolone. Roll up each chicken cutlet starting at tapered end. Secure each roll with toothpick.

3   Heat oil in large nonstick skillet over medium-high heat. Add chicken rolls and cook until golden brown on all sides, about 4 minutes. Add broth and cook, scraping up browned bits from bottom of skillet with wooden spoon. Bring broth to boil; reduce heat and simmer, covered, until chicken is cooked through, about 10 minutes longer.

4   Transfer chicken to platter and keep warm. Increase heat under skillet to high and cook until pan liquid is syrupy, about 5 minutes. Pour over chicken and sprinkle with parsley.

PER SERVING (1 chicken roll and about 2 tablespoons pan sauce): 270 Cal, 12 g Total Fat, 4 g Sat Fat, 0 g Trans Fat, 86 mg Chol, 919 mg Sod, 5 g Carb, 1 g Sugar, 2 g Fib, 36 g Prot, 274 mg Calc.

Healthy Extra   Serve this tasty dish with a side of whole wheat penne topped with chopped tomato and thinly sliced basil (½ cup cooked whole wheat penne per serving will increase the *PointsPlus* value by 2).

Turkey Sausage with Sun-Dried Tomato Couscous

PER SERVING

serves
6

2 teaspoons olive oil

6 sweet Italian-style turkey sausages (about 1 pound)

1 onion, chopped

1 green bell pepper, diced

2 garlic cloves, minced

1¼ cups reduced-sodium chicken broth

1 (6-ounce) bag baby spinach

1 cup whole wheat couscous

6 moist-packed sun-dried tomatoes (not packed in oil), chopped

⅛ teaspoon black pepper

1   Heat oil in large nonstick skillet over medium-high heat. Add sausages and cook, turning often, until browned and cooked through about 6 minutes. Transfer to plate and keep warm.

2   Reduce heat to medium. Add onion, bell pepper, and garlic to skillet; cook, stirring, until onion is softened, about 5 minutes.

3   Return sausages to skillet. Add broth and bring to boil over medium-high heat. Stir in spinach and cook, stirring occasionally, until beginning to wilt, about 2 minutes. Stir in couscous, sun-dried tomatoes, and black pepper. Cover and remove skillet from heat. Let stand until liquid is absorbed and couscous is tender, about 5 minutes. Fluff couscous with fork.

PER SERVING (1 sausage and about ½ cup couscous mixture): 243 Cal, 10 g Total Fat, 0 g Sat Fat, 0 g Trans Fat, 45 mg Chol, 692 mg Sod, 23 g Carb, 4 g Sugar, 5 g Fib, 17 g Prot, 44 mg Calc.

Street Fair Sausage, Potatoes & Peppers

8 PointsPlus® value

PER SERVING

serves **4**

4 sweet or hot Italian-style turkey sausages, pierced with fork

¼ cup water

1 tablespoon olive oil

1 (1-pound) package refrigerated fully cooked cubed potatoes

2 large red or green bell peppers, cut into thick strips

1 large onion, sliced

1 large garlic clove, minced

¼ teaspoon salt

¼ teaspoon black pepper

1 Combine sausages and water in large nonstick skillet and bring to boil. Reduce heat and simmer, covered, 5 minutes. Uncover and cook, turning sausages occasionally, until well browned and cooked through, about 10 minutes longer; transfer to plate. When cool enough to handle, thickly slice sausages. Wipe skillet dry.

2 Add oil to skillet and set over medium heat. Add potatoes, bell peppers, onion, garlic, salt, and black pepper; cook, stirring frequently, until vegetables are tender, about 12 minutes. Return sausages to skillet and cook until heated through, about 3 minutes longer.

PER SERVING (about 1¾ cups): 309 Cal, 13 g Total Fat, 1 g Sat Fat, 0 g Trans Fat, 50 mg Chol, 698 mg Sod, 32 g Carb, 7 g Sugar, 4 g Fib, 17 g Prot, 26 mg Calc.

FYI Using packaged fully cooked cubed potatoes in this dish cuts down on your kitchen time and on the number of pots used. These potatoes are usually found next to other cut-up packaged vegetables in the produce section.

Crisp Cod Cakes with Tomato-Peach Salad

serves
4

1 pound cod or scrod fillets, finely chopped

1 large egg

6 tablespoons plain dried bread crumbs

1 shallot, minced

2 tablespoons chopped fresh parsley

¾ teaspoon salt

¼ teaspoon black pepper

¼ teaspoon hot pepper sauce

3 peaches, halved, pitted, and cut into thin wedges

2 tomatoes, cut into thin wedges

2 scallions, thinly sliced on diagonal

6 large fresh basil leaves, thinly sliced

1 tablespoon lime juice

4 teaspoons olive oil

Lime wedges

1   To make cod cakes, mix together cod, egg, 2 tablespoons of bread crumbs, the shallot, parsley, ½ teaspoon of salt, ⅛ teaspoon of black pepper, and the pepper sauce in large bowl. With damp hands, shape mixture into 4 (3-inch) patties. Transfer patties to wax paper–lined plate; refrigerate until firm, about 30 minutes.

2   Meanwhile, to make salad, gently toss together peaches, tomatoes, scallions, basil, lime juice, and remaining ¼ teaspoon salt and ⅛ teaspoon pepper in serving bowl.

3   Spread remaining 4 tablespoons bread crumbs on sheet of wax paper. Lightly coat patties with crumbs.

4   Heat oil in large nonstick skillet over medium heat. Add patties and cook until golden brown and cooked through, about 5 minutes per side. Serve with salad and lime wedges.

PER SERVING (1 cod cake and about 1 cup salad): 231 Cal, 7 g Total Fat, 1 g Sat Fat, 0 g Trans Fat, 97 mg Chol, 609 mg Sod, 20 g Carb, 3 g Sugar, 3 g Fib, 23 g Prot, 48 mg Calc.

Healthy Extra   Microwave-cooked corn on the cob makes the perfect side for this dish. Remove the husks and silk from 4 medium ears of corn. Place the corn in a microwavable dish and cover with a double thickness of damp paper towels. Microwave on High until the corn is just tender, about 8 minutes. One medium ear of corn per serving will increase the *PointsPlus* value by 2.

Fiery Shrimp with Bok Choy & Rice

Fiery Shrimp with Bok Choy & Rice

serves
4

PER SERVING

3 teaspoons canola oil

1 pound medium shrimp, peeled and deveined

1 cup matchstick-cut carrots

2 baby bok choy, halved lengthwise

6 scallions, cut into 1½-inch lengths

2 tablespoons grated peeled fresh ginger

2 large garlic cloves, minced

½ cup jasmine rice

1½ cups reduced-sodium chicken broth

1 tablespoon reduced-sodium soy sauce

¼–½ teaspoon red pepper flakes

1 Heat 1½ teaspoons of oil in large nonstick skillet over medium-high heat. Add shrimp and cook, turning often, until just opaque in center, about 3 minutes. Transfer to medium bowl.

2 Add remaining 1½ teaspoons oil to skillet. Add carrots, bok choy, scallions, ginger, and garlic; cook, stirring, until fragrant, about 2 minutes. Add rice, tossing to coat. Stir in broth, soy sauce, and pepper flakes; bring to boil. Reduce heat and simmer, covered, until liquid is absorbed and rice is tender, about 20 minutes.

3 Return shrimp to skillet and cook, stirring frequently, until heated through, about 3 minutes.

PER SERVING (about 1½ cups): 231 Cal, 5 g Total Fat, 1 g Sat Fat, 0 g Trans Fat, 168 mg Chol, 613 mg Sod, 18 g Carb, 5 g Sugar, 3 g Fib, 22 g Prot, 83 mg Calc.

FYI Jasmine rice, an aromatic rice once only grown in Thailand, is now also cultivated in the United States. The grains look similar to regular long-grain rice but cook up moister and more tender.

Spaghetti Carbonara with Broccoli & Bacon

 serves 4

PER SERVING

1 (10-ounce) package frozen chopped broccoli, thawed and gently squeezed dry

¾ cup low-fat (1%) milk

½ cup grated Parmesan cheese

1 large egg, lightly beaten

¼ cup fat-free egg substitute

1 tablespoon olive oil

3 garlic cloves, minced

3 slices turkey bacon, chopped

¼ cup dry vermouth or dry white wine

4 cups hot cooked whole wheat spaghetti

1 tablespoon chopped fresh flat-leaf parsley

¼ teaspoon black pepper

1 Mix together broccoli, milk, Parmesan, egg, and egg substitute in medium bowl.

2 Heat oil in large nonstick skillet over medium heat. Add garlic and cook, stirring, until light golden, about 2 minutes. Add bacon and cook, stirring, until crisp, about 4 minutes. Add vermouth and cook until it is almost evaporated, about 30 seconds longer.

3 Reduce heat to medium-low. Add spaghetti and broccoli mixture to skillet; cook, tossing constantly, until eggs are cooked through and mixture is creamy, about 3 minutes. Remove skillet from heat; sprinkle with parsley and pepper; toss to mix well.

PER SERVING (about 1½ cups): 372 Cal, 12 g Total Fat, 4 g Sat Fat, 0 g Trans Fat, 75 mg Chol, 474 mg Sod, 45 g Carb, 4 g Sugar, 9 g Fib, 19 g Prot, 243 mg Calc.

FYI This classic pasta dish works well with whole wheat penne, which makes it even heartier.

No-Fuss Meatless Skillet Lasagna

 serves 4

PER SERVING

1 red onion, finely chopped

1 garlic clove, minced

1 (28-ounce) can whole peeled tomatoes, drained and chopped

¼ cup canned tomato sauce

⅛ teaspoon black pepper

4 tablespoons chopped fresh flat-leaf parsley

6 ounces whole wheat lasagna noodles, broken into 1½-inch pieces and cooked according to package directions

½ cup part-skim ricotta cheese

⅓ cup shredded part-skim mozzarella cheese

2 tablespoons grated Parmesan cheese

1 Spray large nonstick skillet with nonstick spray and set over medium heat. Add onion and cook, stirring, until softened, about 5 minutes. Add garlic and cook, stirring, until fragrant, about 30 seconds. Stir in tomatoes, tomato sauce, and pepper; cook, stirring frequently, until slightly thickened, about 6 minutes; stir in 3 tablespoons of parsley.

2 Stir noodles into skillet. Cook, stirring, until heated through, about 3 minutes. Drop 8 spoonfuls of ricotta, evenly spaced, onto noodle mixture; sprinkle with mozzarella, Parmesan, and remaining 1 tablespoon parsley. Cook, covered, without stirring, until heated through and cheese is melted, about 3 minutes longer.

PER SERVING (1 cup): 297 Cal, 7 g Total Fat, 3 g Sat Fat, 0 g Trans Fat, 17 mg Chol, 639 mg Sod, 44 g Carb, 8 g Sugar, 9 g Fib, 16 g Prot, 229 mg Calc.

Healthy Extra Fresh mushrooms add an enticing earthy quality to the tomato sauce. Add 1 cup of thinly sliced cremini mushrooms to the skillet after the onion is softened and cook until golden.

Lobster Mac 'n' Cheese

serves
6

PER SERVING

1 tablespoon butter

2 tablespoons all-purpose flour

1 (14½-ounce) can diced fire-roasted tomatoes

1 cup shredded reduced-fat Cheddar cheese

½ cup fat-free milk

⅓ cup grated Parmesan cheese

½ teaspoon mustard powder

¼ teaspoon black pepper

4 cups cooked whole wheat elbow macaroni

¾ pound lobster meat, cut into small chunks

2 tablespoons chopped fresh parsley

1   Melt butter in large nonstick skillet over medium-high heat. Add flour and cook, stirring constantly, until roux is golden, about 1 minute. Add tomatoes and cook, stirring constantly, until mixture bubbles and is slightly thickened, about 3 minutes.

2   Add Cheddar, milk, Parmesan, mustard powder, and pepper to flour mixture; cook, stirring, until cheese is melted and sauce is smooth, about 2 minutes. Add macaroni and lobster; cook, tossing, until heated through and mixed well, about 2 minutes. Serve sprinkled with parsley.

PER SERVING (generous 1 cup): 320 Cal, 9 g Total Fat, 5 g Sat Fat, 0 g Trans Fat, 74 mg Chol, 529 mg Sod, 34 g Carb, 4 g Sugar, 3 g Fib, 28 g Prot, 406 mg Calc.

FYI   If you like, an equal amount of chopped cooked shrimp or lump crabmeat can be substituted for the lobster.

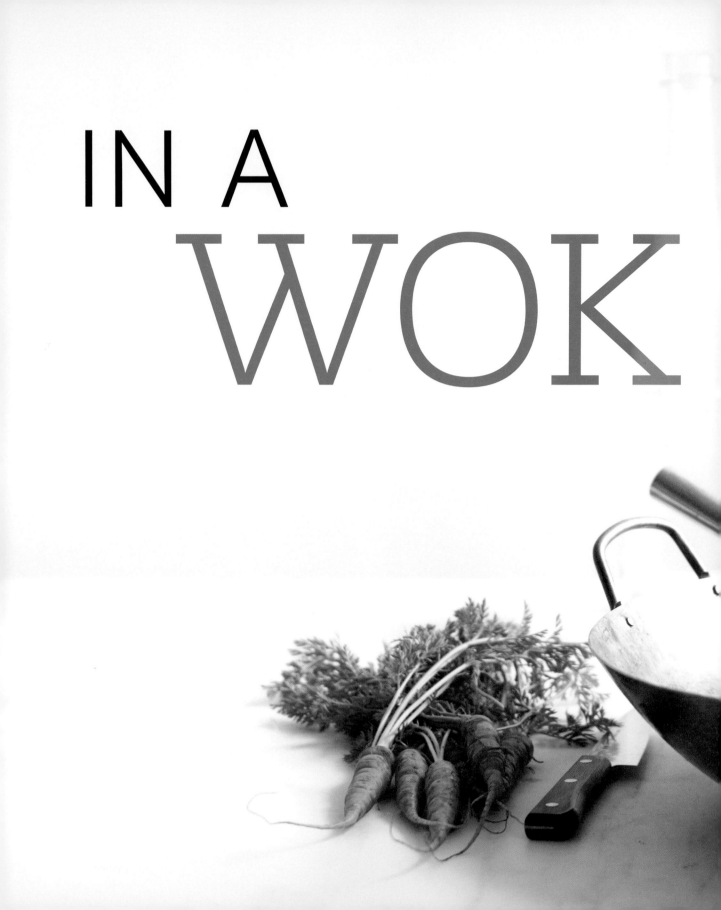

IN A
WOK

CHAPTER 3

IN A WOK

MAKE IT STIR-FRIED FOR DINNER

The word *wok*, synonymous with stir-frying, is a versatile cooking vessel believed to have originated in China around the 10th century. Woks are most often used for stir-frying, but throughout Southeast Asia they are also used for steaming, deep-frying, braising, and stewing. Traditional woks have a round bottom so they can be used on a pit stove. This stove has a hole in which the wok is set so it is surrounded by flames and kept steady. If you buy a round-bottomed wok, be sure to purchase a metal wok ring, which allows you to set the wok inside the ring to keep it stable. Woks also come flat-bottomed, making them a must for electric stoves and a good choice for gas stoves.

Types

Although traditional Chinese woks are made of thin cast iron, **carbon steel woks** are more commonly used today. The more they are used, the more seasoned (nonstick) they become. Carbon steel woks are excellent for stir-frying, as they heat evenly and maintain their temperature. Woks are sold with either a long handle or two short curved handles; both work well.

Stainless steel woks are appreciated for their ability to both quickly heat up and cool down. The best models have an aluminum core sandwiched between two layers of stainless steel for superior heat conduction. These flat-bottomed woks often come with one long handle and a curved helper handle on the opposite side. Stainless steel woks are modern and sleek looking and sometimes come with a lustrous brushed finish.

Nonstick woks make cleanup a snap. Choose one with a petroleum-free ceramic-based interior, which can stand up to high heat and is almost scratchproof. They are more expensive than other nonstick woks.

Electric woks heat up quickly and maintain even cooking temperature. A heat control knob allows them to be heated up to about 425°F, and they often come with a tempered glass cover. Electric woks are available with nonstick and stainless steel interiors.

Sizes

Woks range from 8 inches to 30 inches. A 14-inch-diameter wok is a good choice for 4 to 6 servings.

Basics for Care

A **carbon steel wok** needs a little attention before it is used for the first time. Wash the wok in hot, soapy water, then dry it well and set it over medium heat. Add a little flavorless vegetable oil and wipe it over the surface with a paper towel. Let the wok get very hot, then remove it from the heat and let it cool. Rinse it with hot water and dry it well. After cooking, rinse the wok with hot water and wipe it dry. If needed, lightly rub the interior with a sponge to remove any food particles. Do not use soap, as this will remove the freshly seasoned surface.

A **stainless steel wok** requires the same care as a stainless steel pot. Once it cools down a little, soak it in hot, soapy water for about 30 minutes to loosen any food residue. Wash the wok with a sponge or nylon scrub pad, then rinse well and dry. Do not use a steel wool soap pad, as it can scratch the surface. Stainless steel woks are dishwasher safe.

A **nonstick wok** is easy to care for. Wash it in hot, soapy water using a sponge or nylon scrub pad. This wok is dishwasher safe.

Every part of an **electric wok,** except the temperature control and electric cord, is dishwasher safe. Alternatively, the wok can be washed in hot, soapy water with a sponge or nylon scrub pad.

Szechuan Orange-Ginger Beef

serves
4

2 navel oranges

⅔ cup reduced-sodium chicken broth

3 tablespoons reduced-sodium soy sauce

1 tablespoon cornstarch

½ teaspoon red pepper flakes

1 tablespoon canola oil

1 pound beef top round, trimmed and cut into ⅛ x 2-inch slices

¾ pound green beans, trimmed and cut into 1½-inch lengths

1 yellow bell pepper, cut into thin strips

4 scallions, cut into 2-inch lengths

2 tablespoons minced peeled fresh ginger

2 large garlic cloves, minced

2 cups hot cooked brown rice

1 With vegetable peeler, remove 3 (4-inch) strips zest from one of the oranges; thinly slice strips on diagonal. With knife, remove peel and pith from both oranges. Holding orange over small bowl to catch juice, cut along either side of each membrane to release orange sections, allowing juice to fall into bowl. Repeat.

2 Whisk together ⅓ cup of broth, the orange juice, soy sauce, cornstarch, and pepper flakes in small bowl until blended.

3 Heat wok or large deep nonstick skillet over medium-high heat until a drop of water sizzles in pan. Add oil and swirl to coat wok. Add beef and stir-fry until lightly browned, about 4 minutes; transfer to plate.

4 Add beans, bell pepper, orange zest, and remaining ⅓ cup broth to wok. Cook, covered, 2 minutes. Uncover and add scallions, ginger, and garlic; stir-fry until fragrant, about 30 seconds. Re-whisk cornstarch mixture. Return beef to wok along with orange sections and cornstarch mixture. Stir-fry until sauce bubbles and thickens, about 1 minute. Serve with rice.

PER SERVING (1½ cups orange beef and ½ cup rice): 400 Cal, 10 g Total Fat, 2 g Sat Fat, 0 g Trans Fat, 56 mg Chol, 538 mg Sod, 46 g Carb, 9 g Sugar, 7 g Fib, 33 g Prot, 102 mg Calc.

FYI There are two ways to quickly trim green beans: stack the beans and use a knife to cut off the ends or snap off the ends with your fingers. They will break off at just the right place.

Beef with Tomatoes & Green Beans in Black Bean Sauce

serves
4

¼ cup water

2 tablespoons black bean sauce

1 tablespoon pure maple syrup

2 teaspoons cider vinegar

2 teaspoons canola oil

¾ pound beef top round, trimmed and thinly sliced

3 garlic cloves, thinly sliced

¾ pound green beans, trimmed and cut in half on diagonal

1 pint assorted color mini heirloom tomatoes or cherry tomatoes, halved

2 cups hot cooked brown rice

1   Whisk together water, black bean sauce, maple syrup, and vinegar in small bowl.

2   Heat wok or large deep nonstick skillet over high heat until a drop of water sizzles in pan. Add oil and swirl to coat wok. Add beef and stir-fry until browned, about 4 minutes; transfer to plate.

3   Add garlic to wok and stir-fry until fragrant, about 30 seconds. Add green beans and stir-fry until crisp-tender, about 5 minutes. Add tomatoes and stir-fry 2 minutes.

4   Return beef to wok along with black bean sauce mixture; stir-fry until heated through, about 1 minute longer. Serve over rice.

PER SERVING (1 cup beef mixture and ½ cup rice): 308 Cal, 7 g Fat, 2 g Sat Fat, 0 g Trans Fat, 42 mg Chol, 89 mg Sod, 36 g Carb, 5 g Sugar, 5 g Fib, 25 g Prot, 59 mg Calc.

FYI   During late summer and early fall, farmers' markets offer containers filled with a mix of yellow, green, red, and burgundy mini heirloom tomatoes. They are very sweet and very flavorful.

Beef & Vegetable Sukiyaki

8 PointsPlus value

PER SERVING

serves **8**

4 teaspoons canola oil

2 tablespoons sugar

1 (1-pound) beef tenderloin, trimmed, halved lengthwise, and thinly sliced

8 ounces whole wheat capellini, cooked according to package directions

½ pound Savoy cabbage, cut into 1-inch pieces

½ pound shiitake mushrooms, stemmed and halved

½ pound bean sprouts

1 red bell pepper, diced

8 scallions, cut into 1½-inch lengths

1⅓ cups reduced-sodium chicken broth

⅓ cup sake or dry white wine

¼ cup reduced-sodium soy sauce

½ pound reduced-fat firm tofu, cut into ¾-inch cubes

1 bunch watercress, trimmed

1 Heat oil in large wok or Dutch oven over medium heat. Sprinkle sugar over oil and stir-fry until caramel-colored, about 2 minutes.

2 Increase heat to medium-high; add half of beef and stir-fry until just cooked through, about 2 minutes; transfer to plate. Repeat with remaining beef, reducing heat to medium to prevent sugar from burning, if necessary.

3 Return beef to wok along with capellini, cabbage, mushrooms, bean sprouts, bell pepper, scallions, broth, sake, and soy sauce; bring to boil. Reduce heat and simmer, covered, stirring occasionally, until vegetables are softened, about 5 minutes. Stir in tofu and watercress; cook until watercress is wilted, about 1 minute longer.

PER SERVING (about 1½ cups): 289 Cal, 7 g Total Fat, 2 g Sat Fat, 0 g Trans Fat, 34 mg Chol, 421 mg Sod, 35 g Carb, 7 g Sugar, 7 g Fib, 23 g Prot, 137 mg Calc.

Healthy Extra For dessert, cook 2 or 3 chopped McIntosh apples with 1 cup of fresh or frozen raspberries and a little water until softened. Serve warm or at room temperature, sprinkled with fresh mint.

Beef & Asparagus Stir-Fry

PointsPlus® value **7**
PER SERVING

serves **4**

¾ cup reduced-sodium chicken broth

3 tablespoons reduced-sodium soy sauce

1 tablespoon cornstarch

1 pound asparagus, trimmed

1 tablespoon vegetable oil

1 pound beef top round, trimmed and cut into ⅛ x 2-inch slices

3 garlic cloves, minced

1 red bell pepper, cut into thin strips

6 ounces small shiitake mushrooms, stemmed

1 tablespoon toasted sesame seeds

1   Whisk together broth, soy sauce, and cornstarch in small bowl until smooth.

2   Cut off asparagus tips and put on sheet of foil. Cut asparagus on long diagonal into thin slices; add to asparagus tips.

3   Heat wok or large deep nonstick skillet over high heat until a drop of water sizzles in pan. Add oil and swirl to coat wok. Add beef and stir-fry until lightly browned, about 4 minutes; transfer to plate.

4   Add asparagus and garlic to wok; stir-fry until asparagus is crisp-tender, about 2 minutes. Add bell pepper and mushrooms; stir-fry until mushrooms are softened, about 2 minutes. Return beef and any accumulated juices to wok. Re-whisk broth mixture and add to wok; stir-fry until sauce bubbles and thickens, about 1 minute. Serve sprinkled with sesame seeds.

PER SERVING (about 1½ cups): 279 Cal, 10 g Total Fat, 2 g Sat Fat, 0 g Trans Fat, 56 mg Chol, 549 mg Sod, 16 g Carb, 5 g Sugar, 4 g Fib, 32 g Prot, 53 mg Calc.

Healthy Extra   Serve this stir-fry with red or white quinoa (⅔ cup cooked quinoa per serving will increase the *PointsPlus* value by **3**).

Stir-Fried Beef, Corn & Peppers Tex Mex–Style

serves
4

1 (¾-pound) flank steak, trimmed

1 tablespoon chili powder

1 teaspoon dried oregano

¾ teaspoon salt

2 teaspoons canola oil

2 red bell peppers,
cut into 1-inch chunks

2 yellow bell peppers,
cut into 1-inch chunks

½ cup fresh corn kernels
(about 1 ear of corn)

1 red onion, thinly sliced

3 large garlic cloves, minced

¼ cup chopped fresh cilantro

4 ounces fideo noodles, cooked
according to package directions

1 Cut steak across grain into ¼-inch slices. Cut each slice crosswise into 6 pieces. Mix together chili powder, oregano, and salt on large sheet of foil; add beef and toss until coated evenly.

2 Heat wok or large deep nonstick skillet over high heat until a drop of water sizzles in pan. Add oil and swirl to coat wok. Add steak and stir-fry until lightly browned, about 4 minutes; transfer to plate.

3 Add bell peppers, corn, and onion to wok; stir-fry until bell peppers are crisp-tender, about 5 minutes. Add garlic and stir-fry until fragrant, about 30 seconds. Return beef to wok along with cilantro and stir-fry until heated through, about 1 minute longer. Serve over noodles.

PER SERVING (1¼ cups beef mixture and ½ cup noodles): 325 Cal, 8 g Fat, 2 g Sat Fat, 0 g Trans Fat, 31 mg Chol, 502 mg Sod, 39 g Carb, 8 g Sugar, 5 g Fib, 25 g Prot, 59 mg Calc.

FYI Fideo are Spanish dry vermicelli noodles that are often used in soups and in a paella-like dish called *fideua* (FID-a-wah). The noodles can be found online at spanishtable.com. You can also use spaghetti broken into 2-inch lengths or purchase already-cut dried spaghetti.

Bibimbap

Bibimbap

serves
4

2 tablespoons reduced-sodium soy sauce

1 tablespoon toasted sesame seeds

1 tablespoon packed brown sugar

1 tablespoon grated peeled fresh ginger

¾ pound boneless sirloin steak, trimmed and cut into ½-inch cubes

2 teaspoons canola oil

2 cups matchstick-cut carrots

2 cups bean sprouts

4 cups lightly packed baby spinach

½ cup fat-free egg substitute

2 cups hot cooked brown rice

2 scallions, chopped

Sriracha (chili-garlic) sauce

1   Combine soy sauce, sesame seeds, brown sugar, and ginger in large zip-close plastic bag; add steak. Squeeze out air and seal bag; turn to coat beef. Refrigerate, turning occasionally, at least 30 minutes or up to 2 hours.

2   Meanwhile, heat wok or large deep nonstick skillet over high heat until a drop of water sizzles in pan. Add oil and swirl to coat wok. Add beef and stir-fry until lightly browned, about 4 minutes; transfer to platter.

3   Add carrots to wok and stir-fry until crisp-tender, about 4 minutes; add to platter in separate pile. Add bean sprouts and spinach to wok; stir-fry until spinach is wilted, about 2 minutes. Add to platter. Add egg substitute to wok and cook, without stirring, until almost firm, about 1½ minutes. With edge of spatula, cut egg into small pieces.

4   Spoon rice evenly into 4 bowls. Divide beef, carrots, bean sprouts, spinach, and egg evenly among bowls over rice. Serve sprinkled with scallions and with Sriracha.

PER SERVING (1¾ cups): 339 Cal, 8 g Fat, 2 g Sat Fat, 0 g Trans Fat, 37 mg Chol, 437 mg Sod, 39 g Carb, 8 g Sugar, 6 g Fib, 28 g Prot, 87 mg Calc.

FYI   Bibimbap, which means "mixed rice," is a very popular Korean dish. To make it, warm rice is spooned into a large bowl and topped with cooked vegetables, such as spinach, zucchini, and mushrooms along with chili paste. A fried egg and cooked sliced beef is added, and it is then tossed. Bibimbap can be served hot, warm, or at room temperature.

Hoisin Pork & Mushroom Stir-Fry

5 PointsPlus value
PER SERVING

serves
4

2 tablespoons reduced-sodium
soy sauce

4 teaspoons hoisin sauce

4 teaspoons berry fruit spread
or jelly

1 teaspoon balsamic vinegar

1 teaspoon chili-garlic sauce

1 teaspoon Asian (dark) sesame oil

1 teaspoon canola oil

1 pound pork tenderloin, trimmed
and thinly sliced

½ pound mixed mushrooms, thickly
sliced (remove stems if using
shiitakes)

2 yellow bell peppers,
cut into thin strips

4 scallions, cut lengthwise in half
and cut into 2-inch lengths

1   Whisk together soy sauce, hoisin sauce, fruit spread, vinegar, chili-garlic sauce, and sesame oil in cup until smooth.

2   Heat wok or large deep nonstick skillet over high heat until a drop of water sizzles in pan. Add canola oil and swirl to coat wok. Add pork and stir-fry until lightly browned and cooked through, about 4 minutes; transfer to plate.

3   Add mushrooms to wok and stir-fry until softened, about 2 minutes; add to pork. Add bell peppers, scallions, and soy sauce mixture to wok; stir-fry until bell peppers are crisp-tender, about 4 minutes. Return pork and mushrooms to wok; stir-fry until mixed well, about 1 minute longer.

PER SERVING (about 1¼ cups): 218 Cal, 6 g Fat, 1 g Sat Fat, 0 g Trans Fat, 62 mg Chol, 438 mg Sod, 16 g Carb, 9 g Sugar, 2 g Fib, 25 g Prot, 40 mg Calc.

Healthy Extra   Serve this stir-fry over brown rice (⅔ cup cooked brown rice per serving will increase the *PointsPlus* value by **3**).

Bombay Pork with Basmati Rice

serves
4

2 teaspoons canola oil

4 (¼-pound) boneless pork loin chops, trimmed and cut into ½-inch cubes

½ teaspoon salt

2 sweet onions, thinly sliced

1 small sweet potato, grated

1½ tablespoons yellow mustard seeds

1½ tablespoons curry powder

3 yellow or red tomatoes, diced

¼ cup chopped fresh cilantro

2 cups hot cooked brown basmati rice

1 Heat wok or large deep nonstick skillet over high heat until a drop of water sizzles in pan. Add oil and swirl to coat wok. Sprinkle pork with ¼ teaspoon of salt; add to wok and stir-fry until browned and cooked through, about 4 minutes. Transfer to plate.

2 Add onions to wok and stir-fry 2 minutes. Add potato and stir-fry until crisp-tender, about 4 minutes. Add mustard seeds, curry, and remaining ¼ teaspoon salt; stir-fry 2 minutes. Return pork to skillet along with tomatoes and cilantro; stir-fry until heated through, about 2 minutes longer. Serve with rice.

PER SERVING (1 cup pork mixture and ½ cup rice): 380 Cal, 11 g Fat, 2 g Sat Fat, 0 g Trans Fat, 66 mg Chol, 361 mg Sod, 45 g Carb, 12 g Sugar, 6 g Fib, 27 g Prot, 106 mg Calc.

FYI Yellow mustard seeds are most often used for pickling, canning, and sausage making and are found in many supermarkets. Brown mustard seeds, on the other hand, are smaller, spicier, and used in Asian and African dishes.

Szechuan Chicken with Noodles

serves
4

3 (5-ounce) skinless boneless chicken breasts, cut on diagonal into thin strips

2 tablespoons cornstarch

2 teaspoons canola oil

3 garlic cloves, minced

1 (10-ounce) package broccoli slaw

1 bunch scallions, thinly sliced

½ teaspoon red pepper flakes

4 ounces whole wheat spaghetti, broken in thirds and cooked according to package directions

2 tablespoons reduced-sodium soy sauce

1 tablespoon sherry vinegar

2 teaspoons sugar

2 tablespoons pine nuts, toasted

1 Combine chicken and cornstarch in large zip-close plastic bag. Squeeze out air and seal bag. Shake until chicken is coated evenly.

2 Heat wok or large deep nonstick skillet over high heat until a drop of water sizzles in pan. Add 1 teaspoon of oil and swirl to coat wok. Add chicken and stir-fry until cooked through, about 3 minutes. Add garlic and stir-fry until fragrant, about 30 seconds; transfer to plate.

3 Remove wok from heat; wipe clean with wet paper towel to remove any cornstarch. Set wok over high heat and add remaining 1 teaspoon oil. Add broccoli slaw and stir-fry until crisp-tender, about 4 minutes. Add scallions and pepper flakes; stir-fry 2 minutes.

4 Return chicken to wok along with spaghetti; stir-fry until heated through, about 2 minutes. Add soy sauce, vinegar, and sugar; stir-fry until mixed well, about 1 minute. Serve sprinkled with pine nuts.

PER SERVING (1¾ cups): 324 Cal, 8 g Fat, 1 g Sat Fat, 0 g Trans Fat, 59 mg Chol, 347 mg Sod, 36 g Carb, 4 g Sugar, 7 g Fib, 30 g Prot, 95 mg Calc.

Healthy Extra   Add 1 diced red or orange bell pepper to the skillet along with the broccoli slaw in step 3.

Szechuan Chicken
with Noodles

Garlicky Chicken-Scallion Stir-Fry

serves
4

PER SERVING

⅓ cup reduced-sodium
chicken broth

1 tablespoon reduced-sodium
soy sauce

2 teaspoons cornstarch

3 teaspoons canola oil

1 pound skinless boneless chicken
breasts, cut on diagonal into
thin slices

1 green bell pepper,
cut into thin strips

6 ounces cremini mushrooms,
thickly sliced

½ cup matchstick-cut carrot

¼ pound snow peas, trimmed

6 scallions, cut into
2-inch lengths

4 large garlic cloves, thinly sliced

2 cups hot cooked
brown rice

1 Whisk together broth, soy sauce, and cornstarch in small bowl
until smooth.

2 Heat wok or large deep nonstick skillet over medium-high heat
until a drop of water sizzles in pan. Add 1 teaspoon of oil and swirl to
coat wok. Add half of chicken and stir-fry until cooked through, about
4 minutes; transfer to plate. Add 1 teaspoon of oil to wok along with
remaining chicken; stir-fry until cooked through, about 4 minutes. Add
to chicken on plate.

3 Add remaining 1 teaspoon oil to wok. Add bell pepper, mushrooms,
and carrot; stir-fry until bell pepper is crisp-tender, about 3 minutes.
Add snow peas, scallions, and garlic; stir-fry until snow peas are crisp-
tender and garlic is fragrant, about 1 minute.

4 Re-whisk cornstarch mixture. Return chicken to wok along with
cornstarch mixture. Stir-fry until mixture bubbles and thickens, about
1 minute. Serve with rice.

PER SERVING (about 1 cup chicken mixture and ½ cup rice): 307 Cal, 6 g Total Fat, 1 g Sat Fat,
0 g Trans Fat, 63 mg Chol, 253 mg Sod, 34 g Carb, 4 g Sugar, 4 g Fib, 28 g Prot, 72 mg Calc.

Healthy Extra Double the amount of snow peas and use ½ pound
of mushrooms instead of 6 ounces.

Honey Chicken with Cashews

serves
4

PER SERVING

¾ cup reduced-sodium chicken broth

2 tablespoons reduced-sodium soy sauce

2 tablespoons cornstarch

1½ tablespoons honey

1 pound chicken tenders, cut lengthwise into thin strips

⅛ teaspoon salt

2 garlic cloves, minced

2 red bell peppers, cut into thin strips

¼ cup unsalted cashews, coarsely chopped

2 cups hot cooked whole wheat thin spaghetti

1 Whisk together broth, soy sauce, cornstarch, and honey in small bowl until smooth.

2 Sprinkle chicken with salt. Spray wok or large deep nonstick skillet with nonstick spray and set over high heat until a drop of water sizzles in wok. Add chicken and stir-fry until browned and cooked through, about 3 minutes. Add garlic and stir-fry until fragrant, about 30 seconds; transfer to plate.

3 Add bell peppers to wok and stir-fry until crisp-tender, about 3 minutes. Return chicken to wok along with cashews, stir fry until heated through, about 1 minute. Re-whisk broth mixture; add to wok and stir-fry until sauce bubbles and thickens, about 1 minute longer. Serve over spaghetti.

PER SERVING (1 cup chicken mixture and ½ cup pasta): 310 Cal, 7 g Fat, 2 g Sat Fat, 0 g Trans Fat, 63 mg Chol, 504 mg Sod, 33 g Carb, 10 g Sugar, 5 g Fib, 30 g Prot, 38 mg Calc.

Healthy Extra Add 2 cups trimmed and cut green beans to the wok along with the peppers in step 3.

Stir-Fried Chicken Greek-Style

serves
4

PER SERVING

1 pound chicken tenders, cut lengthwise into thin strips

⅛ teaspoon salt

1 tablespoon olive oil

1 small red onion, thinly sliced

1 cup diced unpeeled cucumber

1 pint grape tomatoes

2 teaspoons dried oregano

2 cups hot cooked whole wheat farfalle (bow ties)

1 teaspoon grated lemon zest

1 tablespoon lemon juice

3 ounces reduced-fat feta cheese, crumbled

1 Sprinkle chicken with salt. Heat wok or large deep nonstick skillet over high heat until a drop of water sizzles in pan. Add oil and swirl to coat wok. Add chicken and stir-fry until browned and cooked through, about 4 minutes; transfer to plate.

2 Add onion to wok and stir-fry 2 minutes. Add cucumber and stir-fry 1 minute. Add tomatoes and oregano; stir-fry 2 minutes. Return chicken to wok along with farfalle and stir-fry until heated through, about 1 minute longer. Remove wok from heat; add lemon zest and juice; toss until mixed well. Serve sprinkled with feta.

PER SERVING (2 cups): 309 Cal, 10 g Fat, 3 g Sat Fat, 0 g Trans Fat, 69 mg Chol, 428 mg Sod, 25 g Carb, 4 g Sugar, 4 g Fib, 32 g Prot, 109 mg Calc.

Moo Shu Chicken

serves **8**

20 min

PER SERVING

3 teaspoons canola oil

½ cup fat-free egg substitute

1 pound chicken tenders, cut lengthwise into thin strips

⅛ teaspoon salt

3 garlic cloves, minced

1 tablespoon minced peeled fresh ginger

1 (1-pound) package coleslaw mix

⅓ cup hoisin sauce

2 tablespoons cider vinegar

8 (6-inch) whole wheat tortillas, warmed

1 Heat wok or large deep nonstick skillet over high heat until a drop of water sizzles in pan. Add 1 teaspoon of oil and swirl to coat wok. Pour in egg substitute and cook, without stirring, until set, about 1 minute. Transfer egg to cutting board; cut into thin strips.

2 Sprinkle chicken with salt. Add remaining 2 teaspoons oil to wok and swirl to coat pan. Add chicken to wok and stir-fry until cooked through, about 3 minutes. Add garlic and ginger; stir-fry until fragrant, about 30 seconds. Transfer to plate. Add coleslaw mix to wok; stir-fry until crisp-tender, about 2 minutes.

3 Return chicken to wok. Add hoisin sauce and vinegar; stir-fry until heated through, about 1 minute. Divide chicken mixture and egg strips evenly among tortillas; roll up to enclose filling.

PER SERVING (1 wrap): 238 Cal, 9 g Fat, 1 g Sat Fat, 0 g Trans Fat, 32 mg Chol, 371 mg Sod, 22 g Carb, 4 g Sugar, 3 g Fib, 16 g Prot, 43 mg Calc.

Healthy Extra Add 1 small red bell pepper, chopped, to the wok along with the coleslaw mix in step 2.

Chicken Strips with Bok Choy & Udon Noodles

serves **4**

PER SERVING

2 tablespoons white miso

1 tablespoon honey

¾ teaspoon chili-garlic sauce

1 pound skinless boneless chicken thighs, cut into thin strips

3 garlic cloves, minced

1 tablespoon minced peeled fresh ginger

6 cups thinly sliced bok choy, stems and tops separated

2 cups hot cooked no-salt-added udon noodles

1 Whisk together miso, honey, and chili-garlic sauce in small bowl until blended.

2 Spray wok or large deep nonstick skillet with nonstick spray and set over high heat until a drop of water sizzles in pan. Add chicken and stir-fry until browned and cooked through, about 4 minutes. Add garlic and ginger; stir-fry until fragrant, about 30 seconds. Transfer to plate.

3 Add bok choy stems to wok and stir-fry 4 minutes. Add bok choy tops and stir-fry until wilted, about 1 minute. Return chicken mixture to wok along with miso mixture. Stir-fry until heated through, about 1 minute. Serve over noodles.

PER SERVING (1 cup chicken mixture and ½ cup noodles): 268 Cal, 9 g Fat, 2 g Sat Fat, 0 g Trans Fat, 74 mg Chol, 426 mg Sod, 22 g Carb, 7 g Sugar, 3 g Fib, 26 g Prot, 112 mg Calc.

FYI Miso, a staple in Japanese cooking, is fermented soybean paste. White miso has a delicate flavor while red miso (which is reddish brown) has a stronger flavor. Miso can be found in health food stores and organic food markets.

Shrimp-Mushroom Egg Fu Yung

serves
4

1 teaspoon canola oil

2 garlic cloves, minced

1½ cups stemmed shiitake mushrooms, sliced

½ red onion, chopped

1 cup bean sprouts

1 tablespoon reduced-sodium soy sauce

3 large eggs

4 large egg whites

6 ounces cooked peeled and deveined shrimp, chopped

¼ cup reduced sodium chicken broth

1 tablespoon dry white wine or dry sherry

1 tablespoon oyster sauce

1 teaspoon cornstarch

1 tablespoon finely chopped fresh parsley

1   Heat oil in nonstick flat-bottomed wok or medium nonstick skillet over medium-high heat. Add garlic and cook, stirring frequently, until fragrant, about 30 seconds. Add mushrooms and onion; cook, stirring frequently, until mushrooms release their liquid and it is evaporated and onion is golden, about 8 minutes. Add bean sprouts and soy sauce; cook, stirring, 1 minute. Remove wok from heat; let cool 15 minutes.

2   Meanwhile, beat eggs and egg whites in large bowl until frothy. Stir in cooled vegetable mixture and shrimp.

3   Spray wok with nonstick spray and set over medium-high heat. Add one-fourth of egg mixture, tilting to cover bottom of pan. Cook until set on bottom, about 1 minute. Place plate on top of wok and invert. Slide omelette back into wok. Cook until lightly browned, about 45 seconds. Slide omelette onto plate and keep warm. Repeat with remaining egg mixture to make 3 more omelettes, spraying wok with nonstick spray between omelettes. Wipe pan clean.

4   Whisk together broth, wine, oyster sauce, and cornstarch in wok until smooth; bring to boil. Reduce heat and cook, whisking occasionally, until sauce bubbles and thickens, about 2 minutes. Drizzle sauce evenly over omelettes; serve sprinkled with parsley.

PER SERVING (1 omelette and about 1 tablespoon sauce): 188 Cal, 6 g Total Fat, 1 g Sat Fat, 0 g Trans Fat, 247 mg Chol, 521 mg Sod, 14 g Carb, 4 g Sugar, 2 g Fib, 21 g Prot, 63 mg Calc.

FYI   Unlike traditional curved-bottomed woks, flat-bottomed woks sit securely on regular stovetop burners and make it easy to cook up the omelettes in this recipe.

Singapore Noodles

9 PointsPlus® value PER SERVING

serves
4

20
min

1 tablespoon canola oil

4 cups thinly sliced napa cabbage

2 tablespoons curry powder

½ teaspoon salt

1 small red bell pepper,
cut into thin strips

2 cups bean sprouts

2 cups thinly sliced scallions
(about 9)

¾ pound cooked skinless fat-free
turkey breast, shredded

6 ounces whole wheat spaghetti,
broken into thirds and cooked
according to package directions

Heat wok or large deep nonstick skillet over high heat until a drop of water sizzles in pan. Add oil and swirl to coat wok. Add cabbage and stir-fry until crisp-tender, about 1 minute. Add curry powder and salt; stir-fry 1 minute. Add bell pepper and bean sprouts; stir-fry 1 minute. Add scallions, turkey, and spaghetti to wok; stir-fry until heated through, about 2 minutes longer.

PER SERVING (2 cups): 356 Cal, 5 g Fat, 1 g Sat Fat, 0 g Trans Fat, 71 mg Chol, 652 mg Sod, 44 g Carb, 7 g Sugar, 10 g Fib, 36 g Prot, 126 mg Calc.

Healthy Extra   Add 2 celery stalks, thinly sliced, and ½ cup matchstick-cut carrot to the wok along with the cabbage.

Singapore Noodles

Wok-Seared Wild Salmon
with Asparagus

Wok-Seared Wild Salmon with Asparagus

serves
4

PER SERVING

2 tablespoons raspberry vinegar

2 tablespoons reduced-sodium soy sauce

1 tablespoon honey

1 tablespoon cornstarch

1 (1-pound) wild or farmed salmon fillet, skinned

⅛ teaspoon salt

2 teaspoons canola oil

1 pound asparagus, trimmed and cut into 2-inch lengths

2 teaspoons minced peeled fresh ginger

2 cups hot cooked brown rice blend

1 Whisk together vinegar, soy sauce, honey, and cornstarch in small bowl until smooth.

2 Cut salmon fillet crosswise into ½-inch slices. Cut each slice crosswise into 4 pieces. Sprinkle with salt.

3 Heat wok or large deep nonstick skillet over high heat until a drop of water sizzles in pan. Add oil and swirl to coat wok. Add salmon and stir-fry until just opaque in center, about 3 minutes; transfer to plate. Add asparagus and ginger; stir-fry until crisp-tender, about 2 minutes.

4 Return salmon to wok. Re-whisk vinegar mixture; add to wok and stir-fry until sauce bubbles and thickens, about 1 minute. Serve over rice.

PER SERVING (1¼ cups salmon mixture and ½ cup rice): 366 Cal, 12 g Fat, 2 g Sat Fat, 0 g Trans Fat, 72 mg Chol, 400 mg Sod, 35 g Carb, 7 g Sugar, 4 g Fib, 31 g Prot, 57 mg Calc.

Healthy Extra To emphasize the raspberry flavor of the vinegar, add ½ cup of fresh raspberries to the salmon mixture just before serving.

Shrimp in Coconut Curry Sauce

6 PointsPlus® value

PER SERVING

serves
6

3 teaspoons canola oil

1½ pounds large shrimp, peeled and deveined, tails left on if desired

½ pound green beans, trimmed and cut into 1½-inch lengths

1 red onion, sliced

1 large red bell pepper, cut into strips

1 tablespoon grated peeled fresh ginger

3 garlic cloves, minced

2 teaspoons Thai red curry paste

1 cup light (reduced-fat) coconut milk

2 large plum tomatoes, chopped

1 tablespoon Asian fish sauce

1 tablespoon lime juice

1 tablespoon sugar

¼ cup lightly packed fresh cilantro leaves

3 cups hot cooked whole wheat couscous

1   Heat wok or large deep nonstick skillet over medium-high heat until a drop of water sizzles in pan. Add 1½ teaspoons of oil and swirl to coat pan. Add shrimp and stir-fry until just opaque in center, about 3 minutes; transfer to plate.

2   Add remaining 1½ teaspoons oil to wok; add beans and stir-fry until slightly softened, about 3 minutes. Add onion and bell pepper; stir-fry until slightly softened, about 3 minutes. Add ginger, garlic, and curry paste; stir-fry until fragrant, about 30 seconds longer.

3   Reduce heat to medium. Add coconut milk, tomatoes, fish sauce, lime juice, and sugar to wok; bring to simmer. Cook, stirring occasionally, until flavors are blended, about 3 minutes. Add shrimp and stir-fry until heated through, about 1 minute longer. Sprinkle with cilantro and serve over couscous.

PER SERVING (1 cup shrimp and vegetable mixture with ½ cup couscous): 243 Cal, 6 g Total Fat, 0 g Sat Fat, 0 g Trans Fat, 168 mg Chol, 496 mg Sod, 26 g Carb, 4 g Sugar, 5 g Fib, 23 g Prot, 71 mg Calc.

Healthy Extra   Start your meal off with a salad of baby lettuces, thinly sliced cucumber, and thinly sliced radishes, dressed with unseasoned rice vinegar.

Lemongrass & Shrimp Fried Rice

8 PointsPlus® value PER SERVING | serves 4

3 teaspoons basil oil

2 small red bell peppers, cut into ½-inch dice

2 tablespoons minced lemongrass or 1 teaspoon grated lemon zest

2 large zucchini, cut into ½-inch dice

3 cups cold cooked white rice

1 cup frozen peas, thawed

½ pound cooked peeled and deveined small shrimp

2 cups lightly packed baby arugula or spinach

3 tablespoons finely chopped Thai or regular basil

2½ tablespoons reduced-sodium soy sauce

1 tablespoon unseasoned rice vinegar

½ teaspoon black pepper

1 Heat wok or large deep nonstick skillet over high heat until a drop of water sizzles in pan. Add 1 teaspoon of oil and swirl to coat wok. Add bell peppers and stir-fry 2 minutes. Add lemongrass and stir-fry until fragrant, about 1 minute. (If using lemon zest, add in step 2 along with the peas.) Add zucchini and stir-fry until crisp-tender, about 2 minutes; transfer to plate.

2 Add remaining 2 teaspoons oil to wok. Add rice and peas; stir-fry until heated through, about 2 minutes. Return vegetables to wok along with remaining ingredients; stir-fry until heated through, about 2 minutes longer.

PER SERVING (1¾ cups): 334 Cal, 5 g Fat, 1 g Sat Fat, 0 g Trans Fat, 115 mg Chol, 563 mg Sod, 50 g Carb, 6 g Sugar, 6 g Fib, 23 g Prot, 105 mg Calc.

FYI Fresh lemongrass is sold loose and in small plastic containers alongside the fresh herbs in the refrigerated produce section of many supermarkets. Any leftover lemongrass can be frozen for up to 3 months in a zip-close plastic freezer bag.

Fiery Scallops & Bok Choy

5 PointsPlus® value PER SERVING | serves 4

1 pound sea scallops

2 tablespoons cornstarch

1 tablespoon grated peeled fresh ginger

Grated zest of ½ orange

½ cup reduced-sodium chicken broth

¼ cup orange juice

3 tablespoons reduced-sodium soy sauce

2 teaspoons sugar

¼–½ teaspoon red pepper flakes

6 ounces broccoli crowns, cut into small florets

6 ounces baby bok choy, cut into 1-inch pieces

3 tablespoons dry white wine or dry sherry

1 Toss together scallops, 1 tablespoon of cornstarch, the ginger, and orange zest on sheet of wax paper until coated evenly.

2 Whisk together remaining 1 tablespoon cornstarch, the broth, orange juice, soy sauce, sugar, and pepper flakes in small bowl until smooth.

3 Spray wok or large deep nonstick skillet with nonstick spray and set over medium-high heat. Add scallop mixture and stir-fry until scallops are just opaque in center, about 3 minutes; transfer to plate.

4 Add broccoli, bok choy, and wine to wok. Cook, covered, until crisp-tender about 3 minutes. Re-whisk broth mixture. Return scallops to wok along with broth mixture. Stir-fry until sauce bubbles and thickens, about 1 minute.

PER SERVING (1¼ cups): 200 Cal, 1 g Total Fat, 0 g Sat Fat, 0 g Trans Fat, 37 mg Chol, 693 mg Sod, 23 g Carb, 2 g Sugar, 6 g Fib, 23 g Prot, 157 mg Calc.

Healthy Extra Enjoy a sweet ending to this tasty main dish by tossing 2 sliced ripe pears with 8 medium litchis and a handful of fresh raspberries.

Scallop Fried Rice

serves
6

PER SERVING

3 tablespoons Asian fish sauce

2 teaspoons seasoned rice vinegar

¼ teaspoon red pepper flakes

4 teaspoons canola oil

1 pound sea scallops

3 large eggs, lightly beaten

4 scallions, thinly sliced

1 tablespoon minced peeled
fresh ginger

1 (10-ounce) package frozen peas

1 orange bell pepper, sliced

½ cup canned straw mushrooms,
drained

4 cups cold cooked brown rice

3 tablespoons chopped
fresh cilantro

1   Stir together fish sauce, vinegar, and pepper flakes in cup.

2   Heat wok or large deep nonstick skillet over medium-high heat until a drop of water sizzles in pan. Add 1 teaspoon of oil and swirl to coat wok. Add scallops and stir-fry until lightly browned and just opaque in center, about 3 minutes; transfer to plate.

3   Reduce heat to medium. Add 1 teaspoon of oil to wok; add eggs and cook until they begin to set, about 1½ minutes, pushing eggs toward center of wok to form large soft curds. Continue cooking eggs until set, about 3 minutes longer. Add to scallops on plate.

4   Heat remaining 2 teaspoons oil in wok. Add scallions and ginger; stir-fry until fragrant, about 30 seconds. Add peas, bell pepper, and mushrooms; stir-fry until softened, about 4 minutes. Stir in rice and fish sauce mixture; stir-fry 1 minute. Return scallops to wok along with scrambled eggs and cilantro; stir-fry until heated through, about 1 minute longer.

PER SERVING (1⅓ cups): 333 Cal, 7 g Total Fat, 1 g Sat Fat, 0 g Trans Fat, 132 mg Chol, 978 mg Sod, 44 g Carb, 4 g Sugar, 6 g Fib, 23 g Prot, 69 mg Calc.

FYI   In China, it is not unusual to be served fried rice that doesn't contain soy sauce. Without the addition of soy, the fried rice takes on a lighter and cleaner flavor that is very appealing, and the sodium level is not raised.

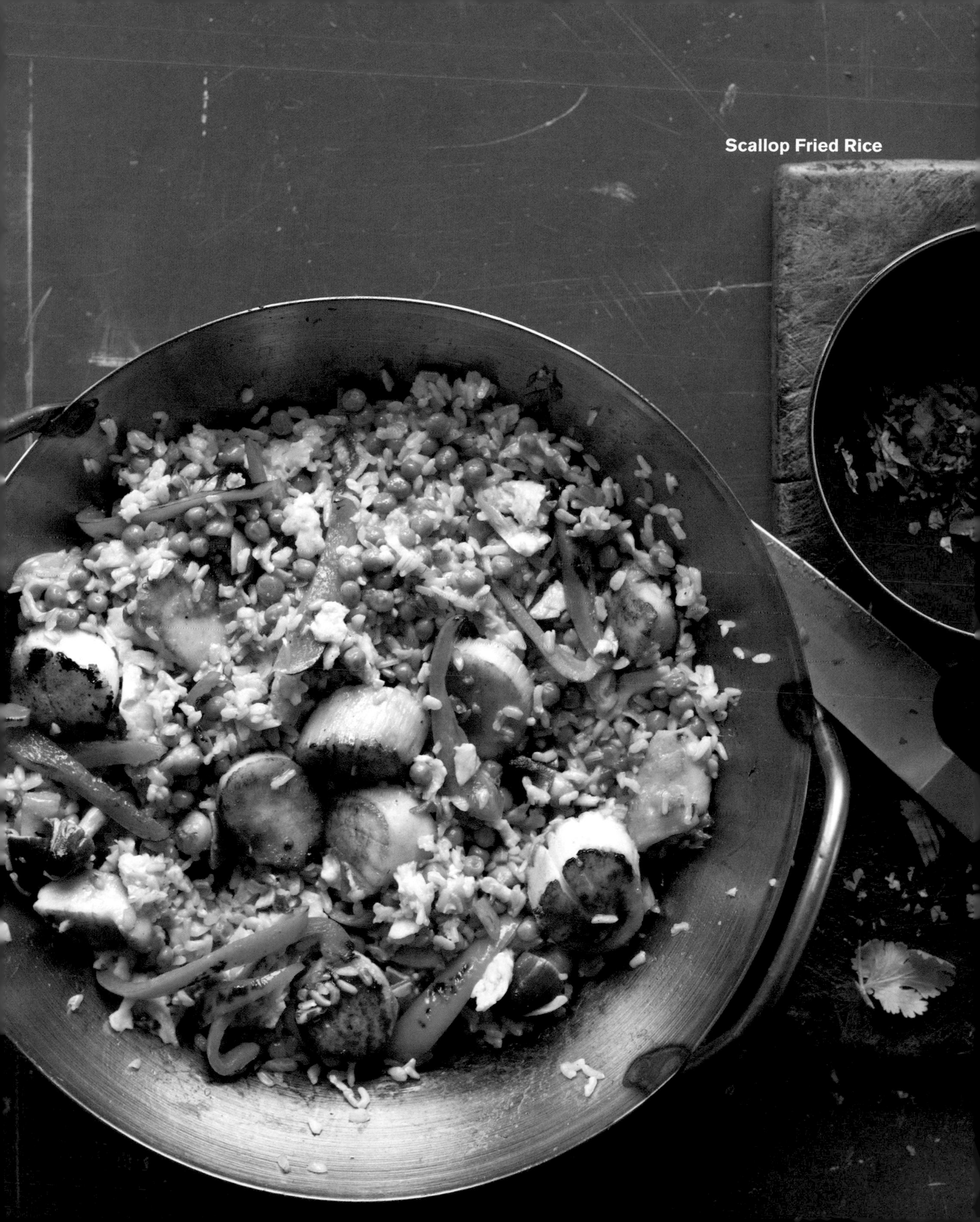

Scallop Fried Rice

Lemon-Infused Scallops with Snow Peas

serves
4

PER SERVING

4 ounces rice stick noodles (vermicelli)

1 tablespoon cornstarch

½ teaspoon cayenne

¼ teaspoon salt

1¼ pounds sea scallops, patted dry and cut horizontally in thirds

2 teaspoons lemon olive oil

1 small red onion, thinly sliced

¼ pound enoki mushrooms

½ pound snow peas, trimmed and cut in half on diagonal

½ small red bell pepper, cut into thin strips

½ green bell pepper, cut into thin strips

½ cup reduced-sodium vegetable broth

½ teaspoon grated lemon zest

1 Put noodles in large bowl and add enough hot water to cover. Cover bowl with plastic wrap and soak until noodles are softened, about 10 minutes. Drain.

2 Mix together cornstarch, cayenne, and ⅛ teaspoon of salt on sheet of wax paper. Add scallops and toss until coated evenly.

3 Heat wok or large deep nonstick skillet over high heat until a drop of water sizzles in pan. Add 1 teaspoon of oil and swirl to coat wok. Add scallops and stir-fry just until opaque in center, about 1 minute; transfer to large bowl. Add onion and mushrooms to wok; stir-fry 2 minutes. Add snow peas, bell peppers, and remaining ⅛ teaspoon salt; stir-fry until vegetables are crisp-tender, about 3 minutes; transfer to scallops.

4 Add remaining 1 teaspoon oil to wok. Add drained noodles and stir-fry until heated through, about 2 minutes. Return scallops and vegetables to wok along with broth and lemon zest; stir-fry until heated through, about 1 minute longer.

PER SERVING (about 1⅔ cups): 311 Cal, 4 g Fat, 1 g Sat Fat, 0 g Trans Fat, 47 mg Chol, 396 mg Sod, 37 g Carb, 4 g Sugar, 3 g Fib, 29 g Prot, 70 mg Calc.

FYI Delicate, long, and thin enoki mushrooms are traditionally enjoyed in soups and salads. They come in small packages and can be refrigerated for up to 1 week. When purchasing them, look for mushrooms that are firm, white, and without any browning or dampness. If you don't have lemon olive oil, use regular olive oil.

Clams & Watercress in Black Bean Sauce

½ cup reduced-sodium chicken broth

1 tablespoon black bean sauce

1½ teaspoons sherry vinegar

1 teaspoon pure maple syrup

1 teaspoon cornstarch

½ teaspoon chili-garlic sauce

1 teaspoon canola oil

2 teaspoons minced peeled fresh ginger

2 large garlic cloves, minced

2 pounds littleneck clams (about 30), scrubbed

1 bunch watercress, trimmed and chopped

1 (8-ounce) package tofu shirataki noodles, drained

1 Whisk together broth, black bean sauce, vinegar, maple syrup, cornstarch, and chili-garlic sauce in small bowl until smooth.

2 Heat wok or large deep nonstick skillet over high heat until a drop of water sizzles in pan. Add oil and swirl to coat wok. Add ginger and garlic; stir-fry until fragrant, about 30 seconds. Add clams and stir-fry until they open, about 4 minutes. Discard any clams that do not open.

3 Add watercress to wok and stir-fry until wilted, about 1 minute. Re-whisk broth mixture. Add to wok and stir-fry until sauce bubbles and thickens, about 1 minute. Add noodles and stir-fry until heated through, about 2 minutes longer.

PER SERVING (2½ cups): 187 Cal, 4 g Fat, 0 g Sat Fat, 0 g Trans Fat, 46 mg Chol, 366 mg Sod, 14 g Carb, 3 g Sugar, 3 g Fib, 22 g Prot, 314 mg Calc.

FYI Tofu shirataki noodles are gluten-free noodles made from a blend of the konjac root plant and tofu. They have a slightly chewy texture and come fully cooked, so they only require reheating. They are usually found in the refrigerated case next to the packaged salad greens.

Black Sesame Tofu with Mixed Vegetables

Thai Vegetable & Tofu Stir-Fry

7 PointsPlus value · serves 6 · PER SERVING

1 cup light (reduced-fat) coconut milk

1 tablespoon reduced-sodium soy sauce

2 teaspoons sugar

1 teaspoon Thai red curry paste

2 teaspoons canola oil

3 garlic cloves, minced

1 tablespoon minced peeled fresh ginger

2 different color bell peppers, cut into 1-inch chunks

½ red onion, thinly sliced

¾ pound baby bok choy, sliced

¼ pound snow peas, trimmed

½ (15-ounce) can baby corn, drained

1 (14-ounce) package reduced-fat firm tofu, drained and cut into ½-inch cubes

3 cups hot cooked brown basmati rice

1 Stir together coconut milk, soy sauce, sugar, and curry paste in small bowl.

2 Heat wok or large deep nonstick skillet over medium-high heat until drop of water sizzles in pan. Add oil and swirl to coat wok. Add garlic and ginger; stir-fry until fragrant, about 30 seconds. Add the bell peppers and onion; stir-fry until crisp-tender, about 4 minutes. Add bok choy and stir-fry until crisp-tender, about 4 minutes.

3 Add snow peas, corn, and coconut milk mixture to wok; bring to boil over high heat. Reduce heat and simmer until snow peas are bright green, about 1 minute. Gently stir in tofu and stir-fry until heated through, about 2 minutes longer. Serve over rice.

PER SERVING (1⅓ cups tofu mixture and ½ cup rice): 263 Cal, 7 g Total Fat, 0 g Sat Fat, 0 g Trans Fat, 0 mg Chol, 184 mg Sod, 41 g Carb, 5 g Sugar, 5 g Fib, 11 g Prot, 208 mg Calc.

Black Sesame Tofu with Mixed Vegetables

5 PointsPlus value · serves 4 · PER SERVING

3 tablespoons sweet orange marmalade

2 tablespoons reduced-sodium soy sauce

1 tablespoon red wine vinegar

1 teaspoon Dijon mustard

2 teaspoons canola oil

1 (14-ounce) package extra-firm tofu, drained and cut into ½-inch cubes

2 teaspoons sesame seeds, preferably black

½ pound snow peas, trimmed and cut in half on diagonal

2 cups matchstick-cut carrots

1 large white turnip, peeled and cut into ½-inch dice

2 celery stalks, thinly sliced crosswise

1 Stir together marmalade, soy sauce, vinegar, and mustard in small bowl.

2 Heat wok or large deep nonstick skillet over high heat until a drop of water sizzles in pan. Add oil and swirl to coat wok. Add tofu and stir-fry 3 minutes. Sprinkle with sesame seeds and stir-fry 1 minute; transfer to plate.

3 Add snow peas, carrots, turnip, and celery to wok; stir-fry until crisp-tender, about 4 minutes. Add tofu mixture and sauce; and stir-fry until heated through, about 1 minute longer.

PER SERVING (1¾ cups): 220 Cal, 8 g Fat, 0 g Sat Fat, 0 g Trans Fat, 0 mg Chol, 399 mg Sod, 25 g Carb, 15 g Sugar, 6 g Fib, 12 g Prot, 261 mg Calc.

Healthy Extra   Serve this unusual tofu stir-fry over brown rice (⅔ cup cooked brown rice per serving will increase the *PointsPlus* value by 3).

IN A   SA

UCEPAN

CHAPTER 4
IN A SAUCEPAN

EASY BREAKFASTS, SOUPS & MORE

Whether you're hard-cooking eggs, heating soup, or warming up leftovers, a saucepan is your pot of choice. A saucepan is a deep, round pot usually with one long handle and sometimes a tight-fitting lid. Saucepans are made from a range of materials, including stainless steel, enamel-coated cast iron, aluminum, and copper.

A Bit of History

Early man simply set meat, fish, or poultry over an open fire to cook it. Finding a way to heat water proved to be a challenge until it was discovered that it could be put into an empty turtle shell or large seashell and set over a fire. Native Americans used gourds and baskets that they made almost waterproof by coating the insides with a layer of clay and letting it dry and harden.

The development of pottery cooking vessels allowed for more possibilities. These vessels could be large or small and short or tall, depending on the specific need. Eventually pottery was coated or glazed, which made it waterproof, a great improvement. These vessels could be suspended over a fire, placed directly in a fire, or set over hot coals.

The development of metal cookware, which conducted heat more efficiently and was fairly indestructible, was the next major advancement in cooking. By the 1600s, many households had a cauldron (a deep cooking pot), a shallow pan, and a metal spit for roasting meats and poultry. By the 1700s, households often had various-size skillets, a kettle, and several wire-handled pots. Skillets were the first cooking vessels to have long handles. Cooking on a stove necessitated pots to be flat-bottomed for stability, while long handles made it easier—and safer—to remove them from the heat.

Types and Sizes

Saucepans range in size from about 2 cups to 4 quarts. Some have somewhat low sides and others have tall sides, but most are straight sided. Other saucepans have flared sides, which is especially useful for reducing liquids, as this allows more surface area to be exposed so the liquid reduces more quickly. When buying saucepans, keep in mind that buying a set is often a better deal than purchasing individual pans. Also, always buy the highest-quality pots your wallet will allow, as they will last longer than lesser-quality saucepans.

Stainless steel saucepans have many good qualities, including being rust-proof, nonreactive (they don't react with acid foods, such as wine or tomatoes), and sturdy. They are not the best conductors of heat, however, so high-quality stainless steel pans have a center core of aluminum or copper; both are excellent heat conductors.

Both **stainless steel and aluminum saucepans** are available with nonstick interiors. When purchasing, look for saucepans that are made of several nonstick layers, which make them more resistant to scratches.

Enamel-coated cast-iron saucepans are another good option. These pots heat evenly and are easy to care for. One downside is that they can be heavy and take more time to cool down.

If you feel like splurging, a **copper saucepan** is your top choice. These French-made pots are appreciated for their superior heat conduction, durability, and good looks. Originally, copper pots were lined with tin, which had to be reapplied from time to time. Now they have stainless-steel interiors, which are nonreactive and easy to care for.

Basics for Care

To clean a **stainless steel saucepan,** immerse it in warm water once it has cooled down slightly. Apply a paste of nonabrasive powder cleanser mixed with water and rub in a circular motion from the center outward using a sponge or nylon scrub pad. Wash the pan with hot, soapy water, rinse it well, and dry it thoroughly. Avoid using steel wool pads, which would scratch the surface. These pots are dishwasher safe.

To ensure that the coating of your **nonstick saucepans** lasts, clean them gently and avoid scratching their surface. Wash them in hot, soapy water with a sponge or nylon scrub pad. The nonstick finish should prevent any food from sticking.

Enamel-coated cast-iron saucepans are easy to care for. Let them cool down before washing them to avoid shocking the enamel due to the change in temperature. Hand-wash them with hot, soapy water, rinse under warm water, and dry them thoroughly. If any food remains stuck, soak the pot for about 15 minutes, then use a nylon scrub pad to remove the residue. Enamel-coated saucepans are dishwasher safe, but it is not recommended, as the detergent will dull the enamel surface over time.

Allow **copper saucepans** to cool down before washing them. Use hot, soapy water and a sponge or nylon scrub pad to remove any stuck-on food particles. To keep the copper looking shiny and new, use copper polish or try this old-fashioned method: squeeze fresh lemon juice all over the exterior of the pot, sprinkle it with kosher salt, and rub with a damp sponge or your fingers until the copper regains its luster.

Dried Fruit & Oat Porridge

6 PointsPlus® value PER SERVING

serves 4

20 min

4 cups water

1⅓ cups quick-cooking (not instant) oats

1 apple, peeled, cored, and diced

¼ cup toasted wheat germ

¼ cup dried cranberries

¼ cup dried blueberries

8 dried apricots, chopped

1 teaspoon pumpkin pie spice

½ teaspoon salt

1 tablespoon unsalted raw or toasted sunflower seeds

Bring water to boil in large saucepan over medium-high heat. Stir in all ingredients except sunflower seeds. Reduce heat to medium-low and simmer, uncovered, stirring occasionally, until water is absorbed, about 10 minutes. Serve porridge sprinkled with sunflower seeds.

PER SERVING (1 cup porridge and ¾ teaspoon sunflower seeds): 227 Cal, 4 g Total Fat, 0 g Sat Fat, 0 g Trans Fat, 1 mg Chol, 306 mg Sod, 43 g Carb, 16 g Sugar, 7 g Fib, 7 g Prot, 43 mg Calc.

All-Week-Long Irish Oatmeal with Dried & Fresh Fruit

4 PointsPlus® value PER SERVING

serves 6

6 cups water

1½ cups Irish or steel-cut oats (not quick-cooking or instant)

½ teaspoon salt

⅔ cup thinly sliced dried apricots, preferably California

⅔ cup dried sour cherries

1 tablespoon pure maple syrup

1½ cups fresh blueberries or raspberries

12 tablespoons low-fat (1%) milk, warmed

1 Combine water, oats, and salt in large saucepan and bring to boil over high heat. Reduce heat and simmer, stirring frequently then almost constantly to prevent oatmeal from sticking to bottom of pan, until oats are softened and liquid is absorbed, about 40 minutes.

2 Remove saucepan from heat and stir in apricots, cherries, and maple syrup. Let oatmeal cool to room temperature, then transfer to covered container and refrigerate up to 1 week.

3 For each serving, spoon 1 cup of oatmeal into microwavable bowl; microwave on High until heated through, about 2 minutes, stirring once or twice. Top with ¼ cup of blueberries and 2 tablespoons of milk.

PER SERVING (1 bowl): 193 Cal, 2 g Total Fat, 0 g Sat Fat, 0 g Trans Fat, 2 mg Chol, 218 mg Sod, 35 g Carb, 18 g Sugar, 7 g Fib, 4 g Prot, 60 mg Calc.

FYI There are two kinds of dried apricots: Turkish and California. Turkish apricots are small, pale whole apricots that are rather sweet. California dried apricot halves have a deep orange color and sweet-tart flavor.

Sunday Morning
Berry Blintzes

serves
4

20
min

PER SERVING

½ cup orange juice

4 cups mixed fresh berries, such as blueberries, raspberries, and quartered strawberries

½ cup fat-free sour cream

1 tablespoon granulated sugar

2 teaspoons grated orange zest

½ teaspoon vanilla extract

4 ready-to-use crêpes

1 tablespoon confectioners' sugar

1   Bring orange juice to boil in large saucepan over high heat; cook until syrupy, about 5 minutes. Remove saucepan from heat and stir in berries.

2   Stir together sour cream, granulated sugar, orange zest, and vanilla in small bowl.

3   Lay crêpes on work surface. Spoon 2 tablespoons of sour cream mixture in center of each crêpe; top each with one-fourth of berry mixture. Fold opposite sides of crêpes over to enclose filling. Dust crêpes evenly with confectioners' sugar.

PER SERVING (1 filled crêpe): 149 Cal, 1 g Total Fat, 0 g Sat Fat, 0 g Trans Fat, 8 mg Chol, 97 mg Sod, 32 g Carb, 12 g Sugar, 8 g Fib, 4 g Prot, 76 mg Calc.

FYI   Ready-to-use crêpes can be found in the refrigerated produce section of supermarkets.

Hungarian Goulash Soup

serves **6**

1 tablespoon olive oil

1 large red onion, quartered and thinly sliced

1¼ pounds beef chuck, trimmed and cut into ¾-inch chunks

1 large red bell pepper, cut into ½-inch pieces

1½ teaspoons paprika, preferably smoked

¾ teaspoon caraway seeds, crushed

½ teaspoon salt

¼ teaspoon black pepper

5 cups reduced-sodium beef broth

1 (14½-ounce) can petite diced tomatoes

½ cup fat-free sour cream

¼ cup chopped fresh flat-leaf parsley

1   Heat oil in large saucepan over medium-high heat. Add onion and cook, stirring, until softened and lightly browned, about 8 minutes. Add beef and cook, stirring, until browned, about 5 minutes.

2   Add bell pepper, paprika, caraway seeds, salt, and black pepper to pot; cook, stirring constantly, until fragrant, about 30 seconds. Add broth and tomatoes; bring to boil. Reduce heat and simmer, covered, until beef is fork-tender, about 1½ hours.

3   Uncover pot and simmer 30 minutes. Remove pot from heat; stir in sour cream and parsley.

PER SERVING (1⅓ cups): 225 Cal, 8 g Total Fat, 2 g Sat Fat, 0 g Trans Fat, 41 mg Chol, 472 mg Sod, 12 g Carb, 5 g Sugar, 2 g Fib, 25 g Prot, 69 mg Calc.

Healthy Extra   Stir 2 cups of sliced cremini or oyster mushrooms into the soup along with the tomatoes in step 2.

Chicken-Tortilla Soup with Corn & Avocado

serves **6**

1 tablespoon olive oil

1 onion, chopped

1 large garlic clove, minced

¾ pound cooked skinless boneless chicken breasts, shredded

2 (6-inch) corn tortillas, coarsely chopped

1 (14½-ounce) can diced fire-roasted tomatoes

1 cup frozen corn kernels

1 large red potato, scrubbed and cut into ½-inch dice

1 (32-ounce) container reduced-sodium chicken broth

½ Hass avocado, pitted, peeled, and cut into ½-inch dice

⅓ cup chopped fresh cilantro

1 jalapeño pepper, seeded and thinly sliced

½ cup shredded reduced-fat Monterey Jack cheese

1   Heat oil in large saucepan over medium heat. Add onion and garlic; cook, stirring, until onion is softened, about 5 minutes.

2   Add chicken, tortillas, tomatoes, corn, potato, and broth to pot; bring to boil over medium-high heat. Reduce heat and simmer, covered, until potato is tender, about 10 minutes.

3   Ladle soup evenly into 6 soup bowls. Top each serving with one-sixth each of avocado, cilantro, jalapeño, and Monterey Jack.

PER SERVING (1 bowl): 278 Cal, 8 g Total Fat, 2 g Sat Fat, 0 g Trans Fat, 49 mg Chol, 631 mg Sod, 27 g Carb, 5 g Sugar, 3 g Fib, 24 g Prot, 179 mg Calc.

FYI   In this soup, the corn tortillas are used as a thickener. Alternatively, the tortillas can be cut into strips and broiled or grilled until crispy, then piled on top of the soup.

Low-Country Gumbo

7 PointsPlus value
PER SERVING

serves
6

1 tablespoon canola oil

½ pound low-fat chicken sausage, sliced

1 onion, chopped

1 green bell pepper, chopped

2 celery stalks, chopped

4 garlic cloves, minced

2 tablespoons all-purpose flour

1 (14½-ounce) can reduced-sodium chicken broth

1 (14½-ounce) can diced tomatoes

1 tablespoon chopped fresh thyme

½ teaspoon salt

½ teaspoon black pepper

¼–½ teaspoon cayenne

2 bay leaves

1 (10-ounce) package frozen sliced okra

½ pound peeled and deveined large shrimp

3 cups hot cooked brown rice

1   Heat oil in large heavy saucepan over medium-high heat. Add sausage and cook, turning, until browned, about 5 minutes. Transfer to medium bowl.

2   Reduce heat to medium. Add onion, bell pepper, celery, and garlic to pot; cook, stirring, until onion is golden, about 8 minutes. Stir in flour and cook, stirring constantly, 1 minute. Gradually stir in broth until mixture is smooth.

3   Add tomatoes, thyme, salt, black pepper, cayenne, and bay leaves to pot; bring to boil over medium-high heat. Reduce heat and simmer, covered, until flavors are blended, about 20 minutes.

4   Return sausage to pot along with okra and shrimp. Simmer, covered, until okra is tender and shrimp is just opaque in center, about 10 minutes. Discard bay leaves. Spoon ½ cup of rice into each of 6 soup bowls. Ladle gumbo evenly over rice.

PER SERVING (about 1½ cups): 284 Cal, 7 g Total Fat, 1 g Sat Fat, 0 g Trans Fat, 85 mg Chol, 668 mg Sod, 37 g Carb, 6 g Sugar, 5 g Fib, 19 g Prot, 102 mg Calc.

Healthy Extra   Add 1 chopped red bell pepper to the soup along with the green bell pepper in step 2.

French Peasant–Style Fish Soup

8 PointsPlus® value
PER SERVING

serves
4

3 tablespoons reduced-fat mayonnaise

2 garlic cloves, minced

2 teaspoons olive oil

1 onion, sliced

1 small fennel bulb, thinly sliced

2 (8-ounce) bottles clam juice

1 cup dry white wine or water

3 (3-inch) strips orange zest, removed with vegetable peeler

½ teaspoon dried thyme

¼ teaspoon black pepper

1 (6-ounce) bag baby spinach

1 pound halibut, cut into 1-inch chunks

Few drops hot pepper sauce

1 (5-ounce) length French baguette, cut into 12 slices and toasted

2 tablespoons coarsely chopped fresh flat-leaf parsley

1   Stir together mayonnaise and garlic in small bowl.

2   Heat oil in large saucepan over medium heat. Add onion and fennel; cook, stirring, until golden, about 8 minutes. Add clam juice, wine, orange zest, thyme, and black pepper; bring to boil. Reduce heat and simmer, covered, until flavors are blended, about 10 minutes.

3   Stir spinach into broth mixture and simmer, covered, until spinach begins to wilt, about 1 minute. Stir about ½ cup of hot broth into mayonnaise mixture. Stir mayonnaise mixture into soup until blended. Add halibut and simmer, covered, until just opaque, about 5 minutes. Stir in pepper sauce.

4   Place 3 toasts in bottom of each of 4 soup bowls. Ladle 1¼ cups of soup into each bowl and sprinkle evenly with parsley.

PER SERVING (1 bowl): 367 Cal, 7 g Total Fat, 1 g Sat Fat, 0 g Trans Fat, 40 mg Chol, 737 mg Sod, 35 g Carb, 4 g Sugar, 6 g Fib, 30 g Prot, 161 mg Calc.

FYI   If the fennel comes with its feathery fronds still attached, chop some and sprinkle over each serving of soup.

Cape Cod Shrimp & Corn Chowder

serves
4

PER SERVING

1 tablespoon canola oil

1 onion, chopped

2 teaspoons fresh thyme leaves

4 cups fresh corn kernels (about 8 ears of corn)

2 (8-ounce) bottles clam juice

1 (14½-ounce) can reduced-sodium chicken broth

¼ teaspoon salt

¼ teaspoon black pepper

¾ pound medium shrimp, peeled and deveined

1 tablespoon snipped fresh chives

1 Heat oil in large saucepan over medium heat. Add onion and thyme; cook, stirring, until onion is softened, about 5 minutes. Add corn, clam juice, broth, salt, and pepper; bring to boil over medium-high heat. Reduce heat and simmer 5 minutes. Remove pot from heat and let soup cool about 5 minutes.

2 Transfer 2 cups of soup to blender and puree. Return puree to saucepan and bring to simmer. Add shrimp and cook until just opaque in center, about 2 minutes. Ladle soup evenly into 4 soup bowls. Serve sprinkled with chives.

PER SERVING (generous 1 cup): 258 Cal, 7 g Total Fat, 1 g Sat Fat, 0 g Trans Fat, 129 mg Chol, 589 mg Sod, 34 g Carb, 7 g Sugar, 5 g Fib, 21 g Prot, 60 mg Calc.

Healthy Extra Add 1 large red potato, scrubbed and cut into ½-inch dice, to the chowder in step 1 along with the corn. This will increase the per-serving *PointsPlus* value by **1**.

Moroccan Lentil & Vegetable Soup

serves
6

PER SERVING

1 tablespoon olive oil

1 large onion, chopped

2 celery stalks, diced

2 carrots, diced

3 garlic cloves, minced

2 teaspoons ground cumin

1 teaspoon ground turmeric

6 cups reduced-sodium vegetable broth

1¼ cups dried brown lentils, picked over, rinsed, and drained

1 small eggplant (about ¾ pound), unpeeled and diced

2 zucchini, diced

2 large plum tomatoes, diced

Grated zest and juice of ½ lime

½ teaspoon salt

¼ teaspoon black pepper

¼ cup chopped fresh cilantro

1 Heat oil in large nonstick saucepan over medium-high heat. Add onion, celery, carrots, and garlic; cook, stirring, until onion is golden, about 8 minutes. Add cumin and turmeric; cook, stirring, until fragrant, about 1 minute.

2 Stir broth and lentils into onion mixture and bring to boil. Reduce heat and simmer, covered, 15 minutes. Add eggplant and simmer, covered, until lentils and eggplant are tender, 15 minutes longer.

3 Add zucchini, tomatoes, lime zest, salt, and pepper to pot; simmer, covered, until zucchini is tender about 5 minutes. Remove pot from heat; stir in lime juice and cilantro.

PER SERVING (about 1½ cups): 225 Cal, 3 g Total Fat, 0 g Sat Fat, 0 g Trans Fat, 0 mg Chol, 381 mg Sod, 39 g Total Carb, 10 g Sugar, 15 g Fib, 13 g Prot, 88 mg Calc.

Thai Seafood Pot

Thai Seafood Pot

PER SERVING

serves
4

2 tablespoons reduced-sodium soy sauce

4 teaspoons lime juice

2 teaspoons packed brown sugar

1 teaspoon Asian (dark) sesame oil

½ teaspoon Sriracha (hot chili sauce) or to taste

6 ounces rice stick noodles (vermicelli)

6 cups reduced-sodium chicken broth

1 pound medium shrimp, peeled and deveined

½ pound shiitake mushrooms, stemmed and sliced

¼ pound snow peas, trimmed and sliced on diagonal

1 cup matchstick-cut carrots

1 tablespoon minced peeled fresh ginger

2 garlic cloves, minced

2 scallions, thinly sliced on diagonal

¼ cup coarsely chopped fresh cilantro

1 Stir together soy sauce, lime juice, brown sugar, oil, and Sriracha in cup until brown sugar is dissolved.

2 Put noodles in large bowl and add enough hot water to cover. Cover bowl with plastic wrap and let stand until noodles are softened, about 10 minutes. Drain.

3 Meanwhile, bring broth to boil in large saucepan over high heat. Add shrimp, mushrooms, snow peas, carrots, ginger, and garlic. Reduce heat and simmer until shrimp are just opaque in center, about 2 minutes.

4 Stir lime juice mixture into soup; return to simmer. Divide noodles evenly among 4 soup bowls and ladle soup evenly on top. Serve sprinkled evenly with scallions and cilantro.

PER SERVING (generous 1½ cups): 388 Cal, 5 g Total Fat, 1 g Sat Fat, 0 g Trans Fat, 168 mg Chol, 608 mg Sod, 55 g Carb, 8 g Sugar, 3 g Fib, 31 g Prot, 86 mg Calc.

Farmers' Market Vegetable Soup

4 PointsPlus® value

PER SERVING

serves **8**

2 Yukon Gold potatoes, scrubbed and cut into ½-inch dice

1 onion, chopped

2 carrots, chopped

2 celery stalks, thinly sliced

6 cups reduced-sodium chicken broth

2 large tomatoes, halved, seeded, and diced

2 zucchini, halved lengthwise and sliced

¾ pound green beans, trimmed and cut into ½-inch pieces

1 cup fresh or frozen peas

1 teaspoon dried oregano

½ teaspoon salt

½ teaspoon black pepper

½ cup chopped fresh basil

½ cup grated Parmesan cheese

1　Combine potatoes, onion, carrots, celery, and broth in large saucepan; bring to boil over medium-high heat. Reduce heat and simmer, covered, until potatoes are just tender, about 10 minutes.

2　Add tomatoes, zucchini, beans, peas, oregano, salt, and pepper to pot; cook, stirring occasionally, until vegetables are tender, about 10 minutes longer. Remove pot from heat and stir in basil. Serve sprinkled with Parmesan.

PER SERVING (1⅓ cups and 1 tablespoon cheese): 135 Cal, 3 g Total Fat, 1 g Sat Fat, 0 g Trans Fat, 4 mg Chol, 326 mg Sod, 22 g Carb, 7 g Sugar, 6 g Fib, 10 g Prot, 122 mg Calc.

Healthy Extra　Add 1 small green bell pepper, cut into ½-inch dice, to the soup along with the tomatoes in step 2.

Farmers' Market
Vegetable Soup

Classic Black Bean Soup

8 PointsPlus® value
PER SERVING

serves **4**

1 cup dried black beans, picked over, rinsed, and drained

1 tablespoon olive oil

1 large onion, chopped

2 celery stalks, thinly sliced

2 carrots, chopped

2 large garlic cloves, minced

2 teaspoons chili powder

1 teaspoon ground cumin

6 cups reduced-sodium chicken broth

½ teaspoon hot pepper sauce

2 hard-cooked large egg whites, chopped

4 tablespoons fat-free sour cream

4 tablespoons chopped fresh cilantro

2 scallions, chopped

1   Put beans in large bowl and add enough boiling water to cover. Cover bowl with plastic wrap and let stand 1 hour; rinse and drain.

2   Heat oil in large nonstick saucepan over medium heat. Add onion, celery, carrots, garlic, chili powder, and cumin; cook, stirring, until vegetables are lightly browned, about 10 minutes.

3   Add soaked beans, broth, and pepper sauce to pot; bring to boil. Reduce heat and simmer, covered, until beans are tender, about 1¼ hours. Remove pot from heat and let soup cool about 5 minutes.

4   Transfer 2 cups of bean soup to blender and puree. Return puree to pot and cook until soup is heated through, about 5 minutes. Serve accompanied by hard-cooked egg whites, sour cream, cilantro, and scallions.

PER SERVING (1⅓ cups soup with 2 tablespoons egg white, 1 tablespoon sour cream, and 1 tablespoon cilantro): 329 Cal, 7 g Total Fat, 1 g Sat Fat, 0 g Trans Fat, 3 mg Chol, 266 mg Sod, 50 g Carb, 6g Sugar, 14 g Fib, 22 g Prot, 140 mg Calc.

FYI   Save a step by not pureeing the bean mixture.

Chock-Full-of-Vegetables Split Pea Soup

serves
8

PER SERVING

1 tablespoon olive oil

1 onion, chopped

1 leek, halved lengthwise and sliced

3 carrots, diced

2 celery stalks, sliced

2 garlic cloves, minced

1 teaspoon dried oregano

1 (1-pound) package yellow split peas, pickod over, rinsed, and drained

1 large all-purpose potato, scrubbed and diced

8 cups reduced-sodium vegetable broth

¾ teaspoon salt

¼ teaspoon black pepper

2 bay leaves

¾ cup fat-free sour cream

1 Heat oil in large nonstick saucepan over medium heat. Add onion, leek, carrots, celery, garlic, and oregano; cook, stirring, until onion is golden, about 8 minutes.

2 Add split peas, potato, broth, salt, pepper, and bay leaves to pot and bring to boil. Reduce heat and simmer, covered, until split peas are almost tender, about 45 minutes. Remove bay leaves. Ladle soup evenly into 8 soup bowls, top with sour cream.

PER SERVING (1 cup soup and 1½ tablespoons sour cream): 313 Cal, 3 g Total Fat, 0 g Sat Fat, 0 g Trans Fat, 2 mg Chol, 429 mg Sod, 57 g Total Carb, 7 g Total Sugar, 21 g Fib, 15 g Prot, 95 mg Calc.

Healthy Extra Add 1 zucchini, cut into ½-inch dice, to the soup along with the split peas in step 2.

Split Pea & Spinach Soup

serves
4

PER SERVING

4 cups reduced-sodium vegetable or chicken broth

½ pound green split peas, picked over, rinsed, and drained

2 carrots, coarsely chopped

2 celery stalks with leaves, coarsely chopped

2 onions, coarsely chopped

½ cup + 1 tablespoon coarsely chopped fresh flat-leaf parsley

3 slices Canadian bacon, coarsely chopped

1 garlic clove, peeled

½ teaspoon salt

⅛ teaspoon black pepper

2 cups lightly packed baby spinach

½ cup frozen peas, thawed

1 Combine broth, split peas, carrots, celery, onions, ½ cup of parsley, the bacon, garlic, salt, and pepper in large saucepan and set over medium-high heat; bring to boil. Reduce heat and simmer, covered, until vegetables and split peas are very soft, about 45 minutes.

2 Stir spinach and peas into pot; cook, stirring, until spinach is wilted, about 2 minutes. Remove pot from heat and let soup cool about 5 minutes.

3 Coarsely puree soup, in batches, in blender. Ladle soup evenly into 4 soup bowls and sprinkle with remaining 1 tablespoon parsley.

PER SERVING (1¾ cups): 265 Cal, 2 g Total Fat, 0 g Sat Fat, 0 g Trans Fat, 8 mg Chol, 412 mg Sod, 47 g Carb, 13 g Sugar, 17 g Fib, 17 g Prot, 98 mg Calc.

FYI Add a bit of smoky flavor to this soup by stirring in a few drops of hickory liquid smoke at the end of the cooking time.

Shrimp & Kielbasa Jambalaya

Shrimp & Kielbasa Jambalaya

PER SERVING

1 tablespoon olive oil

1 large onion, chopped

1 green bell pepper, chopped

1 large celery stalk, chopped

2 large garlic cloves, minced

½ pound turkey kielbasa, thinly sliced

1½ cups long-grain white rice

1 (28-ounce) can diced tomatoes

1 (14½-ounce) can reduced-sodium chicken broth

1 teaspoon dried oregano

¼ teaspoon Creole or Cajun seasoning

1 pound medium shrimp, peeled and deveined, tails left on if desired

1   Heat oil in large nonstick saucepan over medium heat. Add onion, bell pepper, celery, and garlic; cook, stirring, until softened, about 5 minutes. Add kielbasa and cook, stirring, until lightly browned, about 4 minutes.

2   Add rice to pot and cook, stirring frequently, until lightly toasted, about 2 minutes. Add tomatoes, broth, oregano, and Creole seasoning; bring to boil. Reduce heat and simmer, covered, until rice is tender, about 30 minutes.

3   Add shrimp and cook until just opaque in center and liquid is absorbed, about 5 minutes.

PER SERVING (about 1⅓ cups): 351 Cal, 7 g Total Fat, 2 g Sat Fat, 0 g Trans Fat, 136 mg Chol, 814 mg Sod, 48 g Carb, 7 g Sugar, 2 g Fib, 24 g Prot, 68 mg Calc.

Healthy Extra   Seve the jambalaya with steamed whole okra.

Chicken with Saffron Rice

serves
4

PER SERVING

1 teaspoon ground coriander

½ teaspoon ground cumin

½ teaspoon salt

¼ teaspoon cayenne

8 small chicken drumsticks (about 2 pounds), skinned

1 garlic clove, minced

1¼ cups reduced-sodium chicken broth

¾ cup long-grain brown rice

¼ teaspoon saffron threads, crushed

1 (14-ounce) can whole peeled tomatoes, drained and chopped

¾ cup frozen baby peas, thawed

2 tablespoons coarsely chopped fresh flat-leaf parsley or cilantro

1   Combine coriander, cumin, salt, and cayenne on sheet of wax paper; sprinkle all over chicken legs.

2   Spray large nonstick saucepan with nonstick spray and set over medium heat. Add chicken and cook until lightly browned on all sides, about 5 minutes. Add garlic and cook, stirring, until fragrant, about 30 seconds.

3   Stir broth, rice, and saffron into pot and bring to boil. Reduce heat and simmer, covered, 30 minutes. Add tomatoes and cook, covered, until rice is tender, about 35 minutes. Stir in peas and cook, uncovered, until liquid is evaporated, about 5 minutes longer. Serve sprinkled with parsley.

PER SERVING (2 chicken legs with scant 1 cup rice): 417 Cal, 12 g Total Fat, 3 g Sat Fat, 0 g Trans Fat, 115 mg Chol, 640 mg Sod, 36 g Total Carb, 3 g Total Sugar, 3 g Fib, 39 g Prot, 49 mg Calc.

Healthy Extra   Serve with a bowl of fat-free tomatillo salsa for spooning over the chicken and rice.

Barley Risotto with Mushrooms, Sausage & Tomato

PER SERVING

serves
6

1 tablespoon olive oil

1 onion, chopped

2 garlic cloves, minced

¾ pound mixed mushrooms, such as chanterelle and cremini, sliced

⅓ cup dry red wine

1 pound low-fat chicken and spinach sausage, thinly sliced

4 cups reduced-sodium chicken broth

1 cup pearl barley (not quick-cooking) or brown rice

1 large tomato, seeded and diced

¼ cup grated Parmesan cheese

½ teaspoon black pepper

1   Heat oil in large nonstick saucepan over medium-high heat. Add onion and garlic; cook, stirring, until onion is softened, about 5 minutes. Add mushrooms and cook, stirring, until softened, about 5 minutes.

2   Add wine to saucepan and cook, stirring, until wine is evaporated, about 3 minutes. Add sausage and cook, stirring occasionally, until beginning to brown, about 8 minutes. Add broth and barley; bring to boil. Reduce heat and simmer, covered, until barley is tender, about 40 minutes, stirring in tomato about 10 minutes before cooking time is up.

3   Remove saucepan from heat; stir in Parmesan and pepper. Serve at once.

PER SERVING (about 1⅓ cups): 334 Cal, 11 g Total Fat, 4 g Sat Fat, 0 g Trans Fat, 61 mg Chol, 589 mg Sod, 35 g Carb, 4 g Sugar, 6 g Fib, 23 g Prot, 112 mg Calc.

FYI   Barley is one of the oldest grains known and is commonly eaten as cereal, added to yeast breads, and turned into soup, most notably, mushroom-barley. Pearl barley is whole grain barley that has had the bran removed and has been steamed and polished.

Winter Squash & Sage Risotto

PER SERVING

1 tablespoon olive oil

1 shallot, minced

4 fresh sage leaves

1 garlic clove, minced

1 cup short-grain brown rice

¼ cup dry white wine

1 (32-ounce) container reduced-sodium chicken broth, heated to boiling

1 (12-ounce) package frozen cooked winter squash, thawed

¼ teaspoon salt

⅛ teaspoon black pepper

¼ cup grated Parmesan cheese

1 Heat oil in large saucepan over medium-low heat. Add shallot and sage; cook, stirring frequently, until shallot is softened, about 8 minutes. Add garlic and cook, stirring constantly, until fragrant, about 30 seconds; stir in rice.

2 Increase heat to medium and cook, stirring, until rice is translucent, about 3 minutes. Add wine and cook, stirring constantly, until absorbed, about 4 minutes longer.

3 Add broth to rice, ½ cup at a time, stirring until broth is absorbed before adding more, and cooking until rice is tender but slightly chewy in center. Stir in squash, salt, and pepper with last addition of broth and cook, stirring, until broth is absorbed, about 10 minutes longer. Discard sage leaves. Stir in Parmesan and serve at once.

PER SERVING (generous ¾ cup): 311 Cal, 8 g Total Fat, 2 g Sat Fat, 0 g Trans Fat, 4 mg Chol, 295 mg Sod, 52 g Carb, 1 g Sugar, 5 g Fib, 10 g Prot, 89 mg Calc.

FYI When making risotto, it is important to use very hot broth so the rice grains cook thoroughly and evenly. Pour the broth into a large glass measure and microwave on High until boiling, about 4 minutes. Ladle it into the risotto as directed, reheating the broth as needed.

Winter Squash & Sage Risotto

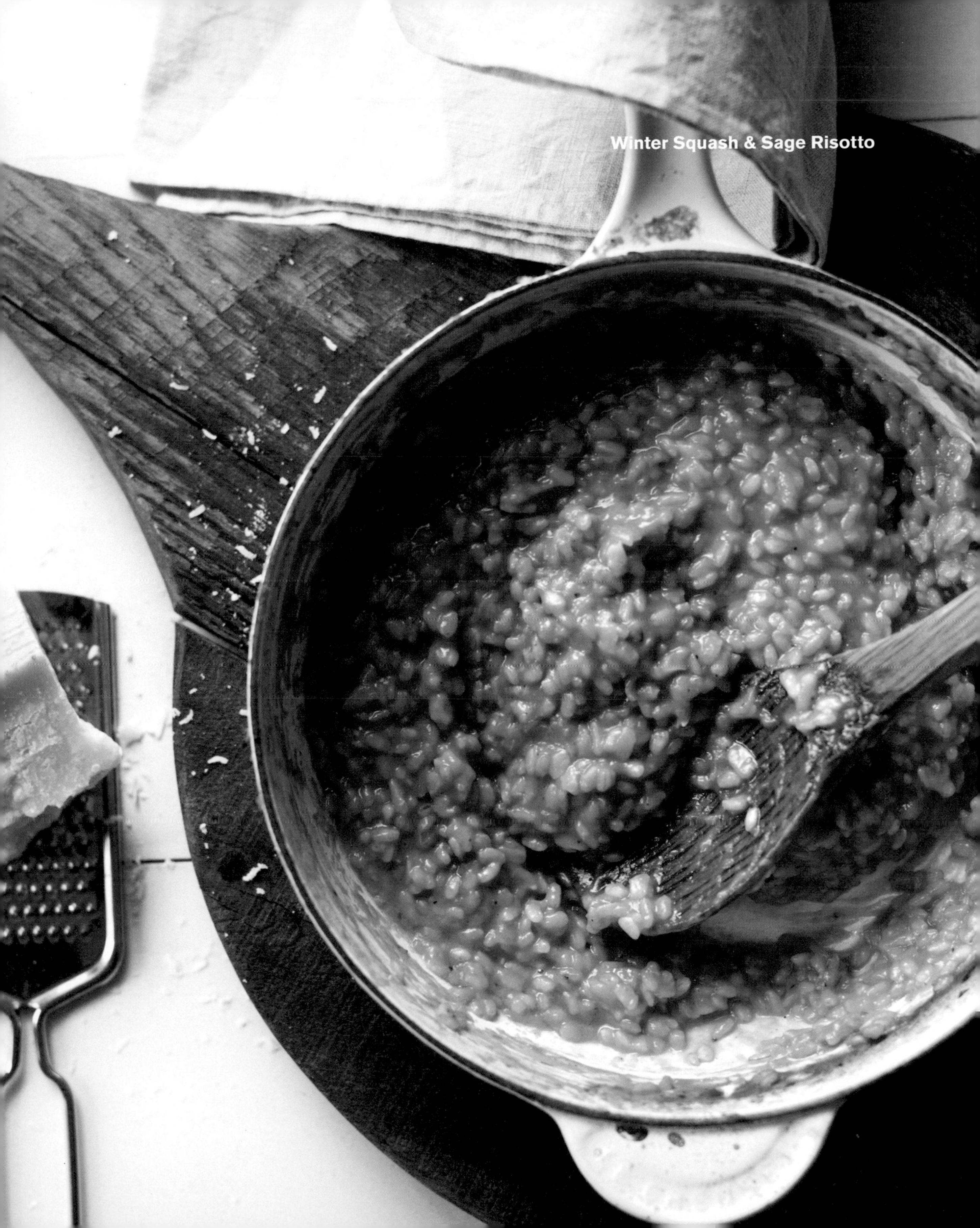

Linguine with Turkey Bolognese

serves
6

PER SERVING

1 tablespoon olive oil

1 small onion, finely chopped

1 small carrot, finely chopped

1 small celery stalk with leaves, finely chopped

1 garlic clove, minced

6 ounces ground skinless turkey breast

¼ teaspoon salt

⅛ teaspoon black pepper

Pinch ground nutmeg

¼ cup dry red wine

1 (14½-ounce) can diced tomatoes, drained

½ cup canned tomato sauce

4 tablespoons reduced-fat (2%) milk

4 tablespoons grated Parmesan cheese

12 ounces whole wheat linguine, cooked according to package directions

1   Heat oil in large heavy saucepan over medium heat. Add onion, carrot, and celery; cook, stirring, until onion is softened, about 5 minutes. Add garlic and cook, stirring constantly, until fragrant, about 30 seconds. Add turkey and cook, breaking it apart with wooden spoon, until browned, about 5 minutes. Stir in salt, pepper, and nutmeg.

2   Add wine to turkey mixture and bring to boil; cook until wine is evaporated, about 4 minutes. Add tomatoes and tomato sauce; simmer, stirring frequently, until tomatoes are broken down and sauce is thickened, about 30 minutes, adding 2 tablespoons of milk after 15 minutes and remaining 2 tablespoons milk 5 minutes later. Stir in 2 tablespoons of Parmesan.

3   Toss sauce with hot linguine in serving bowl until mixed well. Serve sprinkled with remaining 2 tablespoons cheese.

PER SERVING (about 1½ cups): 326 Cal, 5 g Total Fat, 1 g Sat Fat, 0 g Trans Fat, 15 mg Chol, 442 mg Sod, 54 g Carb, 7 g Sugar, 9 g Fib, 19 g Prot, 95 mg Calc.

Healthy Extra   Start your meal off with a radicchio, watercress, red onion, and tomato salad dressed with balsamic vinegar and a pinch of salt.

Saffron Clam Sauce with Capellini

9 PointsPlus value · PER SERVING

serves 4

1 tablespoon olive oil

1 red onion, thinly sliced

¼ teaspoon saffron threads, crushed

1 garlic clove, minced

1 (14½-ounce) can petite diced tomatoes

1 (10-ounce) can whole baby clams, drained

¼ teaspoon black pepper

½ pound whole wheat capellini, cooked according to package directions

⅓ cup chopped fresh flat-leaf parsley

1   Heat oil over medium heat in large saucepan. Add onion and cook, stirring frequently, until softened, about 5 minutes. Add saffron and cook, stirring frequently, until fragrant, about 2 minutes. Add garlic and cook, stirring constantly, until fragrant, about 30 seconds longer.

2   Add tomatoes, clams, and pepper to pot; cook, stirring frequently, until heated through, about 3 minutes longer. Transfer to serving bowl. Add capellini and parsley; toss until mixed well.

PER SERVING (generous 1 cup): 336 Cal, 7 g Total Fat, 1 g Sat Fat, 0 g Trans Fat, 57 mg Chol, 609 mg Sod, 53 g Carb, 6 g Sugar, 9 g Fib, 21 g Prot, 139 mg Calc.

Healthy Extra   Serve this pasta dish with a side of microwave-cooked sliced zucchini and cherry tomatoes tossed with a pinch of dried oregano.

Edamame, Asparagus & Tomatoes with Thin Spaghetti

8 PointsPlus value · PER SERVING

serves 4

½ pound whole wheat penne or other short pasta

1 cup frozen shelled edamame, thawed

¼ pound asparagus, trimmed and cut into 1-inch lengths

¼ cup seasoned rice vinegar

1 tablespoon canola oil

½ teaspoon grated lemon zest

½ teaspoon salt

¼ teaspoon black pepper

1 cup cherry tomatoes, halved

1 small red onion, quartered and thinly sliced

⅓ cup chopped fresh flat-leaf parsley

1   Cook pasta according to package directions in large saucepan, omitting salt if desired. With slotted spoon transfer pasta to colander to drain.

2   Return water to boil; add edamame and asparagus; cook until asparagus is crisp-tender, about 2 minutes. Add to colander; drain. Rinse under cold running water; drain again.

3   Whisk together vinegar, oil, lemon zest, salt, and pepper in serving bowl. Add pasta, edamame, asparagus, and remaining ingredients; toss until mixed well.

PER SERVING (about 2 cups): 295 Cal, 6 g Total Fat, 0 g Sat Fat, 0 g Trans Fat, 0 mg Chol, 600 mg Sod, 53 g Carb, 8 g Sugar, 10 g Fib, 13 g Prot, 64 mg Calc.

FYI   This is a great make-ahead dish, as it is best served at room temperature. Transfer it to a serving bowl; cover and let stand at room temperature for up to 4 hours. Before serving, give it a taste to see if it needs a touch more lemon zest or pepper.

**Fresh Tomato–Red Onion
Sauce with Penne**

Fresh Tomato-Red Onion Sauce with Penne

serves
4

PER SERVING

1 tablespoon olive oil

1 small red onion, finely chopped

1 garlic clove, minced

1¼ pounds cherry tomatoes

½ teaspoon salt

¼ teaspoon black pepper

½ pound whole wheat penne

4 tablespoons grated Parmesan cheese

6 fresh basil leaves, thinly sliced

1   Heat oil in large saucepan over medium heat. Add onion and cook, stirring, until softened, about 5 minutes. Add garlic and cook, stirring constantly, until fragrant, about 30 seconds. Stir in tomatoes, salt, and pepper; cook, stirring occasionally, until tomatoes are collapsed and sauce is slightly thickened, about 10 minutes. Transfer sauce to medium bowl; keep warm. Wash out pot.

2   Cook penne in same pot according to package directions, omitting salt if desired. Drain and return to pot.

3   Add sauce, 2 tablespoons of Parmesan, and the basil to pasta; toss to combine well. Serve sprinkled with remaining 2 tablespoons cheese.

PER SERVING (1 cup): 314 Cal, 7 g Total Fat, 1 g Sat Fat, 0 g Trans Fat, 4 mg Chol, 390 mg Sod, 54 g Carb, 9 g Sugar, 8 g Fib, 11 g Prot, 108 mg Calc.

Healthy Extra   Serve this dish with a side of microwave-cooked broccoli rabe or broccoli drizzled with lemon juice just before serving.

IN A
DUTCH

OVEN

CHAPTER 5

IN A DUTCH OVEN

BOUNTIFUL STEWS, BRAISES & CHILIES

The term *Dutch oven* refers to a heavy pot with a tight-fitting lid that is commonly used for slow-cooked braises and stews. Early Dutch ovens had three legs so they could be placed on top of hot coals. These pots were used for baking, boiling, braising, frying, and roasting.

There are several theories regarding how the Dutch oven got its name. As one story goes, in the 17th century an Englishman named Abraham Darby traveled to the Netherlands to learn about the Dutch process of manufacturing cast-iron cooking vessels. This process created a surface superior to the one developed by the English. In time, Darby patented a similar process for pots that he called Dutch ovens. These early pots were appreciated for their versatility and durability. In fact, they were so coveted that George Washington's mother put her cast-iron cookware in her will.

Types
There are basically two types of Dutch ovens:

A **"camp, cowboy, or chuck wagon"** Dutch oven has three short legs, a heavy wire handle, and a concave lid. Hot coals can be placed in the lid so the food cooks from the top as well as from below, creating an oven-like environment. This Dutch oven is usually made of cast iron but some are also made of heavy aluminum.

Flat-bottomed Dutch ovens can be used on the stovetop and in the oven. They can be made of cast iron, enamel-coated cast iron, aluminum, stainless steel, or stoneware. They all come with a tight-fitting lid so moisture doesn't escape. Stoneware Dutch ovens are very versatile; they can easily go from stovetop to microwave to table.

Sizes and Shapes

Dutch ovens range in size from about 2 quarts to 8 quarts. They are most often round, but some larger ones are oval.

Basics for Care

It is important to season a **cast-iron Dutch oven** before it is used. Wipe the inside with a light coating of flavorless vegetable oil, then place the pot in a 350°F oven for 1 hour. Remove it from the oven and let it cool completely, then wipe it dry with a paper towel. To clean it, rinse it under hot water as soon as it is cool enough to handle to prevent any food from sticking, then use a nonabrasive powder cleaner or kosher salt and a stiff brush to remove any food particles. Dry the pan immediately to prevent rusting and apply a very light coating of vegetable oil while warm. Cast-iron Dutch ovens are not dishwasher safe.

Heavy aluminum Dutch ovens are easy to clean and hard to scratch. Allow them to cool down, then soak in hot, soapy water for about 30 minutes or until the food particles are softened. Scrub the pot using a scrub pad or steel wool soap pad. This type of Dutch oven is dishwasher safe.

Enamel cast-iron Dutch ovens are easy to care for. Allow them to cool completely before washing to avoid shocking the enamel due to the change in temperature. Hand-wash these pots with hot, soapy water, then rinse with warm water and dry well. If any food particles remain, soak these pots for about 15 minutes, then use a nylon scrub pad. These pots are dishwasher safe, but it is not recommended, as detergent will dull the enamel surface over time.

It is recommended to season a **ceramic Dutch oven** before it is used for the first time. Check the manufacturer's instructions for details. This Dutch oven is simple to clean. Soak the cool pot in hot, soapy water for about 30 minutes to help remove any stuck-on food particles. The pot can then be scrubbed clean using a nylon scrub pad. Stoneware Dutch ovens are dishwasher safe.

Yankee Pot Roast

2 tablespoons all-purpose flour

½ teaspoon salt

¼ teaspoon black pepper

1 (1-pound) first-cut brisket, trimmed

1 tablespoon canola oil

2 red onions, thinly sliced

1 (14½-ounce) can reduced-sodium beef broth

1 tablespoon packed brown sugar

6 sprigs + ¼ cup chopped fresh flat-leaf parsley

1 (3-inch) strip lemon zest, removed with vegetable peeler

1 bay leaf

4 carrots, halved lengthwise and cut into 1½-inch lengths

4 parsnips, halved lengthwise and cut into 1½-inch lengths

1 Mix together flour, salt, and pepper on sheet of wax paper; sprinkle all over brisket.

2 Heat oil in medium Dutch oven over medium heat. Add beef and cook until browned on all sides, about 10 minutes; transfer to plate. Add onions to pot and cook, stirring, until softened, about 5 minutes. Add 1 cup of broth, the brown sugar, parsley sprigs, lemon zest, and bay leaf; bring to boil.

3 Return beef and any accumulated juices, the remaining broth, the carrots, and parsnips to pot. Reduce heat to low and cook, covered, at bare simmer, turning roast every 30 minutes, until fork-tender, about 1½ hours. Transfer beef to cutting board and keep warm. With slotted spoon, transfer vegetables to serving bowl. Stir in chopped parsley; keep warm.

4 Place Dutch oven over high heat and bring to boil. Boil, stirring frequently, until juices are thickened, about 8 minutes. Remove and discard parsley sprigs, lemon zest, and bay leaf. Slice pot roast against grain into 12 slices. Serve with vegetables and sauce.

PER SERVING (3 slices pot roast, ¾ cup vegetables, and scant 2 tablespoons sauce): 412 Cal, 11 g Total Fat, 3 g Sat Fat, 0 g Trans Fat, 59 mg Chol, 432 mg Sod, 45 g Carb, 17 g Sugar, 9 g Fib, 34 g Prot, 121 mg Calc.

FYI Alternately, this pot roast—and other braises—can be cooked in the oven, which requires even less attention, as there is no need to turn the meat. After adding the vegetables, cover the Dutch oven and transfer it to a 325°F oven. Braise the roast until fork-tender, about 1½ hours, then reduce the juices and serve as directed in step 4.

Stracotto with Lemon Gremolata

serves
6

PER SERVING

2 tablespoons all-purpose flour

½ teaspoon salt

¼ teaspoon black pepper

1 (2-pound) beef chuck roast, trimmed

1 tablespoon olive oil

3 red onions, thinly sliced

2 garlic cloves, minced

1 (8-ounce) package sliced small white mushrooms

1 (14½-ounce) can petite diced tomatoes

1 cup dry red wine

½ cup chopped fresh flat-leaf parsley

Grated zest of 1 lemon

2 cups hot cooked whole wheat orzo

1   Mix together flour, salt, and pepper on sheet of wax paper; sprinkle all over chuck roast.

2   Heat oil in medium Dutch oven over medium heat. Add beef and cook until browned on all sides, about 10 minutes; transfer to plate. Add onions to pot and cook, stirring, until softened, about 5 minutes. Add half of garlic and cook, stirring constantly, until fragrant, about 30 seconds.

3   Add mushrooms, tomatoes, and wine to Dutch oven; cook, scraping browned bits from bottom of pot, about 3 minutes. Increase heat and bring to boil; reduce heat and simmer until mushrooms are softened, about 10 minutes. Return beef and any accumulated juices to pot; reduce heat and simmer, covered, stirring occasionally and turning beef every 30 minutes, until beef is fork-tender, about 1½ hours. Transfer beef to cutting board and keep warm.

4   Bring vegetable mixture to boil over medium-high heat; boil, stirring frequently at first and then almost constantly, until liquid is almost evaporated, about 12 minutes.

5   To make gremolata, stir together parsley, lemon zest, and remaining garlic in small bowl. Cut beef on diagonal into 12 slices. Serve sprinkled with gremolata and accompanied by vegetables and orzo.

PER SERVING (2 slices beef, generous ⅔ cup vegetables, 1½ tablespoons gremolata, and ⅓ cup orzo): 325 Cal, 9 g Total Fat, 3 g Sat Fat, 0 g Trans Fat, 64 mg Chol, 407 mg Sod, 17 g Carb, 5 g Sugar, 3 g Fib, 35 g Prot, 48 mg Calc.

FYI   Here's how to test meat for "fork-tender" doneness. Take a dinner fork or carving fork and stick it into the thickest part of the meat, then pull it out. If the meat is fork-tender, the fork will go in and out without any resistance.

Sauerbraten

2 cups cider vinegar

2 cups dry white wine

1 cup water

3 red onions, thinly sliced

3 carrots, thinly sliced

6 sprigs fresh flat-leaf parsley

1 teaspoon ground allspice

1 teaspoon salt

½ teaspoon black pepper

1 (2-pound) bottom round beef roast, trimmed

3 tablespoons all-purpose flour

1 tablespoon canola oil

1 bay leaf

¼ cup gingersnap cookie crumbs

2 tablespoons packed brown sugar

1   Combine vinegar, wine, water, onions, carrots, parsley sprigs, allspice, salt, and pepper in medium Dutch oven; bring to boil over high heat. Reduce heat and simmer, covered, 10 minutes. Remove pot from heat; uncover and let cool to room temperature.

2   Transfer marinade and beef roast to gallon zip-close plastic bag. Squeeze out air and seal bag; set in large bowl. Refrigerate at least 1 day or up to 4 days, turning bag two times a day. Remove beef from marinade. Pat beef dry with paper towels; sprinkle with flour.

3   Heat oil in medium Dutch oven over medium heat. Add beef and cook until browned on all sides, about 15 minutes. Pour marinade with vegetables into large sieve set over large bowl; discard parsley. Add 3 cups of marinade, the vegetables, and bay leaf to Dutch oven. Bring to boil over medium heat, stirring and scraping up browned bits from bottom of pot. Reduce heat to low and cook, covered, at bare simmer, stirring and turning roast every 30 minutes to prevent sticking, until beef is fork-tender, about 3½ hours. Transfer beef to cutting board and keep warm.

4   Pour pot liquid through coarse sieve set over large glass measure; discard solids. Wipe Dutch oven clean. Return pot liquid to Dutch oven. Whisk gingersnap crumbs and brown sugar into pot liquid; bring to boil over medium-high heat. Boil, whisking frequently at first and constantly toward end, until sauce is dark and reduced, about 10 minutes. Cut beef into 8 slices and arrange on deep platter; spoon sauce on top.

PER SERVING (1 slice beef and 2 tablespoons sauce): 354 Cal, 9 g Total Fat, 3 g Sat Fat, 0 g Trans Fat, 88 mg Chol, 395 mg Sod, 27 g Carb, 8 g Sugar, 2 g Fib, 30 g Prot, 37 mg Calc.

Healthy Extra   Serve this hearty dish with a side of steamed thinly sliced red cabbage.

Cowboy Stew

serves
4

PER SERVING

2 slices turkey bacon

1 pound beef top round, trimmed and cut into 1-inch chunks

1 tablespoon all-purpose flour

¼ teaspoon salt

¼ teaspoon black pepper

1 tablespoon canola oil

1 large onion, chopped

4 carrots, cut into 2-inch lengths

2 white turnips, cut into 1-inch chunks

1½ cups water

1 cup strong brewed coffee

¼ cup ketchup

1 pound all-purpose potatoes, scrubbed and cut into 1-inch chunks

3 tablespoons coarsely chopped fresh parsley

1   Cook bacon in medium nonstick Dutch oven over medium heat until crisp. Transfer to paper towels to drain. Crumble bacon.

2   Pat beef dry with paper towels. Mix together flour, salt, and ⅛ teaspoon of pepper on sheet of wax paper, sprinkle all over beef.

3   Heat oil in same Dutch oven over medium-high heat. Add beef, in batches, and cook until browned on all sides, about 5 minutes. Transfer to plate.

4   Add onion to Dutch oven; cook, scraping up browned bits from bottom of pot, until onion is golden, about 8 minutes. Return beef to pot along with carrots, turnips, water, coffee, ketchup, and remaining ⅛ teaspoon pepper; bring to boil. Reduce heat and simmer, covered, 1 hour. Add potatoes and simmer, covered, until beef and potatoes are fork-tender, about 20 minutes longer. Serve stew sprinkled with bacon and parsley.

PER SERVING (about 1 cup): 366 Cal, 11 g Total Fat, 3 g Sat Fat, 0 g Trans Fat, 63 mg Chol, 579 mg Sod, 37 g Carb, 11 g Sugar, 5 g Fib, 34 g Prot, 71 mg Calc.

Healthy Extra   Add ½ pound of thickly sliced mushrooms to the Dutch oven along with the carrots in step 4.

No-Fuss French-Style Beef Stew

No-Fuss French-Style Beef Stew

7 PointsPlus value PER SERVING

serves 6

1 tablespoon olive oil

1 large onion, thinly sliced

3 garlic cloves, minced

1½ pounds beef top round, trimmed and cut into 1½-inch chunks

1 sweet potato, peeled and cut into ¾-inch chunks

2 cups dry white wine

1 (14½-ounce) can whole peeled tomatoes, broken up and juice reserved

2 tablespoons Dijon mustard

3 fresh thyme sprigs tied together with kitchen string + 1 tablespoon fresh thyme leaves

½ teaspoon salt

¼ teaspoon black pepper

1 pound oyster, chanterelle, or white mushrooms, halved or quartered if large

1　Heat oil in medium Dutch oven over medium heat. Add onion and garlic; cook, stirring, until onion is softened, about 5 minutes.

2　Reduce heat to medium. Add all remaining ingredients except mushrooms and thyme leaves to Dutch oven; bring to boil. Reduce heat and simmer, covered, 1 hour.

3　Add mushrooms to pot and simmer, covered, until meat is fork-tender, about 1 hour longer. Remove and discard thyme sprigs. Serve sprinkled with thyme leaves.

PER SERVING (about 1 cup stew): 327 Cal, 8 g Total Fat, 2 g Sat Fat, 0 g Trans Fat, 56 mg Chol, 521 mg Sod, 18 g Carb, 5 g Sugar, 3 g Fib, 31 g Prot, 35 mg Calc.

Scandinavian-Style Beef

11 PointsPlus value PER SERVING

serves 4

2 tablespoons all-purpose flour

½ teaspoon salt

¼ teaspoon black pepper

1 pound beef bottom round, trimmed and cut into 1-inch chunks

1 tablespoon canola oil

1 (14½-ounce) can reduced-sodium beef broth

2 large shallots, thinly sliced

2 (6-ounce) red potatoes, scrubbed and cut into ½-inch dice

⅓ cup snipped fresh dill

2 tablespoons reduced-fat sour cream

2 cups hot cooked brown rice

1　Mix together flour, salt, and pepper on sheet of wax paper; sprinkle all over beef.

2　Heat oil in medium Dutch oven over medium heat. Add beef, in batches, and cook until browned on all sides, about 5 minutes per batch; transfer to plate. Add ½ cup of broth and the shallots; cook, stirring frequently and scraping up browned bits from bottom of pot, until shallots are softened, about 5 minutes.

3　Return beef to Dutch oven along with potatoes and remaining broth; bring to boil. Reduce heat and simmer, covered, until beef and potatoes are fork-tender, about 30 minutes. Remove pot from heat; stir in dill and sour cream. Serve over rice.

PER SERVING (1¼ cups stew and ½ cup rice): 438 Cal, 13 g Total Fat, 4 g Sat Fat, 0 g Trans Fat, 91 mg Chol, 373 mg Sod, 43 g Carb, 2 g Sugar, 3 g Fib, 36 g Prot, 48 mg Calc.

Healthy Extra　Serve steamed or roasted whole baby beets alongside the stew.

Classic Pasta with Ragu

serves
6

PER SERVING

3 teaspoons olive oil

1 onion, chopped

1 carrot, diced

1 celery stalk, diced

6 ounces ground lean beef
(7% fat or less)

6 ounces ground lean pork

¼ cup tomato paste

1 (28-ounce) can crushed tomatoes

1 fresh rosemary sprig

½ teaspoon crushed sage

½ teaspoon salt

¼ teaspoon black pepper

1 bay leaf

⅓ cup grated Parmesan cheese

4 cups cooked pasta, such as
gemelli or campanelle

1 Heat 2 teaspoons of oil in medium Dutch oven over medium heat. Add onion, carrot, and celery; cook, stirring, until onion is golden brown, about 8 minutes. Transfer to medium bowl.

2 Add remaining 1 teaspoon oil to Dutch oven. Add beef and pork; cook, breaking meat up with spoon, until no longer pink, about 5 minutes. Return vegetables to pot along with tomato paste; cook, stirring constantly, 1 minute.

3 Add crushed tomatoes, rosemary, sage, salt, pepper, and bay leaf to beef mixture; bring to simmer. Reduce heat and simmer, stirring occasionally, 1 hour.

4 Remove and discard rosemary sprig and bay leaf. Stir in Parmesan and pasta; cook, stirring, until heated through, about 3 minutes longer.

PER SERVING (about 1⅔ cups): 324 Cal, 8 g Total Fat, 2 g Sat Fat, 0 g Trans Fat, 38 mg Chol, 568 mg Sod, 44 g Carb, 4 g Sugar, 6 g Fib, 21 g Prot, 125 mg Calc.

FYI Gemelli pasta is made up of short thick twists, while campanelle pasta resembles trumpet-shaped flowers. These novel shapes hold the sauce especially well.

Cincinnati Four-Way Chili

serves
6

PER SERVING

2 teaspoons canola oil

1 pound ground lean beef
(7% fat or less)

1 large onion, chopped

1 garlic clove, minced

1 (14½-ounce) can petite
diced tomatoes

¼ cup water

1 tablespoon red wine vinegar

1 tablespoon Worcestershire sauce

1 tablespoon unsweetened cocoa

1 tablespoon chili powder

1 teaspoon ground cinnamon

1 teaspoon ground cumin

1 teaspoon ground allspice

¼ teaspoon cayenne

4 cups hot cooked whole wheat
spaghetti

6 tablespoons shredded reduced-
fat sharp Cheddar cheese

6 tablespoons chopped red onion

1   Heat oil in medium Dutch oven over medium-high heat. Add beef and cook, breaking it up with spoon, until no longer pink, about 5 minutes. Add onion and garlic; cook, stirring, until onion is softened, about 5 minutes.

2   Stir tomatoes, water, vinegar, Worcestershire sauce, cocoa, chili powder, cinnamon, cumin, allspice, and cayenne into beef mixture; bring to boil. Reduce heat and simmer, partially covered, stirring occasionally, 1½ hours.

3   Divide spaghetti evenly among 6 plates. Spoon about ⅔ cup chili over each serving of spaghetti. Sprinkle each serving with 1 tablespoon Cheddar and 1 tablespoon onion.

PER SERVING (1 plate): 289 Cal, 8 g Total Fat, 3 g Sat Fat, 0 g Trans Fat, 51 mg Chol, 303 mg Sod, 34 g Carb, 4 g Sugar, 7 g Fib, 23 g Prot, 153 mg Calc.

Healthy Extra   Turn this classic four-way chili into five-way chili by topping each serving with heated canned black beans (¼ cup black beans per serving will increase the *PointsPlus* value by 1).

Succulent Braised Pork Loin Asian-Style

serves
8

PER SERVING

1 cup water

6 scallions, thinly sliced

½ cup reduced-sodium soy sauce

2 tablespoons unseasoned
rice vinegar

2 tablespoons hoisin sauce

1 tablespoon sugar

4 quarter-size slices unpeeled
fresh ginger

4 garlic cloves, peeled

1 whole star anise

1 (2-pound) boneless center-cut
pork loin roast, trimmed

1 teaspoon Asian (dark) sesame oil

2 bunches broccolini, steamed

1   Combine water, 4 scallions, the soy sauce, vinegar, hoisin sauce, sugar, ginger, garlic, and star anise in medium Dutch oven. Add pork and bring to boil over high heat. Reduce heat and simmer, covered, 40 minutes, turning pork after 20 minutes. Turn pork again and simmer until instant-read thermometer inserted into center of pork registers 145°F for medium, about 12 minutes. Transfer to cutting board and let cool to room temperature.

2   Pour pot liquid through sieve set over glass measure or bowl.

3   To make sauce, combine 3 tablespoons of cooking liquid with ½ teaspoon of oil in small bowl. Toss broccolini with ½ cup of cooking liquid and remaining ½ teaspoon oil in medium bowl. Cut pork into 16 slices. Transfer pork and broccolini to platter; drizzle with sauce and sprinkle with remaining 2 scallions. Discard remaining cooking liquid.

PER SERVING (2 slices pork, ¾ cup broccolini, and about 1⅓ tablespoons sauce): 190 Cal, 7 g Total Fat, 2 g Sat Fat, 0 g Trans Fat, 67 mg Chol, 660 mg Sod, 9 g Carb, 3 g Sugar, 2 g Fib, 24 g Prot, 60 mg Calc.

Succulent Braised Pork Loin Asian-Style

Pork Chops with Cabbage, Apple & Caraway

serves
4

PER SERVING

1 tablespoon canola oil

4 (¼-pound) thin-cut bone-in center-cut pork loin chops, trimmed

1 red onion, thinly sliced

4 cups thinly sliced red cabbage (about 1 small head)

¾ cup apple cider or juice

¼ cup cider vinegar

1 small McIntosh apple, unpeeled, cored and cut into ¼-inch dice

2 tablespoons packed dark brown sugar

1 teaspoon mustard seeds

1 teaspoon caraway seeds

½ teaspoon salt

¼ teaspoon black pepper

⅓ cup chopped fresh flat-leaf parsley

1   Heat oil in medium Dutch oven over medium heat. Add pork chops, in batches, and cook, turning frequently, until lightly browned, about 3 minutes per batch; transfer to plate. Add onion and cook, stirring, until softened, about 5 minutes.

2   Add cabbage to Dutch oven and cook, stirring frequently, until wilted, about 4 minutes. Stir in cider and cook, stirring frequently and scraping up browned bits from bottom of pot, until liquid is evaporated, about 6 minutes. Add vinegar and bring to boil. Reduce heat to low; stir in apple, brown sugar, mustard seeds, caraway seeds, salt, and pepper.

3   Nestle pork chops in cabbage mixture; simmer, covered, stirring occasionally, until pork is fork-tender, about 1 hour. Transfer pork chops to platter. Cook cabbage uncovered on high heat, stirring frequently, until liquid is almost evaporated, about 8 minutes. Sprinkle parsley over cabbage and spoon alongside pork chops.

PER SERVING (1 pork chop with ½ cup cabbage mixture): 246 Cal, 8 g Total Fat, 2 g Sat Fat, 0 g Trans Fat, 47 mg Chol, 347 mg Sod, 29 g Carb, 15 g Sugar, 3 g Fib, 17 g Prot, 74 mg Calc.

Healthy Extra   Round out this meal by serving the pork and cabbage with cooked small potatoes (one boiled 3-ounce potato per serving will increase the *PointsPlus* value by 2).

Chunky Pork & Tomato Coconut Green Curry

serves
6

1 tablespoon canola oil

4 small shallots, sliced into thin rings and separated

1 cup (⅜-inch) diced peeled eggplant

1 orange bell pepper, cut into thin strips

1 tablespoon Thai green curry paste

¾ pound boneless pork loin, trimmed and cut into ⅜-inch cubes

2 cups reduced-sodium vegetable or chicken broth

1 (14-ounce) can light (reduced-fat) coconut milk

1 tablespoon Asian fish sauce

1 cup halved cherry tomatoes

½ cup lightly packed fresh cilantro leaves

3 cups hot cooked brown jasmine rice

1 Heat oil in medium Dutch oven over medium-high heat. Add shallots and cook, stirring frequently, until softened, about 5 minutes. Add eggplant and cook, stirring frequently, until lightly browned, about 3 minutes.

2 Reduce heat to medium. Add bell pepper and curry paste to pot; cook, stirring constantly, until fragrant, about 2 minutes. Add pork, broth, coconut milk, and fish sauce. Increase heat to medium-high and bring to boil.

3 Reduce heat and simmer until pork is fork-tender, about 30 minutes. Remove pot from heat; stir in tomatoes and cilantro. Serve over rice.

PER SERVING (1 cup curry and ½ cup rice): 284 Cal, 11 g Total Fat, 1 g Sat Fat, 0 g Trans Fat, 33 mg Chol, 389 mg Sod, 34 g Carb, 3 g Sugar, 3 g Fib, 15 g Prot, 41 mg Calc.

FYI The curry pastes of Southeast Asia are named by their colors, which range from red to green to orange-yellow. Thai green curry paste is made from a combination of various chiles, lemongrass, coriander root, garlic, shrimp paste, kaffir lime, and salt. It is hotter than the more commonly used red curry paste.

Pot-Roasted Lamb with Tomatoes & Garlic

1 (2¼-pound) boneless leg of lamb, trimmed

1 teaspoon salt

¼ + ⅛ teaspoon black pepper

3 red onions, thinly sliced

1 head garlic, cloves separated and peeled

3 red bell peppers, cut into thin strips

¼ cup dry red wine

3 tablespoons water

1 (14½-ounce) can diced tomatoes

1 teaspoon fresh thyme leaves

¼ cup chopped fresh flat-leaf parsley

1   Form lamb into neat shape and tie at 1-inch intervals with kitchen string. Sprinkle with ½ teaspoon of salt and ¼ teaspoon of black pepper. Spray medium Dutch oven with nonstick spray and set over medium heat. Add lamb and brown on all sides, about 10 minutes; transfer to plate.

2   Add onions and garlic to Dutch oven and cook, stirring, until onions are golden brown, about 8 minutes. Add bell peppers and cook, stirring, until beginning to soften, about 3 minutes. Stir in wine, water, tomatoes, thyme, and remaining ½ teaspoon salt and ⅛ teaspoon black pepper; bring to simmer over medium-high heat. Return lamb along with any accumulated juices to Dutch oven; reduce heat and simmer, covered, turning occasionally, until lamb is fork-tender, about 2 hours.

3   Transfer lamb to cutting board and keep warm. Bring liquid to boil over high heat; boil, stirring frequently, until liquid is almost evaporated, about 12 minutes. Stir in parsley. Cut off and discard string from lamb. Cut lamb into 10 slices. Serve with vegetables.

PER SERVING (1 slice lamb and ⅓ cup vegetables): 264 Cal, 11 g Total Fat, 5 g Sat Fat, 0 g Trans Fat, 107 mg Chol, 409 mg Sod, 9 g Carb, 4 g Sugar, 2 g Fib, 30 g Prot, 40 mg Calc.

FYI   Your butcher can easily tie the lamb to save you time in the kitchen.

Moroccan Lamb Stew with Prunes & Cinnamon

serves
4

2 tablespoons all-purpose flour

½ teaspoon salt

¼ teaspoon black pepper

1 pound boneless lamb shoulder, trimmed and cut into 1-inch chunks

1 tablespoon olive oil

1 cup reduced-sodium vegetable or chicken broth

1 red onion, thinly sliced

1 (3-inch) cinnamon stick

1 garlic clove, minced

¾ teaspoon cumin seeds

1 (14½-ounce) can diced tomatoes

½ cup pitted prunes, chopped

3 tablespoons chopped fresh mint

2 cups hot cooked whole wheat couscous

1 Mix together flour, ¼ teaspoon of salt, and ⅛ teaspoon of pepper on sheet of wax paper; sprinkle all over lamb. Heat oil in medium Dutch oven over medium heat. Add lamb, in batches, and cook until browned on all sides, about 5 minutes per batch; transfer to plate.

2 Stir broth and onion into Dutch oven and bring to boil. Cook, stirring constantly and scraping up browned bits from bottom of pan, until onion is softened, about 5 minutes. Stir in cinnamon stick, garlic, and cumin; cook, stirring constantly, until fragrant, about 30 seconds.

3 Stir lamb, tomatoes, prunes, and remaining ¼ teaspoon salt and ⅛ teaspoon pepper into pot. Simmer, covered, stirring occasionally, until lamb is fork-tender, about 45 minutes. Stir in mint; remove and discard cinnamon stick. Serve over couscous.

PER SERVING (1 cup stew and ½ cup couscous): 367 Cal, 12 g Total Fat, 3 g Sat Fat, 68 g Trans Fat, 68 mg Chol, 607 mg Sod, 40 g Carb, 11 g Sugar, 5 g Fib, 25 g Prot, 61 mg Calc.

FYI Another easy way to coat the lamb with the seasoned flour is to put the lamb into a large zip-close plastic bag and add the seasoned flour. Seal the bag and shake it vigorously until the lamb is evenly coated.

Chicken in White Wine

Chicken in White Wine

serves
6

3 slices turkey bacon, chopped

1 (3½-pound) chicken, cut into 8 pieces and skinned

1 onion, chopped

2 celery stalks, sliced

1 head garlic, cloves peeled

1 tablespoon tomato paste

½ pound cremini mushrooms, sliced

1 cup frozen small onions

1 (14½-ounce) can reduced-sodium chicken broth

½ cup dry white wine or dry vermouth

⅓ pound small red potatoes, scrubbed and quartered

4 carrots, cut into 2-inch lengths

2 tablespoons all-purpose flour

2 tablespoons water

2 tablespoons chopped fresh parsley

1   Heat nonstick Dutch oven over medium-high heat. Add bacon and cook, stirring, until crisp, about 5 minutes; transfer to paper towels to drain.

2   Add chicken to Dutch oven, in two batches, and cook until lightly browned on all sides, about 5 minutes per batch. Transfer chicken to plate as it is browned.

3   Reduce heat to medium. Add chopped onion, celery, and garlic to Dutch oven; cook, stirring, until vegetables are lightly browned, about 8 minutes. Stir in tomato paste until smooth. Add mushrooms and frozen onions; cook, stirring, 1 minute. Add broth, wine, potatoes, and carrots; bring to boil, scraping up browned bits from bottom of pot.

4   Return chicken and bacon to Dutch oven. Reduce heat and simmer, covered, until vegetables are tender and juices run clear when chicken thigh is pierced with a fork, about 25 minutes.

5   Meanwhile, whisk together flour and water in small bowl until smooth. Stir in about ¼ cup of hot stew liquid until blended. Add liquid to pot and cook, stirring occasionally, until liquid bubbles and thickens, about 3 minutes. Serve sprinkled with parsley.

PER SERVING (⅙ of chicken and about 1½ cups vegetables with sauce): 295 Cal, 7 g Total Fat, 2 g Sat Fat, 0 g Trans Fat, 96 mg Chol, 360 mg Sod, 22 g Carb, 7 g Sugar, 4 g Fib, 33 g Prot, 76 mg Calc.

FYI   Originally this classic chicken and red wine stew was prepared with a rooster. Slow cooking it in red wine ensured the very flavorful meat would become meltingly tender. Nowadays, chicken stands in for the rooster in this ever-popular recipe.

Provençal Chicken & Mussel Pot

serves
4

PER SERVING

3 teaspoons olive oil

1 pound skinless boneless chicken breasts, cut into 1-inch chunks

2 carrots, coarsely chopped

1 onion, chopped

1 small fennel bulb, cut into ½-inch pieces

2 garlic cloves, minced

¼ teaspoon salt

¼ teaspoon black pepper

¾ pound small Yukon Gold potatoes, scrubbed and quartered

1 large tomato, diced

2 cups reduced-sodium chicken broth

½ cup dry vermouth or dry white wine

2 teaspoons herbes de Provence

24 mussels, scrubbed and debearded

1 Heat 2 teaspoons of oil in medium Dutch oven over medium-high heat. Add chicken, in two batches, and cook until browned on all sides, about 4 minutes per batch; transfer to plate.

2 Add remaining 1 teaspoon oil to Dutch oven and reduce heat to medium. Add carrots, onion, fennel, garlic, salt, and pepper; cook, stirring, until carrots and fennel are crisp-tender, about 8 minutes. Add potatoes, tomato, broth, vermouth, and herbes de Provence; bring to boil. Reduce heat and simmer, covered, until potatoes are almost tender, about 10 minutes.

3 Return chicken to Dutch oven along with mussels; cook, covered, until mussels open and chicken is cooked through, about 5 minutes longer. Discard any mussels that do not open.

PER SERVING (about 2 cups): 396 Cal, 9 g Total Fat, 2 g Sat Fat, 0 g Trans Fat, 90 mg Chol, 572 mg Sod, 33 g Carb, 6 g Sugar, 6 g Fib, 40 g Prot, 108 mg Calc.

FYI Herbes de Provence is a mix of dried herbs that are commonly found in the southern region of Provence in France. This herb blend, often packed in small brown crocks, usually contains basil, lavender, rosemary, sage, savory, fennel, and thyme. It is very flavorful, so a little bit goes a long way.

Provençal Chicken & Mussel Pot

Chicken with Shiitake Mushrooms & Thyme

serves 4

2 tablespoons all-purpose flour

½ teaspoon salt

¼ + ⅛ teaspoon black pepper

4 (½-pound) bone-in chicken breasts, skinned

1 tablespoon olive oil

2 red onions, thinly sliced

1 large garlic clove, minced

½ pound shiitake mushrooms, stemmed and caps thinly sliced

1 cup reduced-sodium chicken broth

½ cup dry red wine

½ teaspoon dried thyme

2 tablespoons chopped fresh flat-leaf parsley

2 cups hot cooked yolk-free whole wheat noodles

1 Mix together flour, ¼ teaspoon of salt, and ¼ teaspoon of pepper on sheet of wax paper; sprinkle all over chicken.

2 Heat oil in medium Dutch oven over medium heat. Add chicken and cook, turning frequently, until golden brown, about 10 minutes; transfer to plate. Add onions and cook, stirring, until softened, about 5 minutes. Add garlic and cook, stirring frequently, until fragrant, about 30 seconds. Add mushrooms and cook, stirring frequently, until softened, about 8 minutes.

3 Stir broth, wine, thyme, and remaining ¼ teaspoon salt and ⅛ teaspoon pepper into Dutch oven; nestle chicken in mushroom mixture. Bring just to boil over medium-high heat. Reduce heat and simmer, covered, turning chicken every 15 minutes, until cooked through, about 45 minutes. With slotted spoon, transfer chicken to platter. Bring vegetable mixture to boil over medium-high heat and boil, stirring frequently, until liquid is almost evaporated, about 10 minutes; stir in parsley. Spoon vegetables over chicken and serve with noodles.

PER SERVING (1 chicken breast, ½ cup vegetables, and ½ cup noodles): 384 Cal, 9 g Total Fat, 2 g Sat Fat, 0 g Trans Fat, 102 mg Chol, 410 mg Sod, 29 g Carb, 5 g Sugar, 4 g Fib, 43 g Prot, 50 mg Calc.

Chicken-Tomatillo Chili with Cilantro & Sour Cream

serves
4

1 tablespoon canola oil

4 (½-pound) bone-in chicken breasts, skinned

1 large sweet onion, quartered and thinly sliced

1 garlic clove, minced

1 teaspoon ground cumin

¼ teaspoon salt

⅛ teaspoon cayenne

½ cup reduced-sodium chicken broth

1 cup fat-free tomatillo salsa

½ cup lightly packed fresh cilantro leaves

2 tablespoons fat-free sour cream

1 Heat oil in medium Dutch oven over medium heat. Add chicken and cook, turning frequently, until golden brown, about 10 minutes; transfer to plate. Add onion and cook, stirring frequently, until lightly browned, about 8 minutes. Stir in garlic, cumin, salt, and cayenne; cook, stirring constantly, until fragrant, about 30 seconds.

2 Add broth to Dutch oven. Cook, stirring constantly, scraping browned bits from bottom of pot, about 3 minutes; stir in salsa. Nestle chicken in onion mixture. Increase heat to medium-high and bring to boil. Reduce heat and simmer, covered, stirring occasionally, until chicken is cooked through, about 25 minutes.

3 Transfer chicken to work surface. When cool enough to handle, shred chicken with two forks; discard bones. Stir chicken, cilantro, and sour cream into chili mixture.

PER SERVING (1 cup): 281 Cal, 9 g Total Fat, 2 g Sat Fat, 0 g Trans Fat, 104 mg Chol, 472 mg Sod, 9 g Carb, 4 g Sugar, 1 g Fib, 38 g Prot, 43 mg Calc.

FYI Sweet onions, such as Vidalia, Walla Walla, Maui, and Texas Sweets, are varieties of onion that are mild in flavor due to their low sulfur and high water content.

Spiced Chicken with Spinach-Almond Couscous

serves
6

PER SERVING

3 teaspoons olive oil

1 pound skinless boneless chicken thighs, trimmed and cut into 1-inch chunks

1 onion, chopped

1 red bell pepper, chopped

1 garlic clove, chopped

2 teaspoons ground cumin

1 teaspoon ground cinnamon

¼ teaspoon red pepper flakes

1 cup reduced-sodium vegetable broth

1 cup orange juice

1 (6-ounce) bag baby spinach

¾ cup golden raisins

¾ teaspoon salt

1 cup spinach couscous

3 tablespoons sliced almonds, preferably toasted

1   Heat 1½ teaspoons of oil in medium Dutch oven over medium-high heat. Add chicken and cook, turning, until browned, about 6 minutes; transfer to plate.

2   Reduce heat to medium. Add remaining 1½ teaspoons oil to Dutch oven. Add onion, bell pepper, and garlic; cook stirring, until onion is softened, about 5 minutes. Add cumin, cinnamon, and pepper flakes; cook, stirring constantly, until fragrant, about 30 seconds.

3   Add broth, orange juice, spinach, raisins, and salt to Dutch oven; bring to boil. Return chicken to pot and bring to simmer. Remove Dutch oven from heat and stir in couscous. Cover and let stand until liquid is absorbed and couscous is tender, about 5 minutes. Fluff couscous mixture with fork. Serve sprinkled with almonds.

PER SERVING (about 1 cup couscous mixture and ½ tablespoon almonds): 370 Cal, 10 g Total Fat, 2 g Sat Fat, 0 g Trans Fat, 50 mg Chol, 416 mg Sod, 50 g Carb, 17 g Sugar, 6 g Fib, 20 g Prot, 77 mg Calc.

FYI   There are several varieties of couscous available in most supermarkets, including semolina, whole wheat, tomato, and spinach. Any variety will work well in this recipe.

Chicken & Dumplings

PER SERVING

serves
8

1⅓ cups + 3 tablespoons all-purpose flour

¾ teaspoon salt

¼ teaspoon black pepper

8 (5-ounce) skinless chicken thighs, trimmed

1 tablespoon canola oil

1 large red onion, thinly sliced

3 cups reduced-sodium chicken broth

4 carrots, cut on diagonal into thin slices

3 celery stalks with leaves, cut on diagonal into thin slices

4 tablespoons chopped fresh flat-leaf parsley

2 teaspoons baking powder

¾ cup + 1 tablespoon low-fat (1%) milk

1 Mix together 3 tablespoons of flour, ½ teaspoon of salt, and the pepper on sheet of wax paper; sprinkle all over chicken.

2 Heat oil in medium Dutch oven over medium-high heat. Cook chicken, in batches, until lightly browned, about 4 minutes per batch; transfer to plate. Reduce heat to medium. Add onion and cook, stirring, until softened, about 5 minutes.

3 Add broth, carrots, and celery to Dutch oven. Bring to boil, stirring constantly and scraping up browned bits from bottom of pot. Return chicken to pot; return to boil. Reduce heat and simmer, partially covered, until chicken is cooked through and vegetables are softened, about 30 minutes. Stir in 2 tablespoons of parsley.

4 Meanwhile, to make dumplings, whisk together remaining 1⅓ cups flour, the baking powder, and remaining ¼ teaspoon salt in medium bowl. With fork, stir in milk and remaining 2 tablespoons parsley just until blended.

5 With large spoon, drop 8 equal spoonfuls of dumpling batter on top of chicken mixture. Simmer, covered, until toothpick inserted into dumpling comes out clean, about 5 minutes.

PER SERVING (1 chicken thigh with scant ⅔ cup stew mixture and 1 dumpling): 300 Cal, 11 g Total Fat, 3 g Sat Fat, 0 g Trans Fat, 72 mg Chol, 495 mg Sod, 25 g Carb, 3 g Sugar, 2 g Fib, 24 g Prot, 70 mg Calc.

Healthy Extra   Start your meal with a salad of crisp greens and tomatoes dressed with red wine vinegar and a pinch of salt.

Easy & Delicious Chicken Mole

Easy & Delicious Chicken Mole

serves
8

PER SERVING

⅓ cup Brazil nuts

1 garlic clove, coarsely chopped

1 (14½-ounce) can diced tomatoes with green chiles

1 small red onion, coarsely chopped

2 teaspoons chili powder

1 teaspoon ground coriander

½ teaspoon salt

⅛ teaspoon black pepper

8 (5-ounce) skinless chicken thighs, trimmed

¼ cup reduced-sodium chicken broth or water

1 ounce semisweet chocolate, finely chopped

½ cup lightly packed fresh cilantro leaves

1   Combine nuts and garlic in food processor and process until nuts are finely ground. Add tomatoes, onion, chili powder, coriander, salt, and pepper; pulse until smooth.

2   Spray medium Dutch oven with nonstick spray and set over medium heat. Add chicken and cook, turning frequently, until golden brown, about 10 minutes; transfer to plate. Add tomato mixture and broth; cook, stirring, 5 minutes. Add chocolate and cook, stirring frequently, until melted, about 4 minutes.

3   Return chicken to pot. Simmer, covered, stirring occasionally, until chicken is cooked through, about 30 minutes. Spoon mole sauce evenly onto 8 plates, top with chicken, and sprinkle with cilantro.

PER SERVING (1 chicken thigh and generous ¼ cup sauce): 230 Cal, 13 g Total Fat, 4 g Sat Fat, 0 g Trans Fat, 72 mg Chol, 245 mg Sod, 7 g Carb, 4 g Sugar, 1 g Fib, 21 g Prot, 32 mg Calc.

Healthy Extra   Enjoy this mole with warm whole wheat tortillas and shredded lettuce. One medium whole wheat tortilla per serving will increase the *PointsPlus* value by 2).

Rabbit in Sour Cream Sauce with Cherry Tomatoes & Noodles

serves
4

PER SERVING

5 cups water

2 cups dry white wine

3 celery stalks, thinly sliced

2 carrots, halved lengthwise
and thinly sliced crosswise

1 onion, quartered

8 sprigs + 3 tablespoons chopped
fresh flat-leaf parsley

½ teaspoon salt

¼ teaspoon black pepper

2 (1½-pound) whole skinless
ready-to-cook fresh or thawed
frozen rabbits

2 cups cooked yolk-free whole
wheat noodles

1 cup halved cherry tomatoes

⅓ cup reduced-fat sour cream

2 teaspoons Dijon mustard

1   Combine water, wine, celery, carrots, onion, parsley sprigs, salt, and pepper in medium Dutch oven. Add rabbits and bring to boil. Reduce heat and simmer, covered, turning rabbits occasionally, until cooked through, about 45 minutes; transfer to platter and let cool.

2   Meanwhile, bring cooking liquid to boil over high heat; boil 20 minutes. Pour cooking liquid and vegetables through fine sieve set over large glass measure or bowl; discard solids. Return liquid to Dutch oven. Return to boil and boil until reduced to 1 cup, about 10 minutes.

3   Meanwhile, with your fingers, shred rabbit and discard bones.

4   Add rabbit and noodles to Dutch oven and cook over medium heat, stirring frequently, until heated through, about 2 minutes. Add tomatoes, chopped parsley, sour cream, and mustard; cook, stirring frequently, until heated through, about 2 minutes longer.

PER SERVING (generous 1 cup): 461 Cal, 13 g Total Fat, 5 g Sat Fat, 0 g Trans Fat, 110 mg Chol, 513 mg Sod, 23 g Carb, 7 g Sugar, 4 g Fib, 38 g Prot, 94 mg Calc.

Healthy Extra   Serve with a side of any favorite dark green vegetable, including green beans, broccoli, Swiss chard, or spinach.

Rabbit in Sour Cream Sauce with
Cherry Tomatoes & Noodles

Posole with Cheddar, Scallions & Cilantro

serves 6

PER SERVING

1¼ pounds skinless boneless chicken thighs, trimmed and cut into 1½-inch chunks

½ teaspoon black pepper

2 teaspoons olive oil

1 onion, chopped

2 garlic cloves, minced

2 (15-ounce) cans hominy, drained

1 (14½-ounce) can diced tomatoes

1½ cups reduced-sodium chicken broth

1 (8-ounce) can tomato sauce

2 teaspoons smoked paprika

1½ teaspoons dried oregano

6 tablespoons shredded fat-free Cheddar cheese

6 scallions, chopped

⅓ cup chopped fresh cilantro

1   Sprinkle chicken with pepper. Heat 1 teaspoon of oil in medium nonstick Dutch oven over medium-high heat. Add chicken, in batches, and cook, turning, until browned, about 6 minutes per batch; transfer to plate.

2   Reduce heat to medium. Add remaining 1 teaspoon oil to Dutch oven. Add onion and garlic; cook, stirring, until onion is golden, about 8 minutes.

3   Return chicken to Dutch oven along with hominy, tomatoes, broth, tomato sauce, paprika, and oregano; bring to boil. Reduce heat and simmer, covered, until flavors are blended and stew is slightly thickened, about 1 hour.

4   Divide posole evenly among 6 bowls; sprinkle each serving with 1 tablespoon Cheddar and one-sixth of scallions and cilantro.

PER SERVING (1⅓ cups stew and 1 tablespoon cheese): 315 Cal, 10 g Total Fat, 3 g Sat Fat, 0 g Trans Fat, 63 mg Chol, 780 mg Sod, 31 g Carb, 8 g Sugar, 6 g Fib, 24 g Prot, 128 mg Calc.

FYI   Hominy is dried white or yellow corn kernels with the germ and hull removed. This is accomplished either mechanically or by soaking the corn in slaked lime or lye. When hominy is ground, it is called hominy grits or grits. It is usually cooked in milk or water and served in a porridge-like form as a side dish for breakfast.

Mixed Seafood Stew with Fennel & Orange

serves
4

1 tablespoon olive oil

2 small red onions, thinly sliced

1 garlic clove, thinly sliced

1 small fennel bulb, cut into ¼-inch dice

1 small yellow bell pepper, cut into thin strips

1 (3-inch) strip orange zest, removed with vegetable peeler

1 (14½-ounce) can petite diced tomatoes

1 cup dry white wine or dry vermouth

½ teaspoon salt

⅛ teaspoon black pepper

½ pound tilapia fillets, cut into 1-inch pieces

½ pound peeled and deveined medium shrimp

4 tablespoons chopped fresh flat-leaf parsley

1 Heat oil in medium Dutch oven over medium-high heat. Add onions and cook, stirring frequently, until softened, about 5 minutes. Add garlic and cook, stirring constantly, until fragrant, about 30 seconds. Add fennel, bell pepper, and orange zest; cook, stirring frequently, until fennel begins to soften, about 3 minutes.

2 Stir tomatoes, wine, salt, and black pepper into Dutch oven and bring to boil. Reduce heat and simmer, covered, 5 minutes. Add tilapia, shrimp, and 2 tablespoons of parsley. Reduce heat and simmer, covered, until fish and shrimp are just opaque in center, about 5 minutes. Remove and discard orange zest. Stir in remaining 2 tablespoons parsley.

PER SERVING (1¼ cups): 247 Cal, 5 g Total Fat, 1 g Sat Fat, 0 g Trans Fat, 112 mg Chol, 681 mg Sod, 17 g Carb, 6 g Sugar, 4 g Fib, 23 g Prot, 87 mg Calc.

Healthy Extra Add red or Yukon Gold potatoes, cut into small dice, to the stew along with the fennel in step 1 (four 3-ounce potatoes will increase the per-serving *PointsPlus* value by *2*).

Saigon-Style Scallops

Saigon-Style Scallops

serves
4

PER SERVING

1 tablespoon canola oil

1 shallot, minced

1 tablespoon minced peeled fresh ginger

2 garlic cloves, minced

2 tablespoons packed brown sugar, preferably dark

1 tablespoon Asian fish sauce

2 teaspoons granulated sugar

¼ teaspoon red pepper flakes

3 tablespoons water

1 pound sea scallops

3 scallions, thinly sliced

6 cups lightly packed mixed baby salad greens or herb salad mix

1   Heat oil in medium Dutch oven over medium-high heat. Add shallot, ginger, and garlic; cook, stirring constantly, until fragrant, about 1 minute. Add brown sugar, fish sauce, granulated sugar, and pepper flakes; simmer 1 minute.

2   Continue to cook until mixture begins to thicken; stir in water and cook, stirring frequently, until sauce is thickened, about 2 minutes. Add scallops and cook, stirring frequently, until just opaque in center, about 3 minutes. With slotted spoon, transfer scallops to medium bowl.

3   Add scallions to sauce and bring to boil. Boil until slightly thickened, about 3 minutes; pour over scallops. Divide salad greens evenly among 4 plates; top evenly with scallops and sauce.

PER SERVING (scant ½ cup scallops with sauce and 1½ cups greens): 191 Cal, 4 g Total Fat, 0 g Sat Fat, 0 g Trans Fat, 37 mg Chol, 567 mg Sod, 18 g Carb, 11 g Sugar, 2 g Fib, 21 g Prot, 49 mg Calc.

FYI   There are two kinds of sea scallops: wet and dry. Wet scallops are treated with a preservative that causes the scallops to absorb water, which is released when the scallops are cooked, leaving the scallops unpleasantly dry. Dry scallops are not treated and remain tender and juicy. It is easy to tell the difference: wet scallops look wet and slippery, while dry scallops look dry and are cream colored.

Shrimp Étouffée

4 PointsPlus value PER SERVING   serves **4**

1 tablespoon canola oil

3 tablespoons all-purpose flour

4 celery stalks with leaves, finely chopped

1 large red bell pepper, finely chopped

1 onion, finely chopped

2 garlic cloves, minced

½ cup water

1 pound peeled and deveined medium shrimp

3 scallions, thinly sliced

¼ cup chopped fresh flat-leaf parsley

1 teaspoon lemon juice

¼ teaspoon salt

⅛ teaspoon cayenne

1 Heat oil in medium Dutch oven over low heat. Gradually add flour and cook, whisking constantly, until light golden brown, about 15 minutes. Increase heat to medium. Add celery, bell pepper, onion, and garlic; cook, stirring frequently, until vegetables are softened, about 15 minutes (mixture may stick to bottom of pot).

2 Add water to Dutch oven and cook, scraping up browned bits from bottom of pot, about 3 minutes. Stir in remaining ingredients. Simmer, stirring constantly, until shrimp are just opaque in center, about 5 minutes.

PER SERVING (1 cup): 177 Cal, 5 g Total Fat, 1 g Sat Fat, 0 g Trans Fat, 168 mg Chol, 404 mg Sod, 14 g Carb, 5 g Sugar, 3 g Fib, 20 g Prot, 85 mg Calc.

FYI The word *étouffée* comes from the French word *étouffer*, which means "to smother." This popular spicy Cajun dish consists of a rich stew of seafood—often crayfish—and vegetables that is smothered in sauce and served over rice. The basis of this dish's deep flavor comes from the browned flour and fat mixture, known as a roux.

Two-Bean Vegetarian Chili

8 PointsPlus value PER SERVING   serves **6**

1 large onion, chopped

1 red bell pepper, diced

1 jalapeño pepper, seeded and minced

3 garlic cloves, chopped

1 (28-ounce) can no-salt-added diced tomatoes

1 (15½-ounce) can cannellini (white kidney) beans, rinsed and drained

1 (15½-ounce) can pinto beans, rinsed and drained

1 (10-ounce) package frozen corn kernels, thawed

2 tablespoons chili powder

1 tablespoon unsweetened cocoa

1 teaspoon dried oregano

¼ teaspoon black pepper

3 cups hot cooked pearl barley

1 Spray medium Dutch oven with nonstick spray and set over medium heat. Add onion, bell pepper, jalapeño, and garlic; cook, stirring, until softened, about 5 minutes.

2 Add all remaining ingredients except barley to Dutch oven; bring to boil. Reduce heat and simmer, stirring occasionally, until chili is slightly thickened, about 15 minutes. Serve over barley.

PER SERVING (1 cup chili and ½ cup barley): 342 Cal, 2 g Total Fat, 0 g Sat Fat, 0 g Trans Fat, 0 mg Chol, 457 mg Sod, 68 g Carb, 8 g Sugar, 13 g Fib, 13 g Prot, 107 mg Calc.

Healthy Extra Serve this satisfying chili accompanied by small bowls of chopped fresh cilantro, chopped scallions, and fat-free sour cream (¼ cup fat-free sour cream per serving will increase the *PointsPlus* value by 1).

Mixed Mushroom–Tempeh Chili

9 PointsPlus® value
PER SERVING

serves
6

1 (3.5-ounce) package dried porcini mushrooms

1 cup boiling water

1 tablespoon olive oil

1 large onion, chopped

1 red bell pepper, diced

2 garlic cloves, minced

3 tablespoons chili powder

2 teaspoons ground cumin

1 pound mixed mushrooms, sliced (remove stems if using shiitakes)

1 (8-ounce) package tempeh, crumbled

1 (14-ounce) can diced fire-roasted tomatoes

2 cups reduced-sodium vegetable broth

1 (15½-ounce) can black beans, rinsed and drained

6 tablespoons shredded reduced-fat Cheddar cheese

⅓ cup chopped red onion

1 Combine dried mushrooms and water in small bowl. Let stand until mushrooms are softened, about 10 minutes. Transfer mushrooms and liquid to sieve set over medium bowl. Reserve 1 cup of liquid. Rinse mushrooms to remove any grit; chop mushrooms.

2 Heat oil in medium Dutch oven over medium heat. Add chopped onion, bell pepper, and garlic; cook, stirring, until softened, about 5 minutes. Stir in chili powder and cumin; cook, stirring, until fragrant, about 30 seconds. Add fresh mushrooms and cook, stirring, until mushrooms release their liquid and it is evaporated, about 8 minutes.

3 Add tempeh, tomatoes, broth, rehydrated mushrooms, and reserved mushroom liquid to Dutch oven; bring to boil. Reduce heat and simmer, covered, until flavors are blended and mixture is slightly thickened, about 45 minutes. Add beans and cook until heated through, about 3 minutes longer. Divide chili evenly among 6 bowls. Serve sprinkled with Cheddar and red onion.

PER SERVING (1¼ cups chili and 1 tablespoon cheese): 358 Cal, 9 g Total Fat, 1 g Sat Fat, 0 g Trans Fat, 1 mg Chol, 536 mg Sod, 48 g Carb, 15 g Sugar, 13 g Fib, 23 g Prot, 204 mg Calc.

Vegetable & Chickpea Couscous

Vegetable & Chickpea Couscous

PER SERVING

serves
4

3 teaspoons olive oil

1 large zucchini, halved lengthwise
and cut into ½-inch slices

3 scallions, sliced

1 cup frozen peas, thawed

1¼ cups water

2 tablespoons lemon juice

1 teaspoon ground cumin

½ teaspoon curry powder

½ teaspoon salt

¼ teaspoon black pepper

1 cup whole wheat couscous

1 (15½-ounce) can chickpeas,
rinsed and drained

3 tablespoons unsalted pistachios,
chopped

1 Heat 2 teaspoons of oil in medium Dutch oven over medium heat.
Add zucchini and cook, stirring, until softened, about 5 minutes. Stir
in scallions and peas. Transfer to medium bowl; keep warm.

2 Combine water, lemon juice, remaining 1 teaspoon oil, the cumin,
curry, salt, and pepper in Dutch oven; bring to boil. Remove pot from
heat; stir in couscous. Cover and let stand 5 minutes; fluff with fork.
Stir in chickpeas and zucchini mixture; let stand 2 minutes. Serve
sprinkled with pistachios.

PER SERVING (about 1½ cups): 307 Cal, 8 g Total Fat, 1 g Sat Fat, 0 g Trans Fat, 0 mg Chol,
579 mg Sod, 49 g Carb, 6 g Sugar, 11 g Fib, 13 g Prot, 72 mg Calc.

Healthy Extra   Add 1 large tomato, diced, to the Dutch oven along
with the chickpeas and zucchini in step 2.

IN A
ROASTING
PAN

CHAPTER 6

IN A ROASTING PAN

HEARTY MAIN DISHES—BEEF, PORK, CHICKEN & MORE

Roasting is a dry-heat cooking method where food is cooked in the oven at a moderate to moderate-high temperature. The ideal cooking vessel is a rectangular roasting pan that has 2- to 3-inch-high sides, which allows the heat to circulate easily, ensuring a crisp surface and good browning. Some pans come with straight sides, others with flared sides; both work equally well. For easy use, roasting pans have handles at both short sides, and some also come with a flat or V-shaped rack that fits inside the pan. These racks are excellent for roasting chicken, turkey, or meat, as they help food to brown—even on the bottom.

Types

Heavy stainless steel roasting pans do a great job of browning and roasting to perfection. They also maintain even heat. These pans can also be used on the stovetop for deglazing and making gravy. And they're broiler-safe.

Stainless steel roasting pans with nonstick interiors are another option. These heavy pans offer an easy-to-care-for surface. Although these pans do a good job of roasting, not as many tasty browned bits—which contribute lots of flavor to sauces and gravies—are produced.

Heavy aluminum roasting pans also do a fine job of browning poultry and meat—*and* caramelizing vegetables.

Glazed porcelain and ceramic roasting pans, sometimes called roasters, also do a good job and are favored by many French cooks. These pans are also used for casseroles and baked fruit desserts. The undersides of these pans are often left unglazed to encourage the maximum amount of heat absorption. Ceramic roasters are microwave- and stovetop-safe, while porcelain roasters are microwave-safe.

Granite Ware, also known as Agate and Enamel Ware, has been around since the 1800s and was often used by cowboys and pioneers. Although it was originally produced in several colors and patterns, the one most commonly found in homes today is black with white speckles. Granite Ware is made of enamel-coated steel and is naturally nonstick. The roasting pans are moderately priced and can be found in hardware stores, chain discount stores, and big box stores.

Sizes

It's nice to have at least two different-size roasting pans on hand: a small roasting pan about 9 x 13 inches, a medium roasting pan about 10 x 14 inches, and/or a large roasting pan at least 11 x 17 inches for roasting a turkey.

Basics for Care

To clean a **stainless steel roasting pan,** first let it cool down, then soak it for about 30 minutes in hot, soapy water to help release any stuck-on food particles. Use a nylon scrub pad and nonabrasive cleaning powder to remove any stains or food residue. Avoid using steel wool soap pads. These pans are also dishwasher safe. If the pan has a nonstick interior, clean it with a sponge or nylon scrub pad to avoid scratching the surface.

Aluminum roasting pans are easy to clean and very durable. Allow the pan to cool, then soak it in hot, soapy water for about 30 minutes. Scrub the pan clean with a nylon scrub pad or steel wool soap pad and dry it well. This roasting pan is also dishwasher safe.

Ceramic roasting pans should be seasoned before they are used the first time. Check the manufacturer's instructions. Glazed porcelain and ceramic roasting pans are easy to clean. Soak the cooled pan in hot, soapy water for about 30 minutes to help to remove any food particles that stick. The pan can then be scrubbed clean using a nylon scrub pad. Ceramic and porcelain roasting pans are dishwasher safe.

To clean a **Granite Ware roasting pan,** first soak it in hot, soapy water for about 30 minutes to dislodge any stubborn food particles. Use a nylon scrub pad to remove any remaining food. Rinse it well and dry it thoroughly to prevent rusting.

Weekend Roast Beef with Crusty Potatoes

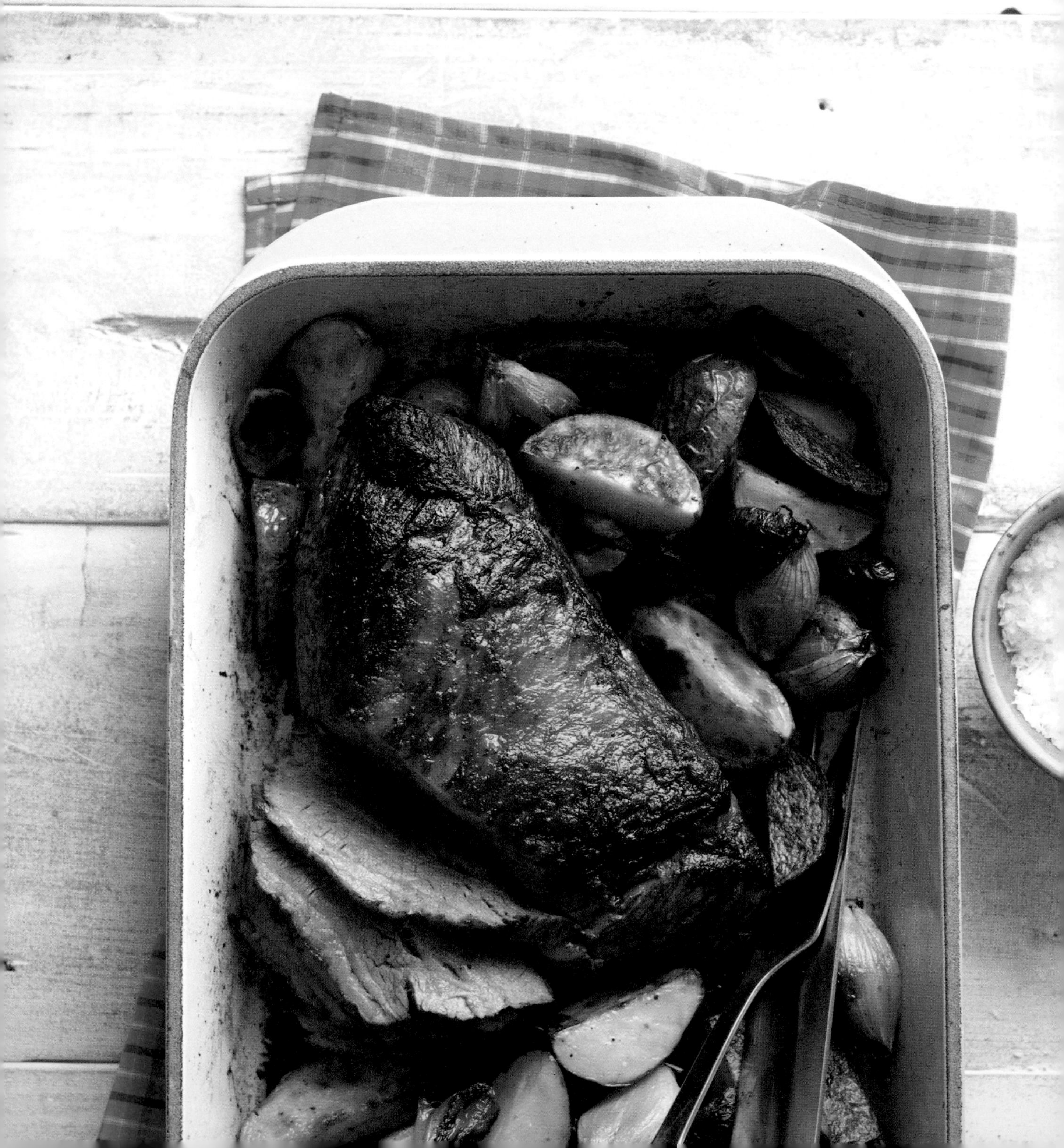

Weekend Roast Beef with Crusty Potatoes

serves
6

PER SERVING

2 teaspoons olive oil

1 teaspoon chopped
fresh rosemary

¾ teaspoon salt

1 (1½-pound) tri-tip beef roast,
trimmed

Grated zest and juice of
1 lemon

2 teaspoons Dijon mustard

2 garlic cloves, minced

1¼ pounds small yellow or white
potatoes, scrubbed and halved
or quartered

8 shallots, peeled

1 Preheat oven to 400°F.

2 Stir together 1 teaspoon of oil, the rosemary, and ¼ teaspoon of salt in cup; rub over top of beef roast. Spray heavy medium roasting pan with nonstick spray and set over medium-high heat. Add roast and cook until browned on all sides, about 8 minutes. Remove pan from heat.

3 Combine lemon zest and juice, mustard, garlic, and remaining 1 teaspoon oil and ½ teaspoon salt in one corner of large zip-close plastic bag, squeezing bag to mix well. Add potatoes and shallots; seal bag and shake until coated well. Scatter potatoes and shallots around beef. Roast until instant-read thermometer inserted into center of beef registers 145°F for medium and potatoes and shallots are tender, about 40 minutes. Transfer roast to cutting board and let stand 10 minutes.

4 Meanwhile, spread potatoes and shallots in roasting pan in even layer; return to oven and roast, turning potatoes and shallots once or twice, until potatoes begin to crisp, about 10 minutes longer. Cut roast across grain into 12 slices and serve with potatoes and shallots.

PER SERVING (2 slices beef and generous ½ cup potatoes and shallots): 240 Cal, 8 g Total Fat, 2 g Sat Fat, 0 g Trans Fat, 50 mg Chol, 379 mg Sod, 22 g Carb, 2 g Sugar, 1 g Fib, 22 g Prot, 32 mg Calc.

FYI Tri-tip roast is a cut of beef from the bottom sirloin. It's also called a triangular roast because of its shape. Not only is it very flavorful, it's also leaner and less expensive than some other cuts.

Eye-Round Roast with Red Wine–Thyme Sauce

3 PointsPlus® value
PER SERVING

serves
6

1 (1½-pound) eye-round roast, trimmed

¾ teaspoon salt

½ teaspoon black pepper

½ cup dry red wine

¼ cup reduced-sodium beef broth

2 teaspoons all-purpose flour

1 teaspoon chopped fresh thyme

1   Preheat oven to 400°F.

2   Sprinkle roast with ½ teaspoon of salt and the pepper. Spray small heavy roasting pan with nonstick spray and set over medium-high heat. Add roast and cook until browned on all sides, about 8 minutes.

3   Transfer roasting pan to oven. Roast until instant-read thermometer inserted into center of beef registers 145°F for medium, about 45 minutes. Transfer roast to cutting board and let stand 10 minutes.

4   Meanwhile, set roasting pan over one burner. Add remaining ¼ teaspoon salt, the wine, broth, flour, and thyme; whisk until blended. Bring to boil over medium-high heat. Reduce heat and simmer, stirring constantly, until sauce bubbles and thickens, about 3 minutes. Remove pan from heat. Cut roast across grain into 18 slices and serve with sauce.

PER SERVING (3 slices beef and 2 tablespoons sauce): 137 Cal, 3 g Fat, 1 g Sat Fat, 0 g Trans Fat, 39 mg Chol, 322 mg Sod, 1 g Carb, 0 g Sugar, 0 g Fib, 21 g Prot, 8 Calc.

FYI   When cooking with wine, choose one that you would also drink. Avoid using cooking wine, which is available in supermarkets, as it is of inferior quality and contains salt.

Beef Tenderloin with Port Wine Pan Sauce

2 teaspoons whole black peppercorns

1 teaspoon fennel seeds

¾ teaspoon salt

1 (1-pound) beef tenderloin, trimmed

2 teaspoons olive oil

1 small onion, finely chopped

2 teaspoons all-purpose flour

⅔ cup ruby port wine

½ cup reduced-sodium beef broth

1 teaspoon coarse-grained mustard

1 teaspoon unsalted butter

1 Preheat oven to 400°F.

2 Combine peppercorns, fennel seeds, and ½ teaspoon of salt in small zip-close plastic bag; press out air and seal bag. With meat mallet or bottom of small heavy saucepan, pound mixture until coarsely ground. Spread spice mixture on sheet of wax paper. Roll tenderloin in spice mixture until coated evenly, pressing it into meat so it adheres.

3 Heat oil in small heavy roasting pan over medium-high heat. Add beef and cook until browned on all sides, about 8 minutes.

4 Transfer roasting pan to oven. Roast until instant-read thermometer inserted into center of beef registers 145°F for medium, about 20 minutes. Transfer beef to cutting board and let stand 10 minutes.

5 Meanwhile, to make sauce, spray same roasting pan with nonstick spray and set over medium heat. Add onion and cook, stirring, until softened, about 5 minutes. Stir in flour and cook, stirring, about 1 minute. Whisk in port, broth, mustard, and remaining ¼ teaspoon salt; bring to boil. Cook, whisking constantly, until sauce bubbles and thickens, about 4 minutes. Remove pan from heat; swirl in butter until melted. Cut beef across grain into 12 slices and serve with sauce.

PER SERVING (3 slices beef and 2 tablespoons sauce): 277 Cal, 10 g Fat, 4 g Sat Fat, 0 g Trans Fat, 70 mg Chol, 517 mg Sod, 9 g Carb, 4g Sugar, 1 g Fib, 25 g Prot, 35 Calc.

FYI A spice grinder or mini food processor is a quick and convenient substitute for a plastic bag and mallet for grinding spices, although a coffee grinder also works well. Just be sure to wipe the inside of the grinder clean when you are finished.

Chili-Rubbed Tenderloin
with Spanish Peppers & Potatoes

serves
4

PER SERVING

1 teaspoon chili powder

¾ teaspoon salt

½ teaspoon dried oregano

1 (1-pound) beef tenderloin, trimmed

2 teaspoons olive oil

1 pound small yellow potatoes, scrubbed and halved

2 red or green bell peppers, cut into strips

1 tablespoon sherry vinegar

1 teaspoon smoked paprika

1 Preheat oven to 425°F.

2 Mix together chili powder, ¼ teaspoon of salt, and oregano on sheet of wax paper. Rub all over tenderloin.

3 Heat oil in heavy medium roasting pan over medium-high heat. Add beef and cook until browned on all sides, about 8 minutes; transfer to plate.

4 Combine potatoes, bell peppers, vinegar, paprika, and remaining ½ teaspoon salt in large bowl. Spray potato mixture with nonstick spray, tossing as you spray to coat evenly. Spread vegetables in same roasting pan in even layer.

5 Transfer roasting pan to oven. Roast, stirring once or twice, until vegetables are partially cooked, about 20 minutes. Push vegetables to sides of pan; place beef in center of pan. Roast until instant-read thermometer inserted into center of beef registers 145°F for medium and vegetables are cooked through, about 20 minutes. Transfer beef to cutting board and let stand 10 minutes. Cut beef across grain into 12 slices and serve with vegetables.

PER SERVING (3 slices beef and ½ cup vegetables): 268 Cal, 9 g Fat, 3 g Sat Fat, 0 g Trans Fat, 67 mg Chol, 500 mg Sod, 19 g Carb, 1g Sugar, 2 g Fib, 27 g Prot, 32 Calc.

Healthy Extra Start your meal off with a refreshing sliced tomato, cucumber, and red onion salad dressed with lemon juice and a bit of salt and pepper. Serve the tenderloin with steamed kale.

**Chili-Rubbed Tenderloin
with Spanish Peppers & Potatoes**

Porcini-Crusted Beef with Lemony Potatoes

8 PointsPlus value

PER SERVING

serves **4**

½ ounce dried porcini mushrooms, broken into pieces

1 tablespoon all-purpose flour

¼ cup fat-free egg substitute

1 (1-pound) beef tenderloin, trimmed

1 teaspoon salt

½ teaspoon black pepper

1 tablespoon olive oil

1 pound small Yukon Gold potatoes, scrubbed and halved

1 tablespoon chopped fresh rosemary

Grated zest of 1 lemon

1   Preheat oven to 400°F.

2   Grind mushrooms to a powder in spice grinder or mini food processor. Spread mushroom powder and flour on separate sheets of wax paper. Pour egg substitute into pie plate.

3   Sprinkle tenderloin with ½ teaspoon of salt and ¼ teaspoon of pepper. Roll beef in flour until coated evenly. Roll beef in egg substitute until coated evenly, allowing excess to drip off. Roll beef in mushroom powder until coated completely.

4   Heat oil in heavy medium roasting pan over medium-high heat. Add beef and cook until browned on all sides, about 8 minutes. Transfer to plate. Remove pan from heat. Spread potatoes in roasting pan in even layer; sprinkle with rosemary and remaining ½ teaspoon salt and ¼ teaspoon pepper. Lightly spray potatoes with nonstick spray.

5   Transfer roasting pan to oven. Roast until potatoes are partially cooked, about 20 minutes. Push potatoes to sides of pan; place beef roast in center of pan. Roast until instant-read thermometer inserted into center of beef registers 145°F for medium and potatoes are cooked through, about 20 minutes longer. Transfer beef to cutting board and let stand 10 minutes. Cut beef across grain into 12 slices. Sprinkle lemon zest over potatoes and serve with beef.

PER SERVING (3 slices beef and ¼ of potatoes): 325 Cal, 11 g Total Fat, 3 g Sat Fat, 0 g Trans Fat, 67 mg Chol, 668 mg Sod, 24 g Carb, 0 g Sugar, 2 g Fib, 30 g Prot, 32 mg Calc.

FYI   Dried sliced porcini mushrooms can be found in specialty food stores. Their rich, earthy flavor makes a little bit go a long way. After they are hydrated in water, the mushrooms can be chopped and added to tomato sauce, risottos, braises, and stews. Be sure to strain the tasty mushroom liquid through a paper towel–lined sieve to remove any grit.

Garlic-Studded Pork Roast with Quick Mustard Sauce

serves
6

PER SERVING

1 (1½-pound) boneless center-cut pork loin, trimmed

2 garlic cloves, thinly sliced

¾ teaspoon salt

½ teaspoon black pepper

1 teaspoon canola oil

1 onion, chopped

2 tablespoons dry vermouth

2 teaspoons all-purpose flour

½ cup reduced-sodium chicken broth

1½ teaspoons coarse-grained Dijon mustard

1 teaspoon chopped fresh parsley

1 Preheat oven to 400°F. Spray small heavy roasting pan with nonstick spray.

2 With small sharp knife, make ¾-inch-deep slits all over pork; push 1 slice of garlic into each slit. Sprinkle pork with ½ teaspoon of salt and the pepper. Place pork in roasting pan. Roast until instant-read thermometer inserted in center of pork registers 145°F for medium, about 1 hour. Transfer pork to cutting board and let stand 10 minutes

3 Meanwhile, to make sauce, pour off and discard fat from roasting pan. Heat oil in roasting pan over medium heat. Add onion and cook, stirring, until softened, about 5 minutes. Add vermouth and bring to boil. Cook, stirring occasionally, until vermouth is evaporated, about 2 minutes. Stir in flour and cook, stirring, until bubbly, about 1 minute. Whisk in broth, mustard, parsley, and remaining ¼ teaspoon salt; bring to boil. Cook, whisking constantly, until sauce bubbles and thickens, about 2 minutes.

4 Cut pork across grain into 12 slices. Serve with sauce.

PER SERVING (2 slices pork and 2 tablespoons sauce): 171 Cal, 7 g Total Fat, 2 g Sat Fat, 0 g Trans Fat, 66 mg Chol, 413 mg Sod, 3 g Carb, 2 g Sugar, 1 g Fib, 22 g Prot, 30 mg Calc.

Healthy Extra Serve the pork with mashed butternut squash mixed with a bit of ground cinnamon and nutmeg.

Roast Pork with Onion-Gingersnap Gravy

serves
6

2½ teaspoons chopped
fresh thyme

1 teaspoon olive oil

1 garlic clove, minced

½ teaspoon salt

1 (1½-pound) boneless center-cut
pork loin, trimmed

1 large onion, cut into
½-inch wedges

½ cup orange juice

1 teaspoon packed brown sugar

1 cup reduced-sodium
chicken broth

4 reduced-fat gingersnap cookies,
crushed

1 tablespoon minced peeled
fresh ginger

1 teaspoon lemon juice

1 teaspoon unsalted butter

1   Preheat oven to 400°F. Spray small heavy roasting pan with nonstick spray.

2   Stir together 2 teaspoons of thyme, the oil, garlic, and ¼ teaspoon of salt in cup; rub all over pork. Place pork in prepared pan; scatter onion around pork. Pour orange juice over onion and sprinkle with brown sugar.

3   Roast until instant-read thermometer inserted into center of pork registers 145°F for medium, about 45 minutes. Transfer pork to cutting board and let stand 10 minutes.

4   Meanwhile, to make gravy, place roasting pan with onion mixture over one burner over medium-high heat. Add broth, gingersnaps, ginger, lemon juice, and remaining ¼ teaspoon salt; bring to boil. Cook, stirring occasionally, until sauce begins to thicken, about 3 minutes. Remove pan from heat; swirl in butter, remaining ½ teaspoon thyme, and any accumulated meat juices until butter is melted. Cut pork across grain into 12 slices and serve with gravy.

PER SERVING (2 slices pork and scant ¼ cup gravy): 201 Cal, 8 g Total Fat, 2 g Sat Fat, 0 g Trans Fat, 68 mg Chol, 363 mg Sod, 9 g Carb, 3 g Sugar, 1 g Fib, 22 g Prot, 36 mg Calc.

Healthy Extra   Accompany the pork and gravy with steamed red or green Swiss chard. Or buy a bunch of rainbow Swiss chard—a tender variety with multicolored stalks of yellow, white, orange, pink, and red.

Tuscan Pork with Cremini Mushrooms & Rosemary

PER SERVING

1 pound cremini mushrooms, halved

1 cup small cherry tomatoes

2 garlic cloves, minced

1 tablespoon balsamic vinegar

2 teaspoons olive oil

¾ teaspoon salt

1 tablespoon chopped
fresh rosemary

Grated zest of 1 lemon

1 (1½-pound) boneless center-cut
pork loin, trimmed

1   Preheat oven to 400°F. Spray heavy medium roasting pan with nonstick spray.

2   Toss together mushrooms, tomatoes, half of garlic, the vinegar, 1 teaspoon of oil, and ½ teaspoon of salt in prepared pan until mixed well. Push vegetables to sides of pan.

3   Stir together rosemary, lemon zest, and remaining garlic, 1 teaspoon oil, and ¼ teaspoon salt in cup; rub all over pork. Place pork in center of roasting pan.

4   Roast until instant-read thermometer inserted into center of pork registers 145°F for medium and vegetables are tender, about 45 minutes. Transfer pork to cutting board and let stand 10 minutes. Cut pork across grain into 12 slices and serve with vegetables.

PER SERVING (2 slices pork and ½ cup vegetables): 187 Cal, 8 g Total Fat, 2 g Sat Fat, 0 g Trans Fat, 66 mg Chol, 342 mg Sod, 5 g Carb, 2 g Sugar, 1 g Fib, 23 g Prot, 41 mg Calc.

FYI   If you want the pork roast to have a very neat shape, ask your butcher to tie it in 1-inch intervals. Be sure to remove the strings before carving the roast.

Chinese Roast Pork & Green Beans

4 PointsPlus© value

PER SERVING

serves **4**

2 tablespoons minced peeled fresh ginger

1 tablespoon reduced-sodium soy sauce

1 tablespoon dry sherry

1 tablespoon hoisin sauce

1 teaspoon chili-garlic sauce

1 teaspoon Asian (dark) sesame oil

1 (1-pound) pork tenderloin, trimmed

¾ pound green beans, trimmed

6 scallions, cut crosswise in half

1   Preheat oven to 425°F. Spray large heavy roasting pan with nonstick spray.

2   Whisk together ginger, soy sauce, sherry, hoisin sauce, chili-garlic sauce, and oil in small bowl until mixed well. Brush half of ginger mixture all over pork. Toss together beans, scallions, and remaining ginger mixture in large bowl.

3   Place pork to one side of prepared pan. Place beans on other side of pan. Roast until instant-read thermometer inserted into center of pork registers 145°F for medium and beans are very tender, about 25 minutes. Transfer pork to cutting board and let stand 10 minutes. Cut pork across grain into 12 slices and serve with beans.

PER SERVING (3 slices pork and ½ cup beans): 184 Cal, 5 g Total Fat, 1 g Sat Fat, 0 g Trans Fat, 62 mg Chol, 329 mg Sod, 11 g Carb, 3 g Sugar, 4 g Fib, 25 g Prot, 55 mg Calc.

Healthy Extra   Combine 1 small diced papaya, 1 diced tomato, and 2 tablespoons chopped fresh basil with a sprinkling of fat-free vinaigrette to round out this meal.

Chinese Roast Pork
& Green Beans

Pork Tenderloin with Thyme-Scented Root Vegetables

1 (1-pound) pork tenderloin, trimmed

¾ teaspoon salt

¼ teaspoon black pepper

4 teaspoons olive oil

4 carrots, thinly sliced

4 celery stalks, thinly sliced

3 parsnips, thinly sliced

2 large garlic cloves, halved

2 tablespoons chopped fresh thyme

¾ cup reduced-sodium chicken broth

1   Preheat oven to 425°F.

2   Sprinkle pork with ½ teaspoon of salt and ⅛ teaspoon of pepper. Fold narrow end of tenderloin under.

3   Heat oil in heavy medium roasting pan over medium-high heat. Add pork and cook until browned on all sides, about 8 minutes. Scatter carrots, celery, parsnips, and garlic around pork; sprinkle with thyme and remaining ¼ teaspoon salt and ⅛ teaspoon pepper. Pour broth over vegetables.

4   Roast, stirring vegetables once or twice, until instant-read thermometer inserted into center of pork registers 145°F for medium and vegetables are tender, about 25 minutes. Transfer pork to cutting board and let stand 5 minutes. Cut pork into ½-inch slices. Serve with vegetables.

PER SERVING (about 3 slices pork and 1 cup vegetables): 286 Cal, 8 g Total Fat, 2 g Sat Fat, 0 g Trans Fat, 62 mg Chol, 700 mg Sod, 29 g Carb, 10 g Sugar, 7 g Fib, 25 g Prot, 102 mg Calc.

Leg of Lamb with Eggplant, Zucchini & Tomato

1 (3½-pound) bone-in leg of lamb, preferably sirloin half, trimmed

1¼ teaspoons salt

½ teaspoon black pepper

1 small eggplant (about ¾ pound), unpeeled, quartered lengthwise and cut into ½-inch slices

2 pounds small red potatoes, scrubbed and halved

4 zucchini, cut into ¾-inch slices

2 large tomatoes, cut into ¾-inch wedges

6 garlic cloves, peeled and halved

2 cups reduced-sodium vegetable broth

1 teaspoon dried oregano

1   Preheat oven to 375°F.

2   Sprinkle lamb with ¾ teaspoon of salt and ¼ teaspoon of pepper. Place lamb in center of large roasting pan.

3   Put eggplant, potatoes, zucchini, tomatoes, and garlic in separate piles around lamb. Pour broth over vegetables; sprinkle with oregano and remaining ½ teaspoon salt and ¼ teaspoon pepper.

4   Roast, basting lamb and vegetables occasionally with pan liquid, until instant-read thermometer inserted into thickest part of lamb (not touching bone) registers 145°F for medium and vegetables are tender, about 45 minutes. Slice lamb and serve with vegetables and pan juices.

PER SERVING (about 3 slices lamb and ⅛ of vegetables): 385 Cal, 11 g Total Fat, 4 g Sat Fat, 0 g Trans Fat, 127 mg Chol, 579 mg Sod, 27 g Carb, 6 g Sugar, 5 g Fib, 45 g Prot, 60 mg Calc.

Mustard & Thyme–Rubbed Lamb Roast with Flageolets

9 PointsPlus value
PER SERVING

serves **8**

8 tablespoons dry white wine

3 tablespoons Dijon mustard

5 garlic cloves, minced

1 tablespoon chopped fresh thyme or rosemary

Grated zest of 1 lemon

1 (2½-pound) boneless leg of lamb, butterflied and trimmed

½ teaspoon black pepper

1 onion, finely chopped

1 cup cherry tomatoes, halved

2 (14½-ounce) cans flageolets or navy beans, rinsed and drained

½ cup reduced-sodium chicken broth

¼ cup coarsely chopped fresh flat-leaf parsley

1   Combine 2 tablespoons of wine, the mustard, half of garlic, the thyme, and lemon zest in corner of large zip-close plastic bag; squeeze ingredients until mixed well. Add lamb; squeeze out air and seal bag. Turn to coat lamb. Refrigerate, turning bag occasionally, at least 4 hours or up to overnight.

2   Preheat oven to 400°F. Place rack in medium roasting pan and spray with nonstick spray.

3   Remove lamb from marinade; discard marinade. Roll lamb up, jelly-roll style and tie with kitchen string at 1-inch intervals; sprinkle with pepper. Place lamb on prepared rack. Roast until instant-read thermometer inserted into center of lamb registers 145°F for medium, about 45 minutes. Transfer lamb to cutting board; loosely cover with sheet of foil.

4   Skim off any fat from pan juices and discard. Place roasting pan over one or two burners over medium-high heat. Add onion, tomatoes, and remaining garlic; cook, stirring often, until onion is golden brown, about 10 minutes. Add remaining 6 tablespoons wine and cook, scraping up browned bits from bottom of pan until wine is evaporated, about 8 minutes. Add flageolets and broth; bring to boil. Reduce heat and simmer until broth is reduced by half, about 5 minutes.

5   Cut off strings from lamb and cut lamb into 32 slices. Sprinkle beans with parsley and serve with lamb.

PER SERVING (4 slices lamb and about ½ cup bean mixture): 378 Cal, 12 g Total Fat, 5 g Sat Fat, 0 g Trans Fat, 112 mg Chol, 723 mg Sod, 26 g Carb, 2 g Sugar, 6 g Fib, 38 g Prot, 90 mg Calc.

FYI   Flageolets are small pale French kidney beans. They are sold dried or canned in specialty food stores and in some supermarkets. Flageolets are best when cooked very simply, which shows off their delicate flavor. Flageolets are often paired with lamb.

Provençal Lamb with
Tomatoes, Onions, & Olives

Provençal Lamb with Tomatoes, Onions & Olives

PER SERVING

serves
10

1 garlic clove, minced + 2 garlic cloves, halved

2 teaspoons minced peeled fresh ginger

2 teaspoons olive oil

¾ teaspoon salt

½ teaspoon ground cumin

¼ teaspoon red pepper flakes

1 (2½-pound) boneless leg of lamb, trimmed, rolled, and tied

6 plum tomatoes, cut into 1-inch chunks

2 onions, each cut into ½-inch wedges

1 lemon, quartered

16 pitted Kalamata olives

¾ cup dry white wine

4 cups hot cooked whole wheat couscous

1 Preheat oven to 400°F. Spray large roasting pan with nonstick spray.

2 Stir together minced garlic, ginger, 1 teaspoon of oil, ½ teaspoon of salt, the cumin, and pepper flakes in cup; rub all over lamb. Place lamb in prepared pan. Scatter tomatoes, onions, lemon, olives, and garlic halves around lamb; drizzle vegetables with remaining 1 teaspoon oil and sprinkle with remaining ¼ teaspoon salt. Pour wine into pan.

3 Roast until instant-read thermometer inserted into center of lamb registers 145°F for medium and vegetables are tender, about 1 hour. Transfer lamb to cutting board and let stand 10 minutes.

4 Meanwhile, skim off and discard any fat from pan juices. Cut lamb into 20 slices. Spoon vegetables into serving bowl; add pan juices and squeeze lemon wedges over. Toss until mixed well. Serve with lamb and couscous.

PER SERVING (2 slices lamb, about ⅓ cup vegetables with pan juices, and generous ⅓ cup couscous): 298 Cal, 12 g Total Fat, 4 g Sat Fat, 0 g Trans Fat, 90 mg Chol, 348 mg Sod, 18 g Carb, 3 g Sugar, 3 g Fib, 26 g Prot, 40 mg Calc.

Healthy Extra   Serve with a bowl of microwave-cooked or steamed whole green beans sprinkled with chopped fresh parsley and grated lemon zest.

Garlic Roast Chicken with Crisp Potatoes & Mushrooms

serves
6

PER SERVING

1½ pounds small Yukon Gold potatoes, scrubbed

2 cups cremini mushrooms

3 small onions, each cut into 6 wedges

6 large garlic cloves, minced

1 tablespoon olive oil

1 teaspoon dried thyme or rosemary

1 teaspoon salt

½ teaspoon black pepper

1 tablespoon poultry seasoning

2 teaspoons paprika

1 (3½-pound) chicken, without giblets

1 cup cherry tomatoes

1   Preheat oven to 425°F. Spray large roasting pan with nonstick spray.

2   Toss together potatoes, mushrooms, onions, half of garlic, the oil, thyme, ½ teaspoon of salt, and ¼ teaspoon of pepper in prepared pan. Push vegetables to sides of pan.

3   Stir together remaining garlic, the poultry seasoning, paprika, and remaining ½ teaspoon salt and ¼ teaspoon pepper in cup; add enough water to make a paste.

4   Rinse chicken inside and out under cold running water. Pat dry with paper towels. Rub garlic paste all over chicken. Tuck wings under and tie legs together with kitchen string. Place chicken, breast side up, in center of pan.

5   Roast, stirring vegetables occasionally, 35 minutes. Scatter tomatoes over vegetables. Roast until instant-read thermometer inserted into thigh (not touching bone) registers 165°F and vegetables are tender, about 20 minutes longer.

6   Transfer chicken to cutting board and let stand 10 minutes. Carve chicken and serve with vegetables. Remove chicken skin before eating.

PER SERVING (⅙ of chicken and vegetables): 304 Cal, 7 g Total Fat, 1 g Sat Fat, 0 g Trans Fat, 89 mg Chol, 498 mg Sod, 29 g Carb, 3 g Sugar, 4 g Fib, 32 g Prot, 60 mg Calc.

FYI   You can use other mushrooms in this dish, including oyster, chanterelle, shiitake (be sure to remove the stems), and white. A mix of mushrooms also works well.

Lemon Chicken with Pan Sauce-Tossed Watercress

serves
6

PER SERVING

1 (3½-pound) chicken, without giblets

¾ teaspoon salt

½ teaspoon black pepper

1 lemon, quartered

6 garlic cloves, peeled

½ cup reduced-sodium chicken broth

2 teaspoons olive oil

1 teaspoon chopped fresh tarragon

1 bunch watercress, trimmed

1   Preheat oven to 400°F. Spray small roasting pan with nonstick spray.

2   Rinse chicken inside and out under cold running water; pat dry with paper towels. Tuck wings under and tie legs together with kitchen string. Place chicken, breast side up, in prepared pan. Sprinkle with ½ teaspoon of salt and ¼ teaspoon of pepper. Scatter lemon quarters and garlic around chicken. Add broth to pan.

3   Roast until instant-read thermometer inserted into thigh (not touching bone) registers 165°F, about 1 hour. Transfer chicken to cutting board and let stand 10 minutes.

4   To make sauce, let lemon and garlic cool slightly. Transfer garlic to blender or mini food processor. Squeeze juice from lemon quarters over garlic. Skim off and discard any fat from pan juices. Add pan juices, oil, tarragon, and remaining ¼ teaspoon salt and ¼ teaspoon pepper to blender; pulse until smooth. Put watercress in serving bowl. Add half of sauce and toss until coated well.

5   Carve chicken. Serve with watercress and remaining sauce. Remove chicken skin before eating.

PER SERVING (⅙ of chicken, 1 cup watercress, and 2 tablespoons sauce): 180 Cal, 6 g Total Fat, 1 g Sat Fat, 0 g Trans Fat, 89 mg Chol, 451 mg Sod, 4 g Carb, 0 g Sugar, 1 g Fib, 29 g Prot, 80 mg Calc.

Healthy Extra   Baked tomato halves make a tasty and colorful addition to the roasted chicken and watercress. Sprinkle the cut sides of 3 halved large tomatoes with a pinch of salt, pepper, and dried oregano. Bake in a foil-lined shallow baking dish alongside the chicken until tender, about 25 minutes.

Roast Chicken with Rustic Bread Stuffing

serves
6

PER SERVING

1 tablespoon olive oil

2 onions, chopped

4 celery stalks, sliced

½ pound shiitake mushrooms, stemmed and sliced

3 cups no-salt-added chicken broth

4 slices whole wheat bread, crusts removed and cut into ¾-inch pieces

1 teaspoon poultry seasoning

1 teaspoon salt

½ teaspoon black pepper

1 (3½-pound) chicken, without giblets

1 tablespoon lemon juice

1 tablespoon all-purpose flour

1   Preheat oven to 375°F.

2   To make stuffing, heat oil in heavy medium roasting pan over medium heat. Add onions, celery, mushrooms, and ½ cup of broth; cook, stirring, until vegetables are softened and liquid is evaporated, about 8 minutes. Transfer to large bowl. Add bread, poultry seasoning, ¼ teaspoon of salt, and ⅛ teaspoon of pepper to vegetables, tossing to combine. Drizzle 1 cup of broth over bread, tossing mixture as you go. If bread is still dry, drizzle with a little water.

3   Lightly spoon some of stuffing into body cavity of chicken. Spoon remaining stuffing into small baking dish. Tuck wings under chicken and tie legs together with kitchen string. Sprinkle chicken with ½ teaspoon of salt and ¼ teaspoon of pepper. Wipe roasting pan clean and lightly spray with nonstick spray.

4   Place chicken, breast side up, in prepared pan. Roast until instant-read thermometer inserted into thickest part of thigh (not touching bone) registers 165°F, about 1 hour 10 minutes. Place baking dish with stuffing in oven after chicken has roasted about 50 minutes; bake until heated through and crusty, about 30 minutes. Transfer chicken to cutting board and let stand 10 minutes.

5   Meanwhile, to make gravy, pour pan juices into 2-cup glass measure; skim off and discard any fat from pan juices. Add enough broth to pan juices to equal 1½ cups. Pour into roasting pan. Whisk in lemon juice, flour, and remaining ¼ teaspoon salt and ⅛ teaspoon pepper until smooth. Set pan over one or two burners over medium-high heat; cook, whisking constantly, until mixture comes to boil. Reduce heat and simmer, whisking constantly, until gravy is slightly thickened, about 2 minutes.

6   Transfer stuffing to serving dish. Carve chicken and serve with gravy. Remove chicken skin before eating.

PER SERVING (⅙ of chicken, ⅔ cup stuffing, and ¼ cup sauce): 288 Cal, 8 g Total Fat, 2 g Sat Fat, 0 g Trans Fat, 105 mg Chol, 697 mg Sod, 20 g Carb, 6 g Sugar, 4 g Fib, 34 g Prot, 67 mg Calc.

FYI   Line the baking dish for the stuffing with foil to cut down on the cleanup.

**Roast Chicken with Rustic
Bread Stuffing**

Crispy Chicken Breasts with Tomatillo-Lime Sauce

serves
6

PER SERVING

6 tomatillos, husked, rinsed, and halved

1 onion, sliced

1 jalapeño pepper, halved and seeded

2 garlic cloves, halved

2 teaspoons olive oil

1 teaspoon salt

1 tablespoon chili powder

Grated zest of 1 lime

3 (¾-pound) bone-in chicken breasts

2 tablespoons chopped fresh cilantro

Juice of 1 lime

1 Preheat oven to 400°F. Spray large shallow roasting pan with nonstick spray.

2 Toss together tomatillos, onion, jalapeño, garlic, oil, and ¼ teaspoon of salt in medium bowl. Spread out along one side of prepared pan.

3 Stir together chili powder, lime zest, and ½ teaspoon of salt on sheet of wax paper. With your fingers, loosen skin on breasts. Rub spice mixture on meat under skin. Press skin back in place. Arrange chicken, skin side up, alongside tomatillo mixture. Roast until instant-read thermometer inserted into breasts (not touching bone) registers 165°F and vegetables are softened, about 35 minutes.

4 To make sauce, transfer tomatillo mixture to food processor. Add cilantro, lime juice, and remaining ¼ teaspoon salt; pulse until smooth. Cut each chicken breast crosswise in half. Serve with sauce. Remove chicken skin before eating.

PER SERVING (1 piece chicken and 2½ tablespoons sauce): 189 Cal, 5 g Total Fat, 1 g Sat Fat, 0 g Trans Fat, 76 mg Chol, 372 mg Sod, 6 g Carb, 3 g Sugar, 2 g Fib, 29 g Prot, 32 mg Calc.

FYI The tomatillo sauce makes a tasty salsa for cut-up vegetables so consider cooking up a double batch. Stored in an airtight container, the sauce can be refrigerated for up to 4 days. For the best flavor, let it come to room temperature before serving.

Shawarma-Spiced Chicken & Green Beans

serves
4

PER SERVING

1 tablespoon grated peeled fresh ginger

1 teaspoon ground cinnamon

¾ teaspoon salt

½ teaspoon ground allspice

½ teaspoon ground coriander

½ teaspoon ground cumin

¼ teaspoon cayenne

1 pound green beans, trimmed

2 teaspoons olive oil

2 (¾-pound) bone-in chicken breasts, skinned and cut crosswise in half

1 Preheat oven to 400°F. Spray large shallow roasting pan with nonstick spray.

2 Stir together ginger, cinnamon, salt, allspice, coriander, cumin, and cayenne in cup.

3 Toss together beans, 1 teaspoon of oil, and half of spice mixture in prepared pan. Push beans to one side of pan.

4 Add remaining 1 teaspoon oil to remaining spice mixture, mixing until it forms a paste. Rub all over chicken. Arrange chicken, meaty side up, alongside beans in pan. Roast, turning green beans occasionally, until instant-read thermometer inserted into thickest part of breasts (not touching bone) registers 165°F and beans are tender, about 35 minutes.

PER SERVING (1 piece chicken and ½ cup green beans): 209 Cal, 6 g Total Fat, 1 g Sat Fat, 0 g Trans Fat, 76 mg Chol, 510 mg Sod, 9 g Carb, 2 g Sugar, 4 g Fib, 30 g Prot, 66 mg Calc.

Healthy Extra   Toss together 2 cups thinly sliced cucumber, 1 thinly sliced red onion, and 2 tablespoons chopped fresh mint with ¼ cup plain fat-free Greek yogurt for a cool accompaniment to this mildly spicy dish.

Indian-Spiced Chicken with
Apple & Onion

Indian-Spiced Chicken with Apple & Onion

serves
4

PER SERVING

½ teaspoon mustard seeds

½ teaspoon cumin seeds

⅛ teaspoon whole black peppercorns

2 garlic cloves, minced

1 tablespoon minced peeled fresh ginger

2 teaspoons olive oil

½ teaspoon salt

4 (7-ounce) bone-in chicken breasts

2 Granny Smith apples, unpeeled, cored, and cut into ¾-inch wedges

1 small sweet onion, thinly sliced

1   Preheat oven to 400°F. Spray large roasting pan with nonstick spray.

2   Combine mustard seeds, cumin seeds, and peppercorns in large zip-close plastic bag; press out air and seal bag. With meat mallet or bottom of small heavy saucepan, finely crush spice mixture. Add garlic, ginger, oil, and salt to crushed spices; seal bag and shake to mix well.

3   With your fingers, loosen skin on chicken breasts; rub 1 tablespoon of spice mixture on meat under skin. Press skin back in place. Place chicken, skin side up, in prepared pan.

4   Add apples and onion to remaining spice mixture; seal bag and shake to coat evenly. Scatter around chicken. Roast, stirring apple mixture once, until instant-read thermometer inserted in thickest part of breasts (not touching bone) registers 165°F and apples are tender, about 30 minutes. Remove chicken skin before eating.

PER SERVING (1 chicken breast and ⅔ cup apple mixture): 254 Cal, 7 g Total Fat, 1 g Sat Fat, 0 g Trans Fat, 89 mg Chol, 371 mg Sod, 15 g Carb, 10 g Sugar, 3 g Fib, 33 g Prot, 33 mg Calc.

Healthy Extra   Serve a bowl of brown rice alongside the chicken (⅔ cup cooked brown rice per serving will increase the *PointsPlus* value by 3).

Lemon-Oregano Drumsticks with Artichokes & Potatoes

serves
6

PER SERVING

½ cup lemon juice (about 3 lemons)

1 tablespoon + 2 teaspoons olive oil

3 garlic cloves, minced

2 teaspoons dried oregano

1 teaspoon salt

½ teaspoon black pepper

Pinch cayenne

6 (5-ounce) chicken drumsticks, skinned

1½ pounds baking potatoes, scrubbed and cut lengthwise into 1-inch wedges

1 (10-ounce) package frozen artichoke hearts, thawed and patted dry

6 large shallots, sliced

18 pitted Kalamata olives

1   Preheat oven to 425°F. Spray large shallow roasting pan with nonstick spray.

2   Whisk together lemon juice, oil, garlic, oregano, salt, pepper, and cayenne in small bowl.

3   Place drumsticks in center of prepared pan. Scatter potatoes, artichokes, shallots, and olives around chicken; drizzle with lemon juice mixture. Roast, stirring vegetables occasionally, until chicken is cooked through and vegetables are tender and lightly browned, about 50 minutes.

PER SERVING (1 drumstick and ⅙ of vegetables): 290 Cal, 10 g Total Fat, 2 g Sat Fat, 0 g Trans Fat, 61 mg Chol, 676 mg Sod, 33 g Carb, 4 g Sugar, 6 g Fib, 22 g Prot, 72 mg Calc.

FYI   Chicken drumsticks are a little tricky to skin as they can be slippery. To make it easier, grab hold of the edge of the skin with a paper towel, then pull the skin off.

Butterflied Quail with Fresh Raspberry Sauce

serves
4

PER SERVING

1¼ teaspoons hot paprika

½ teaspoon + pinch salt

8 (4½-ounce) bone-in quail, split and flattened

1 cup red wine, such as Beaujolais or Pinot Noir

3 tablespoons seedless raspberry jam

1 cup fresh raspberries

1 Preheat oven to 450°F. Spray medium roasting pan with nonstick spray.

2 Stir together 1 teaspoon of paprika and ½ teaspoon of salt on sheet of wax paper. With your fingers, loosen skin on breasts and thighs of quail; rub some of spice mixture on meat under skin. Press skin back in place; rub remaining spice mixture all over quail.

3 Place quail, skin side up, in prepared pan. Spray with nonstick spray. Roast until quail are just cooked through, about 10 minutes. Transfer to sheet of foil; keep warm.

4 To make sauce, set roasting pan over one or two burners over medium-high heat; add wine and bring to boil. Reduce heat and simmer until wine is reduced by half, about 3 minutes. Add jam and cook, stirring constantly, until sauce is smooth, about 1 minute. Add raspberries and remaining ¼ teaspoon paprika and pinch of salt; cook, stirring often, until raspberries are softened, about 2 minutes longer. Stir in any accumulated quail juices. Serve sauce with quail. Remove skin before eating.

PER SERVING (2 quail and 3 tablespoons sauce): 340 Cal, 9 g Total Fat, 3 g Sat Fat, 0 g Trans Fat, 136 mg Chol, 427 mg Sod, 9 g Carb, 4 g Sugar, 2 g Fib, 43 g Prot, 34 mg Calc.

Healthy Extra Microwave-cooked cubed pumpkin or butternut squash makes the perfect fall accompaniment for the quail and raspberry sauce. Be sure to drizzle it with some of the jewel-toned sauce.

Orange-Brined Turkey Breast with Fresh Cranberry Sauce

serves
8

PER SERVING

1½ cups orange juice

1½ cups water

2 tablespoons + ⅓ cup honey

1 tablespoon kosher salt

1 (2½-pound) frozen boneless turkey breast roast, thawed

1 small onion, chopped

2 garlic cloves, chopped

½ teaspoon black pepper

1 (12-ounce) bag fresh or thawed frozen cranberries

2 teaspoons grated orange zest

1   To make turkey brine, combine orange juice, water, 2 tablespoons of honey, and the salt in deep large bowl, stirring until salt is dissolved. Add turkey, onion, and garlic, adding water to bowl to cover turkey completely, if needed. Cover bowl and refrigerate about 8 hours.

2   Preheat oven to 350°F. Spray heavy medium roasting pan with nonstick spray.

3   Remove turkey from brine; discard brine. Pat turkey dry with paper towels; sprinkle with pepper. Set prepared roasting pan over medium-high heat. Add turkey and cook until browned on all sides, about 6 minutes.

4   Transfer roasting pan to oven. Roast until instant-read thermometer inserted into center of turkey roast registers 165°F, 1 hour to 1 hour 15 minutes. Transfer turkey to cutting board and let stand 10 minutes.

5   Meanwhile, to make sauce, put cranberries in food processor and pulse until coarsely chopped; transfer to serving bowl. Stir in remaining ⅓ cup honey and the orange zest. Cut turkey into 24 slices and serve with cranberry sauce. Remove turkey skin before eating.

PER SERVING (3 slices turkey and ¼ cup sauce): 256 Cal, 1 g Total Fat, 0 g Sat Fat, 0 g Trans Fat, 93 mg Chol, 751 mg Sod, 27 g Carb, 18 g Sugar, 2 g Fib, 34 g Prot, 29 mg Calc.

FYI   A turkey breast roast is a boneless turkey breast that has been rolled and tied into a neat shape. It comes frozen, so plan ahead and leave enough time for defrosting it in the refrigerator, which will take about 3 days. Lightly grilled treviso radicchio or Belgian endive is the perfect side dish.

Orange-Brined Turkey Breast with Fresh Cranberry Sauce

Thyme-Scented Halibut
with Roasted Mixed Mushrooms

serves
4

PER SERVING

1 pound mixed mushrooms, such as cremini, oyster, and shiitake, sliced (remove stems if using shiitakes)

3 teaspoons chopped fresh thyme

2 teaspoons olive oil

½ teaspoon salt

¼ teaspoon black pepper

4 (6-ounce) halibut fillets

1 teaspoon grated lemon zest

1 teaspoon lemon juice

1   Preheat oven to 400°F. Spray medium roasting pan with nonstick spray.

2   Toss together mushrooms, 2 teaspoons of thyme, the oil, ¼ teaspoon of salt, and ⅛ teaspoon of pepper in prepared pan; spread to form even layer. Roast 15 minutes.

3   Meanwhile, sprinkle halibut with remaining 1 teaspoon thyme, ¼ teaspoon salt, and ⅛ teaspoon pepper.

4   Remove roasting pan from oven. Arrange halibut fillets on top of mushrooms. Roast until halibut is just opaque in center, about 10 minutes. Place halibut on plates. Sprinkle lemon zest and juice over mushrooms and toss to mix well. Divide mushrooms evenly among plates.

PER SERVING (1 fish fillet and ½ cup mushrooms): 232 Cal, 6 g Total Fat, 1 g Sat Fat, 0 g Trans Fat, 52 mg Chol, 386 mg Sod, 5 g Carb, 2 g Sugar, 1 g Fib, 37 g Prot, 101 mg Calc.

Healthy Extra   Add more flavor and color by tossing 1 small thinly sliced onion and 1 diced small red bell pepper into the mushroom mixture in step 2.

Tomato & Basil–Topped Halibut with Golden Onions

 serves **4**

PER SERVING

1 pound red potatoes, scrubbed, halved, and sliced

2 onions, cut into thin wedges

5 teaspoons olive oil

1 teaspoon salt

¼ teaspoon black pepper

2 tomatoes, chopped

1 (1½-pound) halibut steak

6 fresh basil leaves, torn

2 tablespoons coarsely chopped fresh flat-leaf parsley

1   Preheat oven to 450°F. Spray large roasting pan with nonstick spray.

2   Toss together potatoes, onions, 3 teaspoons of oil, ½ teaspoon of salt, and ⅛ teaspoon of pepper in prepared pan. Spread to form even layer. Roast, stirring occasionally, until vegetables are slightly softened, about 20 minutes.

3   Meanwhile, mix together tomatoes with remaining 2 teaspoons oil, ½ teaspoon salt, and ⅛ teaspoon pepper.

4   Push potatoes and onions to one side of roasting pan. Place halibut alongside vegetables; spoon tomato mixture on top of fish. Roast until fish is just opaque in center and potatoes are tender and lightly browned, about 15 minutes. Serve sprinkled with basil and parsley.

PER SERVING (¼ of halibut and 1 cup vegetables): 323 Cal, 7 g Total Fat, 1 g Sat Fat, 0 g Trans Fat, 54 mg Chol, 687 mg Sod, 27 g Carb, 7 g Sugar, 4 g Fib, 39 g Prot, 122 mg Calc.

FYI   Other firm-fleshed fish work well in this dish, including cod, wild salmon, and mahi mahi.

Wild Salmon with Strawberry-Avocado Salsa

 serves **4**

PER SERVING

4 (¼-pound) wild salmon fillets

1 teaspoon grated lime zest

¾ teaspoon ground cumin

½ teaspoon + pinch salt

⅛ teaspoon black pepper

2 cups strawberries, hulled and diced

½ avocado, pitted, peeled, and diced

½ jalapeño pepper, seeded and minced

1 tablespoon lime juice

2 tablespoons snipped fresh chives

2 tablespoons chopped fresh cilantro

1   Preheat oven to 400°F. Spray heavy medium roasting pan with nonstick spray.

2   Sprinkle salmon with lime zest, ½ teaspoon of cumin, ½ teaspoon of salt, and the black pepper. Arrange salmon, skin side down, in prepared pan. Roast until salmon is just opaque in center, about 10 minutes.

3   Meanwhile, to make salsa, toss together strawberries, avocado, jalapeño, lime juice, chives, cilantro, and remaining ¼ teaspoon cumin and pinch of salt in serving bowl. Serve with salmon. Remove salmon skin before eating.

PER SERVING (1 salmon fillet and ½ cup salsa): 240 Cal, 11 g Total Fat, 2 g Sat Fat, 0 g Trans Fat, 72 mg Chol, 387 mg Sod, 8 g Carb, 4 g Sugar, 3 g Fib, 27 g Prot, 35 mg Calc.

FYI   Wild-caught salmon from Alaska comes from well-managed fisheries and is low in contaminants. It is a better choice than farm-raised salmon, which is associated with environmental concerns, including chemical use, parasites, and disease.

Striped Bass Fillets with Fresh Artichokes & Cherry Tomatoes

serves
4

PER SERVING

4 artichokes

3 tablespoons lemon juice

2 teaspoons olive oil

2 teaspoons chopped fresh rosemary

½ teaspoon salt

¼ teaspoon black pepper

4 (6-ounce) striped bass fillets

2 cups cherry tomatoes

1 teaspoon grated lemon zest

1   Preheat oven to 400°F. Spray large roasting pan with nonstick spray.

2   To prepare artichokes, fill large bowl with water and add 2 tablespoons of lemon juice. Working with one artichoke at a time, bend back and snap off leaves. Using teaspoon or melon baller, scrape out fuzzy choke and discard. With vegetable peeler, peel stem, then trim end. Cut artichoke hearts lengthwise into quarters. Drop in lemon water.

3   Drain artichokes and pat dry with paper towels; transfer to prepared pan. Add oil, 1 teaspoon of rosemary, ¼ teaspoon of salt, and ⅛ teaspoon of pepper; toss to coat evenly. Roast, stirring once, until artichokes are almost tender, about 30 minutes.

4   Meanwhile, sprinkle bass with remaining 1 teaspoon rosemary, ¼ teaspoon salt, and ⅛ teaspoon pepper.

5   Add tomatoes to artichokes, tossing to combine. Push vegetables to sides of pan; place fish, skin side down, in center of pan. Roast until fish is just opaque in center and tomatoes begin to burst, about 10 minutes longer. Sprinkle vegetables with lemon zest and fish with remaining 1 tablespoon lemon juice.

PER SERVING (1 fish fillet and ¾ cup vegetables): 232 Cal, 7 g Total Fat, 1 g Sat Fat, 0 g Trans Fat, 140 mg Chol, 484 mg Sod, 10 g Carb, 3 g Sugar, 4 g Fib, 34 g Prot, 37 mg Calc.

Healthy Extra   Serve the fish and vegetables with whole wheat couscous (⅔ cup cooked whole wheat couscous per serving will increase the *PointsPlus* value by 3).

Slashed Bass with Parsley-Caper Vinaigrette

PER SERVING

serves 4

1 (2-pound) whole sea bass or other white-fleshed fish, cleaned

1 small lemon, thinly sliced

1 teaspoon grated lemon zest

2 tablespoons lemon juice

1 tablespoon olive oil

½ teaspoon Dijon mustard

⅛ teaspoon black pepper

2 tablespoons chopped fresh flat-leaf parsley

1 tablespoon capers, rinsed, drained, and minced

1 small garlic clove, minced

1   Preheat oven to 400°F. Spray medium roasting pan with nonstick spray.

2   Rinse fish inside and out under cold running water; pat dry with paper towels. With sharp knife, make 3 equally spaced diagonal slashes, cutting almost to bone on each side of fish. Place fish in prepared pan. Fill cavity of fish with lemon slices. Roast just until fish is opaque in center, about 20 minutes.

3   Meanwhile, to make vinaigrette, whisk together lemon zest and juice, oil, mustard, and pepper in small bowl. Stir in parsley, capers, and garlic. Serve with fish.

PER SERVING (¼ of fish and 1 tablespoon sauce): 142 Cal, 6 g Total Fat, 1 g Sat Fat, 0 g Trans Fat, 43 mg Chol, 167 mg Sod, 4 g Carb, 0 g Sugar, 1 g Fib, 20 g Prot, 34 mg Calc.

Healthy Extra   Serve the fish with steamed broccoli or broccolini.

Moroccan Fish with Potatoes & Tomatoes

6 PointsPlus value PER SERVING · serves 4

½ teaspoon ground cumin

½ teaspoon paprika

½ teaspoon ground ginger

½ teaspoon salt

¼ teaspoon black pepper

⅛ teaspoon ground cinnamon

Pinch cayenne

1 pound small red potatoes, scrubbed and thinly sliced

2 teaspoons olive oil

2 garlic cloves, minced

4 (6-ounce) cod or other mild white-fleshed fish fillets

4 plum tomatoes, each cut into 8 wedges

1 teaspoon grated lemon zest

2 tablespoons chopped fresh flat-leaf parsley

1 Preheat oven to 400°F. Spray large roasting pan with nonstick spray.

2 Combine cumin, paprika, ginger, salt, pepper, cinnamon, and cayenne on sheet of wax paper.

3 Combine potatoes, 1¼ teaspoons of spice mixture, the oil, and garlic in large zip-close plastic bag. Seal bag and shake until potatoes are coated evenly. Transfer potato mixture to prepared pan and spread evenly. Roast, stirring once, until potatoes are almost tender, about 15 minutes.

4 Meanwhile, sprinkle fish with remaining spice mixture.

5 Add tomatoes to potatoes, stirring to combine. Push vegetables to sides of pan; arrange fish in center of pan. Sprinkle with lemon zest. Roast until fish is just opaque in center, about 10 minutes longer. Serve sprinkled with parsley.

PER SERVING (1 fish fillet and ⅔ cup vegetables): 242 Cal, 4 g Total Fat, 1 g Sat Fat, 0 g Trans Fat, 65 mg Chol, 394 mg Sod, 22 g Carb, 3 g Sugar, 3 g Fib, 30 g Prot, 44 mg Calc.

Penne with Feta, Roasted Zucchini & Fennel

8 PointsPlus value PER SERVING · serves 4

2 zucchini, halved lengthwise and cut into ½-inch slices

1 large fennel bulb, thinly sliced

1 large red onion, thinly sliced

2 teaspoons olive oil

½ teaspoon salt

¼ teaspoon black pepper

4 cups hot cooked whole wheat penne

1 teaspoon grated lemon zest

2 tablespoons lemon juice

2 tablespoons snipped fresh dill

½ cup crumbled reduced-fat feta cheese

1 Preheat oven to 400°F. Spray large shallow roasting pan with nonstick spray.

2 Combine zucchini, fennel, onion, oil, ¼ teaspoon of salt, and ⅛ teaspoon of pepper in prepared pan. Spread to form even layer. Roast, stirring occasionally, until vegetables are tender, about 35 minutes.

3 Spoon vegetables into serving bowl; add penne, lemon zest and juice, dill, and remaining ¼ teaspoon salt and ⅛ teaspoon pepper; toss until mixed well. Sprinkle with feta.

PER SERVING (1¾ cups): 306 Cal, 6 g Total Fat, 2 g Sat Fat, 0 g Trans Fat, 5 mg Chol, 573 mg Sod, 50 g Carb, 5 g Sugar, 8 g Fib, 13 g Prot, 126 mg Calc.

FYI To get 4 cups of cooked penne, you will need 8 ounces (about 2⅔ cups) dry pasta.

Warm Butternut Squash Salad with Ham & Bitter Greens

serves 4

PER SERVING

2 ounces sliced prosciutto

1 (1¾-pound) butternut squash, peeled, seeded, and cut into ¾-inch pieces

3 teaspoons olive oil

½ teaspoon salt

¼ teaspoon black pepper

1 tablespoon cider vinegar

1 tablespoon water

2 teaspoons Dijon mustard

1 teaspoon dark molasses

8 cups lightly packed torn frisée or escarole (about 1 large head)

1 Preheat oven to 400°F. Spray large shallow roasting pan with nonstick spray,

2 Arrange prosciutto in single layer in prepared pan. Roast until lightly browned, about 8 minutes. Transfer prosciutto to paper towels to drain; coarsely chop.

3 Combine squash, 1 teaspoon of oil, ¼ teaspoon of salt, and ⅛ teaspoon of pepper in large bowl; toss until mixed well. Spread squash in same pan. Roast, stirring once, until tender, about 30 minutes. Let cool slightly.

4 To make dressing, whisk together vinegar, water, mustard, molasses, and remaining 2 teaspoons oil, ¼ teaspoon salt, and ⅛ teaspoon pepper in large serving bowl. Add frisée, squash, and prosciutto; toss until mixed well.

PER SERVING (generous 2 cups): 155 Cal, 6 g Total Fat, 1 g Sat Fat, 0 g Trans Fat, 11 mg Chol, 760 mg Sod, 24 g Carb, 5 g Sugar, 8 g Fib, 7 g Prot, 130 mg Calc.

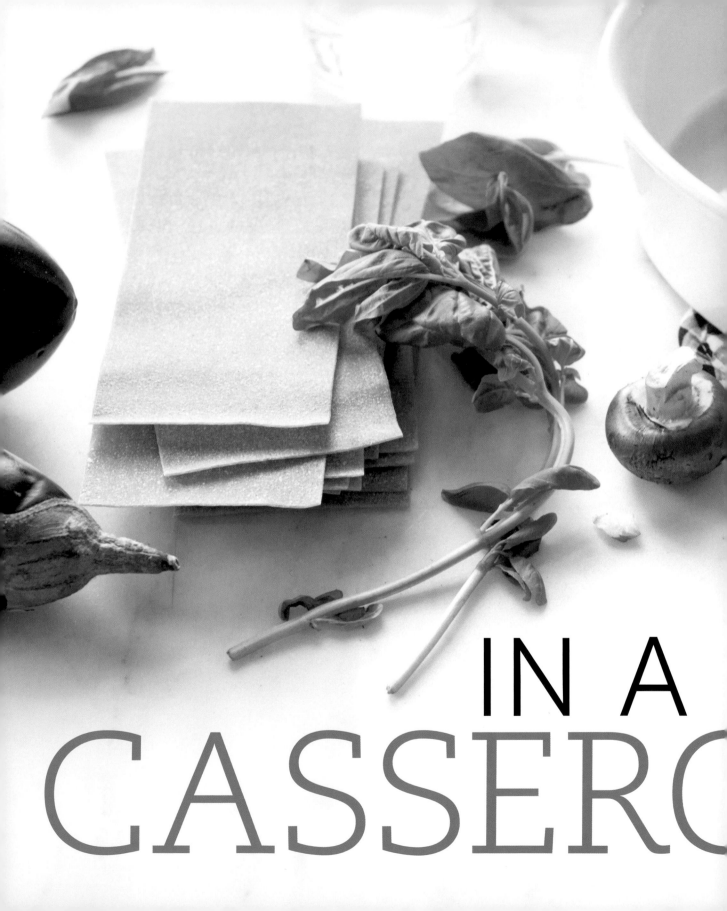

IN A
CASSERO

LE DISH

CHAPTER 7

IN A CASSEROLE DISH

COMFORT-FOOD ENTRÉES

A casserole dish is a type of bakeware that can withstand long cooking without drying out or burning the food. A typical casserole dish is round with a tight-fitting lid and two handles, which allows it to go from oven to table with ease. The term *casserole* also refers to a type of recipe.

Types

Casserole dishes can be ovenproof, flameproof, or both.

Ovenproof casseroles are usually made of glass, porcelain, or stoneware. They can be used in the oven but not on the stovetop. Some are also freezer- and microwave-safe; check with the manufacturer. A baking dish (see page 316) can usually be substituted.

Flameproof casserole dishes can be used on the stovetop over direct heat and in the oven. They are often made of cast iron, enameled cast iron, or stainless steel. When it comes to one-pot cooking, using a flameproof casserole dish is great because it saves having to use an extra pot or pan for sautéing or browning. A Dutch oven is often a good alternative (just be sure the handle or knob is ovenproof).

Sizes and Shapes

Casserole dishes are available in a range of shapes (round, square, oval, and rectangular) and sizes (from a few cups to several quarts) and come shallow or deep. Choose the shape and size that best fits what you are preparing.

Basics for Care

For easy cleaning, once a casserole dish has cooled down, soak it for about 15 minutes in hot, soapy water to help loosen any food particles that cling. If needed, use a nonabrasive cleaner or nylon scrub pad, which won't scratch its surface.

Picadillo-Style Shepherd's Pie with Chipotle Mashed Potatoes

serves
6

PER SERVING

1 pound ground lean beef (7% fat or less)

2 teaspoons canola oil

1 onion, chopped

1 small zucchini, diced

1 small yellow squash, diced

2 garlic cloves, minced

1 (14½-ounce) can diced tomatoes

2 tablespoons golden raisins, chopped

8 pimiento-stuffed green olives, chopped

1 teaspoon ground cinnamon

1 teaspoon ground cumin

1 (24-ounce) package refrigerated mashed potatoes

1 tablespoon chipotles en adobo, chopped

1   Preheat oven to 375°F.

2   Spray 2-quart flameproof casserole dish with nonstick spray and set over medium heat. Add beef, and cook, breaking it apart with spoon, until browned, about 10 minutes. Transfer to large bowl.

3   Add oil to casserole dish. Add onion, zucchini, yellow squash, and garlic; cook, stirring, until vegetables are softened, about 6 minutes. Return beef to casserole. Stir in tomatoes, raisins, olives, cinnamon, and cumin; bring to boil. Wipe bowl clean.

4   Mix together mashed potatoes and chipotles in same large bowl. Spread potato topping over beef mixture. Transfer casserole to oven and bake until potato topping is browned and filling is bubbly along edge, about 25 minutes. Let stand 5 minutes before serving.

PER SERVING (generous 1 cup): 266 Cal, 7 g Total Fat, 2 g Sat Fat, 0 g Trans Fat, 46 mg Chol, 692 mg Sod, 31 g Carb, 7 g Sugar, 4 g Fib, 19 g Prot, 86 mg Calc.

Healthy Extra   Serve this shepherd's pie with a side of steamed broccoli sprinkled with lemon juice.

Cheese, Beef & Noodle Casserole

serves
6

2 teaspoons olive oil

1 onion, chopped

2 garlic cloves, minced

¼ teaspoon red pepper flakes

¾ pound ground lean beef
(7% fat or less)

4 cups hot cooked whole
wheat penne

2 cups fat-free marinara sauce

¼ cup chopped fresh parsley

¾ cup shredded reduced-fat
Monterey Jack cheese

1 Preheat oven to 375°F.

2 Heat oil in 2-quart flameproof casserole dish over medium heat. Add onion, garlic, and pepper flakes; cook, stirring, until onion is softened, about 5 minutes. Add beef and cook, breaking it apart with spoon, until browned, about 10 minutes.

3 Stir penne, marinara sauce, ½ cup of Monterey Jack, and the parsley into beef mixture and spread evenly; sprinkle with remaining ¼ cup cheese. Transfer casserole to oven and bake until cheese is melted and filling is bubbly around edge, about 20 minutes.

PER SERVING (about 1 cup): 298 Cal, 8 g Total Fat, 3 g Sat Fat, 0 g Trans Fat, 42 mg Chol, 473 mg Sod, 35 g Carb, 2 g Sugar, 5 g Fib, 22 g Prot, 256 mg Calc.

Healthy Extra Start your meal off with a torn escarole salad dressed with lemon juice and sprinkled with thinly sliced radishes and the radish tops, chopped, if attached. The tops make a tasty addition to almost any salad.

Cheese, Beef & Noodle Casserole

Reuben Casserole

serves
4

2 teaspoons canola oil

1 onion, thinly sliced

½ (16-ounce) package sauerkraut, rinsed, drained, and squeezed dry

½ teaspoon caraway seeds

½ pound lean corned beef, cut into ¾-inch dice

1 cup refrigerated cooked diced potatoes (from 18-ounce package)

1 cup water

2 tablespoons fat-free Thousand Island dressing

½ cup shredded reduced-fat Jarlsberg cheese

1 thin slice seedless rye bread, crust removed and torn into small pieces (about ½ cup)

1 Preheat oven to 375°F.

2 Heat oil in 2-quart flameproof casserole dish over medium heat. Add onion and cook, stirring, until golden, about 8 minutes. Add sauerkraut and caraway seeds; cook, stirring occasionally, until liquid is evaporated and sauerkraut is lightly browned, about 8 minutes.

3 Stir corned beef, potatoes, and water into sauerkraut mixture and bring to boil. Drizzle dressing over and sprinkle with Jarlsberg.

4 Pulse bread in food processor until coarse crumbs form. Sprinkle over cheese and lightly spray with nonstick spray. Transfer casserole to oven and bake until cheese is melted and crumbs are browned, about 20 minutes.

PER SERVING (about 1 cup): 199 Cal, 6 g Total Fat, 2 g Sat Fat, 0 g Trans Fat, 37 mg Chol, 935 mg Sod, 19 g Carb, 4 g Sugar, 4 g Fib, 16 g Prot, 155 mg Calc.

FYI Be sure to use packaged—not canned—sauerkraut. Packaged sauerkraut is also called fresh sauerkraut and is much milder than canned.

Lamb, Eggplant & Orzo Casserole

serves
4

1 (1-pound) eggplant, unpeeled and cut into 1-inch cubes

½ cup water

2 teaspoons olive oil

2 shallots, thinly sliced

2 garlic cloves, minced

¾ pound ground lean lamb

2 cups chunky marinara sauce

1 cup hot cooked whole wheat orzo

¼ cup chopped fresh mint

2 tablespoons plain fat-free Greek yogurt

Grated zest of 1 lemon

¼ cup crumbled fat-free feta cheese

1 Preheat oven to 375°F.

2 Combine eggplant and water in 1½-quart microwavable dish. Cover bowl with plastic wrap; poke a few holes in wrap. Microwave on High until eggplant is tender, about 6 minutes; drain.

3 Meanwhile, heat oil in 2-quart flameproof casserole dish over medium heat. Add shallots and garlic; cook, stirring, until softened, about 4 minutes. Add lamb and cook, breaking it apart with spoon, until browned, about 8 minutes. Add marinara sauce and bring to boil. Reduce heat and simmer, covered, until flavors are blended and mixture begins to thicken, about 8 minutes longer.

4 Remove casserole dish from heat. Stir in eggplant, orzo, mint, yogurt, and lemon zest; sprinkle with feta. Transfer casserole to oven and bake until filling is bubbly and cheese is softened, about 15 minutes.

PER SERVING (1 cup): 302 Cal, 12 g Total Fat, 3 g Sat Fat, 0 g Trans Fat, 49 mg Chol, 911 mg Sod, 29 g Carb, 10 g Sugar, 7 g Fib, 23 g Prot, 109 mg Calc.

Healthy Extra   Start your meal off with a Greek-inspired salad of thickly sliced unpeeled cucumber, thick wedges of ripe tomato, and thinly sliced red onion dressed with lemon juice and sprinkled with feta cheese (1 ounce of fat-free feta cheese per serving will increase the *PointsPlus* value by 1).

Chicken & Tomatillo Enchilada Casserole

 serves 6

PER SERVING

2½ pounds tomatillos, husked, rinsed, and chopped

1 cup chopped scallions (about 4 scallions)

½ cup chopped fresh cilantro

1 or 2 jalapeño peppers, seeded and minced

2 large garlic cloves, minced

¾ teaspoon salt

¼ teaspoon black pepper

12 (6-inch) corn tortillas

2½ cups shredded cooked skinless chicken breast

12 tablespoons shredded reduced-fat Mexican cheese blend

12 tablespoons fat-free sour cream

1 Preheat oven to 350°F. Spray 9 x 13-inch baking dish with nonstick spray.

2 Puree half of tomatillos in food processor. Stir together chopped tomatillos, pureed tomatillos, scallions, cilantro, jalapeño, garlic, salt, and black pepper in large shallow bowl.

3 Dip both sides of 1 tortilla in tomatillo mixture. Place tortilla on sheet of foil on work surface; top with about 3 tablespoons of chicken, ½ tablespoon of cheese, and 1 tablespoon of sour cream. Fold two opposite sides of tortilla over to enclose filling. Place enchilada, seam side down, in prepared baking dish. Repeat with remaining tortillas, chicken, cheese, and sour cream, making total of 12 enchiladas. Pour remaining tomatillo mixture over enchiladas and sprinkle with remaining 6 tablespoons cheese.

4 Cover baking dish with foil. Bake 20 minutes; uncover and bake until edges of enchiladas begin to brown and cheese is melted, about 10 minutes longer. Let stand 5 minutes before serving.

PER SERVING (2 enchiladas and ⅙ of sauce): 390 Cal, 9 g Total Fat, 3 g Sat Fat, 0 g Trans Fat, 78 mg Chol, 589 mg Sod, 44 g Carb, 6 g Sugar, 5 g Fib, 33 g Prot, 278 mg Calc.

FYI Tomatillos, also called Mexican green tomatoes, belong to the tomato family. They look very much like small tomatoes except for their papery husk, which indicates that tomatillos are also related to the cape gooseberry. This slightly tart, firm vegetable is available year-round. Tomatillos can be eaten raw or cooked.

Chicken & Tomatillo
Enchilada Casserole

Crispy Chicken Parmesan Casserole

serves 4

2 tablespoons reduced-fat mayonnaise

1 large egg white

16 multigrain club crackers, finely crushed (about ½ cup crumbs)

2 tablespoons grated Parmesan cheese

2 tablespoons chopped fresh flat-leaf parsley

4 (¼-pound) chicken cutlets

8 tablespoons fat-free marinara sauce

8 tablespoons shredded part-skim mozzarella cheese

1 Preheat oven to 425°F. Spray 7 x 11-inch baking dish with nonstick spray.

2 Whisk together mayonnaise and egg white in shallow bowl or pie plate. Mix together cracker crumbs, Parmesan, and parsley on sheet of wax paper.

3 Dip 1 cutlet into mayonnaise mixture, then coat with crumb mixture, shaking off excess. Place cutlet in prepared baking dish. Repeat with remaining cutlets.

4 Top each cutlet with 2 tablespoons of marinara sauce and 2 tablespoons of mozzarella. Bake until chicken is cooked through and cheese is melted and bubbly, about 12 minutes.

PER SERVING (1 chicken cutlet): 370 Cal, 13 g Total Fat, 4 g Sat Fat, 2 g Trans Fat, 72 mg Chol, 630 mg Sod, 27 g Carb, 3 g Sugar, 2 g Fib, 31 g Prot, 155 mg Calc.

Healthy Extra Round out your meal with steamed kale, mustard greens, or beet greens—delicious ways to include antioxidants and vitamins in your diet.

Chicken & Mixed Mushroom Tetrazzini

serves 6

2 teaspoons olive oil

¾ pound mixed mushrooms, sliced

1 onion, thinly sliced

3 tablespoons all-purpose flour

1½ cups fat-free milk

1 cup reduced-sodium chicken broth

2 cups shredded cooked skinless chicken breast

1½ cups hot cooked whole wheat thin spaghetti

¾ teaspoon salt

¼ cup fresh whole wheat bread crumbs (about ½ slice bread)

2 tablespoons grated Parmesan cheese

1 Preheat oven to 350°F.

2 Heat oil in 2-quart flameproof casserole dish over medium heat. Add mushrooms and onion; cook, stirring, until mushrooms are softened, about 8 minutes. Sprinkle flour over vegetables; cook, stirring, 2 minutes.

3 Gradually stir milk and broth into vegetable mixture; bring to boil. Reduce heat and simmer, stirring occasionally, until sauce is thickened and bubbly, about 5 minutes.

4 Stir chicken, spaghetti, and salt into vegetable mixture. Mix together bread crumbs and Parmesan on sheet of wax paper. Sprinkle over chicken mixture. Transfer casserole to oven and bake until filling is bubbly and topping is browned, about 20 minutes.

PER SERVING (¾ cup): 230 Cal, 5 g Total Fat, 1 g Sat Fat, 0 g Trans Fat, 42 mg Chol, 423 mg Sod, 25 g Carb, 6 g Sugar, 3 g Fib, 23 g Prot, 135 mg Calc.

Healthy Extra Serve the tetrazzini along with a bowl of steamed baby carrots and snow peas.

Panko-Topped Chicken & Sausage Cassoulet

serves
6

PER SERVING

1 pound sweet Italian-style turkey sausage, cut into ½-inch slices

2 teaspoons canola oil

2 carrots, chopped

1 onion, chopped

2 garlic cloves, minced

¼ cup dry white wine or vermouth

1 (15½-ounce) can cannellini (white kidney) beans, rinsed and drained

1 (14½-ounce) can petite diced tomatoes

1 cup reduced-sodium chicken broth

1 cup (½-inch) diced cooked skinless chicken breast

1 tablespoon chopped fresh thyme

½ cup whole wheat panko (Japanese bread crumbs)

1   Preheat oven to 350°F.

2   Spray 2½-quart flameproof casserole dish with nonstick spray and set over medium heat. Add sausage and cook until browned, about 10 minutes. Transfer to medium bowl.

3   Add oil to casserole dish. Add carrots, onion, and garlic; cook, stirring, until onion is golden, about 8 minutes. Add wine and bring to boil, scraping up browned bits from bottom of casserole. Cook, stirring occasionally, until wine is evaporated, about 2 minutes. Return sausage to casserole. Add all remaining ingredients except panko; bring to boil.

4   Sprinkle panko over cassoulet and lightly spray with nonstick spray. Transfer casserole to oven and bake until heated through and bread crumbs are browned, about 25 minutes.

PER SERVING (generous 1 cup): 307 Cal, 11 g Total Fat, 0 g Sat Fat, 0 g Trans Fat, 65 mg Chol, 880 mg Sod, 24 g Carb, 7 g Sugar, 6 g Fib, 27 g Prot, 66 mg Calc.

Healthy Extra   Accompany the cassoulet with a plate of thickly sliced tomatoes topped with alfalfa sprouts and a sprinkling of vinegar and sea salt.

Coconut Curry, Chicken, & Rice Casserole

Coconut Curry, Chicken & Rice Casserole

serves
6

2 teaspoons canola oil

1 onion, chopped

1 red bell pepper, chopped

2 tablespoons minced peeled fresh ginger

2 garlic cloves, minced

1 tablespoon curry powder

1 teaspoon garam masala

¾ teaspoon salt

1 cup brown rice

2 cups cubed cooked skinless chicken thighs

2 cups reduced-sodium chicken broth

1 (14½-ounce) can diced tomatoes

½ cup light (reduced-fat) coconut milk

1 cup frozen peas

2 tablespoons chopped fresh cilantro

1 Preheat oven to 350°F.

2 Heat oil in 2½-quart flameproof casserole dish with lid over medium heat. Add onion and bell pepper; cook, stirring occasionally, until onion is golden, about 8 minutes. Add ginger, garlic, curry powder, garam masala, and salt; cook, stirring constantly, until fragrant, about 1 minute.

3 Stir rice into onion mixture and cook until coated evenly, about 2 minutes. Stir in chicken, broth, tomatoes, and coconut milk; bring to boil. Transfer casserole to oven and bake, covered, until liquid is absorbed and rice is tender, about 45 minutes, sprinkling peas over rice mixture after 35 minutes of baking. Serve sprinkled with cilantro.

PER SERVING (generous 1 cup): 308 Cal, 10 g Total Fat, 2 g Sat Fat, 0 g Trans Fat, 44 mg Chol, 533 mg Sod, 37 g Carb, 6 g Sugar, 4 g Fib, 19 g Prot, 48 mg Calc.

FYI   Garam masala is a blend of warm spices that originated in the colder northern regions of India. The mix of spices is dependent upon the cook, but the rule of thumb is to include black pepper, cardamom, cinnamon, cloves, coriander, cumin, dried chiles, fennel, mace, and nutmeg. Consider mixing up your own blend at home.

Sausage & Pepper Bread Pudding

serves
6

PER SERVING

2 cups low-fat (1%) milk

2 large eggs

1 large egg white

1 (8-ounce) loaf whole wheat
French bread, crust removed
and cut into 1½-inch cubes
(about 5 cups)

⅓ cup shredded reduced-fat
Cheddar cheese

2 teaspoons olive oil

½ pound sweet or hot Italian-style
turkey sausages, thinly sliced

2 red bell peppers, cut into
thin strips

1 onion, thinly sliced

2 garlic cloves, minced

1   Preheat oven to 375°F.

2   Whisk together milk, eggs, and egg white in large bowl. Add bread and Cheddar, tossing until mixed well. Let stand 15 minutes.

3   Meanwhile, heat 1 teaspoon of oil in 1½-quart shallow flameproof casserole dish over medium heat. Add sausages and cook until browned, about 8 minutes. Add to bread mixture.

4   Add remaining 1 teaspoon oil to casserole dish. Add bell peppers, onion, and garlic; cook, stirring, until peppers and onion are softened, about 5 minutes.

5   Add bell pepper mixture to bread mixture, stirring until mixed well. Spoon into casserole dish and spread evenly. Transfer casserole to oven and bake until topping is browned and knife inserted into center comes out clean, about 25 minutes. Serve hot or warm.

PER SERVING (about 1 cup): 269 Cal, 10 g Total Fat, 2 g Sat Fat, 0 g Trans Fat, 100 mg Chol, 541 mg Sod, 29 g Carb, 9 g Sugar, 3 g Fib, 17 g Prot, 204 mg Calc.

FYI   The bread pudding can be prepared ahead and refrigerated overnight, then baked as directed. Since the pudding will go into the oven cold, allow a little extra baking time or set the pudding out at room temperature about 45 minutes before baking so it has a chance to warm up.

Pizza-Style Baked Pasta

serves
8

12 ounces whole wheat penne, cooked according to package directions

½ pound hot Italian-style turkey sausage, thinly sliced

2 cups fat-free marinara sauce

1 cup shredded part-skim mozzarella cheese

4 tablespoons grated Parmesan cheese

¼ cup thinly sliced fresh basil

½ teaspoon dried oregano

2 tablespoons Italian-seasoned dried bread crumbs

1   Preheat oven to 350°F. Spray 7 x 11-inch baking dish with nonstick spray.

2   Toss together penne, sausage, 1 cup of marinara sauce, ½ cup of mozzarella, 2 tablespoons of Parmesan, the basil, and oregano in prepared baking dish. Top with remaining 1 cup marinara sauce, then sprinkle with remaining ½ cup mozzarella, 2 tablespoons Parmesan, and the bread crumbs.

3   Lightly spray sheet of foil with nonstick spray; place, sprayed side down, over baking dish. Bake 20 minutes. Uncover and bake until sausage is cooked through and mozzarella is melted, about 15 minutes longer.

PER SERVING (⅛ of casserole): 300 Cal, 8 g Total Fat, 2 g Sat Fat, 0 g Trans Fat, 27 mg Chol, 588 mg Sod, 40 g Carb, 2 g Sugar, 5 g Fib, 17 g Prot, 173 mg Calc.

Baked Cod with Spinach, Feta & Dill

serves
4

2 teaspoons olive oil

4 scallions, thinly sliced

2 garlic cloves, minced

2 (6-ounce) bags baby spinach

1 tablespoon water

½ teaspoon salt

2 tablespoons Italian-seasoned dried bread crumbs

Grated zest of 1 lemon

1 tablespoon snipped fresh dill

4 (6-ounce) cod fillets

2 tablespoons crumbled reduced-fat feta cheese

1   Preheat oven to 425°F.

2   Heat 1½ teaspoons of oil in 2-quart shallow flameproof casserole dish over medium heat. Add scallions and cook, stirring, until softened, about 2 minutes. Add garlic and cook, stirring frequently, until fragrant, about 30 seconds.

3   Add handful of spinach, the water, and ¼ teaspoon of salt to casserole dish, stirring just until spinach is wilted. Add remaining spinach in batches, stirring until spinach is wilted before adding more. Remove casserole dish from heat. Stir in breadcrumbs.

4   Stir together lemon zest, dill, and remaining ½ teaspoon oil and ¼ teaspoon salt in small bowl. Rub herb mixture on both sides of cod. Place fillets, in one layer, on top of spinach. Sprinkle with feta. Transfer casserole to oven and bake until fish is opaque in center, about 12 minutes.

PER SERVING (1 cod fillet and ¼ of spinach mixture): 209 Cal, 4 g Total Fat, 1 g Sat Fat, 0 g Trans Fat, 66 mg Chol, 638 mg Sod, 14 g Carb, 1 g Sugar, 5 g Fib, 31 g Prot, 112 mg Calc.

Lighter Tuna-Noodle Casserole

5 PointsPlus® value

PER SERVING

serves **6**

2 cups water

½ pound green beans, trimmed and cut into 1-inch pieces

2 teaspoons canola oil

1 (8-ounce) package white mushrooms, sliced

1 onion, finely chopped

½ teaspoon salt

¼ cup dry sherry or vermouth

3 tablespoons all-purpose flour

2 cups fat-free milk

1 cup reduced-sodium chicken broth

2 cups cooked wide whole wheat egg noodles

1 (5-ounce) can chunk white tuna in water, drained and flaked

½ cup shredded reduced-fat Jarlsberg cheese

6 reduced-fat whole grain wheat crackers (such as Triscuits), coarsely crushed

1   Preheat oven to 350°F.

2   Bring water to boil in 2-quart flameproof casserole dish over medium-high heat. Add beans and bring to boil. Cook, covered, just until tender, about 3 minutes; drain.

3   To make sauce, heat oil in same casserole dish over medium heat. Add mushrooms, onion, and salt; cook, stirring occasionally, until mushrooms are tender, about 8 minutes. Add sherry and bring to boil, scraping up browned bits from bottom of skillet. Cook, stirring, until sherry is evaporated, about 3 minutes. Sprinkle flour over mushroom mixture; cook, stirring, 2 minutes. Gradually stir in milk and broth; bring to boil. Cook, stirring, until mixture bubbles and thickens, about 4 minutes.

4   Stir beans, noodles, and tuna into mushroom sauce. Mix together Jarlsberg and crackers on sheet of wax paper; sprinkle over casserole. Transfer casserole to oven and bake until casserole is bubbly and top is golden, about 25 minutes.

PER SERVING (generous 1 cup): 199 Cal, 4 g Total Fat, 1 g Sat Fat, 0 g Trans Fat, 19 mg Chol, 425 mg Sod, 23 g Carb, 7 g Sugar, 3 g Fib, 16 g Prot, 220 mg Calc.

Healthy Extra   Enjoy this classic from the '50s with a retro salad of iceberg lettuce and cherry tomato wedges.

Lighter Tuna-Noodle Casserole

Cajun Shrimp & Chile–Corn Bread Casserole

serves
8

PER SERVING

FILLING

2 teaspoons canola oil

¼ pound cremini mushrooms, sliced

1 onion, chopped

1 green bell pepper, chopped

1 celery stalk, chopped

3 garlic cloves, minced

½ teaspoon reduced-sodium Cajun or Creole seasoning

¾ pound peeled and deveined medium shrimp

2 (14½-ounce) cans no-salt-added stewed tomatoes

1 cup fresh or thawed frozen okra

½ cup fat-free tomatillo salsa

CORN BREAD TOPPING

1 cup all-purpose flour

1 cup yellow cornmeal

2 teaspoons baking powder

1 teaspoon sugar

½ teaspoon salt

¾ cup low-fat buttermilk

3 tablespoons canola oil

1 large egg

1 Preheat oven to 400°F.

2 To make filling, heat oil in 3-quart flameproof casserole dish over medium heat. Add mushrooms, onion, bell pepper, celery, garlic, and Cajun seasoning; cook, stirring, until vegetables are softened, about 8 minutes. Add shrimp, tomatoes, okra, and salsa; bring to boil. Reduce heat and simmer, stirring occasionally, until mixture is slightly thickened, about 5 minutes.

3 Meanwhile, to make corn bread topping, whisk together flour, cornmeal, baking powder, sugar, and salt in large bowl. Make a well in center of flour mixture. Combine buttermilk, oil, and egg in well, whisking until blended well. Stir flour mixture into buttermilk mixture just until blended.

4 Spoon batter, by heaping tablespoonfuls, over shrimp mixture. Transfer casserole to oven and bake until shrimp mixture is bubbly and corn bread is golden, about 20 minutes.

PER SERVING (about ¾ cup): 288 Cal, 8 g Total Fat, 1 g Sat Fat, 0 g Trans Fat, 90 mg Chol, 482 mg Sod, 41 g Carb, 8 g Sugar, 4 g Fib, 12 g Prot, 112 mg Calc.

Roasted Eggplant & Mushroom Lasagna

serves
8

1 (1-pound) eggplant, unpeeled and cut into ½-inch rounds

8 ounces assorted mushrooms, such as oyster, chanterelle, and cremini, halved

½ teaspoon salt

1 (24-ounce) jar fat-free marinara or tomato sauce

9 no-boil whole wheat lasagna noodles

¾ cup shredded part-skim mozzarella cheese

3 tablespoons chopped fresh basil

3 tablespoons grated Parmesan cheese

1 Set racks in upper and lower thirds of oven. Preheat oven to 400°F. Spray 9 x 13-inch baking dish and large baking sheet with olive oil nonstick spray.

2 Spread eggplant on baking sheet and mushrooms in prepared baking dish. Lightly spray vegetables with nonstick spray and sprinkle with salt; toss to coat evenly. Roast, stirring occasionally, until eggplant and mushrooms are tender and lightly browned, about 25 minutes. Transfer vegetables to sheet of foil.

3 Reduce oven temperature to 375°F. Spread ½ cup of marinara sauce in same baking dish. Arrange 3 noodles over sauce. Top with one-third of eggplant mixture, 1 cup of marinara sauce, ¼ cup of mozzarella, 1 tablespoon of basil, and 1 tablespoon of Parmesan. Repeat layering twice.

4 Transfer lasagna to oven and bake until mixture is bubbly around edges and topping is browned, about 45 minutes. Let stand 10 minutes before serving.

PER SERVING (⅛ of lasagna): 214 Cal, 4 g Total Fat, 2 g Sat Fat, 0 g Trans Fat, 7 mg Chol, 596 mg Sod, 32 g Carb, 2 g Sugar, 8 g Fib, 12 g Prot, 146 mg Calc.

Three-Cheese Polenta Lasagna

PointsPlus® value 6

serves
6

PER SERVING

1 cup fat-free ricotta cheese

¼ cup grated Parmesan cheese

3 tablespoons chopped fresh flat-leaf parsley

½ teaspoon black pepper

1½ cups fat-free marinara sauce

2 (16-ounce) tubes fat-free mushroom polenta, each cut into 12 rounds

12 fresh basil leaves

1 cup shredded part-skim mozzarella cheese

1   Preheat oven to 375°F. Spray 9 x 13-inch baking dish with nonstick spray.

2   Stir together ricotta, Parmesan, parsley, and pepper in medium bowl.

3   Spread ½ cup of marinara sauce in prepared baking dish. Arrange 12 polenta rounds over sauce; top each round with scant 2 tablespoons of ricotta mixture and 1 basil leaf. Arrange remaining 12 polenta rounds on top. Spoon remaining 1 cup marinara sauce over polenta and sprinkle with mozzarella.

4   Spray sheet of foil with nonstick spray; use, sprayed side down, to loosely cover baking dish. Bake until lasagna is heated through and sauce is bubbly, about 30 minutes. Remove foil; let stand 10 minutes before serving.

PER SERVING (⅙ of lasagna): 243 Cal, 5 g Total Fat, 3 g Sat Fat, 0 g Trans Fat, 17 mg Chol, 913 mg Sod, 31 g Carb, 3 g Sugar, 3 g Fib, 16 g Prot, 333 mg Calc.

FYI   Tubes of mushroom polenta are found in supermarkets in the produce or organic food section. Look for other varieties including plain and Italian herb, which would work equally well in this lasagna.

Monterey Jack, Green Chile & Bean Casserole

serves 6

PER SERVING

1 (16-ounce) can fat-free refried beans

4 scallions, sliced

½ cup chopped fresh cilantro

⅓ cup fat-free sour cream

1 (4-ounce) can chopped mild green chiles, drained

1½ teaspoons chili powder

1 (14½-ounce) can no-salt-added diced tomatoes

1 (16-ounce) tube fat-free plain polenta, cut into 12 rounds

¾ cup shredded reduced-fat Monterey Jack cheese

1 Preheat oven to 375°F. Spray 9 x 13-inch baking dish with nonstick spray.

2 Stir together beans, scallions, cilantro, sour cream, chiles, and chili powder in medium bowl.

3 Spread half of tomatoes in prepared baking dish. Arrange polenta rounds over sauce. Spoon bean mixture evenly over polenta. Top with remaining tomatoes; sprinkle with Monterey Jack. Bake until heated through and cheese is melted, about 25 minutes. Let stand 5 minutes before serving.

PER SERVING (⅙ of casserole): 191 Cal, 3 g Total Fat, 2 g Sat Fat, 0 g Trans Fat, 0 mg Chol, 814 mg Sod, 30 g Carb, 1 g Sugar, 0 g Fib, 10 g Prot, 269 mg Calc.

Healthy Extra   Add some extra protein to this casserole by topping the first layer of tomatoes with 4 (3-ounce) cooked skinless boneless chicken breasts that have been shredded or diced. This will increase the per-serving *PointsPlus* value by *2*.

Easy Tomato, Rice & Corn Casserole

serves 6

PER SERVING

1 tablespoon canola oil

1 red bell pepper, diced

1 onion, chopped

2 garlic cloves, minced

1 cup long-grain white rice

1 tablespoon chili powder

2 cups frozen corn kernels

1 (14½-ounce) can diced tomatoes

1 (14½-ounce) can reduced-sodium vegetable broth

3 plum tomatoes, seeded and chopped

¾ cup shredded reduced-fat Cheddar cheese

1 Preheat oven to 350°F.

2 Heat oil in 3-quart flameproof casserole dish with lid over medium heat. Add bell pepper, onion, and garlic; cook, stirring, until softened, about 5 minutes. Add rice and chili powder; cook, stirring, until well coated, about 1 minute.

3 Add corn, diced tomatoes, and broth to rice mixture; bring to boil. Transfer casserole to oven and bake, covered, until most of liquid is absorbed and rice is tender, about 20 minutes.

4 Sprinkle casserole with chopped tomatoes and Cheddar. Bake, uncovered, until cheese is melted, about 5 minutes longer. Let stand 5 minutes before serving.

PER SERVING (generous 1 cup): 257 Cal, 6 g Total Fat, 2 g Sat Fat, 0 g Trans Fat, 10 mg Chol, 324 mg Sod, 44 g Carb, 6 g Sugar, 3 g Fib, 8 g Prot, 233 mg Calc.

Healthy Extra   A chopped salad of fresh tomatoes and cucumber seasoned with lime juice makes a refreshing accompaniment to the casserole.

Tortilla Casserole with
Tomatillo Salsa

Tortilla Casserole with Tomatillo Salsa

5 PointsPlus® value
PER SERVING

serves
6

1 large onion, chopped

1 red bell pepper, chopped

2 garlic cloves, minced

1½ teaspoons ground cumin

¾ teaspoon dried oregano

1 (14¾-ounce) can
cream-style corn

2 large eggs

3 large egg whites

⅔ cup shredded reduced-fat
Mexican cheese blend

2 tablespoons mild pepper sauce
(such as Frank's)

4 (6-inch) corn tortillas,
cut into 1-inch strips

¾ cup fat-free tomatillo salsa

1   Preheat oven to 375°F.

2   Spray 1½-quart flameproof casserole dish or heavy ovenproof nonstick skillet with nonstick spray and set over medium heat. Add onion, bell pepper, and garlic; cook, stirring, until softened, about 5 minutes. Stir in cumin and oregano. Remove casserole from heat; transfer vegetable mixture to sheet of foil and let cool.

3   Mix together corn, eggs, egg whites, ⅓ cup of cheese, and the pepper sauce in large bowl. Stir in vegetable mixture. Spoon half of mixture into cooled casserole dish. Arrange half of tortilla strips on top. Repeat with remaining vegetable mixture and tortilla strips. Sprinkle with the remaining ⅓ cup cheese. Transfer casserole to oven and bake until golden and set in center, about 35 minutes. Serve with salsa.

PER SERVING (⅙ of casserole and 2 tablespoons of salsa): 199 Cal, 5 g Total Fat, 2 g Sat Fat, 0 g Trans Fat, 79 mg Chol, 607 mg Sod, 29 g Carb, 6 g Sugar, 2 g Fib, 9 g Prot, 201 mg Calc.

Healthy Extra   Serve the casserole with additional fat-free tomatillo salsa.

Cauliflower, Zucchini & Chickpea Biryani

7 PointsPlus® value

PER SERVING

serves
6

2 teaspoons canola oil

1 onion, thinly sliced

2 garlic cloves, minced

1 tablespoon curry powder

1 teaspoon garam masala

1 teaspoon Thai red curry paste

¾ cup brown basmati rice

2½ cups reduced-sodium chicken broth

1 (14½-ounce) can petite diced tomatoes

2 cups cauliflower florets

1 (15½-ounce) can chickpeas, rinsed and drained

¼ cup golden raisins

1 zucchini, diced

3 tablespoons unsalted cashews, coarsely chopped

1   Preheat oven to 350°F.

2   Heat oil in 2½-quart round flameproof casserole dish with lid over medium heat. Add onion and garlic; cook, stirring, until onion is softened, about 5 minutes.

3   Stir curry powder, garam masala, and curry paste into onion mixture; cook, stirring, until fragrant, about 1 minute. Add rice and cook, stirring until coated well, about 2 minutes.

4   Add broth, tomatoes, cauliflower, chickpeas, and raisins to onion mixture; bring to boil. Transfer casserole to oven and bake, covered, until rice is almost tender, about 45 minutes. Stir in zucchini and bake, covered, until rice and zucchini are tender and liquid is absorbed, about 5 minutes longer. Serve sprinkled with cashews.

PER SERVING (1⅓ cups): 256 Cal, 6 g Total Fat, 1 g Sat Fat, 0 g Trans Fat, 0 mg Chol, 396 mg Sod, 44 g Carb, 12 g Sugar, 7 g Fib, 10 g Prot, 60 mg Calc.

FYI   Biryani is a rice-based dish that is popular in India and its surrounding countries. It typically consists of meat, fish, or poultry, rice, vegetables, and a variety of herbs and spices that are either cooked together or layered and cooked. There are also vegetarian versions.

Crustless Corn & Tomato Quiche

serves
6

PER SERVING

2 teaspoons olive oil

1 onion, chopped

1 green bell pepper, diced

1 cup fresh or thawed frozen corn kernels

½ teaspoon salt

1½ cups fat-free milk

2 large eggs

2 large egg whites

2 tablespoons fat-free ricotta cheese

½ teaspoon dried oregano

1 cup shredded reduced-fat Cheddar cheese

1 cup cherry tomatoes, halved

1   Preheat oven to 425°F. Spray 1½-quart shallow casserole dish or 9-inch quiche dish with nonstick spray.

2   Heat oil in large nonstick skillet over medium-high heat. Add onion, bell pepper, corn, and ¼ teaspoon of salt; cook, stirring, until onion is softened, about 5 minutes. Remove skillet from heat; let cool slightly.

3   Meanwhile, whisk together milk, eggs, egg whites, ricotta, oregano, and remaining ¼ teaspoon of salt in large bowl until blended. Stir in onion mixture and Cheddar. Pour into prepared casserole dish. Scatter tomatoes evenly over filling (tomatoes will sink slightly).

4   Bake quiche 15 minutes. Reduce oven temperature to 350°F and bake until filling is set and knife inserted into center comes out clean, about 20 minutes longer. Let stand 10 minutes before serving.

PER SERVING (⅙ of quiche): 162 Cal, 8 g Total Fat, 3 g Sat Fat, 0 g Trans Fat, 87 mg Chol, 422 mg Sod, 14 g Carb, 6 g Sugar, 1 g Fib, 12 g Prot, 380 mg Calc.

FYI   Add some unexpected color to this flavorful quiche by using assorted color heirloom cherry tomatoes.

Pie-Style Spanakopita

serves
6

PER SERVING

1 (10-ounce) package frozen chopped spinach, thawed and squeezed dry

4 scallions, finely chopped

1 cup fat-free ricotta cheese

⅓ cup crumbled reduced-fat feta cheese

¼ cup snipped fresh dill

1 large egg, lightly beaten

¼ teaspoon salt

10 (9 x 14-inch) sheets frozen phyllo dough, thawed

1 Preheat oven to 375°F. Spray shallow 1½-quart shallow casserole dish or 9-inch deep-dish pie plate with nonstick spray.

2 Mix together all ingredients except phyllo in large bowl.

3 Lay 1 sheet of phyllo in prepared casserole dish, allowing it to extend over rim of dish; lightly spray with nonstick spray. (Keep remaining phyllo covered with damp paper towel and plastic wrap to keep it from drying out.) Repeat with 3 more sheets of phyllo, placing corners at different angles and lightly spraying each sheet with nonstick spray. Fold edges of phyllo in to form 1½-inch-high rim.

4 Spread spinach mixture over phyllo. Lightly spray 1 of remaining sheets of phyllo with nonstick spray; crumple loosely and place on top of filling. Repeat with remaining 5 sheets of phyllo. Bake until filling is heated through and phyllo is golden, about 30 minutes. Let stand 10 minutes before serving.

PER SERVING (⅙ of pie): 176 Cal, 5 g Total Fat, 2 g Sat Fat, 0 g Trans Fat, 41 mg Chol, 455 mg Sod, 22 g Carb, 2 g Sugar, 2 g Fib, 12 g Prot, 231 mg Calc.

Healthy Extra   Enjoy a dessert of sliced star fruit, strawberries, and kiwifruit.

Pie-Style Spanakopita

Creamy Corn & Broccoli Spoon Bread

serves
6

PER SERVING

1 (16-ounce) tube fat-free plain polenta, cut into chunks

2 tablespoons water

2 cups small broccoli florets, steamed

1 (8¼-ounce) can cream-style corn

½ cup fat-free milk

½ cup shredded reduced-fat Jarlsberg cheese

¼ cup all-purpose flour

2 large egg yolks

4 large egg whites, at room temperature

½ teaspoon cream of tartar

1 Preheat oven to 400°F. Spray 2-quart casserole dish with nonstick spray.

2 Combine polenta and water in food processor and pulse until smooth, about 15 seconds. Transfer to large bowl. Add broccoli, corn, milk, Jarlsberg, flour, and egg yolks, stirring until mixed well.

3 With electric mixer on high speed, beat egg whites until foamy. Add cream of tartar and beat until soft peaks form when beaters are lifted. Stir about one-fourth of beaten egg whites into polenta mixture to lighten it. With rubber spatula, gently fold in remaining egg whites just until blended.

4 Gently scrape batter into prepared casserole dish. Bake until spoon bread is slightly puffed and golden, about 45 minutes. Serve at once.

PER SERVING (1 cup): 201 Cal, 3 g Total Fat, 1 g Sat Fat, 0 g Trans Fat, 77 mg Chol, 536 mg Sod, 30 g Carb, 4 g Sugar, 3 g Fib, 12 g Prot, 255 mg Calc.

FYI Serve the spoon bread accompanied by an escarole, tomato, and red onion salad dressed with a squeeze of lime juice.

TVP Bolognese & Pasta Casserole

10 PointsPlus value
PER SERVING

serves
6

2 teaspoons olive oil

3 garlic cloves, thinly sliced

¼ teaspoon red pepper flakes

1 (14-ounce) tube refrigerated textured vegetable protein (TVP)

1 (28-ounce) can Italian peeled whole tomatoes

½ cup reduced-sodium chicken broth

¼ teaspoon salt

4 cups hot cooked whole wheat penne

½ cup chopped fresh basil

1 cup shredded reduced-fat Italian four-cheese blend

1 Preheat oven to 375°F.

2 Heat oil in 1½-quart flameproof casserole dish over medium heat. Add garlic and pepper flakes; cook, stirring constantly, until fragrant, about 1 minute. Increase heat to medium-high. Add TVP and cook, breaking it up with spoon, until browned, about 6 minutes.

3 Add tomatoes to TVP mixture, breaking them up with spoon. Add broth and salt; bring to boil. Reduce heat and simmer, stirring occasionally, until flavors are blended and sauce begins to thicken, about 15 minutes. Remove casserole dish from heat. Stir in penne and basil.

4 Spoon half of pasta mixture into prepared casserole dish; sprinkle with ½ cup of cheese. Top with remaining pasta mixture and sprinkle with remaining ½ cup cheese. Bake until edge is bubbly and topping is browned, about 25 minutes.

PER SERVING (1⅓ cups): 437 Cal, 6 g Total Fat, 2 g Sat Fat, 0 g Trans Fat, 10 mg Chol, 554 mg Sod, 51 g Carb, 12 g Sugar, 15 g Fib, 45 g Prot, 400 mg Calc.

Healthy Extra Serve a seasonal fresh fruit compote as a light and refreshing way to end the meal. In the fall, use diced apples, diced pears, and pomegranate seeds; in the winter, try mandarin orange segments tossed with fresh mint and raspberries; in the spring, use a mix of strawberries and kiwifruit; and in the summer, combine wedges of peaches and apricots with blackberries.

IN A SLOW COOKER

CHAPTER 8

IN A SLOW COOKER

EASY-DOES-IT MAIN DISHES

For over 30 years, the slow cooker has been a favorite way to cook one-pot meals. Originally it was marketed as the modern way to cook baked beans, with its slogan "Cooks all day while the cook's away." Eighty million pots later, the slow cooker remains a favorite among cooks. At its most basic, this lidded pot has electric coils wrapped inside an outer shell, a ceramic liner, and a dial for on/off, high, and low. At the low setting food can be ready in 4 to 6 hours, while at the high setting food is ready in 8 to 12 hours.

Types

There are four types of slow cookers:

Manual slow cookers usually have three heat settings (on/off, high, and low), a removable ceramic insert that's dishwasher safe and doubles as a serving dish, and a glass lid.

Programmable slow cookers offer one-touch control with multiple time and temperature settings, a dishwasher-safe ceramic insert, and a glass lid. These cookers automatically shift to the warm setting when the cooking is finished and can be programmed to cook for as little as 30 minutes or up to 20 hours.

Cook and carry slow cookers are perfect for taking food on the road. They usually have two or three

cook settings, a dishwasher-safe ceramic insert, and a glass lid that locks securely in place to help get food to its destination safely.

Top-of-the-line slow cookers offer the ability to brown meat or sauté vegetables on the stovetop in an aluminum insert. Two handles make it easy to transfer the insert to and from the slow cooker or to the table for serving. These slow cookers are more expensive.

Sizes and Shapes

Slow cookers range in size from 1½ quarts to 7 quarts, with the most useful from 4 to 6 quarts. Depending on the size of the cooker, at least 2 or up to 12 people can be served.

Meat Loaf with Parmesan & Tomato

serves
4

PER SERVING

1 pound ground skinless
turkey breast

½ cup grated zucchini

¼ cup grated Parmesan cheese

¼ cup plain dried
bread crumbs

4 tablespoons fresh
flat-leaf parsley

2 tablespoons fat-free egg
substitute

1 garlic clove, minced

½ teaspoon salt

¼ teaspoon black pepper

½ cup canned tomato sauce

1   Line bottom and part way up side of 5- or 6-quart slow cooker with sheet of nonstick foil.

2   Mix together turkey, zucchini, Parmesan, bread crumbs, 3 tablespoons of parsley, the egg substitute, garlic, salt, and pepper in medium bowl just until mixed well. Shape mixture into loaf about 6 inches long x 3½ inches wide x 1½ inches high; place in slow cooker and spoon tomato sauce on top.

3   Cover and cook 1 hour on high. Reduce heat to low and cook until instant-read thermometer inserted into center of loaf registers 160°F, about 4 hours longer.

4   Carefully lift meat loaf from slow cooker using foil as handles and transfer to cutting board; let stand covered with foil 10 minutes. Sprinkle meat loaf with remaining 1 tablespoon parsley and cut into 8 slices.

PER SERVING (2 slices): 184 Cal, 3 g Total Fat, 1 g Sat Fat, 0 g Trans Fat, 49 mg Chol, 663 mg Sod, 8 g Carb, 2 g Sugar, 1 g Fib, 32 g Prot, 81 mg Calc.

Healthy Extra   Keep the Italian theme going and serve this full-flavored loaf with steamed broccolini sprinkled with diced roasted red pepper (not packed in oil), red pepper flakes, and dried or chopped fresh oregano.

Rustic Beef Short Ribs with Mustard Sauce

Rustic Beef Short Ribs with Mustard Sauce

PER SERVING

6 tablespoons fat-free sour cream

1½ tablespoons Dijon mustard

1 tablespoon snipped fresh chives

3 tablespoons all-purpose flour

½ teaspoon salt

½ teaspoon black pepper

1¼ pounds boneless beef short ribs, trimmed and cut into 2-inch chunks

1 pound red potatoes, scrubbed and cut into 1-inch chunks

1 large onion, coarsely chopped

1½ cups baby or baby-cut carrots

3 garlic cloves, minced

1 cup reduced-sodium beef broth

2 tablespoons Worcestershire sauce

1 To make mustard sauce, stir together sour cream, mustard, and chives in serving bowl. Cover and refrigerate until ready to serve.

2 Mix together flour, salt, and pepper on sheet of wax paper. Coat beef with seasoned flour, shaking off excess.

3 Spray large nonstick skillet with nonstick spray and set over medium-high heat. Add beef, in batches, and cook until browned on all sides, about 8 minutes per batch, transferring beef to 5- or 6-quart slow cooker as it is browned.

4 Add remaining ingredients to slow cooker. Cover and cook until meat and vegetables are tender, 4–5 hours on high or 8–10 hours on low. Serve with mustard sauce.

PER SERVING (1⅓ cups stew and 1½ tablespoons mustard sauce): 325 Cal, 13 g Total Fat, 5 g Sat Fat, 0 g Trans Fat, 67 mg Chol, 441 mg Sod, 25 g Carb, 4 g Sugar, 3 g Fib, 26 g Prot, 54 mg Calc.

Italian Pot Roast

PER SERVING

serves
8

¼ cup all-purpose flour

1 teaspoon salt

¼ teaspoon black pepper

1 (2¾-pound) bottom round beef roast, trimmed

1 tablespoon olive oil

4 small red onions, thinly sliced

4 garlic cloves, minced

2 teaspoons finely chopped dried porcini or other dried mushrooms

½ teaspoon dried rosemary, crumbled

½ cup reduced-sodium beef broth

1 (14½-ounce) can diced tomatoes

8 fresh flat-leaf parsley sprigs

1   Combine flour, salt, and pepper on sheet of wax paper. Roll beef in seasoned flour, shaking off excess.

2   Heat oil in large nonstick skillet over medium heat. Add beef and cook until browned on all sides, about 10 minutes. Transfer to 5- or 6-quart slow cooker.

3   Add onions to skillet and cook, stirring, until softened, about 5 minutes. Add garlic, porcini mushrooms, and rosemary; cook, stirring constantly, until fragrant, about 1 minute. Add broth and bring to boil, scraping up browned bits from bottom of skillet. Transfer to slow cooker; stir in tomatoes and parsley sprigs.

4   Cover and cook until beef is fork-tender, 4–6 hours on high or 8–10 hours on low. Transfer beef to cutting board; let stand 10 minutes. Discard parsley. Cut beef into 16 slices and serve with vegetables and sauce.

PER SERVING (2 slices beef and 3 tablespoons vegetables with sauce): 313 Cal, 11 g Total Fat, 3 g Sat Fat, 0 g Trans Fat, 122 mg Chol, 463 mg Sod, 10 g Carb, 3 g Sugar, 1 g Fib, 42 g Prot, 31 mg Calc.

FYI   In Italy, slow-cooked pot roast is called *stracotto*, which means "overcooked." The dish is appreciated for the fact that once the ingredients are put together, the cook's work is done. Enjoy it as Italians do with a side of soft polenta (½ cup of cooked polenta per serving will increase the *PointsPlus* value by 2).

Beef Stew Burgundy-Style

serves
4

PER SERVING

2 tablespoons all-purpose flour

¾ teaspoon salt

¼ teaspoon black pepper

1 pound boneless beef bottom round, trimmed and cut into 2-inch chunks

1 tablespoon olive oil

1½ cups reduced-sodium beef broth

½ cup dry red wine

¾ pound Yukon Gold potatoes, peeled and cut into 1-inch chunks

½ pound cremini mushrooms, halved or quartered if large

4 carrots, cut into 1-inch chunks

1 cup frozen small onions

2 garlic cloves, minced

1½ teaspoons dried savory or thyme

1 Mix together flour, salt, and pepper on sheet of wax paper. Coat beef with seasoned flour, shaking off excess.

2 Heat oil in large nonstick skillet over medium-high heat. Add beef, in batches, and cook until browned on all sides, about 6 minutes per batch, transferring beef to 5- or 6-quart slow cooker as it is browned.

3 Add remaining ingredients to slow cooker. Cover and cook until beef and vegetables are tender, 4–5 hours on high or 8–10 hours on low.

PER SERVING (1½ cups): 390 Cal, 11 g Total Fat, 3 g Sat Fat, 0 g Trans Fat, 88 mg Chol, 557 mg Sod, 30 g Carb, 6 g Sugar, 4 g Fib, 35 g Prot, 54 mg Calc.

Healthy Extra   Stir 2 cups of turnip chunks into the stew along with the potatoes in step 3 and increase the amount of mushrooms to ¾ pound.

Chunky Beef & Bean Chili

serves
4

PER SERVING

1 pound lean beef chuck, trimmed and cut into ¾-inch cubes

1 (15½-ounce) can pinto beans, rinsed and drained

1 (14½-ounce) can petite diced tomatoes

1¼ cups reduced-sodium beef broth

1 onion, finely chopped

2 tablespoons cornmeal

1 jalapeño pepper, seeded and minced

2 teaspoons chili powder

1 teaspoon ground cumin

¼ teaspoon anise seeds, crushed

¼ teaspoon cayenne

1 cup lightly packed fresh cilantro leaves

Combine all ingredients except cilantro in 5-or 6-quart slow cooker. Cover and cook until beef is fork-tender, 4–6 hours on high or 8–10 hours on low. Stir in ¾ cup of cilantro. Serve sprinkled with remaining ¼ cup cilantro.

PER SERVING (1½ cups): 310 Cal, 6 g Total Fat, 2 g Sat Fat, 0 g Trans Fat, 48 mg Chol, 636 mg Sod, 29 g Carb, 6 g Sugar, 8 g Fib, 32 g Prot, 83 mg Calc.

Healthy Extra   Serve this chili with a side of brown rice and steamed spinach (⅔ cup cooked brown rice per serving will increase the *PointsPlus* value by 3).

Pulled Pork & Cabbage Sandwiches

PER SERVING

1½ cups thinly sliced green cabbage

1½ red onions, thinly sliced

¼ cup cider vinegar

¼ cup ketchup

¼ cup packed light brown sugar

2 tablespoons water

1 tablespoon tomato paste

½ teaspoon hot paprika, preferably smoked

½ teaspoon chili powder

¼ teaspoon ground cumin

¼ teaspoon salt

1 (1-pound) pork tenderloin, trimmed

4 (3½-ounce) whole wheat rolls, split and warmed

1 Combine 1 cup of cabbage, 1 onion, vinegar, ketchup, brown sugar, water, and tomato paste in 5- or 6-quart slow cooker.

2 Combine paprika, chili powder, cumin, and salt on sheet of wax paper; rub all over pork. Place in slow cooker. Cover and cook until pork is fork-tender, 6–8 hours on low. Transfer to cutting board.

3 When cool enough to handle, with two forks, shred pork; stir back into sauce in slow cooker. Spoon ¾ cup of pork mixture onto bottom half of each roll. Top each serving with one-fourth of remaining cabbage and red onion. Cover with tops of rolls.

PER SERVING (1 sandwich): 339 Cal, 4 g Total Fat, 1 g Sat Fat, 0 g Trans Fat, 62 mg Chol, 667 mg Sod, 48 g Carb, 18 g Sugar, 3 g Fib, 27 g Prot, 38 mg Calc.

FYI Smoked paprika, *pimentón* in Spanish, is made by slowly cooking red chile pods over a wood fire. It is available both sweet and hot and adds a delicious authentic smoky flavor to foods.

Pork Chop & Bean Cassoulet

serves
6

PER SERVING

3 (15½-ounce) cans cannellini (white kidney) beans, rinsed and drained

1 (8-ounce) can tomato sauce

1 cup reduced-sodium beef broth

½ teaspoon salt

¼ teaspoon black pepper

6 (¼-pound) boneless pork loin chops, trimmed

4 small carrots, halved lengthwise and thinly sliced

2 onions, thinly sliced

4 garlic cloves, minced

1 cup fresh whole wheat bread crumbs (about 2 slices bread)

¼ cup grated Parmesan cheese

⅓ cup chopped fresh flat-leaf parsley

1 Stir together beans, tomato sauce, broth, ¼ teaspoon of salt, and ⅛ teaspoon of pepper in 5- or 6-quart slow cooker.

2 Season pork with remaining ¼ teaspoon salt and ⅛ teaspoon pepper. Spray large nonstick skillet with nonstick spray and set over medium heat. Add pork and cook until lightly browned on all sides, about 6 minutes; transfer to slow cooker. Add carrots and onions to skillet; cook, stirring, until onions are softened, about 5 minutes. Stir in garlic and cook, stirring constantly, until fragrant, about 30 seconds; add to slow cooker.

3 Cover and cook until pork is fork-tender, 4–6 hours on high or 8–10 hours on low. About 30 minutes before cooking time is up, sprinkle cassoulet evenly with bread crumbs, Parmesan, and parsley; cover and cook 30 minutes longer.

PER SERVING (1 pork chop and about ¾ cup vegetable mixture): 415 Cal, 9 g Total Fat, 3 g Sat Fat, 0 g Trans Fat, 69 mg Chol, 614 mg Sod, 45 g Carb, 9 g Sugar, 12 g Fib, 36 g Prot, 187 mg Calc.

Healthy Extra Serve the cassoulet with a side of steamed whole green beans and wax beans.

Lamb & Apricot Tagine

11 PointsPlus® value
PER SERVING

serves
4

3 tablespoons all-purpose flour

½ teaspoon salt

¼ teaspoon black pepper

1 pound boneless leg of lamb, trimmed and cut into 1-inch chunks

4 small onions, thinly sliced

2 garlic cloves, thinly sliced

¾ teaspoon cumin seeds

1 cup reduced-sodium vegetable or beef broth

1 (15½-ounce) can chickpeas, rinsed and drained

½ cup lightly packed fresh cilantro leaves

½ cup dried apricots, cut into thin strips

2 cups hot cooked whole wheat couscous

1 Mix together flour, salt, and pepper on sheet of wax paper. Coat lamb with seasoned flour, shaking off excess.

2 Spray large nonstick skillet with nonstick spray and set over medium-high heat. Add lamb, in batches, and cook until well browned on all sides, about 5 minutes per batch, transferring lamb to 5- or 6-quart slow cooker as it is browned.

3 Add onions to skillet and cook, stirring constantly, until browned, about 4 minutes. Add garlic and cumin; cook, stirring constantly, until fragrant, about 30 seconds. Add broth to skillet and bring to boil, scraping up browned bits from bottom of skillet.

4 Transfer onion mixture to slow cooker; stir in chickpeas. Cover and cook until lamb is fork-tender, 4–6 hours on low. Just before serving, stir in cilantro and apricots. Serve with couscous.

PER SERVING (scant 1 cup stew and ½ cup couscous): 436 Cal, 11 g Total Fat, 4 g Sat Fat, 0 g Trans Fat, 89 mg Chol, 650 mg Sod, 53 g Carb, 14 g Sugar, 9 g Fib, 33 g Prot, 75 mg Calc.

FYI Tagines are slow-simmered North African stews that can contain meat or poultry, vegetables, dried fruits, preserved lemons and spices, including ginger, cumin, turmeric, cayenne, and cinnamon. These stews are cooked in heavy clay pots also called tagines. A tagine consists of a flat base with low sides and a tall cone-shaped top, which is designed to promote condensation and keep the stew moist. Once the cover is removed, the bottom of the tagine becomes the serving dish.

Irish Stew with Potatoes, Pearl Onions & Carrots

serves
8

PER SERVING

2 cups reduced-sodium vegetable or beef broth

2 pounds boneless leg of lamb, trimmed and cut into 1-inch chunks

8 small red potatoes, scrubbed and halved

2 cups pearl onions, peeled

2 parsnips, quartered lengthwise and cut into ⅜-inch slices

3 carrots, cut into chunks

1 small turnip, halved, each half cut into 8 wedges

1 bay leaf

½ teaspoon salt

¼ teaspoon black pepper

3 tablespoons all-purpose flour

2 cups frozen peas, thawed

¼ cup chopped fresh flat-leaf parsley or mint

1   Reserve 2 tablespoons of broth in small bowl. Combine remaining broth, the lamb, potatoes, onions, parsnips, carrots, turnip, bay leaf, salt, and pepper in 5- or 6-quart slow cooker. Cover and cook until lamb is fork-tender and vegetables are softened, about 4 hours on high or 8 hours on low.

2   About 30 minutes before cooking time is up, whisk together reserved 2 tablespoons broth and the flour until smooth. Whisk in ¼ cup hot stew liquid until blended well. Stir back into slow cooker until blended. Cover and cook on high until mixture bubbles and thickens, about 30 minutes longer. Discard bay leaf and stir in peas and parsley.

PER SERVING (2 cups): 419 Cal, 10 g Total Fat, 4 g Sat Fat, 0 g Trans Fat, 89 mg Chol, 394 mg Sod, 52 g Carb, 9 g Sugar, 7 g Fib, 31 g Prot, 74 mg Calc.

FYI   Here's the easiest way to peel pearl onions: Bring a large glass bowl half-filled with water to a boil in the microwave. Add the onions and cover the bowl with plastic wrap; let stand 5 minutes. Drain off the water, and when cool enough to handle, trim the root end and slip off the skin with the help of a small knife.

**Irish Stew with Potatoes, Pearl
Onions & Carrots**

French Country-Style Chicken Stew

serves
4

2 tablespoons all-purpose flour

½ teaspoon salt

¼ teaspoon black pepper

4 skinless chicken thighs, trimmed

1 tablespoon olive oil

2 red onions, thinly sliced

2 cups lightly packed thinly sliced green cabbage

¾ cup reduced-sodium chicken broth

½ teaspoon fresh thyme leaves

2 carrots, quartered lengthwise and cut into ¼-inch slices

1 parsnip, quartered lengthwise and cut into ¼-inch slices

3 tablespoons chopped fresh flat-leaf parsley

1 Combine flour, salt, and pepper on sheet of wax paper. Coat chicken with seasoned flour, shaking off excess.

2 Heat oil in large heavy skillet, such as cast iron, over medium-high heat. Add chicken and cook until browned on all sides, about 10 minutes. Transfer to plate. Add onions to skillet and cook, stirring frequently, until browned, about 4 minutes; transfer to 5- or 6-quart slow cooker.

3 Reduce heat to medium; add cabbage to skillet and cook, stirring frequently, until wilted, about 3 minutes. Transfer to slow cooker. Add broth and thyme to skillet; bring to boil, stirring to scrape up any browned bits from bottom of skillet. Transfer to slow cooker. Add carrots and parsnip to slow cooker; nestle chicken in vegetables. Cover and cook until chicken is cooked through and vegetables are softened, about 4 hours on low. Serve sprinkled with parsley.

PER SERVING (1 chicken thigh and ½ cup vegetables): 233 Cal, 10 g Total Fat, 2 g Sat Fat, 0 g Trans Fat, 49 mg Chol, 384 mg Sod, 21 g Carb, 6 g Sugar, 4 g Fib, 17 g Prot, 68 mg Calc.

Healthy Extra Serve the chicken and vegetables with a side of mashed rutabaga sprinkled with chopped fresh parsley.

Chicken Pot au Feu

11 PointsPlus® value
PER SERVING

serves **4**

1 (32-ounce) container reduced-sodium chicken broth

12 small red potatoes, halved

6 small carrots, cut on diagonal into 2-inch lengths

1 turnip, cut into 8 wedges

2 leeks (white parts only), cleaned and thinly sliced

8 sprigs + 1 tablespoon chopped fresh flat-leaf parsley

4 garlic cloves, peeled

1 bay leaf

½ teaspoon salt

¼ teaspoon black pepper

4 (5-ounce) skinless chicken thighs, trimmed

4 teaspoons Dijon mustard

1 Combine broth, potatoes, carrots, turnip, leeks, parsley sprigs, garlic, bay leaf, salt, and pepper in 5- or 6-quart slow cooker; nestle chicken in vegetables. Cover and cook until chicken is cooked through and vegetables are softened, about 4 hours on low.

2 With slotted spoon, transfer chicken and vegetables to separate bowls. Pour broth through fine sieve set over large glass measure; discard solids. Serve broth in soup bowls sprinkled with half of chopped parsley; sprinkle chicken and vegetables with remaining parsley and serve with mustard.

PER SERVING (1 cup broth, 1 chicken thigh, and 1 cup vegetables): 425 Cal, 9 g Total Fat, 2 g Sat Fat, 0 g Trans Fat, 60 mg Chol, 633 mg Sod, 61 g Carb, 9 g Sugar, 8 g Fib, 28 g Prot, 113 mg Calc.

FYI Pot au feu, which means "pot on fire" in French, is a dish consisting of meat and vegetables cooked in a liquid, such as water. The resulting rich broth is served as the first course, followed by the meat and vegetables as the main course. Our lighter chicken version is equally satisfying.

Shredded Chicken Ragu with Pasta

8 PointsPlus® value
PER SERVING

serves **4**

1 (28-ounce) can crushed tomatoes packed in thick puree with basil

1 onion, finely chopped

3 fresh basil sprigs or 1 teaspoon dried basil

2 garlic cloves, minced

1 bay leaf

¼ teaspoon salt

¼ teaspoon black pepper

2 (5-ounce) skinless chicken thighs, trimmed

4 cups hot cooked whole wheat rotini

¼ cup grated Parmesan cheese

1 Combine tomatoes, onion, basil, garlic, bay leaf, salt, and pepper in 5- or 6-quart slow cooker; nestle chicken in vegetables. Cover and cook until chicken is cooked through, about 4 hours on low. Discard basil sprigs and bay leaf.

2 With slotted spoon, transfer chicken to cutting board. With two forks, shred chicken; discard bones. Return chicken to slow cooker along with rotini; toss until mixed well. Serve sprinkled with Parmesan.

PER SERVING (1¾ cups chicken mixture and 1 tablespoon cheese): 329 Cal, 5 g Total Fat, 2 g Sat Fat, 0 g Trans Fat, 29 mg Chol, 561 mg Sod, 51 g Carb, 10 g Sugar, 5 g Fib, 20 g Prot, 166 mg Calc.

Healthy Extra Begin your meal with a refreshing arugula, orange segment, and radicchio salad dressed with balsamic vinegar and a sprinkling of dried oregano.

Chicken Thighs Osso Buco

serves **4**

PER SERVING

1 (14½-ounce) can diced tomatoes

¼ cup reduced-sodium chicken broth

1 small carrot, cut into ¼-inch slices

1 small onion, finely chopped

3 sprigs + 1½ tablespoons chopped fresh flat-leaf parsley

2 garlic cloves, minced

¼ teaspoon salt

¼ teaspoon black pepper

4 (5-ounce) skinless chicken thighs, trimmed

½ teaspoon grated lemon zest

1   Combine tomatoes, broth, carrot, onion, parsley sprigs, half of garlic, the salt, and pepper in 5- or 6-quart slow cooker; nestle chicken in vegetables. Cover and cook until chicken is cooked through and vegetables are softened, about 4 hours on low.

2   With slotted spoon, transfer chicken to platter; discard parsley sprigs. With slotted spoon, transfer vegetables to bowl.

3   Mix together chopped parsley, the lemon zest, and remaining garlic; stir half of parsley mixture into vegetables. Serve chicken and vegetables sprinkled with remaining parsley mixture.

PER SERVING (1 chicken thigh, ¼ cup vegetables, and 1 tablespoon sauce): 150 Cal, 6 g Total Fat, 2 g Sat Fat, 0 g Trans Fat, 49 mg Chol, 436 mg Sod, 9 g Carb, 5 g Sugar, 2 g Fib, 15 g Prot, 38 mg Calc.

Healthy Extra   Serve the osso buco with a bowl of whole wheat couscous (⅔ cup cooked whole wheat couscous per serving will increase the *PointsPlus* value by 3).

Sausage & Bean Chili

serves **6**

PER SERVING

1 (20-ounce) package sweet or hot Italian-style turkey sausage, casings removed

1 tablespoon olive oil

1 large onion, thinly sliced

2 jalapeño peppers, seeded and minced

2 tablespoons chili powder

1 tablespoon ground coriander or cumin

2 garlic cloves, minced

4 (14½-ounce) cans no-salt-added diced tomatoes

2 (15½-ounce) cans no-salt-added small red or white beans, rinsed and drained

6 tablespoons shredded reduced-fat Monterey Jack cheese

6 tablespoons fat-free sour cream

1   Put sausage in large nonstick skillet and set over medium heat. Cook, breaking sausage apart with spoon, until beginning to brown, about 8 minutes. Transfer sausage to 5- or 6-quart slow cooker.

2   Add oil to skillet. Add onion and jalapeños; cook, stirring, until onion is softened, about 5 minutes. Stir in chili powder, coriander, and garlic; cook, stirring constantly, until fragrant, about 30 seconds. Transfer to slow cooker. Stir in tomatoes and beans. Cover and cook 4–6 hours on high or 8–10 hours on low.

3   Spoon chili evenly into 6 bowls; top evenly with Monterey Jack and sour cream.

PER SERVING (1⅔ cups chili, 1 tablespoon cheese, and 1 tablespoon sour cream): 386 Cal, 12 g Total Fat, 1 g Sat Fat, 0 g Trans Fat, 61 mg Chol, 775 mg Sod, 40 g Carb, 12 g Sugar, 9 g Fib, 28 g Prot, 222 mg Calc.

Healthy Extra   Serve this robust chili with bowls of diced red or yellow bell peppers, diced red onion, and coarsely chopped fresh cilantro.

Spicy Fisherman's Stew

4 PointsPlus value

PER SERVING

serves **4**

1 (14½-ounce) can diced tomatoes

½ cup bottled clam juice

1 small fennel bulb, finely chopped

1 onion, finely chopped

2 (3-inch) strips lemon zest, removed with vegetable peeler

1 garlic clove, minced

¼ teaspoon salt

¼ teaspoon cayenne

¾ pound tilapia fillets, cut into 1-inch pieces

½ pound large shrimp, peeled and deveined

½ pound mussels, scrubbed and debearded

⅓ cup chopped fresh flat-leaf parsley

1   Combine tomatoes, clam juice, fennel, onion, lemon zest, garlic, salt, and cayenne in 5- or 6-quart slow cooker. Cover and cook until vegetables are softened, about 4 hours on high.

2   About 30 minutes before cooking time is up, stir tilapia and shrimp into slow cooker; arrange mussels on top. Cover and cook until fish and shrimp are just opaque in center, about 30 minutes longer. Discard lemon zest and any mussels that do not open. Stir in parsley.

PER SERVING (1½ cups): 192 Cal, 2 g Total Fat, 1 g Sat Fat, 0 g Trans Fat, 131 mg Chol, 650 mg Sod, 13 g Carb, 6 g Sugar, 4 g Fib, 30 g Prot, 96 mg Calc.

FYI   You can use other mild white-fleshed fish in the tasty stew, including catfish, halibut, and monkfish.

Shrimp & Sausage Gumbo

6 PointsPlus value

PER SERVING

serves **4**

1 tablespoon canola oil

2 tablespoons all-purpose flour

2¼ cups no-salt-added chicken broth

4 celery stalks, halved lengthwise and cut into ½-inch slices

2 onions, cut into ½-inch pieces

1 green bell pepper, cut into ½-inch pieces

6 garlic cloves, minced

1 bay leaf

½ pound turkey kielbasa, cut on diagonal into thin slices

½ pound medium shrimp, peeled and deveined

6 scallions, thinly sliced

1   Heat oil in large nonstick skillet over medium heat; add flour and stir until blended. Cook, stirring constantly, until golden brown, about 12 minutes. Add 1 cup of broth and bring to boil, stirring frequently. Boil until slightly thickened, about 2 minutes (mixture will still be lumpy).

2   Add celery, onions, bell pepper, garlic, and bay leaf to skillet; cook, stirring constantly, until vegetables are softened, about 5 minutes.

3   Transfer vegetable mixture to 5- or 6-quart slow cooker. Stir in kielbasa and remaining 1¼ cups broth. Cover and cook 4–6 hours on high or 8–10 hours on low. About 30 minutes before cooking time is up, stir in shrimp and cook until just opaque in center, about 20 minutes longer. Discard bay leaf. Serve gumbo sprinkled with scallions.

PER SERVING (1½ cups): 248 Cal, 10 g Total Fat, 2 g Sat Fat, 0 g Trans Fat, 134 mg Chol, 741 mg Sod, 18 g Carb, 8 g Sugar, 4 g Fib, 22 g Prot, 85 mg Calc.

Healthy Extra   Serve this gumbo with a bowl of brown rice (⅔ cup cooked brown rice per serving will increase the *PointsPlus* value by 3).

Risotto with Shrimp, Peas & Parmesan

serves 4

PER SERVING

1 tablespoon olive oil

1 cup short-grain brown rice

2 cups reduced-sodium vegetable broth

2 large shallots, minced

¼ cup dry white wine

½ teaspoon salt

¼ teaspoon black pepper

¾ pound shrimp, peeled and deveined

1¼ cups frozen peas, thawed

½ cup grated Parmesan cheese

1   Heat oil in 5- or 6-quart slow cooker until hot, about 15 minutes on high. Add rice, stirring until coated. Stir in broth, shallots, wine, salt, and pepper.

2   Cover and cook until rice is tender but slightly chewy in center, about 1¾ hours on high. Stir in shrimp and cook, covered, until shrimp is just opaque in center, about 20 minutes longer. Stir in peas and Parmesan. Serve at once.

PER SERVING (1 cup): 389 Cal, 8 g Total Fat, 2 g Sat Fat, 0 g Trans Fat, 135 mg Chol, 696 mg Sod, 50 g Carb, 4 g Sugar, 5 g Fib, 24 g Prot, 184 mg Calc.

Healthy Extra   A bowl of diced peaches, plums, and mango is a light and flavorful way to end this meal.

Tuscan White Beans with Tomatoes, Basil & Shrimp

serves

4

PER SERVING

1 (15½-ounce) can cannellini (white kidney) beans, rinsed and drained

1 (14½-ounce) can petite diced tomatoes

1 small red onion, cut into ¼-inch dice

2 slices Canadian bacon, cut into ¼-inch pieces

1 garlic clove, minced

¼ teaspoon black pepper

¾ pound medium shrimp, peeled and deveined

2 tablespoons thinly sliced fresh basil

Combine beans, tomatoes, onion, bacon, garlic, and pepper in 5- or 6-quart slow cooker. Cover and cook 4–6 hours on high or 8–10 hours on low. Stir in shrimp, cover, and cook on high until shrimp is just opaque in center, about 20 minutes longer. Transfer to serving bowl; stir in basil. Serve hot or warm.

PER SERVING (scant 1 cup): 211 Cal, 2 g Total Fat, 1 g Sat Fat, 0 g Trans Fat, 133 mg Chol, 845 mg Sod, 24 g Carb, 6 g Sugar, 6 g Fib, 24 g Prot, 101 mg Calc.

Healthy Extra   Start your meal off with a salad of drained canned artichoke hearts tossed with baby arugula, halved cherry tomatoes, and thinly sliced scallions dressed with balsamic vinegar.

Summer Vegetable Risotto

serves

4

PER SERVING

1 tablespoon olive oil

1 shallot, minced

1 cup short-grain brown rice

1 garlic clove, minced

¼ cup dry white wine or vermouth

2 cups reduced-sodium vegetable broth

1 zucchini, grated

½ cup fresh corn kernels (about 1 ear of corn)

¼ teaspoon salt

⅛ teaspoon black pepper

1 cup halved cherry tomatoes

½ cup grated Parmesan cheese

3 tablespoons chopped fresh flat-leaf parsley

1   Heat oil in medium nonstick skillet over medium heat. Add shallot and cook, stirring frequently, until softened, about 5 minutes. Add rice and garlic; cook, stirring frequently, until rice is translucent, about 2 minutes. Add wine and cook until it is evaporated, about 2 minutes.

2   Transfer rice mixture to 5- or 6-quart slow cooker. Stir in broth, zucchini, corn, salt, and pepper. Cover and cook until rice is tender but slightly chewy in center, about 2 hours on high.

3   Stir tomatoes, Parmesan, and 2 tablespoons of parsley into risotto. Serve at once, sprinkled with remaining 1 tablespoon parsley.

PER SERVING (1 cup): 312 Cal, 8 g Total Fat, 2 g Sat Fat, 0 g Trans Fat, 9 mg Chol, 381 mg Sod, 49 g Carb, 4 g Sugar, 4 g Fib, 10 g Prot, 161 mg Calc.

Healthy Extra   Increase the cherry tomatoes to 1½ cups and use 2 zucchini.

Tomato-Mushroom Bolognese with Whole Grain Linguine

 serves 4

PER SERVING

1 (14½-ounce) can diced tomatoes

¾ cup canned tomato sauce

1 small onion, finely chopped

1 small carrot, finely chopped

1 small celery stalk with leaves, finely chopped

½ cup finely chopped cremini or white mushrooms

½ cup finely chopped fresh fennel

1 garlic clove, minced

⅛ teaspoon black pepper

½ cup grated Parmesan cheese

¼ cup reduced-fat (2%) milk, at room temperature

12 ounces whole grain linguine, cooked according to package directions

1   Combine tomatoes, tomato sauce, onion, carrot, celery, mushrooms, fennel, garlic, and pepper in 5- or 6-quart slow cooker. Cover and cook until vegetables are softened, about 3½ hours on low.

2   Stir together ¼ cup of Parmesan and the milk in small bowl; stir into vegetable mixture. Cook 30 minutes longer. Add linguine and toss until mixed well. Serve sprinkled with remaining ¼ cup cheese.

PER SERVING (1½ cups): 432 Cal, 5 g Total Fat, 2 g Sat Fat, 0 g Trans Fat, 10 mg Chol, 657 mg Sod, 83 g Carb, 11 g Sugar, 14 g Fib, 20 g Prot, 207 mg Calc.

FYI   A food processor makes quick work of finely chopping the vegetables. Process the hard vegetables first, then the soft ones.

Pasta, Bacon & Roasted Pepper Frittata

 serves 4

PER SERVING

2¼ cups fat-free egg substitute

½ cup grated Parmesan cheese

¼ teaspoon black pepper

1 cup frozen peas, thawed

5 slices Canadian bacon, halved and cut crosswise into matchsticks

½ cup coarsely chopped roasted red pepper

4 cups cooked whole wheat spaghetti

⅓ cup shredded part-skim mozzarella cheese

1   Whisk together egg substitute, Parmesan, and black pepper in large bowl. Stir in peas, bacon, and roasted pepper. Add spaghetti, stirring to combine.

2   Generously spray ceramic insert of 5- or 6-quart slow cooker with nonstick spray. Pour in egg mixture, making sure pasta is submerged. Sprinkle mozzarella over egg mixture, leaving 1-inch border all around to prevent frittata from sticking. Cover and cook until knife inserted into center of frittata comes out clean, about 2 hours on high.

3   Remove lid and lift out ceramic insert; let stand 15 minutes. With rubber spatula, loosen edges of frittata. Cut crosswise into thick slices. With inverted long metal spatula, transfer slices to platter. Serve hot, warm, or at room temperature.

PER SERVING (¼ of frittata): 261 Cal, 6 g Total Fat, 3 g Sat Fat, 0 g Trans Fat, 21 mg Chol, 619 mg Sod, 31 g Carb, 3 g Sugar, 7 g Fib, 23 g Prot, 181 mg Calc.

Healthy Extra   A dish of steamed asparagus, especially in the spring when it is at its most flavorful, makes a tasty side dish for the frittata.

Pasta, Bacon & Roasted Pepper Frittata

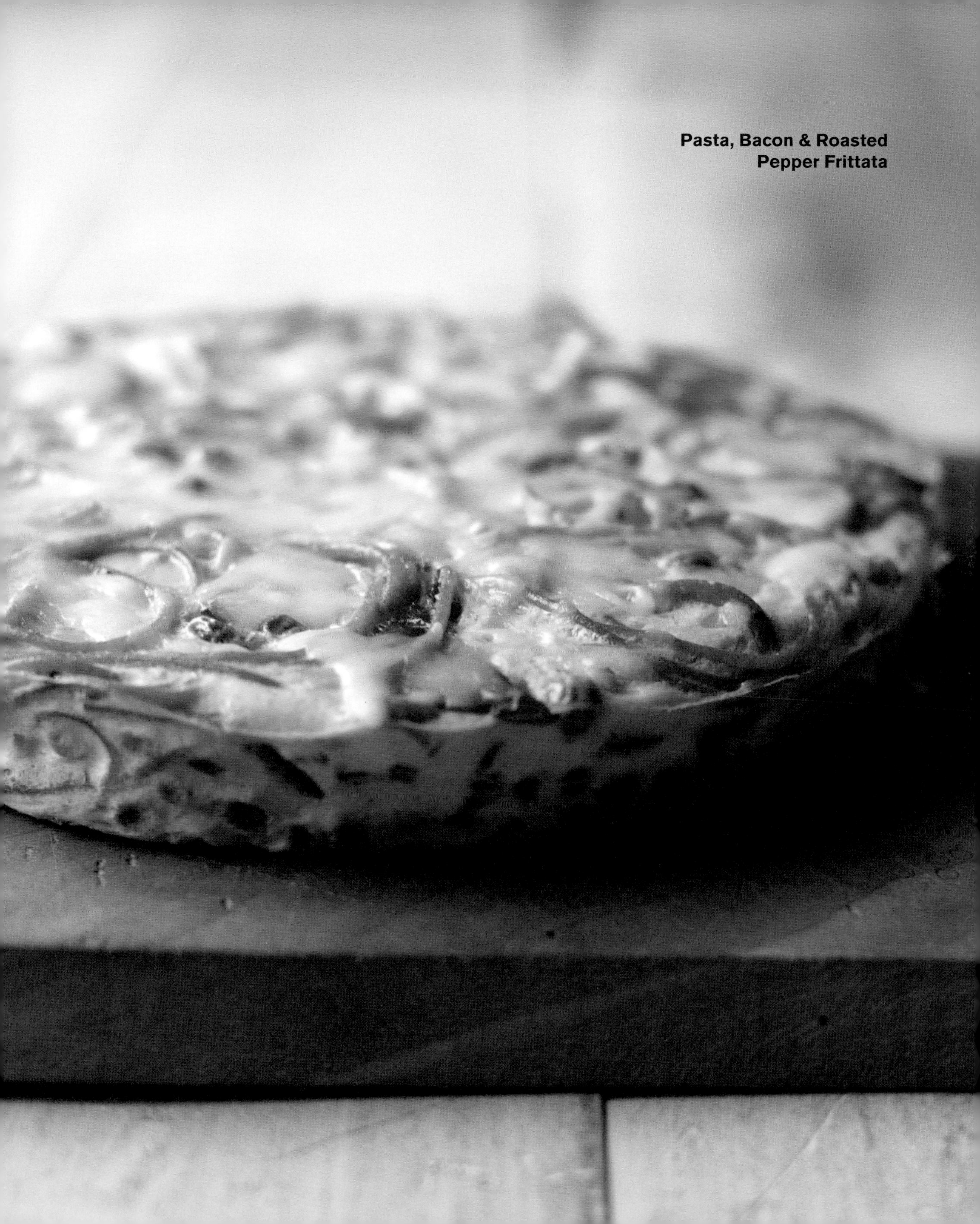

Turkey-Parmesan Meatball &
Escarole Soup

Turkey-Parmesan Meatball & Escarole Soup

6 PointsPlus® value
PER SERVING

serves **8**

2 slices whole wheat bread, crusts removed and cut into ½-inch pieces

¼ cup low-fat (1%) milk

1 (20½-ounce) package ground skinless turkey breast

½ cup grated Parmesan cheese

¼ cup fat-free egg substitute

1 large shallot, minced

3 tablespoons chopped fresh flat-leaf parsley

1 teaspoon salt

½ teaspoon black pepper

Pinch ground nutmeg

1 tablespoon olive oil

2 (32-ounce) containers reduced-sodium chicken broth

4 cups lightly packed thinly sliced escarole, Swiss chard, or kale

1 (15½-ounce) can cannellini (white kidney) beans, rinsed and drained

1   Mix together bread and milk in large bowl; let stand until softened, about 5 minutes. Add turkey, ¼ cup of Parmesan, the egg substitute, shallot, 2 tablespoons of parsley, the salt, pepper, and nutmeg, stirring until mixed well but not overmixed.

2   With damp hands, shape mixture into 24 meatballs, using about 2 tablespoons of turkey mixture for each meatball, transferring meatballs to sheet of foil as they are shaped. Wash bowl.

3   Heat oil in large nonstick skillet over medium-high heat. Add meatballs, in two batches, and cook until well browned on all sides, about 5 minutes per batch. Transfer to cleaned bowl as they are browned.

4   Combine broth, escarole, and beans in 5- or 6-quart slow cooker; add meatballs. Cover and cook until meatballs are cooked through, about 4 hours on low. Serve soup sprinkled with remaining ¼ cup cheese and 1 tablespoon parsley.

PER SERVING (1⅓ cups and 3 meatballs): 227 Cal, 6 g Total Fat, 2 g Sat Fat, 0 g Trans Fat, 34 mg Chol, 675 mg Sod, 16 g Carb, 2 g Sugar, 4 g Fib, 30 g Prot, 126 mg Calc.

Healthy Extra   Add 1 cup of sliced white or cremini mushrooms to the soup along with the meatballs in step 4.

Hanoi Chicken Pho

5 PointsPlus® value
PER SERVING

serves
6

3 scallions

2 (32-ounce) containers reduced-sodium chicken broth

3 (5-ounce) skinless boneless chicken breasts

2 slices crystallized ginger

2 garlic cloves, lightly crushed

1½ teaspoons coriander seeds, crushed

1 whole star anise or 3-inch cinnamon stick

½ teaspoon whole black peppercorns

¼ teaspoon salt

4 ounces rice stick noodles (vermicelli)

2½ cups lightly packed baby spinach

1½ cups halved cherry tomatoes

½ cup bean sprouts

¼ cup coarsely chopped fresh cilantro

2 tablespoons torn fresh mint leaves

Lime wedges

1 Thinly slice scallions, keeping white and green parts separated. Combine broth, chicken, white parts of scallions, the ginger, garlic, coriander, star anise, peppercorns, and salt in 5- or 6-quart slow cooker. Cover and cook 4–6 hours on high or 8–10 hours on low.

2 Meanwhile, put rice noodles in large bowl and add enough hot tap water to cover; cover bowl with plastic wrap and soak noodles until softened, about 10 minutes. Drain in colander; rinse under cold running water and drain again.

3 With slotted spoon, transfer chicken to cutting board. When cool enough to handle, shred chicken. Pour broth through fine sieve set over same large bowl; discard solids. Return chicken to broth along with noodles.

4 Divide spinach evenly among 6 soup bowls. Ladle 1⅔ cups soup into each bowl. Top each serving with one-sixth each of tomatoes, scallion greens, bean sprouts, cilantro, and mint. Serve with lime wedges.

PER SERVING (1¾ cups): 211 Cal, 4 g Total Fat, 1 g Sat Fat, 0 g Trans Fat, 39 mg Chol, 251 mg Sod, 24 g Carb, 2 g Sugar, 1 g Fib, 21 g Prot, 47 mg Calc.

FYI Pho, pronounced fuh, is a traditional Vietnamese noodle dish that usually consists of meat and wide rice noodles in a broth flavored with seasonings that include star anise, ginger, and onion.

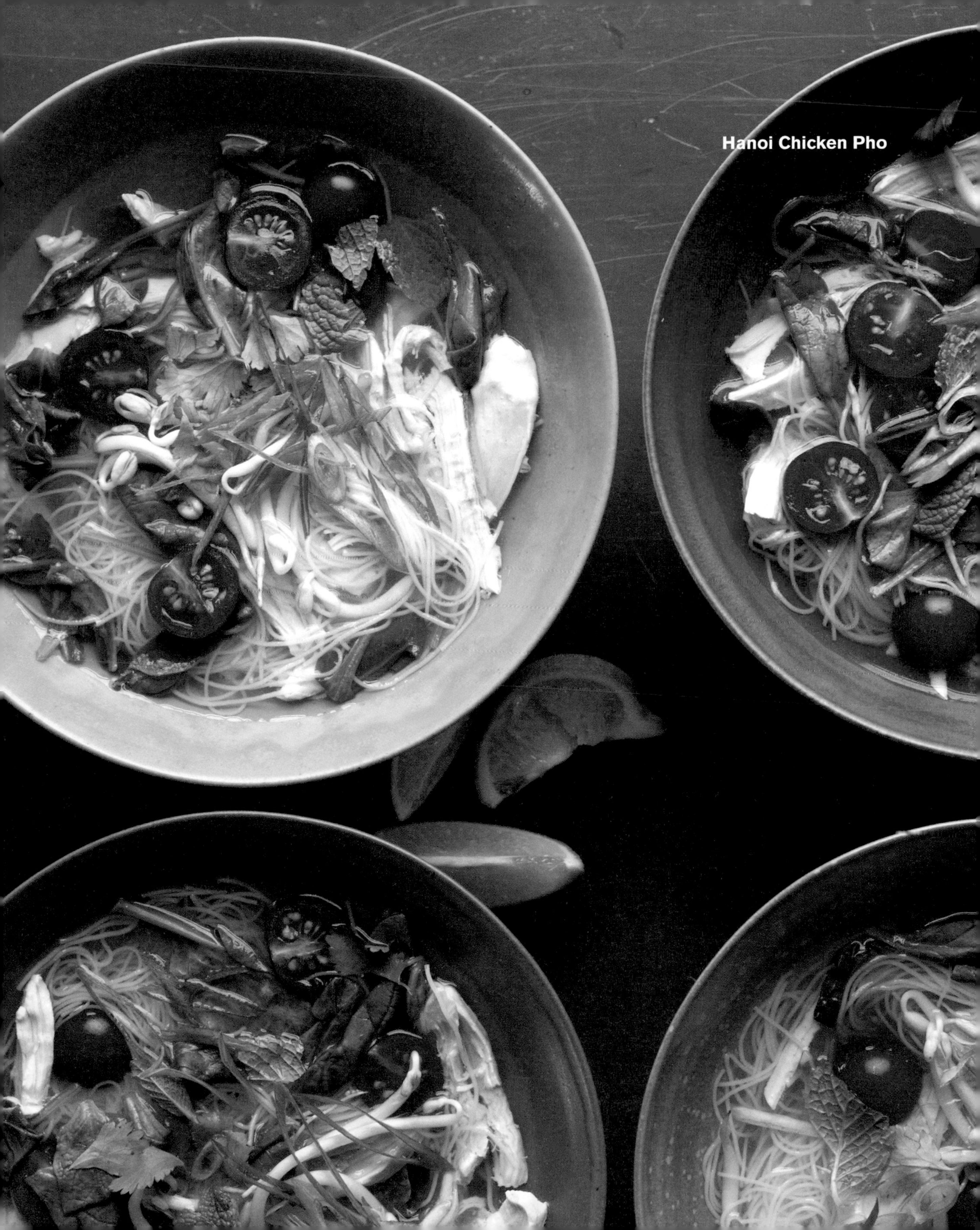

Hanoi Chicken Pho

Double Mushroom Soup

Double Mushroom Soup

serves
4

PER SERVING

1 (.35-ounce) package dried mushrooms, preferably porcini

½ cup boiling water

3 cups reduced-sodium beef or vegetable broth

½ pound small white mushrooms, sliced

1 carrot, halved lengthwise and sliced

1 celery stalk with leaves, thinly sliced

1 small red onion, quartered and thinly sliced

1 small bay leaf

¾ teaspoon dried dill

½ teaspoon salt

⅛ teaspoon black pepper

2 tablespoons chopped fresh flat-leaf parsley

8 tablespoons reduced-fat sour cream

2 slices Canadian bacon, cut into matchsticks

1   Combine dried mushrooms and water in small bowl. Let stand until softened, about 20 minutes. Transfer mushrooms and liquid to sieve set over medium bowl. Reserve mushroom liquid. Rinse mushrooms to remove any grit; pat dry with paper towels and finely chop. Pour mushroom liquid into 5- or 6-quart slow cooker.

2   Add broth, dried mushrooms, fresh mushrooms, carrot, celery, onion, bay leaf, dill, salt, and pepper to slow cooker. Cover and cook 3 hours on high or 6 hours on low. Discard bay leaf. Stir in 1 tablespoon of parsley.

3   Ladle soup evenly into each of 4 soup bowls. Top each serving with 2 tablespoons of sour cream and one-fourth of bacon; sprinkle evenly with remaining 1 tablespoon parsley.

PER SERVING (1¼ cups): 145 Cal, 7 g Total Fat, 3 g Sat Fat, 0 g Trans Fat, 18 mg Chol, 581 mg Sod, 10 g Carb, 4 g Sugar, 2 g Fib, 11 g Prot, 79 mg Calc.

FYI   Be sure to rinse the dried mushrooms thoroughly to remove all the grit.

Hearty Moroccan Lamb-Vegetable Soup

PER SERVING

serves
6

1 tablespoon olive oil

2 red onions, thinly sliced

2 garlic cloves, minced

1½ teaspoons ground coriander

1 teaspoon ground ginger

1 teaspoon ground cumin

1 teaspoon ground turmeric

½ teaspoon salt

¼ teaspoon black pepper

¾ pound boneless leg of lamb, trimmed and cut into ½-inch pieces

1 (32-ounce) container reduced-sodium vegetable or chicken broth

1 (15½-ounce) can chickpeas, rinsed and drained

1 (14½-ounce) can diced tomatoes

2 carrots, quartered lengthwise and thinly sliced

1 cup lightly packed fresh cilantro leaves

1   Heat oil in large nonstick skillet over medium-high heat. Add onions and cook, stirring frequently, until lightly browned, about 8 minutes. Add garlic, coriander, ginger, cumin, turmeric, salt, and pepper; cook, stirring constantly, until fragrant, about 30 seconds.

2   Transfer onion mixture to 5- or 6-quart slow cooker; add lamb, broth, chickpeas, tomatoes, and carrots. Cover and cook until vegetables are softened, 4–6 hours on high or 8–10 hours on low. Stir in cilantro.

PER SERVING (1⅓ cups): 223 Cal, 8 g Total Fat, 2 g Sat Fat, 0 g Trans Fat, 45 mg Chol, 650 mg Sod, 21 g Carb, 7 g Sugar, 5 g Fib, 16 g Prot, 62 mg Calc.

FYI   This robust soup is known as harira. It is often served for dinner during Ramadan to break the fast.

Manhattan Clam-Bacon Chowder

4 PointsPlus® value
PER SERVING

serves
4

3 cups reduced-sodium vegetable broth

1 (14½-ounce) can petite diced tomatoes

1 (10-ounce) can baby clams

1 red potato, scrubbed and cut into ½-inch dice

1 red onion, quartered and thinly sliced

1 celery stalk with leaves, thinly sliced

2 slices Canadian bacon, finely chopped

6 sprigs + ⅓ cup chopped fresh flat-leaf parsley

⅛ teaspoon black pepper

Combine broth, tomatoes, clams with their juice, potato, onion, celery, bacon, parsley sprigs, and pepper in 5- or 6-quart slow cooker. Cover and cook until vegetables are softened, 4–6 hours on high or 8–10 hours on low. Discard parsley sprigs. Serve sprinkled with chopped parsley.

PER SERVING (1½ cups): 180 Cal, 3 g Total Fat, 1 g Sat Fat, 0 g Trans Fat, 64 mg Chol, 908 mg Sod, 22 g Carb, 7 g Sugar, 3 g Fib, 16 g Prot, 143 mg Calc.

Healthy Extra   Add 1 carrot, cut into small dice, to the soup along with the celery.

Squash Soup with Tuscan White Beans

5 PointsPlus® value
PER SERVING

serves
4

5 cups reduced-sodium vegetable or chicken broth

2 cups (½-inch) cubes butternut or acorn squash

1 (15½-ounce) can cannellini (white kidney) beans, rinsed and drained

1 (14½-ounce) can diced tomatoes

2 slender carrots, thinly sliced

2 small red onions, thinly sliced

2 garlic cloves, minced

¼ teaspoon salt

¼ teaspoon black pepper

⅓ cup chopped fresh flat-leaf parsley

¼ cup grated Parmesan cheese

Combine broth, squash, beans, tomatoes, carrots, onions, garlic, salt, and pepper in 5- or 6- quart slow cooker. Cover and cook 4–6 hours on high or 8–10 hours on low. Stir in parsley and serve sprinkled with Parmesan.

PER SERVING (2 cups): 196 Cal, 2 g Total Fat, 1 g Sat Fat, 0 g Trans Fat, 4 mg Chol, 713 mg Sod, 36 g Carb, 9 g Sugar, 9 g Fib, 10 g Prot, 193 mg Calc.

Healthy Extra   Start your meal with an autumn salad of crisp greens topped with ½ cup of drained canned unsweetened mandarin orange segments and ⅓ cup of pomegranate seeds sprinkled with lime juice and a touch of salt and black pepper.

ON THE
GRILL

CHAPTER 9

ON THE GRILL

NO-FUSS MEAT, CHICKEN, FISH & VEGETARIAN DISHES

Grilling imparts incomparable flavor to food, which is just one reason why it is a favorite American pastime. Whether the food is cooked on a state-of-the-art gas grill, a tabletop hibachi, or a kettle grill, all grills are pretty much the same. By definition a grill is a cooking unit that has parallel metal bars or rungs on which food is placed and is fueled underneath by charcoal or gas. Cooking over an open wood fire is also considered grilling, but nothing beats the convenience of a modern-type grill.

Types

Americans love **gas grills.** Since introduced in the 1960s, gas grills have become the most popular way of grilling—and for good reason. They are easy to ignite, heat up quickly, and maintain constant heat. Lastly, they are a snap to clean. The simplest gas grill has two burners, propane ignition, a small end table, a storage bin, and a thermometer, which indicates the cooking temperature. Midpriced models have three burners, a built-in thermometer, propane ignition, a funnel and tray that collect the fat that drips off, and a warming rack at the back of the grill. High-end models resemble stoves with their sleek stainless-steel exterior, four powerful burners, smoker box, rotisserie attachment, side shelves, and storage cabinets. These grills are great for grilling a large amount of food at one time.

Charcoal grills are another way to cook outdoors. The most popular charcoal grill is the kettle grill, which was invented by George Stephen, a metalworker. He fashioned two halves of a nautical buoy together and the kettle grill was born. The concept behind this grill is simplicity itself: The coals are piled in the bottom half of the grill and a rack is placed on top. The domed lid, which has vents, allows the user to slow-cook whole chickens or large pieces of meat, as well as to smoke foods over indirect heat (not directly over the coals). When using a charcoal grill, allow about 30 minutes for the coals to become ashed over (light gray all over). Also available are portable kettle grills, great for tailgate parties and picnics.

The **hibachi** is a small Japanese tabletop grill that is fueled by charcoal. It consists of a small firebox for the charcoal and two square adjustable grates that can be moved closer to or farther away from the heat. Hibachis are best for grilling smaller foods, such as steaks, kebabs, chops, chicken parts, shrimp, and vegetables.

Newer to the market are **electric grills,** which resemble inverted broilers with the heating element underneath—instead of above—the food. The heat is regulated using a knob or touch-pad control, with tabletop as well as full-size models available. These grills deliver lots of heat and the ability to sear food well and provide grill marks. The drawbacks are a lack of authentic fire flavor and the inability to cook whole chickens or large pieces of meat using the indirect method.

Caring for Your Grill

When your gas or charcoal grill is at temperature but before you begin grilling, take a metal bristle barbecue brush and run it back and forth over the grill rack until all of the charred particles are removed. Alternatively, you can scrub the grill clean as soon as the food is removed (while the grill is still hot). Depending on how much you use your grill, the interior will need to be cleaned from time to time. Refer to the manufacturer's instructions.

Fueling the Fire

Charcoal briquettes are the most common fuel used. They are available in supermarkets, hardware stores, and some kitchenware stores. Also available are self-starting briquettes that have been infused with lighter fluid; a long match ignites them instantly. (Do not mix them with regular briquettes.)

Hardwood charcoal, also known as lump charcoal, is made from logs that are burned and broken into chunks. It is the fuel of choice for many grilling aficionados for its ability to burn very hot and because it is all natural.

Apple, mesquite, hickory, and oak wood chunks are another fuel option. They burn hot and impart tempting smoky flavor. Apple, hickory, and oak lend food a delicate smokiness, while mesquite lends food a more intense smoky flavor.

Lighting up the Grill

To light a gas grill, follow the manufacturer's instructions. For charcoal grills, there are several options:

A **chimney starter** is a large open-ended metal cylinder with a handle on the side. Crumpled newspaper is put into the bottom and topped with charcoal. The paper is lit through a hole in the bottom of the cylinder and glowing coals are ready in about 15 minutes.

An **electric starter** is a loop-shaped heating element that is nestled into the charcoal until the coals burn red, which takes about 5 minutes. The starter is then removed and the coals are given time to become ashed over (light gray all over). Be sure to cool the starter on a heatproof surface, such as cement, safely away from where it could be accidentally touched.

Paraffin starters are small waxy cubes that can be used in place of newspaper in a chimney starter.

Lighter fluid is an easy and popular way to get a charcoal fire going. For safety's sake, douse the charcoal with fluid, then close the can and put it away before lighting the grill with a match or butane grill lighter.

Adding More Flavor to a Gas or Charcoal Grill

Apple, hickory, mesquite, and cherry wood chips add smoky flavor to grilled food without a lot of fuss. Soak about 1 cup of chips in water for at least 30 minutes or up to 1 hour and drain well. Toss the chips directly onto the hot coals or, if using a gas grill, put them in a smoker box or foil package with some holes poked in and place on the lit burners.

Lemon-Soy Marinated London Broil with Celery Salad

serves
6

⅓ cup lemon juice

2 tablespoons reduced-sodium soy sauce

1 tablespoon extra-virgin olive oil

2 garlic cloves, minced

1 teaspoon dried oregano

½ teaspoon dried thyme

1 (1¼-pound) top round steak, trimmed

1 teaspoon salt

¼ + ⅛ teaspoon black pepper

2 cups sliced celery with leaves

½ cup halved cherry tomatoes

4 large radishes, thinly sliced

¼ cup lightly packed fresh flat-leaf parsley leaves

1 To make marinade, whisk together lemon juice, soy sauce, oil, garlic, oregano, and thyme in small bowl; reserve 2 tablespoons for celery salad. Transfer remaining marinade to large zip-close plastic bag; add steak. Squeeze out air and seal bag; turn to coat steak. Refrigerate, turning bag occasionally, at least 2 hours or up to 6 hours.

2 Spray grill rack with nonstick spray. Preheat grill to medium-high or prepare medium-high fire.

3 Remove steak from marinade; discard marinade. Sprinkle steak with ¾ teaspoon of salt and ¼ teaspoon of pepper. Place steak on grill rack and grill until instant-read thermometer inserted into center of steak registers 145°F for medium, about 6 minutes per side. Transfer steak to cutting board and let stand 10 minutes.

4 Meanwhile, to make salad, toss together celery, tomatoes, radishes, parsley, reserved marinade, and remaining ¼ teaspoon salt and ⅛ teaspoon pepper in serving bowl.

5 Cut steak on angle against grain into 18 slices. Serve with salad.

PER SERVING (3 slices steak and ½ cup salad): 181 Cal, 9 g Total Fat, 3 g Sat Fat, 0 g Trans Fat, 40 mg Chol, 626 mg Sod, 4 g Carb, 1 g Sugar, 1 g Fib, 22 g Prot, 32 mg Calc.

Healthy Extra   Add a 15½-ounce can of rinsed and drained chickpeas to the celery salad. This will increase the per-serving *PointsPlus* value by 2.

**Lemon-Soy Marinated London Broil
with Celery Salad**

Pepper-Rubbed Filets Mignons with Hobo-Pack Potatoes

serves
4

4 garlic cloves, minced

2 teaspoons coarsely ground rainbow peppercorns

1 teaspoon salt

4 (¼-pound) filets mignons, about 1 inch thick, trimmed

1 pound Yukon Gold potatoes, scrubbed and cut into ½-inch slices

1 tablespoon chopped fresh rosemary

2 teaspoons olive oil

1 teaspoon grated lemon zest

1   Spray grill rack with nonstick spray. Preheat grill to high or prepare hot fire.

2   Mix together half of garlic, the peppercorns, and ½ teaspoon of salt on sheet of wax paper; rub on both sides of steaks; let stand at room temperature while cooking potatoes.

3   Tear off 4 sheets of heavy-duty foil. Toss together potatoes, rosemary, oil, lemon zest, remaining garlic, and ½ teaspoon salt in large bowl until coated evenly. Divide potatoes evenly among foil sheets and loosely wrap to enclose potatoes.

4   If using gas grill, place foil packs on grill rack and reduce heat to medium-low; if using charcoal grill, place packs along edges of grill rack where it is cooler. Grill until potatoes are tender, about 25 minutes, turning packs over after 15 minutes. Transfer to cooler part of grill and keep warm.

5   If using gas grill, increase heat to high. Place steaks on grill rack and grill until instant-read thermometer inserted into side of steak registers 145°F for medium, about 5 minutes per side. Transfer steaks to cutting board and let stand 5 minutes. Serve with potatoes.

PER SERVING (1 steak and 1 hobo pack): 286 Cal, 9 g Total Fat, 3 g Sat Fat, 0 g Trans Fat, 67 mg Chol, 673 mg Sod, 21 g Carb, 0 g Sugar, 2 g Fib, 27 g Prot, 26 mg Calc.

FYI   Rainbow pepper is a mix of pink, white, and black peppercorns. It can be found in many supermarkets and specialty food stores. Pink peppercorns are not a true peppercorn but the berry of a rose plant. White peppercorns are black peppercorns that have ripened and been skinned, while black peppercorns are picked when the berries are not quite ripe, then dried.

Grilled Colombian-Style Flank Steak & Okra with Creamy Avocado

serves
4

PER SERVING

½ cup dark beer

2 tablespoons Worcestershire sauce

1 teaspoon ground cumin

¾ teaspoon salt

½ teaspoon black pepper

1 (1-pound) flank steak, trimmed

½ pound okra

1 Hass avocado, halved and pitted

2 scallions, finely chopped

1 jalapeño pepper, seeded and minced

2 tablespoons lime juice

1   Combine beer, Worcestershire sauce, cumin, ¼ teaspoon of salt, and ¼ teaspoon of black pepper in large zip-close plastic bag and add steak. Squeeze out air and seal bag. Refrigerate, turning bag occasionally, at least 1 hour or up to 6 hours.

2   Spray grill rack with nonstick spray. Preheat grill to high or prepare hot fire. If using wooden skewers, soak 8 (8-inch) skewers in water 30 minutes.

3   Remove steak from marinade; discard marinade. Wipe off excess marinade from steak. Place steak on grill rack and grill until instant-read thermometer inserted into side of steak registers 145°F for medium, about 5 minutes per side. Transfer to cutting board; keep warm.

4   Meanwhile, thread okra evenly onto 2 parallel skewers, holding skewers about ¾-inch apart. Lightly spray okra with nonstick spray and sprinkle with ¼ teaspoon of salt. Place skewers on grill rack and grill until okra is lightly charred and softened, about 4 minutes. Transfer to platter.

5   Scoop avocado into serving bowl and coarsely mash. Stir in scallions, jalapeño, lime juice, and remaining ¼ teaspoon salt and ¼ teaspoon pepper.

6   Cut steak into 12 slices; transfer to platter with okra. Serve with avocado mixture.

PER SERVING (3 slices steak, ¼ of okra, and ¼ cup avocado mixture): 255 Cal, 12 g Total Fat, 3 g Sat Fat, 0 g Trans Fat, 42 mg Chol, 732 mg Sod, 10 g Carb, 1 g Sugar, 5 g Fib, 26 g Prot, 78 mg Calc.

Beef-Mushroom Yakitori

5 PointsPlus value
PER SERVING

serves
4

3 tablespoons reduced-sodium soy sauce

2 tablespoons packed brown sugar

1 tablespoon yellow miso

2 teaspoons canola oil

1 teaspoon Asian (dark) sesame oil

1 large garlic clove, minced

¾ pound beef tenderloin, trimmed and cut into ¾-inch chunks

6 ounces cremini mushrooms, halved

3 scallions, cut into 1½-inch lengths

1 teaspoon toasted sesame seeds

1 Spray grill rack with nonstick spray. Preheat grill to medium-high or prepare medium-high fire. If using wooden skewers, soak 4 (10-inch) skewers in water about 30 minutes.

2 To make glaze, whisk together soy sauce, brown sugar, miso, canola oil, sesame oil, and garlic in small bowl until brown sugar is dissolved.

3 Alternately thread beef, mushrooms, and scallions onto skewers. Place skewers on grill rack and grill, turning and brushing with glaze, until beef is lightly charred and cooked to medium doneness and mushrooms and scallions are tender, about 6 minutes. Transfer to platter and sprinkle with sesame seeds.

PER SERVING (1 skewer): 216 Cal, 9 g Total Fat, 2 g Sat Fat, 0 g Trans Fat, 50 mg Chol, 580 mg Sod, 12 g Carb, 9 g Sugar, 1 g Fib, 21 g Prot, 39 mg Calc.

Healthy Extra   Round out the meal with a bowl of brown rice (⅔ cup cooked brown rice per serving will increase the *PointsPlus* value by 3).

Rosemary-Rubbed Pork Tenderloin with Grilled Tomatoes

serves
4

1 (1-pound) pork tenderloin, trimmed

3 tablespoons chopped fresh parsley

2 tablespoons lemon juice

1 tablespoon finely chopped fresh rosemary

3 garlic cloves, minced

1 large shallot, minced

1 tablespoon extra-virgin olive oil

1 teaspoon salt

¼ teaspoon black pepper

2 tomatoes, cut crosswise in half

1   Place pork between 2 sheets of wax paper. With meat mallet or bottom of small heavy saucepan, pound to ½-inch thickness.

2   To make marinade, whisk together all remaining ingredients except tomatoes in small bowl; reserve 1 tablespoon marinade. Transfer remaining marinade to large zip-close plastic bag; add pork. Squeeze out air and seal bag; turn to coat pork. Refrigerate, turning bag occasionally, at least 2 hours or up to 6 hours.

3   Spray grill rack with nonstick spray. Preheat grill to medium-high or prepare medium-high fire.

4   Remove pork from marinade; discard marinade. Place pork on grill rack and grill, turning, until instant-read thermometer inserted into center of pork registers 145°F for medium, about 20 minutes. Transfer to cutting board and let stand 10 minutes.

5   Meanwhile, brush cut sides of tomatoes with reserved marinade. Place tomatoes on grill rack, cut sides down, and grill until lightly charred and softened, about 5 minutes. Cut pork on diagonal into 12 slices and serve with tomatoes.

PER SERVING (3 slices pork and 1 tomato half): 177 Cal, 7 g Total Fat, 2 g Sat Fat, 0 g Trans Fat, 62 mg Chol, 636 mg Sod, 5 g Carb, 2 g Sugar, 1 g Fib, 23 g Prot, 25 mg Calc.

Healthy Extra   Serve bulgur sprinkled with chopped fresh parsley alongside the pork and tomatoes (½ cup cooked bulgur per serving will increase the *PointsPlus* value by 2).

**Mojo Pork Chops with Grilled
Plantains**

Mojo Pork Chops with Grilled Plantains

serves 4

PER SERVING

2 garlic cloves, minced

1 teaspoon dried oregano

¾ teaspoon salt

4 (6-ounce) bone-in pork rib chops, ½ inch thick, trimmed

2 very ripe plantains, unpeeled

¼ cup lime juice

1 teaspoon grated orange zest

2 tablespoons orange juice

1 tablespoon chopped fresh cilantro

½ serrano pepper, seeded and minced

1 teaspoon extra-virgin olive oil

1 Spray grill rack with nonstick spray. Preheat grill to medium-high or prepare medium-high fire.

2 Stir together half of garlic, the oregano, and ½ teaspoon of salt in small bowl. Rub on both sides of pork chops. Place chops on grill rack and grill until instant-read thermometer inserted into side of chop registers 145°F for medium, about 5 minutes per side. Transfer to platter; keep warm. Leave grill on.

3 Cut plantains lengthwise in half. Place plantains on grill rack and grill, turning occasionally, until tender, about 8 minutes. Add plantains to platter.

4 To make sauce, whisk together lime juice, orange zest and juice, remaining garlic, the cilantro, serrano, oil, and remaining ¼ teaspoon salt in small bowl. Spoon over pork and plantains.

PER SERVING (1 pork chop, ½ plantain, and 1½ tablespoons sauce): 283 Cal, 8 g Total Fat, 2 g Sat Fat, 0 g Trans Fat, 71 mg Chol, 488 mg Sod, 31 g Carb, 14 g Sugar, 2 g Fib, 24 g Prot, 33 mg Calc.

Healthy Extra Serve a dish of grilled red onion wedges and cherry tomatoes alongside the succulent pork chops.

Leg of Lamb with Aleppo Pepper & Lemony Couscous Salad

serves
8

1 cup plain fat-free yogurt

2 garlic cloves, minced

1½ teaspoons salt

1 teaspoon dried mint

1 teaspoon Aleppo pepper or ¼ teaspoon red pepper flakes

1 (2-pound) boneless leg of lamb, trimmed and butterflied

2 red bell peppers

2 zucchini, cut into ½-inch lengthwise slices

1 small eggplant (about ¾ pound) unpeeled and cut into ½-inch rounds

3 cups hot cooked whole wheat couscous

¼ cup lemon juice

¼ cup chopped fresh flat-leaf parsley

1 Combine yogurt, garlic, 1 teaspoon of salt, the mint, and ¼ teaspoon of Aleppo pepper in large zip-close plastic bag; add lamb. Squeeze out air and seal bag; turn to coat lamb. Refrigerate, turning bag occasionally, at least 4 hours or up to overnight.

2 Spray grill rack with nonstick spray. Preheat grill to medium-high or prepare medium-high fire.

3 Place bell peppers on grill rack and grill, turning occasionally, until peppers are softened and skins are blackened, about 10 minutes. Transfer to clean large zip-close plastic bag; seal bag. Let peppers steam 10 minutes.

4 Meanwhile, lightly spray zucchini and eggplant with nonstick spray. Place on grill rack and grill, turning, until softened and lightly browned, about 6 minutes. Transfer to cutting board; let cool.

5 Wipe off excess yogurt mixture from lamb. Place on grill rack and grill, turning, until instant-read thermometer inserted into thickest part of lamb registers 145°F for medium, about 25 minutes. Transfer to cutting board. Let stand 10 minutes.

6 Meanwhile, peel and seed roasted bell peppers and coarsely chop. Transfer to serving bowl. Chop zucchini and eggplant and add to bowl along with couscous, lemon juice, parsley, and remaining ½ teaspoon salt and ¾ teaspoon Aleppo pepper. Toss until mixed well. Cut lamb across grain into 32 slices. Serve with couscous salad.

PER SERVING (4 slices lamb and 1 cup couscous salad): 284 Cal, 10 g Total Fat, 4 g Sat Fat, 0 g Trans Fat, 90 mg Chol, 541 mg Sod, 21 g Carb, 6 g Sugar, 4 g Fib, 29 g Prot, 98 mg Calc.

FYI Aleppo pepper comes from northern Syria near the town of Aleppo. It has a medium level of heat with fruity undertones, as well as hints of cumin and salt. Use it to add authentic chile flavor to Mediterranean dishes. It can be purchased online at thespicehouse.com and at kalustyans.com.

Jerk Pork Kebabs with Mango & Bell Pepper

PER SERVING

2 tablespoons lime juice

1 teaspoon sugar

½ teaspoon curry powder

1 pound boneless pork loin chops, trimmed and cut into 1-inch chunks

2 teaspoons jerk seasoning

1 red bell pepper, cut into 2-inch pieces

1 yellow bell pepper, cut into 2-inch pieces

4 scallions, cut into 2-inch lengths

1 mango, pitted, peeled, and cut into 1-inch chunks

1 Spray grill rack with nonstick spray. Preheat grill to medium-high or prepare medium-high fire. If using wooden skewers, soak 8 (8-inch) skewers in water 30 minutes.

2 To make sauce, whisk together lime juice, sugar, and curry powder in small bowl.

3 Sprinkle pork with jerk seasoning. Alternately thread pork, bell peppers, scallions, and mango onto skewers. Place skewers on grill rack and grill, turning occasionally, until pork is cooked through and vegetables and mango are well marked and tender, about 8 minutes. Transfer skewers to platter and spoon sauce over top.

PER SERVING (2 skewers and about 2 teaspoons sauce): 209 Cal, 6 g Total Fat, 2 g Sat Fat, 0 g Trans Fat, 66 mg Chol, 190 mg Sod, 16 g Carb, 11 g Sugar, 2 g Fib, 23 g Prot, 44 mg Calc.

Healthy Extra Serve these skewers accompanied by brown or brown basmati rice (⅔ cup cooked brown rice per serving will increase the *PointsPlus* value by 3).

Kofta Kebabs over Blueberry-Mint Couscous

PER SERVING

1 pound ground lean lamb

¼ cup snipped fresh dill

2 garlic cloves, minced

2 teaspoons dried oregano

1½ teaspoons ground cumin

1 teaspoon salt

½ teaspoon black pepper

⅛ teaspoon cayenne

2 cups cooked whole wheat couscous, at room temperature

½ cup fresh blueberries

¼ cup chopped fresh mint

2 teaspoons extra-virgin olive oil

Grated zest of ½ lemon

Lemon wedges

1 Spray grill rack with olive oil nonstick spray. Preheat grill to medium or prepare medium fire.

2 Mix together lamb, dill, garlic, oregano, cumin, ¾ teaspoon of salt, ¼ teaspoon of black pepper, and cayenne in large bowl until mixed well but not overmixed. With damp hands, shape into 8 equal meatballs; thread evenly onto 4 (8-inch) metal skewers. Spray with nonstick spray.

3 Place skewers on grill rack and grill, turning, until meatballs are cooked through, about 10 minutes.

4 Meanwhile, mix together couscous, blueberries, mint, oil, lemon zest, and remaining ¼ teaspoon salt and ¼ teaspoon black pepper in large bowl. Spoon couscous mixture onto platter and top with kebabs. Serve with lemon wedges.

PER SERVING (1 skewer and ¾ cup couscous mixture): 257 Cal, 10 g Total Fat, 3 g Sat Fat, 0 g Trans Fat, 64 mg Chol, 644 mg Sod, 20 g Carb, 2 g Sugar, 4 g Fib, 23 g Prot, 49 mg Calc.

Lamb Burgers with Charred Onions & Feta

serves
4

4 (½-inch) onion slices

¾ pound ground lean lamb

½ pound ground lean pork, such as tenderloin

¼ cup minced onion

2 large garlic cloves, minced

1 teaspoon dried oregano

1 teaspoon dried dill

1 teaspoon ground cumin

¼ teaspoon salt

¼ teaspoon black pepper

4 whole wheat hamburger buns, split

12 arugula leaves

2 tomatoes, thinly sliced

8 tablespoons crumbled fat-free feta cheese

1   Spray grill rack with nonstick spray. Preheat grill to medium-high or prepare medium-high fire.

2   Spray onion slices with olive oil nonstick spray. Place onion on grill rack and grill, turning once, until lightly charred and softened, about 6 minutes. Transfer to cutting board; chop.

3   Mix together lamb, pork, minced onion, garlic, oregano, dill, cumin, salt, and pepper in large bowl until mixed well but not overmixed. With damp hands, shape into 4 equal patties.

4   Place patties on grill rack and grill until instant-read thermometer inserted into side of burger registers 160°F for well done, about 5 minutes per side. Meanwhile, place buns, cut sides down, on grill rack and grill until toasted, about 2 minutes.

5   Place 3 arugula leaves and one-fourth of tomatoes on bottom half of each bun; top each with burger. Top each burger with one-fourth of charred onion and 2 tablespoons of feta. Cover with tops of buns.

PER SERVING (1 garnished burger): 355 Cal, 10 g Total Fat, 3 g Sat Fat, 0 g Trans Fat, 83 mg Chol, 582 mg Sod, 31 g Carb, 7 g Sugar, 5 g Fib, 35 g Prot, 167 mg Calc.

Healthy Extra   Serve a fresh cucumber salad of thinly sliced unpeeled English (seedless) cucumber, snipped fresh dill, minced garlic, and a splash of unseasoned rice vinegar.

Lamb Burgers with Charred
Onions & Feta

Applewood-Smoked Chicken with Caramelized Lemons

PER SERVING

serves
6

2 cups applewood or hickory wood chips

¼ cup lightly packed fresh cilantro leaves

2 garlic cloves, coarsely chopped

Grated zest of 1 lemon

2 teaspoons olive oil

1 teaspoon ground coriander

1½ teaspoons salt

¾ teaspoon black pepper

1 (4-pound) chicken, without giblets

3 small lemons, cut crosswise in half

1 Remove grill rack and preheat grill to medium or prepare medium fire. Soak wood chips in bowl of water about 30 minutes.

2 Meanwhile, combine cilantro, garlic, lemon zest, oil, coriander, salt, and pepper in mini food processor; pulse until it forms a paste. With your fingers, loosen skin on chicken breasts, legs, and thighs. Rub herb mixture on meat under skin; press skin back into place. Place chicken in disposable foil roasting pan.

3 Drain wood chips. If using gas grill, turn heat under one burner to low. Place chips in small disposable foil pan with a few holes poked in and set on top of hotter burner. If using charcoal grill, push coals to one side of grill and scatter chips over coals. Set grill rack on grill and spray with nonstick spray.

4 Place pan with chicken on cooler portion of grill rack and grill, covered, until instant-read thermometer inserted into thigh (not touching bone) registers 165°F, about 1 hour 20 minutes. Transfer chicken to carving board; let stand 10 minutes.

5 Meanwhile, place lemon halves, cut sides down, on hotter side of grill rack and grill until caramelized, about 5 minutes. Carve chicken and arrange on platter; squeeze lemon juice on top. Remove chicken skin before eating.

PER SERVING (⅙ of chicken): 201 Cal, 6 g Total Fat, 1 g Sat Fat, 0 g Trans Fat, 102 mg Chol, 695 mg Sod, 7 g Carb, 0 g Sugar, 3 g Fib, 32 g Prot, 57 mg Calc.

Healthy Extra   Put some thickly sliced zucchini on the grill alongside the lemons. They will take about the same amount of time to become softened and nicely marked.

Low & Slow Barbecued Chicken

serves 6

PER SERVING

¼ cup ketchup

2 tablespoons pomegranate molasses

1 teaspoon Worcestershire sauce

½ teaspoon mustard powder

Pinch cayenne

1 (3½-pound) chicken, cut into 6 pieces and skinned

½ teaspoon salt

¼ teaspoon black pepper

2 large zucchini, cut on diagonal into ¼-inch slices

1   Spray grill rack with nonstick spray. Preheat grill to medium-low or prepare medium-low fire.

2   Whisk together ketchup, pomegranate molasses, Worcestershire sauce, mustard, and cayenne in small bowl.

3   Sprinkle chicken with salt and black pepper. Place chicken on grill rack and grill, turning once or twice, 12 minutes. Baste chicken with sauce and grill, turning once or twice, until browned and cooked through, about 12 minutes longer. Spray zucchini with nonstick spray; place on grill during last 12 minutes of grilling time and grill, turning once, until softened.

PER SERVING (1 piece chicken and ⅙ of zucchini): 183 Cal, 4 g Total Fat, 1 g Sat Fat, 0 g Trans Fat, 89 mg Chol, 416 mg Sod, 8 g Carb, 6 g Sugar, 0 g Fib, 27 g Prot, 32 mg Calc.

Healthy Extra   Grill ears of corn alongside the chicken (1 small or medium ear of corn per serving will increase the *PointsPlus* value by 2).

Sweet Chili–Glazed Chicken Breasts with Pineapple & Cilantro

serves 4

PER SERVING

2 tablespoons lime juice

2 tablespoons reduced-sodium soy sauce

1 tablespoon packed brown sugar

1 tablespoon sweet chili sauce

3 (5-ounce) skinless boneless chicken breasts, cut on diagonal into 1-inch strips

8 (½-inch) slices peeled pineapple, cored

1 tablespoon chopped fresh cilantro

1   Spray grill rack with nonstick spray. Preheat grill to medium-high or prepare medium-high fire.

2   Combine lime juice, soy sauce, brown sugar, and chili sauce in large zip-close plastic bag and add chicken. Squeeze out air and seal bag; turn to coat chicken. Refrigerate, turning occasionally, at least 30 minutes or up to 1 hour.

3   Remove chicken from marinade; discard marinade. Place chicken and pineapple on grill rack and grill, turning occasionally, until chicken is cooked through, about 10 minutes, and pineapple is well marked and softened, about 2 minutes per side. Transfer chicken and pineapple to platter. Serve sprinkled with cilantro.

PER SERVING (about 3 chicken strips and 2 slices pineapple): 187 Cal, 3 g Total Fat, 1 g Sat Fat, 0 g Trans Fat, 59 mg Chol, 374 mg Sod, 18 g Carb, 14 g Sugar, 1 g Fib, 23 g Prot, 33 mg Calc.

Healthy Extra   A bowl of brown basmati rice sprinkled with thinly sliced scallion rounds out this meal (⅔ cup cooked brown basmati rice per serving will increase the *PointsPlus* value by 3).

**Margarita Chicken
with Charred Corn**

Margarita Chicken with Charred Corn

7 PointsPlus® value

PER SERVING

serves
4

2 tablespoons chopped
fresh cilantro stems
+ 2 tablespoons chopped
fresh cilantro leaves

2 tablespoons lime juice

2 tablespoons Triple Sec
or Cointreau

2 garlic cloves, coarsely chopped

½ jalapeño pepper, seeded
and coarsely chopped

1 teaspoon olive oil

½ teaspoon salt

¼ teaspoon black pepper

4 (5-ounce) skinless boneless
chicken breasts

4 teaspoons reduced-fat
mayonnaise

2 teaspoons chili powder

4 ears of corn, silk removed

1   Combine cilantro stems, lime juice, Triple Sec, garlic, jalapeño, oil, salt, and black pepper in food processor or blender and puree. Transfer to large zip-close plastic bag and add chicken. Squeeze out air and seal bag; turn to coat chicken. Refrigerate, turning bag occasionally, at least 20 minutes or up to 2 hours.

2   Meanwhile, stir together chopped cilantro leaves, mayonnaise, and chili powder in small bowl.

3   Spray grill rack with nonstick spray and preheat grill to medium-high or prepare medium-high fire.

4   Remove chicken from marinade; discard marinade. Spray corn with nonstick spray. Place chicken and corn on grill rack and grill, turning occasionally, until chicken is cooked through and corn is tender and lightly charred, about 10 minutes. Transfer chicken to platter. Brush chili mayonnaise over corn and place on platter.

PER SERVING (1 chicken breast and 1 ear of corn): 284 Cal, 7 g Total Fat, 1 g Sat Fat, 0 g Trans Fat, 78 mg Chol, 429 mg Sod, 23 g Carb, 6 g Sugar, 3 g Fib, 32 g Prot, 24 mg Calc.

FYI   Fresh cilantro stems are just as flavorful as cilantro leaves. The whole stems can be placed in a zip-close freezer plastic bag and frozen for up to several months. Remove as much as you need, then chop for use in marinades, soups, and stews.

Korean-Style Soft Tacos

serves
4

4 cups lightly packed thinly sliced romaine lettuce

2 scallions, chopped

3 tablespoons kimchi, thinly sliced

2 tablespoons mirin or rice wine

2 tablespoons lime juice

1½ tablespoons sugar

1 tablespoon reduced-sodium soy sauce

2 garlic cloves, minced

¼ teaspoon Asian (dark) sesame oil

1 pound skinless boneless chicken breasts, cut into ½-inch strips

4 (6-inch) reduced-fat whole wheat tortillas

¼ cup reduced-fat Monterey Jack cheese

Lime wedges

1 Spray grill rack with nonstick spray. Preheat grill to medium-high or prepare medium-high fire.

2 Toss together lettuce, scallions, and kimchi in large bowl.

3 Combine mirin, lime juice, sugar, soy sauce, garlic, and oil in large zip-close plastic bag and add chicken. Squeeze out air and seal bag; turn to coat chicken. Refrigerate, turning occasionally, at least 20 minutes or up to 1 hour.

4 Remove chicken from marinade; discard marinade. Place chicken on grill rack and grill, turning, until well marked and cooked through, about 8 minutes. Transfer to plate. Place tortillas on grill rack and grill until warmed through, about 30 seconds per side.

5 Place 1 tortilla on each of 4 plates and top each with one-fourth of chicken and kimchi mixture. Serve with Monterey Jack and lime wedges.

PER SERVING (1 taco): 291 Cal, 7 g Total Fat, 2 g Sat Fat, 0 g Trans Fat, 66 mg Chol, 621 mg Sod, 24 g Carb, 7 g Sugar, 11 g Fib, 33 g Prot, 137 mg Calc.

FYI In the 7th century, kimchi—fermented cabbage—was developed as a way to preserve cabbage by pickling it. By the 16th century, chile peppers were added to the mix, turning kimchi into the Korean condiment that is familiar to us today. It is sold in jars in many supermarkets, health food stores, and Asian markets.

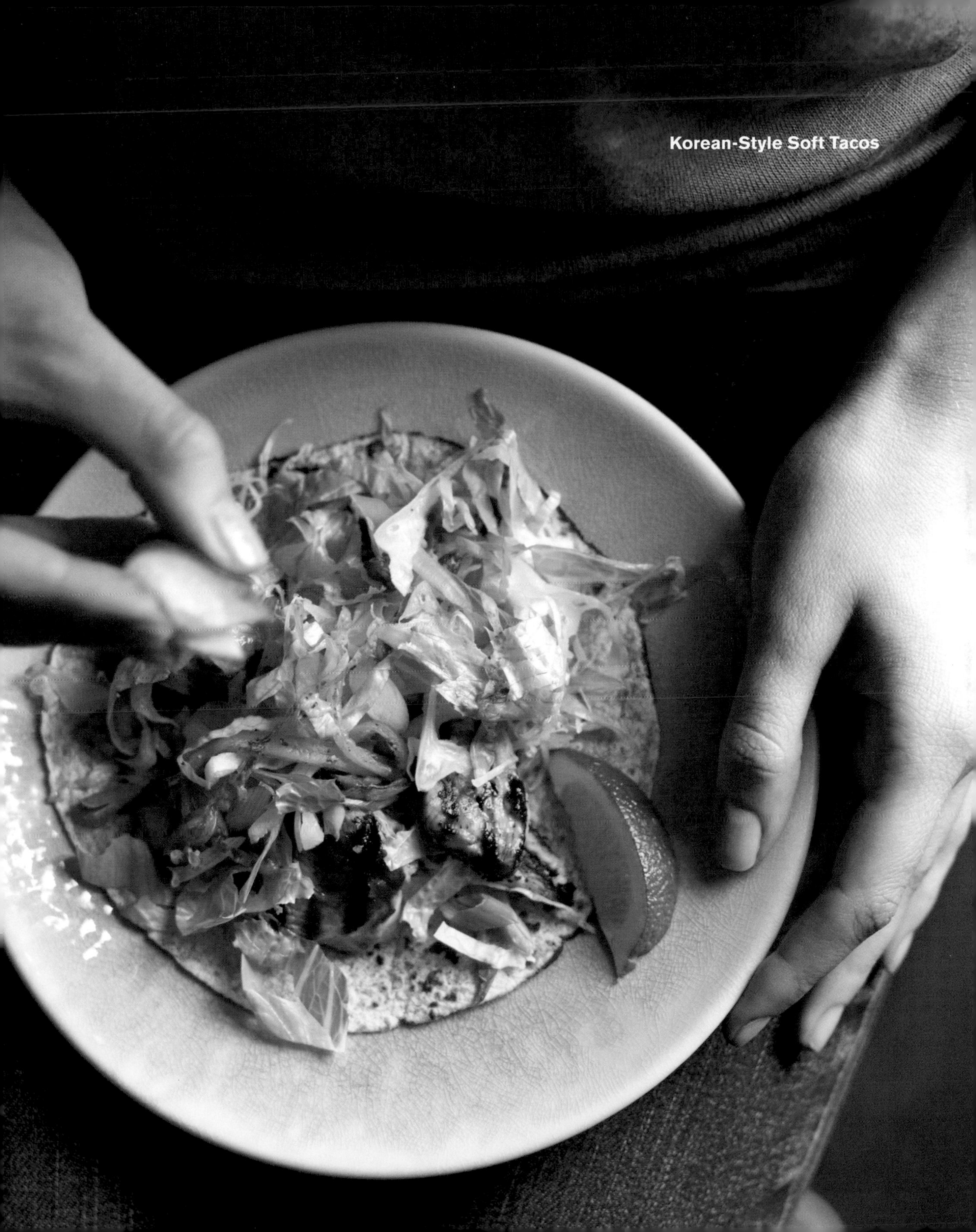
Korean-Style Soft Tacos

Chicken with Basil Dressing & Grilled Tomatoes

serves
4

PER SERVING

1 tablespoon grated lemon zest

4 large garlic cloves, minced

¾ teaspoon salt

½ teaspoon black pepper

4 (5-ounce) skinless boneless chicken breasts

12 large fresh basil leaves

3 tablespoons lemon juice

2 tablespoons water

1 teaspoon extra-virgin olive oil

4 plum tomatoes (about 1 pound), halved lengthwise

1 To make marinade, combine lemon zest, garlic, ½ teaspoon of salt, and ¼ teaspoon of pepper in large zip-close plastic bag and add chicken. Squeeze out air and seal bag; turn to coat chicken. Refrigerate, turning occasionally, at least 1 hour or up to overnight.

2 Spray grill rack with nonstick spray. Preheat grill to medium-high or prepare medium-high fire.

3 Meanwhile, to make dressing, combine, basil, lemon juice, water, oil, and remaining ¼ teaspoon salt and ¼ teaspoon pepper in food processor or blender and puree. Transfer to serving bowl.

4 Lightly spray cut sides of tomatoes with nonstick spray. Place chicken on grill rack and grill, turning, until cooked through, about 10 minutes. After 5 minutes of grilling time, place tomatoes on grill rack, cut sides down, and grill, without turning, until tender and lightly charred, about 4 minutes. Transfer chicken and tomatoes to platter; drizzle chicken with basil dressing.

PER SERVING (1 chicken breast, 1 tablespoon dressing, and 2 tomato halves): 185 Cal, 5 g Total Fat, 1 g Sat Fat, 0 g Trans Fat, 78 mg Chol, 508 mg Sod, 5 g Carb, 2 g Sugar, 1 g Fib, 29 g Prot, 33 mg Calc.

Healthy Extra   Serve the tomatoes on a bed of arugula or watercress.

Chicken & Fresh-Tomato Parmesan

serves **4**

20 min

PER SERVING

4 (5-ounce) skinless boneless chicken breasts

1 teaspoon dried oregano

½ teaspoon salt

¼ teaspoon black pepper

1 large red or yellow tomato, cut into 8 slices

8 tablespoons shredded part-skim mozzarella cheese

2 tablespoons grated Parmesan cheese

4 large fresh basil leaves

1   Spray grill rack with olive oil nonstick spray. Preheat grill to medium-high or prepare medium-high fire.

2   Lightly spray chicken with nonstick spray and sprinkle with oregano, salt, and pepper. Place chicken on grill rack and grill, turning occasionally, until browned, about 5 minutes.

3   Top each chicken breast with 2 tomato slices and 2 tablespoons of mozzarella; grill, covered, until chicken is cooked through and cheese is melted and bubbly, about 4 minutes longer. Transfer chicken to platter; sprinkle evenly with Parmesan and top each with 1 basil leaf.

PER SERVING (1 chicken breast): 217 Cal, 7 g Total Fat, 3 g Sat Fat, 0 g Trans Fat, 88 mg Chol, 474 mg Sod, 3 g Carb, 1 g Sugar, 1 g Fib, 34 g Prot, 156 mg Calc.

Healthy Extra   Serve the chicken Parmesan along with a bowl of cooked whole wheat spaghetti topped with diced fresh tomatoes, thinly sliced basil, and a drizzle of red wine vinegar (½ cup cooked whole wheat spaghetti per serving will increase the *PointsPlus* value by 2).

Grilled Chicken with Thai Coleslaw

serves **4**

PER SERVING

3 cups lightly packed thinly sliced green cabbage

¼ pound green beans, trimmed and cut into 1-inch pieces

4 radishes, thinly sliced

3 tablespoons lime juice

1 large shallot, minced

2 garlic cloves, minced

1 tablespoon Asian fish sauce

1 small Thai chile or 2 serrano peppers, seeded and chopped

2 teaspoons sugar

4 (5-ounce) skinless boneless chicken breasts

¼ teaspoon salt

¼ teaspoon black pepper

1   Spray grill rack with nonstick spray. Preheat grill to medium-high or prepare medium-high fire.

2   To make coleslaw, toss together cabbage, beans, radishes, lime juice, shallot, garlic, fish sauce, chile, and sugar in large bowl until mixed well.

3   Sprinkle chicken with salt and black pepper. Place chicken on grill rack and grill, turning, until chicken is cooked through, about 10 minutes. Transfer chicken to cutting board; let stand 10 minutes. Thinly slice on diagonal; divide evenly among 4 plates. Spoon coleslaw on top

PER SERVING (1 chicken breast and ¾ cup coleslaw): 194 Cal, 4 g Total Fat, 1 g Sat Fat, 0 g Trans Fat, 78 mg Chol, 577 Sod, 10 g Carb, 3 g Sugar, 2 g Fib, 30 g Prot, 60 mg Calc.

Healthy Extra   Serve a plate of thickly sliced tomatoes and very thinly sliced red onion and cucumber alongside.

Tandoori-Style Kebabs with Zucchini-Tomato Salad

5 PointsPlus value PER SERVING

serves 4

1 (6-ounce) container plain fat-free Greek yogurt

1 tablespoon grated peeled fresh ginger

2 garlic cloves, minced

½ teaspoon garam masala

1 pound skinless boneless chicken breasts, cut into 1-inch chunks

4 zucchini or yellow squash, halved lengthwise and cut into 1-inch slices

32 cherry tomatoes (about 1½ pints)

2 tablespoons lime juice

¼ teaspoon salt

¼ teaspoon black pepper

1   Combine yogurt, ginger, garlic, and garam masala in large zip-close plastic bag and add chicken. Squeeze out air and seal bag; turn to coat chicken. Refrigerate, turning bag occasionally, at least 1 hour or up to 6 hours.

2   Spray grill rack with nonstick spray. Preheat grill to medium-high or prepare medium-high fire.

3   Alternately thread zucchini and tomatoes onto 4 (8-inch) metal skewers; lightly spray with nonstick spray. Thread chicken onto 4 (8-inch) metal skewers. Place skewers on grill rack and grill, turning, until chicken is cooked through and vegetables are softened and lightly charred, about 8 minutes. With fork, slide vegetables off skewers into serving bowl. Add lime juice, salt, and pepper; toss gently until mixed well. Serve with chicken skewers.

PER SERVING (1 kebab and 1 cup vegetable mixture): 207 Cal, 3 g Total Fat, 1 g Sat Fat, 0 g Trans Fat, 63 mg Chol, 243 mg Sod, 15 g Carb, 9 g Sugar, 4 g Fib, 30 g Prot, 87 mg Calc.

Healthy Extra   Round out the meal with a bowl of brown basmati rice cooked with a couple of cardamom pods tucked in (⅔ cup cooked brown basmati rice per serving will increase the *PointsPlus* value by *3*).

Hoisin-Glazed Drumsticks & Cabbage Salad

 serves 4

PER SERVING

1 small red onion, thinly sliced (about 1 cup)

4 cups lightly packed thinly sliced Napa or Savoy cabbage

2 tablespoons unseasoned rice vinegar

2 tablespoons lime juice

1 teaspoon sugar

½ teaspoon salt

⅛ teaspoon coarsely ground Szechuan pepper or black pepper

2 tablespoons + 2 teaspoons hoisin sauce

6 drops hot pepper sauce or sambal oelek

8 (¼-pound) chicken drumsticks, skinned

1   Spray grill rack with nonstick spray. Preheat grill to medium or prepare medium fire.

2   To make salad, combine onion with enough water to cover in large bowl. Let stand 10 minutes; drain. Add cabbage, vinegar, 1 tablespoon of lime juice, the sugar, salt, and pepper to onion; toss until coated well.

3   To make glaze, stir together hoisin sauce, remaining 1 tablespoon lime juice, and the pepper sauce in pie plate. Add drumsticks, turning until coated well. Place chicken on grill rack and grill, turning, until instant-read thermometer inserted in drumstick registers 165°F, about 20 minutes. Serve with salad.

PER SERVING (2 drumsticks and 1¼ cups salad): 206 Cal, 5 g Total Fat, 1 g Sat Fat, 0 g Trans Fat, 98 mg Chol, 599 mg Sod, 12 g Carb, 6 g Sugar, 3 g Fib, 28 g Prot, 47 mg Calc.

FYI   Sambal oelek is a blend of chiles, brown sugar, and salt. Other variations of sambal include kaffir lime, galangal, tamarind, and coconut.

Smoked Paprika–Rubbed Cornish Hens with Caraway Onions

serves
4

3 tablespoons finely chopped fresh parsley

2 garlic cloves, minced

2 teaspoons olive oil

1 teaspoon smoked sweet paprika

¾ teaspoon salt

2 (1½-pound) Cornish game hens

2 large Walla Walla, Hawaiian Sweet, or Vidalia onions, cut into ½-inch rounds

2 tablespoons sherry vinegar

½ teaspoon caraway seeds, crushed

1   Spray grill rack with nonstick spray. Preheat grill to medium or prepare medium fire.

2   Mix together parsley, garlic, oil, paprika, and ½ teaspoon of salt in small bowl.

3   With kitchen shears, cut along each side of backbones of hens; discard backbones. Turn hens, breast sides up, and open flat. Use palm of your hand to flatten breasts slightly. With fingers, carefully loosen skin on breasts, legs, and thighs. Rub herb mixture on meat under skin; press skin back into place; tuck wings under.

4   Place hens, skin side up on grill rack and grill 15 minutes. Turn hens and grill until instant-read thermometer inserted into thigh (not touching bone) registers 165°F, about 20 minutes longer. Transfer hens to cutting board; let stand 10 minutes. Cut each hen lengthwise in half.

5   Meanwhile, spray onion slices with nonstick spray. Place onions on grill rack and grill until softened and lightly browned, about 4 minutes per side. Transfer onions to large bowl and separate into rings. Add vinegar, caraway seeds, and remaining ¼ teaspoon salt; toss until mixed well. Serve with hens. Remove skin before eating.

PER SERVING (½ Cornish hen and 1¼ cups onion mixture): 266 Cal, 8 g Total Fat, 2 g Sat Fat, 0 g Trans Fat, 146 mg Chol, 539 mg Sod, 14 g Carb, 8 g Sugar, 2 g Fib, 34 g Prot, 61 mg Calc.

Healthy Extra   A bowl of whole wheat couscous turns the hens and onions into a satisfying meal (⅔ cup cooked whole wheat couscous per serving will increase the *PointsPlus* value by 3).

Turkey Sausage Fajitas with Mushrooms & Peppers

 serves 4

PER SERVING

½ pound sweet or hot Italian-style turkey sausages

2 red bell peppers, cut into thick strips

1 large portobello mushroom, stemmed

1 large red onion, sliced

4 (8-inch) reduced-fat whole wheat tortillas

½ teaspoon dried oregano

1 Spray grill rack with nonstick spray. Preheat grill to medium or prepare medium fire.

2 Place sausages, bell peppers, mushroom, and onion on grill rack and grill, turning, until sausages are cooked through, about 15 minutes, and vegetables are softened, about 8 minutes. Transfer sausages and vegetables to cutting board. Cut sausages into ½-inch slices and mushroom into ¼-inch slices. Coarsely chop onion.

3 Place tortillas on grill rack and grill just until warmed, about 30 seconds on each side. Pile one-fourth of sausages and vegetables on each tortilla; sprinkle evenly with oregano. Fold tortillas in half.

PER SERVING (1 fajita): 245 Cal, 9 g Total Fat, 0 g Sat Fat, 0 g Trans Fat, 34 mg Chol, 655 mg Sod, 23 g Carb, 5 g Sugar, 12 g Fib, 18 g Prot, 16 mg Calc.

Healthy Extra Grill 2 portobello mushrooms instead of 1.

Grilled Tuna with Tonnato Sauce

 serves 4

PER SERVING

1 (6-ounce) can chunk light tuna packed in water, drained

¼ cup reduced-fat mayonnaise

1 tablespoon capers, rinsed and drained

2 anchovy fillets, rinsed and drained

2 tablespoons chopped fresh parsley

3 drops hot pepper sauce

2 (½-pound) tuna steaks, 1 inch thick

½ teaspoon black pepper

1 small head green leaf lettuce, thinly sliced (about 4 cups lightly packed)

4 small tomatoes, each cut into 4 slices

1 Spray grill rack with nonstick spray. Preheat grill to high or prepare hot fire.

2 To make sauce, coarsely flake canned tuna into blender or food processor. Add mayonnaise, capers, anchovies, parsley, and pepper sauce; blend until smooth and creamy.

3 Sprinkle tuna steaks with pepper. Place on grill rack and grill until well marked but still pink in center, about 4 minutes per side for medium-rare. Transfer tuna to cutting board; let stand 5 minutes. Thinly slice tuna.

4 Divide lettuce and tomatoes evenly among 4 plates; top evenly with tuna and drizzle with sauce.

PER SERVING (½ tuna steak, 4 tomato slices, 1 cup lettuce, and about ¼ cup sauce): 185 Cal, 6 g Total Fat, 1 g Sat Fat, 0 g Trans Fat, 45 mg Chol, 526 mg Sod, 8 g Carb, 4 g Sugar, 2 g Fib, 25 g Prot, 56 mg Calc.

Tea-Smoked Salmon with Bok Choy & Radishes

serves
4

PER SERVING

¼ cup + 1 tablespoon loose black tea (such as Lapsang Souchong)

¼ cup + 1 teaspoon packed brown sugar

¼ cup raw jasmine rice

½ teaspoon salt

4 (¼-pound) wild salmon fillets with skin

4 baby bok choy, trimmed and cut lengthwise in half

1 tablespoon reduced-sodium soy sauce

1 tablespoon unseasoned rice vinegar

1 teaspoon toasted sesame seeds

5 radishes, thinly sliced

1 Remove grill rack and preheat grill to high or prepare hot fire. Tear off 1 (12-inch) sheet of heavy-duty foil.

2 Combine ¼ cup of tea, ¼ cup of brown sugar, and the rice in center of foil. Fold foil over to make sealed packet. Poke several holes in top of foil to allow smoke to escape. If using gas grill, place packet on lit burner. If using charcoal grill, place packet on coals. Spray grill rack with nonstick spray and place on grill; close lid and wait 10 minutes. If using charcoal grill, leave vents partially open. Open lid and check for smoke. If needed, wait a few minutes longer.

3 Combine remaining 1 tablespoon tea and the salt in spice grinder or mini food processor; pulse until finely ground. Sprinkle salmon with 2 teaspoons of salt mixture; lightly spray with nonstick spray. (Reserve remaining salt mixture for another time.)

4 Place fillets, skin side down, on grill rack (not directly over packet) and grill until lightly browned and just opaque in center, about 4 minutes per side. After 4 minutes of grilling time, place bok choy on grill rack and grill, turning, until tender and lightly charred, about 4 minutes.

5 Meanwhile, to make sauce, whisk together soy sauce, vinegar, and remaining 1 teaspoon brown sugar in small bowl until sugar is dissolved. Add sesame seeds. Divide bok choy and radishes evenly among 4 plates. Place 1 salmon fillet on each plate; drizzle evenly with sauce.

PER SERVING (1 salmon fillet and ¼ of vegetables): 210 Cal, 9 g Total Fat, 1 g Sat Fat, 0 g Trans Fat, 72 mg Chol, 531 mg Sod, 4 g Carb, 3 g Sugar, 2 g Fib, 27 g Prot, 21 mg Calc.

FYI The jasmine rice adds subtle flavor and some weight to the foil smoking packet. Discard the packet after the grill cools down.

Tea-Smoked Salmon with Bok Choy & Radishes

Arctic Char with Watermelon, Nectarine & Basil Salad

serves
4

PER SERVING

4 (5-ounce) arctic char fillets

¾ teaspoon salt

¼ teaspoon black pepper

2 cups (½-inch) diced seedless watermelon

2 nectarines, pitted and cut into ½-inch dice

4 large fresh basil leaves, thinly sliced

1 large shallot, minced

1 tablespoon balsamic vinegar

1 Spray grill rack with nonstick spray. Preheat grill to medium-high or prepare medium-high fire.

2 Spray arctic char fillets with olive oil nonstick spray; sprinkle with ½ teaspoon of salt and ⅛ teaspoon of pepper. Place fillets on grill rack and grill just until opaque in center, about 4 minutes per side.

3 Meanwhile, to make salad, gently stir together watermelon, nectarines, basil, shallot, vinegar, and remaining ¼ teaspoon salt and ⅛ teaspoon pepper in medium bowl.

4 Place 1 fish fillet on each of 4 plates; top evenly with salad.

PER SERVING (1 arctic char fillet and about ¾ cup salad): 163 Cal, 5 g Total Fat, 1 g Sat Fat, 0 g Trans Fat, 34 mg Chol, 485 mg Sod, 15 g Carb, 11 g Sugar, 2 g Fib, 16 g Prot, 15 mg Calc.

Healthy Extra Serve a bowl of hot cooked whole wheat orzo alongside (½ cup of cooked whole wheat orzo per serving will increase the *PointsPlus* value by 2).

Grilled Shrimp with Warm Mushroom & Frisée Salad

serves
4

PER SERVING

4 teaspoons red wine vinegar

4 teaspoons extra-virgin olive oil

½ teaspoon salt

¼ teaspoon black pepper

1 pound large shrimp, peeled and deveined, tails left on if desired

½ pound shiitake mushrooms, stemmed

1 bunch frisée, torn, or 4 cups lightly packed mixed baby salad greens

¼ cup chopped red onion or scallions

1   Spray grill rack with olive oil nonstick spray. Preheat grill to medium-high or prepare medium-high fire.

2   Meanwhile, to make vinaigrette, whisk together vinegar, oil, ¼ teaspoon of salt, and ⅛ teaspoon of pepper in salad bowl.

3   Spray shrimp and mushrooms with olive oil nonstick spray; sprinkle with remaining ¼ teaspoon salt and ⅛ teaspoon pepper. Place shrimp and mushrooms on grill rack and grill, turning once, until shrimp are just opaque in center and mushrooms are tender, about 5 minutes.

4   Add frisée, mushrooms, and onion to vinaigrette; toss until mixed well. Serve with shrimp.

PER SERVING (about 8 shrimp and 1 cup salad): 166 Cal, 6 g Total Fat, 1 g Sat Fat, 0 g Trans Fat, 168 mg Chol, 490 mg Sod, 10 g Carb, 2 g Sugar, 2 g Fib, 19 g Prot, 41 mg Calc.

Healthy Extra   Enjoy the shrimp and mushroom salad with a bowl of room-temperature bulgur tossed with chopped peaches and fresh mint (½ cup cooked bulgur per serving will increase the *PointsPlus* value by 2).

Super-Crispy Eggplant & Mushroom Parmesan

serves
4

1 small eggplant (about 1 pound), unpeeled and cut into ½-inch rounds

2 large portobello mushrooms, stemmed and cut into ½-inch slices

4 plum tomatoes, each cut lengthwise in half

½ teaspoon salt

¼ teaspoon black pepper

12 large fresh basil leaves

½ cup shredded part-skim mozzarella cheese

3 tablespoons whole wheat panko (Japanese bread crumbs)

¼ cup grated Parmesan cheese

2 teaspoons extra-virgin olive oil

1 Spray grill rack with nonstick spray. Preheat grill to high or prepare hot fire.

2 Combine eggplant, mushrooms, and tomatoes in jelly-roll pan. Lightly spray with nonstick spray and sprinkle with salt and pepper; toss until coated evenly.

3 Place eggplant and mushrooms on grill rack, in batches, and grill, turning, until lightly charred and softened, about 5 minutes, returning eggplant and mushrooms to pan when they are done. Place tomatoes, skin side down, on grill rack and grill, without turning, until lightly charred, about 4 minutes. Transfer tomatoes to cutting board; cut each lengthwise in half.

4 Arrange half of eggplant slices in 9-inch heavy skillet, such as cast iron. Layer with mushrooms, tomatoes, half of basil, and half of mozzarella. Arrange remaining eggplant on top and cover with remaining basil and mozzarella. Sprinkle evenly with panko and Parmesan; drizzle with oil.

5 Cover skillet with foil and place on grill rack. Grill 5 minutes. Remove foil and continue to grill until cheese is melted and bread crumbs are browned, about 5 minutes longer.

PER SERVING (¼ of dish): 144 Cal, 7 g Total Fat, 3 g Sat Fat, 0 g Trans Fat, 12 mg Chol, 453 mg Sod, 14 g Carb, 5 g Sugar, 6 g Fib, 9 g Prot, 182 mg Calc.

Healthy Extra   A side of hot cooked whole wheat pasta of your choice sprinkled with chopped fresh parsley turns this dish into a hearty meal (½ cup of cooked whole wheat pasta will increase the *PointsPlus* value by 2).

**Super-Crispy Eggplant &
Mushroom Parmesan**

Grilled Tofu-Vegetable Stacks

serves
4

PER SERVING

5 tablespoons balsamic vinegar

2 teaspoons extra-virgin olive oil

1 garlic clove, minced

½ teaspoon salt

¼ teaspoon black pepper

4 portobello mushrooms, stemmed

2 Japanese eggplants, unpeeled, trimmed and each cut lengthwise into 4 slices

1 red bell pepper, cut into 4 slabs

1 (12-ounce) package extra-firm reduced-fat tofu, cut crosswise into 8 slices

1 tablespoon lemon juice

1   Spray grill rack with nonstick spray. Preheat grill to high or prepare hot fire.

2   To make dressing, whisk together 3 tablespoons of vinegar, the oil, garlic, salt, and black pepper in small bowl. Arrange mushrooms, eggplants, bell pepper, and tofu in jelly-roll pan. Drizzle dressing over vegetables and tofu, turning vegetables and tofu until coated well on both sides.

3   Place vegetables on grill rack and grill, turning, until softened and lightly charred, about 8 minutes. Transfer to platter. Place tofu on grill rack and grill until lightly marked, about 2 minutes per side. Transfer to platter.

4   Meanwhile, to make sauce, combine remaining 2 tablespoons vinegar and the lemon juice in small saucepan. Place saucepan on grill rack and cook, stirring occasionally, until heated through, about 5 minutes.

5   Place 1 mushroom, curved side down, on each of 4 plates. Top each with 1 slice of tofu, 2 slices of eggplant, 1 piece of bell pepper, and 1 slice of tofu. Drizzle evenly with sauce.

PER SERVING (1 stack): 157 Cal, 5 g Total Fat, 0 g Sat Fat, 0 g Trans Fat, 0 mg Chol, 334 mg Sod, 18 g Carb, 9 g Sugar, 5 g Fib, 11 g Prot, 340 mg Calc.

FYI   There are several varieties of eggplants available: the common large, deep purple eggplant known as Black Beauty; small, curved Sicilian eggplant; large ivory eggplant; Asian eggplant that ranges in color from ivory to variegated lavender to deep purple; and long and slender Japanese eggplant, which is tender and delicate.

Vegetable Sandwiches with Lemon-Basil Goat Cheese

PointsPlus® value 5

serves 4

PER SERVING

½ cup reduced-fat soft goat cheese

2 tablespoons chopped fresh basil

Grated zest of ½ lemon

1 small eggplant (¾ pound), unpeeled and cut into ¼-inch rounds

2 zucchini, cut on diagonal into ¼-inch slices

¾ teaspoon black pepper

8 (1-ounce) slices whole wheat Italian bread

1 large tomato, thinly sliced

8 large watercress sprigs, trimmed

1   Spray grill rack with nonstick spray. Preheat grill to medium-high or prepare medium-high fire.

2   Stir together goat cheese, basil, and lemon zest in small bowl.

3   Spray eggplant and zucchini with olive oil nonstick spray; sprinkle with pepper. Place on grill rack and grill, turning, until lightly browned and tender, about 8 minutes. Transfer to plate and let cool slightly.

4   Meanwhile, place slices of bread on grill rack and grill until well marked and crisp on one side, about 2 minutes (do not turn bread).

5   Spread goat cheese mixture evenly on ungrilled side of 4 slices of bread. Top evenly with eggplant, zucchini, tomato, and watercress. Cover with remaining slices of bread, grilled sides facing up.

PER SERVING (1 sandwich): 220 Cal, 4 g Total Fat, 1 g Sat Fat, 0 g Trans Fat, 0 mg Chol, 671 mg Sod, 35 g Carb, 7 g Sugar, 8 g Fib, 7 g Prot, 151 mg Calc.

FYI   The vegetables can be grilled up to several hours ahead and stored, covered, at room temperature.

IN SOME
DIFFERE

CHAPTER 10

IN SOMETHING DIFFERENT

WAFFLES, PANINI DISHES, PRESSURE COOKER SPECIALS & FONDUES

Besides the pots and pans needed for day-to-day cooking, there is specialty cookware, such as waffle bakers, panini makers, pressure cookers, and fondue pots, that makes cooking special, fancier, easier, faster, or simply more fun.

Waffle Bakers

Although Thomas Jefferson hosted waffle parties in the 1700s using waffle irons brought back from Europe, the waffle iron wasn't patented in the U.S. until 1869. It consisted of two hinged iron plates that fit together and were heated on a wood or gas stove.

Since then, waffle bakers (also known as waffle makers and waffle irons) have come a long way. They are electric and have a nonstick interior that ensures the easy removal of waffles. There is a dial to set the degree of doneness and an indicator light that signals when it is preheated. The batter is ladled onto the preheated grid, the lid is closed, and the waffles bake until a doneness indicator light illuminates. Waffle bakers can bake up waffles in a variety of shapes, including square, heart, and round, as well as Mickey Mouse.

To protect the nonstick interior from scratches, silicone, heat-safe nylon, or wooden utensils are recommended for removing waffles. Always allow the waffle baker to cool down before cleaning it. To clean the interior, brush away any crumbs, then wipe the grid clean with a damp sponge or dishcloth. Wipe the exterior clean with a damp sponge. To keep the exterior shiny, use a nonabrasive cleanser, such as Bar Keeper's Friend.

Panini Makers

Paninis are Italian-style sandwiches. These sandwiches are often grilled in an electric press that has top and bottom ridged grill plates that give the bread grill marks, make it crisp, and heat the filling through. Paninis are versatile; they can be served for breakfast, lunch, or dinner, as well as for dessert or as an appetizer.

When buying a panini maker, look for a model that has a hinged top plate that allows for various sandwich thicknesses. Most models come with easy-to-care-for nonstick interiors, stainless steel exteriors, and variable temperature controls. Panini makers also do an excellent job of grilling fish steaks and fillets, chicken breasts, chops, and vegetables.

To clean a panini maker, let it cool down, then use the cleaning "fork" the manufacturer provided or a nylon or wooden utensil to remove any food particles that cling to the grids. Then use a damp sponge or cloth to wipe the interior clean.

Pressure Cookers

Pressure cookers are a cooking marvel, allowing food to cook in one-third or less the amount of usual time. The concept behind this appliance is simple: Once the lid is locked into place, the liquid inside the pot heats up and becomes steam. Since the steam is trapped, the pressure within the pot builds to the point where water boils at 250° instead of 212°F. At this higher pressure, food cooks much more quickly.

While the first generation of pressure cookers, with their jiggle-topped pressure regulators, does a good job, the newest models are considerably improved. There is no guesswork when high pressure is reached, the pots are made of heavy stainless steel, often with an aluminum or copper core for even heating, and some are nonstick.

If you take the time to care for your pressure cooker, it will last for many years. Here are some tips: Be sure to remove and clean the gasket (refer to the manufacturer's instructions). After washing the lid in hot, soapy water, check the vent area and wipe or scrub away any dirt. Clean the interior with a nonabrasive cleaning powder and a sponge or nylon scrub pad. Dry the lid and bottom of the cooker with a kitchen towel.

Fondue Pots

The word *fondue* comes from the French word *fondre*, which means "melt." Classic fondues are made of cheese or chocolate. For a cheese fondue, the cheese, seasoning, and wine are melted in a pot on the stove. The fondue is then transferred to a fondue pot and set over a burner to keep the cheese mixture hot. Diners spear cubes of bread with long-stemmed fondue forks and dip them into the melted cheese until coated. Fondue parties were all the rage in the 1960s. Recently this fun, communal way to share food with friends has regained popularity.

Fondue pots are usually made of enameled cast iron, stainless steel, or stoneware. The simplest models consist of a small pot, stand, burner, and six to eight fondue forks. Some stainless steel models come with nonstick interiors, while high-end models have cast-aluminum cooking inserts that are stovetop-safe, so the fondues can be cooked and served in the same pot. There are also electric fondue pots that have an adjustable temperature control, as well as a probe to check the temperature in the pot.

To clean enamel-coated cast-iron or stainless steel fondue pots, let the pot cool down, then soak it for about 15 minutes in hot, soapy water. Use a sponge or nylon scrub pad to remove any food particles and wipe it dry. Do not use steel wood soap pads. To keep the outside of stainless steel pots looking shiny, use a nonabrasive cleaning powder. Let a stoneware fondue pot cool down, then soak it for about 15 minutes in hot, soapy water. The pot can then be scrubbed clean with a nylon scrub pad. They're dishwasher safe. If using an electric fondue pot, refer to the manufacturer's instructions.

Lots of Whole Grains & Honey Waffles

Lots of Whole Grains & Honey Waffles

serves
6

PER SERVING

1 cup white whole wheat flour

¼ cup toasted wheat germ

¼ cup millet

2 teaspoons baking powder

¼ teaspoon salt

1 cup fat-free ricotta cheese

1 large egg

1 large egg white

1 cup low-fat (1%) milk

2 tablespoons honey

3 cups quartered strawberries

1 tablespoon confectioner's sugar

1   Spray waffle baker with nonstick spray. Preheat according to manufacturer's directions.

2   Whisk together flour, wheat germ, millet, baking powder, and salt in large bowl. Stir together ricotta, egg, egg white, milk, and honey in medium bowl. Stir ricotta mixture into flour mixture just until combined.

3   When waffle baker is ready, ladle in 1 cup of batter for 4 (4-inch) waffles. Close lid and bake until golden brown, about 5 minutes. Transfer waffles to platter and keep warm. Repeat with remaining batter, spraying waffle baker between batches, making total of 12 waffles. Serve waffles topped with strawberries and sprinkled with confectioner's sugar.

PER SERVING (2 waffles and ½ cup strawberries): 245 Cal, 3 g Total Fat, 1 g Sat Fat, 0 g Trans Fat, 41 mg Chol, 374 mg Sod, 42 g Carb, 14 g Sugar, 6 g Fib, 14 g Prot, 233 mg Calc.

FYI   To freeze any leftover waffles, let them cool to room temperature, then place, in a single layer, in a shallow baking pan and freeze until hard. Stack the frozen waffles between sheets of wax paper and transfer to a zip-close freezer plastic bag; seal and date. Freeze for up to 2 months.

Wild Blueberry–Cornmeal Waffles

5 PointsPlus® value

PER SERVING

serves **8**

1 cup white whole wheat flour

1 cup stone-ground yellow cornmeal

2 teaspoons baking powder

1 teaspoon baking soda

2 cups low-fat buttermilk

1 large egg

2 large egg whites

1 tablespoon canola oil

1 cup fresh or frozen wild or regular blueberries

8 teaspoons pure maple syrup, warmed

1 Spray waffle baker with nonstick spray. Preheat according to manufacturer's directions.

2 Whisk together flour, cornmeal, baking powder, and baking soda in large bowl. Make a well in middle of flour mixture. Whisk together buttermilk, egg, egg whites, and oil in well. With rubber spatula, stir flour mixture into buttermilk mixture until flour mixture is moistened; stir in blueberries.

3 When waffle baker is ready, ladle in 1 cup of batter for 4 (4-inch) waffles. Close lid and bake until golden brown, about 5 minutes. Transfer waffles to platter and keep warm. Repeat with remaining batter, spraying waffle baker between batches, making total of 16 waffles. Serve with maple syrup.

PER SERVING (2 waffles and 1 teaspoon maple syrup): 217 Cal, 3 g Total Fat, 1 g Sat Fat, 0 g Trans Fat, 29 mg Chol, 382 mg Sod, 39 g Carb, 9 g Sugar, 3 g Fib, 7 g Prot, 104 mg Calc.

FYI To keep the waffles warm, preheat the oven to 200°F and set a large wire rack in a jelly-roll pan. Place the waffles on the rack and keep warm in the oven while baking up the remaining waffles.

Oatmeal–Cottage Cheese Waffles

4 PointsPlus® value

PER SERVING

serves **6**

1 cup white whole wheat flour

¾ cup old-fashioned oats

2 teaspoons baking powder

¼ teaspoon salt

1 cup fat-free milk

1 cup small curd 1% cottage cheese

1 tablespoon packed brown sugar

1 large egg

1 large egg white

1 teaspoon vanilla extract

1 Spray waffle baker with nonstick spray. Preheat according to manufacturer's directions.

2 Combine flour, oats, baking powder, and salt in large zip-close plastic bag. Seal bag and shake until mixed well. Whisk together milk, cottage cheese, brown sugar, egg, egg white, and vanilla in large bowl. Add flour mixture and stir just until combined.

3 When waffle baker is ready, ladle in 1 cup of batter for 4 (4-inch) waffles. Close lid and bake until golden brown, about 5 minutes. Transfer waffles to platter and keep warm. Repeat with remaining batter, spraying waffle baker between batches, making total of 12 waffles.

PER SERVING (2 waffles): 187 Cal, 2 g Total Fat, 1 g Sat Fat, 0 g Trans Fat, 38 mg Chol, 470 mg Sod, 29 g Carb, 5 g Sugar, 4 g Fib, 12 g Prot, 111 mg Calc.

Healthy Extra Top the waffles with a mix of fresh berries and sliced peaches.

Pumpkin Belgian Waffles

6 PointsPlus® value
PER SERVING

serves **4**

1 cup white whole wheat flour

2 tablespoons packed light brown sugar

2¼ teaspoons baking powder

1 teaspoon baking soda

1 teaspoon pumpkin pie spice

1½ cups salt-free, fat-free buttermilk

½ cup canned pumpkin puree

¼ cup fat-free egg substitute

1 tablespoon canola oil

1 Spray Belgian waffle baker with nonstick spray. Preheat according to manufacturer's directions.

2 Whisk together flour, brown sugar, baking powder, baking soda, and pumpkin pie spice in large bowl. Make a well in middle of flour mixture. Combine buttermilk, pumpkin, egg substitute, and oil in well. With rubber spatula, stir until flour mixture is moistened.

3 When waffle baker is ready, ladle ⅓ cup of batter into each waffle grid. Close lid and bake until golden brown, about 5 minutes. Transfer waffles to platter and keep warm. Repeat with remaining batter, spraying waffle baker between batches, making total of 8 waffles.

PER SERVING (2 waffles): 234 Cal, 5 g Total Fat, 1 g Sat Fat, 0 g Trans Fat, 4 mg Chol, 650 mg Sod, 39 g Carb, 11 g Sugar, 5 g Fib, 9 g Prot, 178 mg Calc.

Healthy Extra   Serve the waffles with fat-free sour cream and fresh raspberries (¼ cup fat-free sour cream per serving will increase the *PointsPlus* value by 1).

Decadent Chocolate Dessert Waffles

5 PointsPlus® value
PER SERVING

serves **10**

1¼ cups white whole wheat flour

⅓ cup granulated sugar

⅓ cup Dutch process cocoa

6 amaretti cookies, finely crushed

1 ounce bittersweet or semisweet chocolate, finely chopped

1½ teaspoons baking powder

¼ teaspoon baking soda

Pinch salt

1¼ cups low-fat (1%) milk

¼ cup fat-free egg substitute

3 tablespoons butter, melted

1 teaspoon vanilla extract

1 tablespoon confectioners' sugar

1 Spray waffle baker with nonstick spray. Preheat waffle baker according to manufacturer's directions.

2 Combine flour, granulated sugar, cocoa, cookie crumbs, chocolate, baking powder, baking soda, and salt in zip-close plastic bag. Seal bag and shake until mixed well. Whisk together milk, egg substitute, butter, and vanilla in large bowl. Add flour mixture to milk mixture bowl and stir just until combined.

3 When waffle baker is ready, ladle ⅓ cup of batter onto each waffle grid. Close lid and bake until golden brown, about 5 minutes. Transfer waffles to platter and keep warm. Repeat with remaining batter, spraying waffle baker between batches, making total of 10 waffles. Serve sprinkled with confectioners' sugar.

PER SERVING (1 waffle): 178 Cal, 6 g Total Fat, 3 g Sat Fat, 0 g Trans Fat, 11 mg Chol, 179 mg Sod, 27 g Carb, 14 g Sugar, 2 g Fib, 4 g Prot, 54 mg Calc.

Healthy Extra   Top the waffles with a mix of fresh berries or a mix of diced fresh fruit.

Lemony Arctic Char with Arugula-Cucumber Salad

  serves 4 · 20 min

PER SERVING

4 (5-ounce) arctic char or wild salmon fillets

Grated zest and juice of 1 large lemon

½ teaspoon salt

¼ teaspoon black pepper

1 bunch arugula, trimmed

½ cup very thinly sliced English (seedless) cucumber

¼ cup thinly sliced red onion

2 teaspoons extra-virgin olive oil

1 Spray panini maker with nonstick spray and preheat to high.

2 Sprinkle arctic char with lemon zest, salt, and pepper. Place fish in panini maker. Close lid and cook just until opaque in center, about 4 minutes.

3 Meanwhile toss together arugula, cucumber, and onion in serving bowl. Drizzle with oil and lemon juice; toss again. Divide evenly among 4 plates. Serve fish alongside.

PER SERVING (1 arctic char fillet and 1½ cups salad): 238 Cal, 11 g Total Fat, 3 g Sat Fat, 0 g Trans Fat, 69 mg Chol, 400 mg Sod, 4 g Carb, 2 g Sugar, 1 g Fib, 31 g Prot, 99 mg Calc.

Healthy Extra Add 1 cup rinsed and drained canned cannellini (white kidney) beans to the salad. This will increase the per-serving *PointsPlus* value by **1**.

Open-Face Chicken Paninis Vietnamese-Style

 7 PointsPlus® value
PER SERVING

| serves |
| 4 |

2 (5-ounce) skinless boneless chicken breasts

¼ teaspoon black pepper

4 (2-ounce) whole grain rolls, split

2 tablespoons lime juice

1 tablespoon Asian fish sauce

1 tablespoon sugar

2 cups lightly packed coleslaw mix

1 cucumber, shredded (about 1 cup)

5 large radishes, shredded

½ jalapeño pepper, minced

¼ cup lightly packed fresh cilantro leaves

2 tablespoons chopped fresh mint

1 Spray panini maker with nonstick spray and preheat to high.

2 Sprinkle chicken with black pepper. Place chicken in panini maker. Close lid and cook until just cooked through, about 10 minutes. Transfer to cutting board and let cool. Wipe panini maker clean.

3 Place rolls in panini maker; close lid and cook until toasted, about 3 minutes.

4 Meanwhile, to make slaw, whisk together lime juice, fish sauce, and sugar in large bowl until sugar is dissolved. Add coleslaw mix, cucumber, radishes, jalapeño, cilantro, and mint; toss until mixed well.

5 Thinly slice chicken. Place 1 roll, cut sides up, on each of 4 plates. Divide chicken evenly among rolls; top each with one-fourth of coleslaw mixture.

PER SERVING (1 sandwich): 255 Cal, 5 g Total Fat, 1 g Sat Fat, 0 g Trans Fat, 39 mg Chol, 666 mg Sod, 36 g Carb, 8 g Sugar, 6 g Fib, 20 g Prot, 96 mg Calc.

Turkey, Chutney & Cheddar Paninis

 **5** PointsPlus® value
PER SERVING

| serves |
| 8 |

| 20 |
| min |

8 (1-ounce) slices rye bread

½ pound thinly sliced skinless smoked turkey breast

4 ounces shredded fat-free Cheddar cheese

8 large watercress sprigs, trimmed

¼ cup Major Grey's chutney

4 teaspoons fat-free mayonnaise

1 Preheat panini maker to high.

2 Spray one side of each slice of bread with nonstick spray. Place, sprayed side down, on work surface. Divide turkey evenly among 4 slices of bread. Top evenly with Cheddar and watercress. Stir together chutney and mayonnaise in small bowl; spread evenly on remaining 4 slices of bread. Cover each sandwich with slice of bread, sprayed side facing up. Place sandwiches in panini maker. Close lid and cook until bread is well marked and crisp and cheese is melted, about 4 minutes. Cut each sandwich in half.

PER SERVING (½ sandwich): 184 Cal, 6 g Total Fat, 3 g Sat Fat, 0 g Trans Fat, 23 mg Chol, 740 mg Sod, 22 g Carb, 6 g Sugar, 1 g Fib, 12 g Prot, 153 mg Calc.

Healthy Extra Add 2 thin slices of red onion to each sandwich.

Shrimp, Avocado & Greens Paninis

PER SERVING

4 slices turkey bacon, halved

¾ pound shelled and deveined large shrimp

2 teaspoons chili powder

8 (1-ounce) slices whole grain bread

½ Hass avocado, pitted, peeled, and mashed

2 cups lightly packed baby spinach

1   Spray panini maker with nonstick spray and preheat to high.

2   Place bacon in panini maker. Close lid and cook until browned and crisp, about 6 minutes. Drain on paper towels.

3   Meanwhile, toss together shrimp and chili powder on sheet of foil. Place shrimp in panini maker. Close lid and cook until just opaque in center, about 1 minute.

4   Spray one side of each slice of bread with olive oil nonstick spray. Place, sprayed side down, on work surface. Spread avocado evenly on 4 slices of bread. Top each with 2 pieces of bacon, one-fourth of shrimp, and ½ cup of spinach. Cover with remaining slices of bread, sprayed side facing up.

5   Place sandwiches in panini maker. Close lid and cook until bread is well marked and crisp, about 4 minutes.

PER SERVING (1 sandwich): 302 Cal, 10 g Total Fat, 2 g Sat Fat, 0 g Trans Fat, 140 mg Chol, 736 mg Sod, 28 g Carb, 4 g Sugar, 6 g Fib, 26 g Prot, 96 mg Calc.

Healthy Extra   Add 2 slices of tomato to each sandwich.

Shrimp, Avocado & Greens Paninis

Tomato, Basil & Ricotta Paninis

 serves 4 | 20 min

PER SERVING

1 cup fat-free ricotta cheese

½ cup shredded part-skim mozzarella cheese

4 large fresh basil leaves, thinly sliced

1 teaspoon grated lemon zest

½ teaspoon salt

¼ teaspoon black pepper

8 thin slices ciabatta or other country-style bread

2 plum tomatoes, sliced

1 Spray panini maker with nonstick spray and preheat to high.

2 Stir together ricotta, mozzarella, basil, lemon zest, salt, and pepper in small bowl. Spread evenly over 4 slices of bread. Divide slices of tomato among sandwiches and cover with remaining 4 slices of bread.

3 Place sandwiches in panini maker. Close lid and cook until bread is well marked and crisp and mozzarella is melted, about 3 minutes.

PER SERVING (1 sandwich): 170 Cal, 4 g Total Fat, 2 g Sat Fat, 0 g Trans Fat, 13 mg Chol, 607 mg Sod, 20 g Carb, 3 g Sugar, 1 g Fib, 14 g Prot, 309 mg Calc.

FYI Ciabatta, which means "carpet slipper" in Italian, is a yeast bread that is fairly long, wide, and flat and great for sandwiches.

Strawberry, Mozzarella & Thyme Paninis

 serves 4 | 20 min

PER SERVING

4 tablespoons reduced-sugar strawberry fruit spread

8 (1-ounce) slices whole wheat bread

½ cup shredded part-skim mozzarella cheese

1 teaspoon chopped fresh thyme

1 teaspoon confectioners' sugar

1 Spray panini maker with nonstick spray and preheat to high.

2 Spread 1 tablespoon of fruit spread on each of 4 slices of bread. Sprinkle evenly with mozzarella and thyme; top with remaining 4 slices of bread.

3 Place sandwiches in panini maker. Close lid and cook until bread is well marked and crisp and cheese is melted, about 4 minutes. Dust evenly with confectioners' sugar. Cut each sandwich into quarters.

PER SERVING (1 sandwich): 227 Cal, 5 g Total Fat, 2 g Sat Fat, 0 g Trans Fat, 8 mg Chol, 342 mg Sod, 35 g Carb, 12 g Sugar, 4 g Fib, 11 g Prot, 165 mg Calc.

Healthy Extra Enjoy a salad of red and green leaf lettuce topped with thinly sliced radicchio and drizzled with fresh lemon juice.

Grilled Vegetable & Goat Cheese Paninis with Fresh Tarragon

PER SERVING

2 Japanese eggplants, unpeeled and cut into ½-inch lengthwise slices

2 small zucchini, cut into 8 (¼-inch) lengthwise slices

¼ teaspoon salt

8 (1-ounce) slices whole wheat bread

8 tablespoons soft goat cheese with black pepper

1 tablespoon chopped fresh tarragon

¼ cup chopped roasted red pepper (not packed in oil)

1   Spray panini maker with nonstick spray and preheat to high.

2   Spray eggplants and zucchini with nonstick spray and sprinkle with salt; place in panini maker. Close lid and cook until vegetables are softened, about 5 minutes. Transfer to sheet of foil to cool slightly.

3   Spread each of 4 slices of bread with 2 tablespoons of goat cheese; sprinkle evenly with tarragon. Top evenly with eggplants, zucchini, and roasted pepper. Cover with remaining 4 slices of bread.

4   Place sandwiches in panini maker. Close lid and cook until bread is well marked and crisp and filling is heated through, about 4 minutes.

PER SERVING (1 sandwich): 207 Cal, 5 g Total Fat, 3 g Sat Fat, 0 g Trans Fat, 7 mg Chol, 524 mg Sod, 30 g Carb, 7 g Sugar, 6 g Fib, 12 g Prot, 94 mg Calc.

FYI   Japanese eggplant is one of the several varieties of eggplant available in some supermarkets, produce, and specialty food stores. Long, thin, purple Japanese eggplants have bright green stems (known as calyxes). They are tender and sweet tasting.

Beef & Root Vegetable Stew

6 PointsPlus® value
PER SERVING

serves
6

1 pound bottom round steak, trimmed and cut into 1-inch chunks

½ teaspoon salt

¼ teaspoon black pepper

1 tablespoon canola oil

2 large onions, chopped

3 garlic cloves, minced

1 tablespoon chopped fresh thyme

1 (14½-ounce) can reduced-sodium beef broth

4 carrots, cut lengthwise in half and into 1-inch chunks

1 (1-pound) celery root, peeled and cut into 1-inch chunks

¾ pound small red potatoes, scrubbed and quartered

¼ cup chopped fresh parsley

1   Sprinkle steak with salt and pepper. Heat oil in large pressure cooker over medium-high heat. Add steak and cook until browned on all sides, about 6 minutes. Add onions, garlic, thyme, and broth; lock lid in place. Bring to high pressure over high heat. Reduce heat just enough to maintain pressure; cook 5 minutes.

2   Quick-release pressure according to manufacturer's directions. Add all remaining ingredients to pressure cooker except parsley. Lock lid in place. Bring to high pressure. Reduce heat just enough to maintain high pressure; cook 5 minutes. Quick-release pressure according to manufacturer's directions. Stir in parsley.

PER SERVING (1 cup): 247 Cal, 7 g Total Fat, 2 g Sat Fat, 0 g Trans Fat, 44 mg Chol, 358 mg Sod, 26 g Carb, 6 g Sugar, 5 g Fib, 20 g Prot, 77 mg Calc.

FYI   Celery root, also called celeriac, knob celery, and turnip-rooted celery, has a subtle celery flavor and dense, fibrous flesh. Choose a celery root that is very firm and fresh looking. To prepare it, cut off the top and base, then cut away all the outer peel. Immediately dip the celery root into cold water to prevent browning, then cut as directed in recipe.

Chicken Gumbo

5 PointsPlus value PER SERVING | serves **6** | **20** min

2 teaspoons canola oil

½ pound turkey kielbasa, cut into ½-inch slices

1 pound skinless boneless chicken breasts, cut into 1-inch chunks

1 (14½-ounce) can no-salt-added diced tomatoes

1 bunch scallions, thinly sliced (white and green parts separated)

½ pound okra, cut into 1-inch pieces, or 1 (10-ounce) package frozen sliced okra

4 garlic cloves, chopped

1 tablespoon Worcestershire sauce

1 teaspoon dried oregano

2 tablespoons quick-cooking polenta

¼ teaspoon black pepper

Few drops hot pepper sauce or to taste

1 Heat oil in pressure cooker over medium-high heat. Add kielbasa and chicken; cook until browned on all sides, about 5 minutes. Stir in tomatoes, white parts of scallions, okra, garlic, Worcestershire sauce, and oregano; lock lid in place. Bring to high pressure over high heat. Reduce heat just enough to maintain pressure; cook 4 minutes.

2 Quick-release pressure according to manufacturer's directions. Stir in polenta and black pepper; simmer until gumbo is thickened, about 1 minute. Stir in green parts of scallions and pepper sauce.

PER SERVING (1 cup): 211 Cal, 7 g Total Fat, 2 g Sat Fat, 0 g Trans Fat, 66 mg Chol, 451 mg Sod, 13 g Carb, 4 g Sugar, 3 g Fib, 23 g Prot, 82 mg Calc.

Healthy Extra Serve the gumbo over hot cooked brown rice (⅔ cup cooked brown rice per serving will increase the *PointsPlus* value by 3).

Curried Lentil-Vegetable Stew

Curried Lentil-Vegetable Stew

4 PointsPlus® value | serves **6**

PER SERVING

2 teaspoons olive oil

1 large onion, chopped

1 leek, cleaned and chopped

1 (32-ounce) container reduced-sodium vegetable or chicken broth, warmed

1 pound butternut squash, peeled, halved, seeded, and cut into 1½-inch chunks

1 cup brown lentils, picked over, rinsed, and drained

1 tablespoon curry powder

½ teaspoon ground cumin

½ teaspoon salt

¼ teaspoon black pepper

2 cups lightly packed coarsely chopped kale

1 Heat oil in pressure cooker over high heat. Add onion and leek; cook, stirring, until softened about 3 minutes. Stir in broth, squash, lentils, curry powder, cumin, salt, and pepper; lock lid in place. Bring to high pressure over high heat. Reduce heat just enough to maintain pressure; cook 10 minutes.

2 Quick-release the pressure according to the manufacturer's directions. Stir in kale; simmer until tender, about 5 minutes longer.

PER SERVING (1¼ cups): 190 Cal, 2 g Total Fat, 0 g Sat Fat, 0 g Trans Fat, 0 mg Chol, 300 mg Sod, 35 g Carb, 5 g Sugar, 14 g Fib, 10 g Prot, 108 mg Calc.

Healthy Extra Add 2 cups of diced zucchini to the soup along with the kale in step 2.

Triple-Berry Bread Pudding

5 PointsPlus® value | serves **4**

PER SERVING

2 large eggs

2 large egg whites

¾ cup fat-free half-and-half

⅓ cup sugar

1 teaspoon grated lemon zest

1 teaspoon vanilla extract

¼ teaspoon salt

Pinch ground allspice

3 cups lightly packed (½-inch) cubes whole wheat bread (about 3 slices)

1½ cups fresh blueberries, raspberries, and blackberries

1 Lightly beat eggs, egg whites, half-and-half, sugar, lemon zest, vanilla, salt, and allspice in 1½-quart soufflé or other heatproof dish that will fit into pressure cooker. Add bread, stirring until coated completely. Stir in berries and press down to form even layer on top.

2 Set dish in middle of 24-inch-long sheet of heavy-duty foil; bring ends up to meet over top of dish. Fold ends over to seal, creating tent and leaving enough room for pudding to puff. Fold short ends of foil together and press against side of dish to seal.

3 Set trivet or wire rack in bottom of cooker; place pudding on top. Pour in enough water to reach halfway up side of dish; lock lid in place. Bring to high pressure over high heat. Reduce heat enough to maintain pressure; cook 15 minutes. Let pressure drop naturally 10 minutes; release any remaining pressure. Remove lid and carefully remove pudding from cooker. Let cool at least 10 minutes. Serve warm or refrigerate to serve chilled later.

PER SERVING (¾ cup): 187 Cal, 3 g Total Fat, 1 g Sat Fat, 0 g Trans Fat, 108 mg Chol, 342 mg Sod, 30 g Carb, 19 g Sugar, 3 g Fib, 9 g Prot, 101 mg Calc.

Milk Chocolate Fondue

serves **8**

20 min

PER SERVING

1⅓ cups milk chocolate chips

⅔ cup fat-free half-and-half

1 teaspoon vanilla extract

¼ teaspoon instant espresso powder

4 cups strawberries with their stems attached

4 bananas, cut into thick slices

1   Put chocolate chips in food processor.

2   Put half-and-half in glass measure and microwave on High until it simmers, about 1 minute. With motor running, pour into feed tube of food processor; add vanilla and espresso powder. Process until chocolate is melted and mixture is smooth, about 1 minute longer.

3   Transfer chocolate mixture to fondue pot with flame under it to keep it warm. Serve with strawberries and bananas.

PER SERVING (2 tablespoons fondue, ½ cup strawberries, and ½ banana): 254 Cal, 9 g Total Fat, 6 g Sat Fat, 0 g Trans Fat, 6 mg Chol, 41 mg Sod, 42 g Carb, 29 g Sugar, 9 g Fib, 4 g Prot, 95 mg Calc.

Healthy Extra   Other fondue-friendly fruits include thick slices of kiwifruit, pineapple wedges, and orange segments.

Southwestern Cheese Fondue

serves **8**

20 min

PER SERVING

¾ cup dry white wine

1½ tablespoons cornstarch

½ cup water

8 ounces shredded reduced-fat Monterey Jack cheese

¼–½ teaspoon chipotle chile powder

½ teaspoon salt

4 cups broccoli florets

4 cups white and purple cauliflower florets

1   Whisk together ¼ cup of wine and the cornstarch in small bowl until smooth.

2   Combine remaining ½ cup wine and the water in medium heavy saucepan and bring to simmer over medium-high heat. Stir in Monterey Jack and whisk constantly until melted. Whisk in cornstarch mixture and simmer, whisking constantly, until mixture bubbles and thickens, about 1 minute.

3   Stir chile powder and salt into fondue; transfer to fondue pot with flame under it to keep it warm. Serve with broccoli and cauliflower.

PER SERVING (¼ cup fondue and 1 cup vegetables): 128 Cal, 5 g Total Fat, 4 g Sat Fat, 0 g Trans Fat, 15 mg Chol, 405 mg Sod, 7 g Carb, 1 g Sugar, 2 g Fib, 9 g Prot, 434 mg Calc.

FYI   This savory fondue works well as an appetizer or light bite. Serve it with other dippers, including thickly sliced mushrooms, pieces of bell pepper, or asparagus spears.

Southwestern Cheese Fondue

Bittersweet Chocolate–Orange Fondue

serves
8

20
min

PER SERVING

⅔ cup fat-free half-and-half

2 (3-inch) strips orange zest, removed with vegetable peeler

1⅓ cups chopped bittersweet chocolate

1 tablespoon Grand Marnier or Triple Sec

2 cups raspberries

2 cups sliced kiwifruit

2 cups clementine segments (about 4 clementines)

1 Combine half-and-half and orange zest in small saucepan and bring to simmer over medium-high heat. Add chocolate and remove from heat; let stand 1 minute. Whisk until chocolate is melted and mixture is smooth. Discard orange zest; stir in Grand Marnier.

2 Transfer chocolate mixture to fondue pot with flame under it to keep it warm. Serve with raspberries, kiwifruit, and clementines.

PER SERVING (2 tablespoons fondue, ¼ cup raspberries, ¼ cup kiwifruit, and ¼ cup clementine): 220 Cal, 9 g Total Fat, 5 g Sat Fat, 0 g Trans Fat, 0 mg Chol, 20 mg Sod, 36 g Carb, 27 g Sugar, 6 g Fib, 3 g Prot, 70 mg Calc.

FYI Use chocolate chips and avoid having to chop the chocolate.

Bittersweet Chocolate–
Orange Fondue

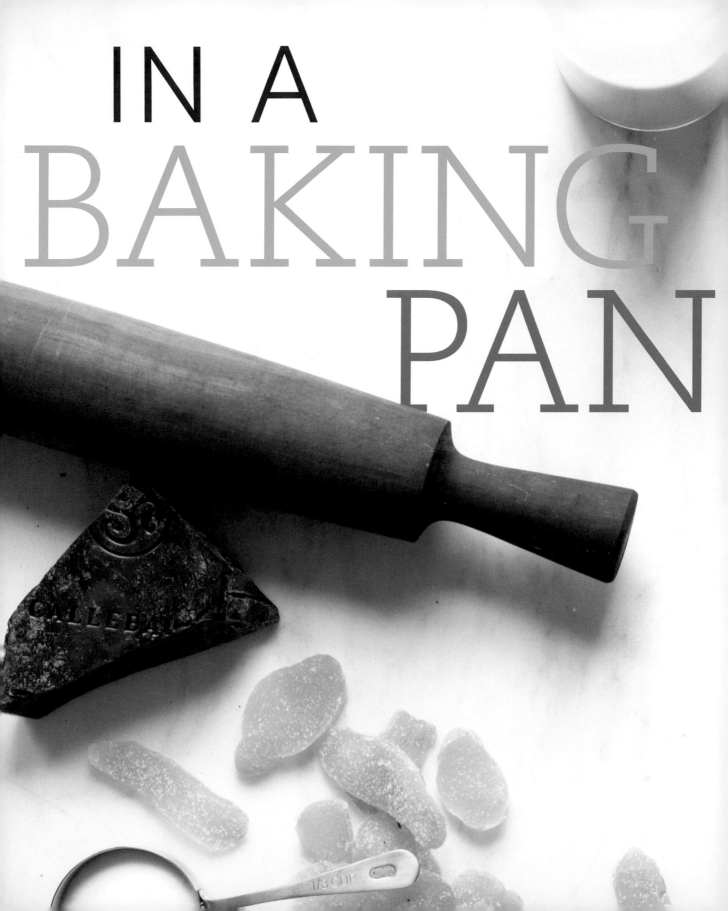

IN A
BAKING
PAN

CHAPTER 11

IN A BAKING PAN

MAKE IT SWEET: CAKES, QUICK BREADS, BUCKLES & BAR COOKIES

Whether baking a Bundt cake, quick bread, fruit pie, or favorite cookie, using the right pan can make all the difference when it comes to baking success. Baking pans come in a variety of shapes and sizes, so it's easy to find just the right pan to suit every baking need.

Types

Round, square, and rectangular baking pans are the go-to pans for brownies, bar cookies, cake layers, old-fashioned pan cakes, and some coffeecakes. These metal pans are often made of aluminum, although some have a nonstick interior or a nonstick finish both inside and out. For the best results, choose a heavier pan over a lighter one to prevent uneven baking. By definition, a baking pan is metal, but glass or ceramic baking dishes can often be substituted.

A **springform pan** is the pan of choice for cheesecakes. The base (bottom) and side are separate pieces clamped together by a latch on the outside of the pan. The side of the pan expands when the clamp is released, making it easy to remove a cake. Also available are glass-bottomed springform pans, which are especially nice as the base can be used as a serving plate.

A **tube pan** is a baking pan with a center tube. A *Bundt pan* is a fluted round-bottomed tube pan.

It gained in popularity in 1966 when Pillsbury sponsored a baking contest in which the second-place winner was a Bundt cake. Since then, nearly 60 million of these pans have been sold. Most Bundt pans are made of heavy cast aluminum (liquid aluminum that is poured into a mold, which produces a pan with a very thick wall) with a nonstick finish. An *angel food cake pan* is another kind of tube pan. This tall slope-sided removable bottom pan is the only pan for angel food cake. The tall center tube ensures the middle of the cake bakes in the same amount of time as the rest of the cake, while the removable bottom ensures that the cake can be easily lifted out of the pan. Some angel food cake pans come with small "feet" at the bottom. Since this cake is cooled upside down (so it doesn't collapse), the feet ensure that air can circulate freely around the cake. A *kugelhopf pan* is a tall fluted pan with an angled ridged pattern all around. It is typically used for baking a sweet raisin-filled yeast bread of the same name, a specialty of the Alsace region of France. These pans were originally made of tin, but now most are made of heavy cast aluminum with a nonstick finish.

A **loaf pan** is a metal or glass rectangular pan used for baking quick breads, loaf cakes, and yeast breads.

Pie plates—also known as a pie pans—are shallow round pans made of metal or glass, although many bakers prefer glass for its ability to brown. There are also deep-dish pie plates for extra-deep pies that usually only have a top crust.

A **tart pan** has shallow sides that are usually fluted and a bottom that is often removable, which makes for easy serving. The most common shape is round but you can also find rectangular tart pans, as well as mini pans for individual desserts.

Baking sheets come with and without rims. A *jelly-roll pan* is a rimmed baking sheet used for making a jelly roll, a filled sponge cake rolled up like a log. *Cookie sheets* are baking sheets with one or two low rims. Their design makes it easy to slide cookies onto wire racks. When purchasing baking sheets, choose heavy aluminum pans to ensure uniform baking.

A **muffin pan** (also called a muffin tin) is a baking pan with cup-shaped depressions that hold either 6 or 12 sweet or savory muffins. Muffin pans are typically made of stainless steel or aluminum. There are also soft, flexible silicone muffin pans and individual silicone muffin cups that don't need to be floured or greased.

Baking Pan Sizes

When it comes to **round baking pans,** the most useful sizes are 8 and 9 inches in diameter and 2 inches deep; larger and smaller pans are available. For most baking needs, 8- and 9-inch square baking pans are ideal; most are 2 inches high. A standard rectangular baking pan is 9 x 13 x 2 inches. Some have covers, which is great when taking baked goods on the road.

Springform pans range in diameter from about 6 inches to 12 inches. The most useful size is 9 inches across and 2½ to 3 inches deep.

A traditional **Bundt pan** holds 12 cups of batter and is about 10 inches in diameter. Many recipes call for Bundt pans by their cup capacity. To measure it, put the pan on the counter or in the sink and add enough measured water to reach the top of the pan. Bundt pans are also available in 6- or 15-cup capacity. A standard angel food cake pan has a 10-inch diameter, while kugelhopf pans range from 6- to 10-cup capacity.

Standard **loaf pans** are 4½ x 8½ x 3 inches (6 cups) and 5 x 9 x 3 inches (8 cups). Mini loaf pans and extra-large loaf pans are also available.

A standard **pie plate** has a 9-inch diameter and is 1½ inches deep, while a deep-dish pie plate has a 9-inch diameter and is 2 inches deep.

The most useful **removable bottom round tart pan** is 9 inches in diameter, although they range from about 4 inches to 11 inches.

A standard **jelly-roll pan** is 10 x 15 inches. Most cookie sheets are 12 x 16 inches or 14 x 18 inches.

Recipes call for **regular (standard) muffin pans, mini (gem) muffin pans, or jumbo muffin pans.** Standard pans are about 2½ inches in diameter, mini pans are 1¼ to 2 inches in diameter, and jumbo pans are 3¼ inches in diameter.

Basics for Care

Metal and glass baking pans are easy to care for. Once cooled down, soak them for about 15 minutes in hot, soapy water, then use a nylon scrub pad to dislodge any remaining food. Rinse with warm water and dry well.

Nonstick baking pans require gentle cleaning. Once cool, soak it in hot, soapy water for about 15 minutes, then use a sponge or nylon scrub pad to clean it well.

Fallen Chocolate Cake

Fallen Chocolate Cake

¾ cup granulated sugar

¼ cup + 1 tablespoon unsweetened cocoa

4 ounces bittersweet or semisweet chocolate, finely chopped

2 tablespoons butter

1 tablespoon instant espresso powder

¼ teaspoon salt

½ cup boiling water

2 large egg yolks

¼ cup all-purpose flour

4 large egg whites, at room temperature

¼ teaspoon cream of tartar

1   Preheat oven to 375°F. Line bottom of 9-inch springform pan with wax paper; spray with nonstick spray.

2   Whisk together ½ cup of granulated sugar, ¼ cup of cocoa, the chocolate, butter, espresso powder, and salt in medium bowl. Add boiling water and stir until chocolate is melted and mixture is smooth; let cool slightly. Whisk egg yolks into chocolate mixture until smooth. Gradually add flour, stirring just until blended.

3   With electric mixer on medium speed, beat egg whites and cream of tartar in large bowl until soft peaks form when beaters are lifted. Add remaining ¼ cup granulated sugar, 1 tablespoon at a time, beating until stiff, glossy peaks form when beaters are lifted.

4   With rubber spatula, stir one-fourth of beaten egg whites into chocolate mixture to lighten it, then gently fold in remaining whites just until no streaks of white remain. Scrape batter into prepared pan.

5   Bake until toothpick inserted into center of cake comes out with moist crumbs clinging, about 35 minutes. Let cool completely in pan on wire rack (cake will sink slightly in center). Run thin knife around side of cake to loosen from pan; release and remove side of pan. Just before serving, dust top of cake with remaining 1 tablespoon cocoa.

PER SERVING (¹⁄₁₂ of cake): 144 Cal, 7 g Total Fat, 4 g Sat Fat, 0 g Trans Fat, 40 mg Chol, 83 mg Sod, 21 g Carb, 17 g Sugar, 1 g Fib, 3 g Prot, 8 mg Calc.

Healthy Extra   Accompany each slice of cake with sliced fresh strawberries, raspberries, and blackberries.

Olive Oil–Cornmeal Cake with Strawberries

serves
12

1¼ cups all-purpose flour

½ cup yellow cornmeal, preferably stone-ground

2 teaspoons baking powder

½ teaspoon salt

¾ cup + 1 tablespoon sugar

½ cup low-fat buttermilk

⅓ cup olive oil

2 large eggs

1 tablespoon grated lemon zest

2 tablespoons sliced almonds

2 (1-pound) containers fresh strawberries, hulled and sliced

¼ cup orange liqueur or orange juice

1   Preheat oven to 350°F. Spray 8-inch round cake pan with nonstick spray.

2   Combine flour, cornmeal, baking powder, and salt in large zip-close plastic bag; seal bag and shake until mixed well. Whisk together ¾ cup of sugar, the buttermilk, oil, eggs, and lemon zest in large bowl. Add flour mixture to buttermilk mixture, stirring just until combined. Pour batter into prepared pan. Scatter almonds over batter and sprinkle with remaining 1 tablespoon sugar.

3   Bake until toothpick inserted into center of cake comes out with moist crumbs clinging, 25–30 minutes. Let cool in pan on wire rack 15 minutes. Remove cake from pan and let cool completely on rack.

4   Meanwhile, stir together strawberries and liqueur in serving bowl. Serve with cake.

PER SERVING (¹⁄₁₂ of cake and ½ cup strawberries): 223 Cal, 8 g Total Fat, 1 g Sat Fat, 0 g Trans Fat, 36 mg Chol, 211 mg Sod, 34 g Carb, 16 g Sugar, 2 g Fib, 4 g Prot, 49 mg Calc.

FYI   Use a mild-flavored olive oil that has a grassy flavor rather than one that has a peppery bite.

**Olive Oil–Cornmeal Cake
with Strawberries**

Chocolate-Ginger Bundt Cake

 serves 24 PER SERVING

2 cups white whole wheat flour

1¼ cups sugar

2 teaspoons baking powder

1 teaspoon ground cinnamon

½ teaspoon baking soda

½ teaspoon salt

½ cup unsweetened cocoa

1 ounce bittersweet or semisweet chocolate, finely chopped

½ cup boiling water

½ cup low-fat (1%) milk

⅓ cup canola oil

¼ cup light molasses

2 large eggs

1 large egg white

1 tablespoon grated peeled fresh ginger

1   Preheat oven to 350°F. Spray 10-inch Bundt pan with nonstick spray.

2   Combine flour, sugar, baking powder, cinnamon, baking soda, and salt in large zip-close plastic bag. Seal bag and shake until mixed well.

3   Combine cocoa and chocolate in large bowl. Add boiling water and stir until chocolate is melted and mixture is smooth; let cool. Add milk, oil, molasses, eggs, egg white, and ginger to cocoa mixture; whisk until blended well. Add flour mixture, stirring just until combined. Pour batter into prepared pan.

4   Bake until toothpick inserted into center of cake comes out clean, 45–50 minutes. Let cool in pan on wire rack 10 minutes. Invert cake onto rack and let cool completely.

PER SERVING (¹⁄₂₄ of cake): 138 Cal, 4 g Total Fat, 1 g Sat Fat, 0 g Trans Fat, 18 mg Chol, 133 mg Sod, 23 g Carb, 14 g Sugar, 2 g Fib, 3 g Prot, 30 mg Calc.

FYI   When choosing ginger, look for firm fresh-looking ginger without any wrinkles.

Apricot-Glazed Yogurt Loaf Cake

 serves 16 PER SERVING

2 cups white whole wheat flour

2 teaspoons baking powder

1 teaspoon ground ginger

½ teaspoon salt

1 cup plain reduced-fat Greek yogurt

1 cup sugar

2 large eggs

¼ cup canola oil

Grated zest of 1 orange

¼ teaspoon vanilla extract

2 tablespoons apricot preserves

1 teaspoon lemon juice

1   Preheat oven to 350°F. Spray 4½ x 8½-inch loaf pan with nonstick spray.

2   Combine flour, baking powder, ginger, and salt in zip-close plastic bag; seal bag and shake until mixed well. Whisk together yogurt, sugar, eggs, oil, orange zest, and vanilla in large bowl until blended well. Stir in flour mixture just until combined. Scrape batter into prepared pan and spread evenly.

3   Bake until toothpick inserted into center of cake comes out clean, 45–50 minutes. Let cool in pan on wire rack 10 minutes. Run thin knife around sides of cake to loosen from pan. Remove cake from pan and let cool on rack until warm, about 30 minutes.

4   Meanwhile, to make glaze, stir together preserves and lemon juice in small microwavable bowl. Microwave on High until melted, about 30 seconds. Brush hot glaze over top of warm cake. Let cool completely.

PER SERVING (¹⁄₁₆ of cake): 147 Cal, 4 g Total Fat, 0 g Sat Fat, 0 g Trans Fat, 27 mg Chol, 156 mg Sod, 24 g Carb, 11 g Sugar, 2 g Fib, 4 g Prot, 27 mg Calc.

Old-Fashioned Applesauce Cake

serves
12

1½ cups all-purpose flour

½ cup whole wheat pastry flour

2 tablespoons unsweetened cocoa

2 teaspoons baking powder

1½ teaspoons pumpkin pie spice

½ teaspoon baking soda

½ teaspoon salt

¾ cup low-fat buttermilk

½ cup unsweetened applesauce

¾ cup packed light brown sugar

¼ cup canola oil

1 large egg

¼ cup chopped walnuts

1   Preheat oven to 375°F. Spray 8-inch square baking pan with nonstick spray.

2   Combine all-purpose flour, pastry flour, cocoa, baking powder, pumpkin pie spice, baking soda, and salt in large zip-close plastic bag; seal bag and shake until mixed well. Whisk together buttermilk, applesauce, brown sugar, oil, and egg in large bowl. Add flour mixture to buttermilk mixture and stir just until combined. Stir in walnuts. Pour batter into prepared pan.

3   Bake until toothpick inserted into center of cake comes out clean, about 35 minutes. Let cool in pan on wire rack 10 minutes. Run thin knife around edges of cake to loosen from pan. Invert onto rack; let cool 10 minutes. Invert again and let cool completely.

PER SERVING (¹⁄₁₂ of cake): 192 Cal, 7 g Total Fat, 1 g Sat Fat, 0 g Trans Fat, 19 mg Chol, 267 mg Sod, 30 g Carb, 15 g Sugar, 1 g Fib, 4 g Prot, 56 mg Calc.

FYI   There are two kinds of unsweetened cocoa powder: natural and Dutch process. Natural cocoa has rich chocolate flavor and is used most often in baking. Dutch-process cocoa is treated with an alkali, which mellows its flavor and lends baked goods a deep, dark color.

Fresh Blueberry–Vanilla Cake

serves
24

3 cups all-purpose flour

2 cups sugar

1 teaspoon baking powder

¾ teaspoon baking soda

½ teaspoon salt

¼ teaspoon ground nutmeg

1 cup low-fat buttermilk

½ cup olive oil

3 large eggs

1 tablespoon vanilla extract

2 cups fresh blueberries
(about 1 pint)

1 Preheat oven to 350°F. Spray 10-inch tube pan with nonstick spray. Dust with flour, shaking out excess.

2 Combine flour, sugar, baking powder, baking soda, salt, and nutmeg in large zip-close plastic bag. Seal bag and shake until mixed well. Whisk together buttermilk, oil, eggs, and vanilla in large bowl. Add flour mixture to buttermilk mixture, stirring just until blended; gently stir in blueberries. Scrape batter into prepared pan and spread evenly.

3 Bake until toothpick inserted into center of cake comes out clean, about 1 hour 10 minutes. Let cool in pan on wire rack 15 minutes. Remove cake from pan and let cool completely on rack.

PER SERVING (¹⁄₂₄ of cake): 159 Cal, 6 g Total Fat, 1 g Sat Fat, 0 g Trans Fat, 27 mg Chol, 130 mg Sod, 27 g Carb, 14 g Sugar, 1 g Fib, 3 g Prot, 22 mg Calc.

FYI You can also use frozen blueberries in this cake. Consider stocking up on pints of fresh blueberries when they are in season and reasonably priced. Wrap each pint container (do not wash the berries) in heavy-duty foil and place in a zip-close plastic bag. Freeze for up to one year.

Fresh Blueberry–Vanilla Cake

Raspberry Cheesecake Cups

serves
12

PER SERVING

½ cup reduced-fat gingersnap cookie crumbs (about 12 cookies)

1 tablespoon butter, softened

¼ cup raspberry fruit spread

2 (8-ounce) packages light cream cheese (Neufchâtel), softened

½ cup sugar

1 large egg

1 large egg white

1 teaspoon grated lemon zest

1 teaspoon vanilla extract

1   Preheat oven to 350°F. Spray regular 12-cup muffin pan with nonstick spray. Line each cup with 2 x 6-inch foil strip, allowing foil to extend above rim.

2   Stir together cookie crumbs and butter in small bowl until mixed well. Press 2 teaspoons of crumb mixture onto bottom of each cup; refrigerate until firm, about 15 minutes. Spread about 1 teaspoon of fruit spread over crumb mixture in each cup. Refrigerate while making filling.

3   With electric mixer on medium speed, beat cream cheese in medium bowl until very smooth, about 2 minutes. Gradually add sugar, beating until fluffy, about 2 minutes. Beat in egg, egg white, lemon zest, and vanilla until blended. Divide batter evenly among cups.

4   Bake until edges of cheesecakes are set and centers jiggle slightly, about 20 minutes. Let cool in pan on wire rack 30 minutes. Cover cakes with foil and refrigerate until chilled and set, at least 4 hours or up to 2 days. Lift cheesecakes from their cups using foil strips as handles.

PER SERVING (1 cheesecake cup): 178 Cal, 11 g Total Fat, 6 g Sat Fat, 0 g Trans Fat, 48 mg Chol, 189 mg Sod, 17 g Carb, 12 g Sugar, 0 g Fib, 5 g Prot, 53 mg Calc.

FYI   These little cakes can also be baked in 1 x 2½-inch-deep silicone cupcake molds. Heatproof and nonstick, they make it a breeze to bake and remove baked goods from the molds. They can also be reused hundreds of times. Fill the molds as directed above and place on a baking sheet. Once the cheesecakes are baked and cooled, simply pop them out of the molds.

Raspberry Cheesecake Cups

Apple & Dried Fruit Galette

5 PointsPlus® value

PER SERVING

serves **10**

CRUST

1 ¼ cups white whole wheat flour

1 tablespoon sugar

½ teaspoon salt

3 tablespoons canola oil

1 tablespoon cold unsalted butter, cut into pieces

3-4 tablespoons ice water

FILLING

½ cup pitted prunes, quartered

½ cup dried apricots, quartered

½ cup unsweetened apple juice

¼ cup water

¼ cup sugar

Pinch salt

2 Golden Delicious apples, peeled, halved, cored, and cut into ½-inch slices

TOPPING

2 teaspoons fat-free milk

1 teaspoon sugar

1   To make crust, combine flour, sugar, and salt in food processor; pulse until blended. Add oil and butter; pulse until mixture resembles coarse crumbs. Pour 3 tablespoons of water through feed tube, pulsing just until dough forms. (If dough doesn't come together, add remaining 1 tablespoon water.) Shape dough into disk. Wrap in plastic wrap and refrigerate until firm, at least 30 minutes or up to 1 day.

2   To make filling, combine all filling ingredients except apples in medium saucepan; bring to boil. Reduce heat and simmer, partially covered, stirring occasionally, until fruit is softened, about 10 minutes. Add apples and cook, partially covered, stirring occasionally, until apples are softened and mixture is thickened, about 10 minutes. Remove saucepan from heat. Let cool 15 minutes.

3   Meanwhile, preheat oven to 375°F. Line large baking sheet with parchment paper.

4   On lightly floured work surface with a lightly floured rolling pin, roll dough into 13-inch round. Transfer to prepared baking sheet. Mound filling over crust, leaving 3-inch border. Fold edge of dough over filling, pleating it as you go around. Lightly brush edge of dough with milk and sprinkle with sugar.

5   Bake until filling bubbles slightly and crust is browned, about 35 minutes. Let cool 10 minutes. Slide galette with parchment onto wire rack. With metal spatula, separate galette from parchment; slip out parchment and discard. Let galette cool completely. Cut into wedges.

PER SERVING (⅒ of galette): 182 Cal, 6 g Total Fat, 1 g Sat Fat, 0 g Trans Fat, 3 mg Chol, 133 mg Sod, 32 g Carb, 16 g Sugar, 4 g Fib, 3 g Prot, 12 mg Calc.

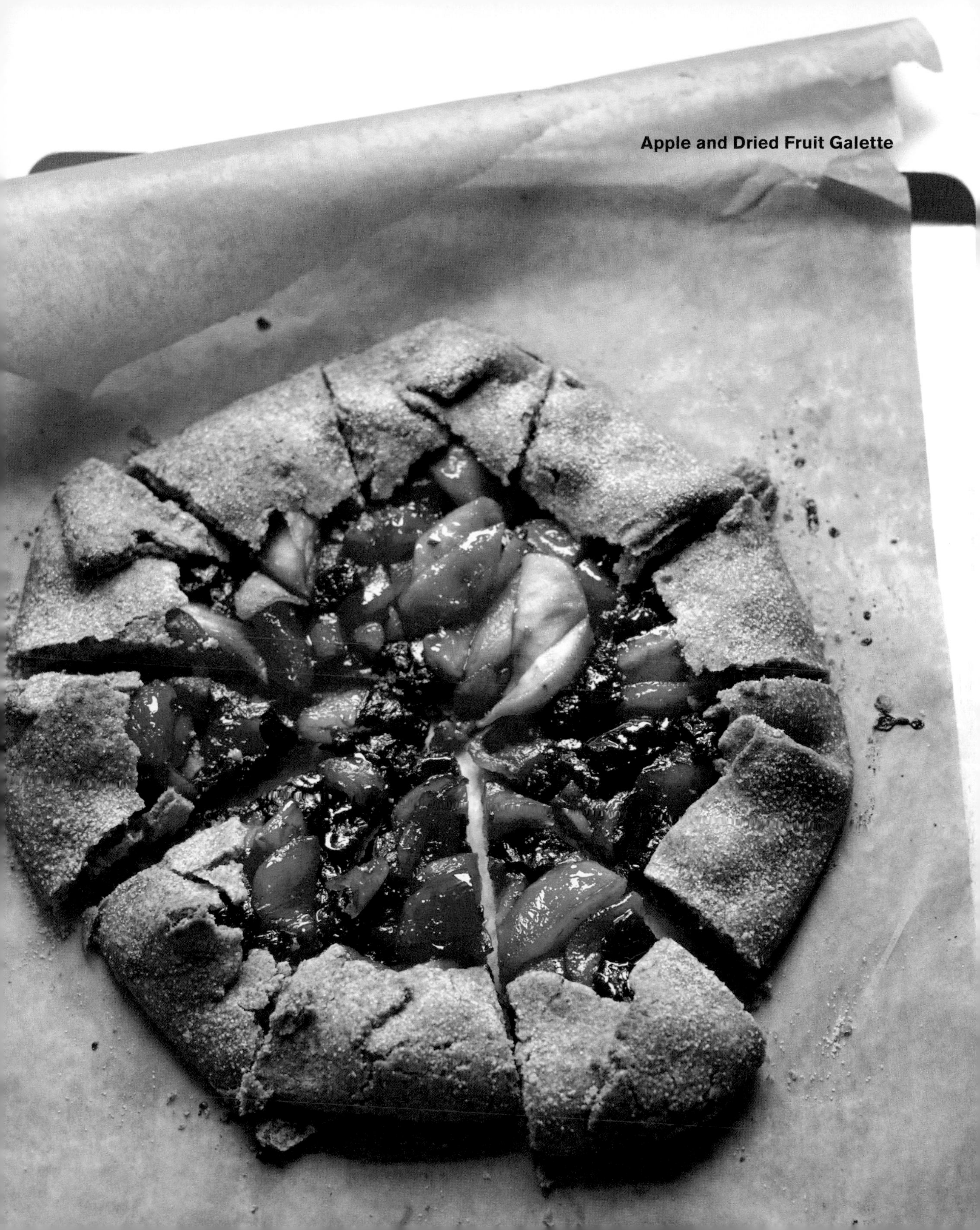
Apple and Dried Fruit Galette

Plum-Apricot Buckle

Plum-Apricot Buckle

serves
10

PER SERVING

FILLING

1 cup cake flour (not self-rising)

1 teaspoon baking powder

½ teaspoon salt

½ cup low-fat buttermilk

½ cup sugar

1 large egg

¼ cup canola oil

1 teaspoon vanilla extract

6 Italian plums, halved, pitted, and cut into ½-inch wedges

6 small apricots, halved and pitted

TOPPING

1 tablespoon sugar

½ teaspoon ground cinnamon

1　Preheat oven to 375°F. Spray 9-inch springform pan with nonstick spray.

2　To make filling, combine flour, baking powder, and salt in zip-close plastic bag. Seal bag and shake until mixed well. Whisk together buttermilk, sugar, egg, oil, and vanilla in large bowl. Add flour mixture, stirring just until combined. Pour batter into prepared pan. Scatter plums and apricots over batter.

3　To make topping, mix together sugar and cinnamon in cup; sprinkle evenly over fruit.

4　Bake until buckle is browned and bubbly, about 35 minutes. Let cool on wire rack about 20 minutes. Serve warm or at room temperature.

PER SERVING (⅒ of buckle): 169 Cal, 7 g Total Fat, 1 g Sat Fat, 0 g Trans Fat, 22 mg Chol, 191 mg Sod, 27 g Carb, 15 g Sugar, 1 g Fib, 3 g Prot, 35 mg Calc.

FYI　A buckle is a cake-like dessert, so named because the cake bakes up around the fruit and "buckles." If you can't find Italian plums, use red or black plums instead.

Marbled Chocolate-Orange Angel Food Cake

4 PointsPlus® value
PER SERVING

serves
12

12 large egg whites, at room temperature

1 teaspoon cream of tartar

¼ teaspoon salt

1¼ cups sugar

Grated zest of 2 oranges

1 cup cake flour (not self-rising), sifted

¼ cup unsweetened cocoa

¼ cup semisweet chocolate chips

1 tablespoon fat-free milk

1   Place rack in lower third of oven. Preheat oven to 350°F.

2   With electric mixer on medium speed, beat egg whites, cream of tartar, and salt in large bowl until soft peaks form when beaters are lifted. Add sugar, 2 tablespoons at a time, beating until egg whites form stiff, glossy peaks when beaters are lifted. Beat in orange zest.

3   Sift flour, one-third at a time, over egg whites, gently folding it in with rubber spatula just until flour is no longer visible (do not overmix). Transfer half of batter to medium bowl and sift cocoa over batter. With rubber spatula, gently fold in cocoa until mixed well. Spoon batters alternately into ungreased 10-inch tube pan. With table knife, swirl batter to create marbled effect.

4   Bake until cake springs back when lightly pressed, about 35 minutes. Invert pan onto its legs or neck of bottle. Let cool completely.

5   Combine chocolate chips and milk in small microwavable bowl. Microwave on High until chocolate is melted, 30–40 seconds; stir until smooth. Run thin knife around edge of cake to loosen from side and center tube of pan. Invert cake onto serving plate. Drizzle glaze over top of cake, allowing it to drip down side of cake. Let stand until glaze sets.

PER SERVING (¹⁄₁₂ of cake): 139 Cal, 2 g Total Fat, 1 g Sat Fat, 0 g Trans Fat, 0 mg Chol, 105 mg Sod, 29 g Carb, 18 g Sugar, 1 g Fib, 5 g Prot, 13 mg Calc.

FYI   Sifting the flour is important when making an angel food cake as it removes any small lumps and also aerates it, making the cake lighter. You can use an old-fashioned sifter or a sieve.

Soufléd Apple-Pear Pancake

PointsPlus value 3 PER SERVING

serves
6

2 teaspoons canola oil

2 firm-ripe red Bartlett pears, halved, cored, and cut into thin wedges

1 Granny Smith apple, peeled, halved, cored, and cut into thin wedges

2 tablespoons granulated sugar

½ teaspoon ground cinnamon

1 cup fat-free milk

2 large eggs

½ teaspoon vanilla extract

¼ teaspoon salt

¼ cup all-purpose flour

1 tablespoon confectioners' sugar

1 Preheat oven to 400°F.

2 Heat oil in medium ovenproof skillet, such as cast iron, over medium heat. Add pears, apple, 1 tablespoon of granulated sugar, and the cinnamon. Cook, stirring occasionally, until pears and apple are tender and most of liquid is evaporated, about 10 minutes.

3 Whisk together milk, eggs, vanilla, salt, and remaining 1 tablespoon granulated sugar in medium bowl. Gradually whisk in flour until smooth. Pour batter over hot fruit mixture.

4 Bake until pancake is puffed and golden brown, 20–25 minutes. Cool pancake in skillet on wire rack 10 minutes. Dust with confectioners' sugar and cut into 6 wedges. Serve warm or at room temperature.

PER SERVING (1 wedge): 129 Cal, 3 g Total Fat, 1 g Sat Fat, 0 g Trans Fat, 72 mg Chol, 136 mg Sod, 22 g Carb, 13 g Sugar, 2 g Fib, 4 g Prot, 67 mg Calc.

Healthy Extra This special pancake is also a great choice for breakfast. Top each serving with fat-free cottage cheese for some healthful protein (⅓ cup fat-free cottage cheese per serving will increase the *PointsPlus* value by **1**).

Amaretti-Berry Crumble

serves
6

¼ cup sugar

1 tablespoon all-purpose flour

1½ teaspoons cornstarch

½ teaspoon ground cinnamon

⅛ teaspoon salt

2 (6-ounce) containers fresh blueberries

2 (6-ounce) containers fresh raspberries

2 (6-ounce) containers fresh blackberries

2 teaspoons lemon juice

¾ teaspoon almond extract

8 amaretti cookies, coarsely crushed (½ cup)

1 tablespoon unsalted butter, melted

1   Preheat oven to 375°F. Spray 1½-quart baking dish with nonstick spray.

2   Combine sugar, flour, cornstarch, cinnamon, and salt in small zip-close plastic bag. Seal bag and shake until mixed well. Gently toss together flour mixture, blueberries, raspberries, blackberries, lemon juice, and almond extract in prepared baking dish; spread evenly. Sprinkle with amaretti and drizzle with butter.

3   Bake until topping is browned and mixture is bubbly, about 30 minutes. Let crumble cool on wire rack about 20 minutes. Serve warm or at room temperature.

PER SERVING (1 cup): 153 Cal, 3 g Total Fat, 1 g Sat Fat, 0 g Trans Fat, 5 mg Chol, 52 mg Sod, 31 g Carb, 20 g Sugar, 8 g Fib, 2 g Prot, 37 mg Calc.

Healthy Extra   Top each serving of crumble with plain fat-free yogurt and a few fresh berries (1/3 cup of plain fat-free yogurt per serving will increase the *PointsPlus* value by 1).

Amaretto Fudge Brownies

serves
16

¾ cup all-purpose flour

¾ teaspoon baking powder

¼ teaspoon salt

1 large egg

1 large egg white

3 tablespoons almond-flavored liqueur (Amaretto)

1 teaspoon vanilla extract

¾ cup sugar

3 tablespoons butter, melted

2 tablespoons hot water

½ cup unsweetened cocoa

1 tablespoon instant espresso powder

½ cup chopped walnuts

1   Preheat oven to 350°F. Spray 8-inch square baking pan with nonstick spray.

2   Combine flour, baking powder, and salt in small zip-close plastic bag. Seal bag and shake until mixed well. Whisk together egg, egg white, liqueur, and vanilla in large bowl. Add sugar, butter, and hot water; whisk until blended well. Whisk in cocoa and espresso powder. Add flour mixture, stirring just until blended; stir in walnuts. Scrape batter into prepared pan and spread evenly.

3   Bake until toothpick inserted into center of brownies comes out with a few moist crumbs clinging, about 20 minutes. (Do not overbake.) Let cool completely in pan on wire rack. Cut into 16 squares.

PER SERVING (1 square): 111 Cal, 5 g Total Fat, 2 g Sat Fat, 0 g Trans Fat, 19 mg Chol, 86 mg Sod, 15 g Carb, 7 g Sugar, 1 g Fib, 3 g Prot, 14 mg Calc.

FYI   Brownies can be cakey or fudgy. Ours are somewhere in between. If you like, you can bake them for a few minutes less to make them more fudgy or a few minutes more to make them more cakey.

Dried Fruit-Cornmeal Quick Bread

serves
16

2 cups white whole wheat flour

¾ cup sugar

½ cup yellow cornmeal

1½ teaspoons baking powder

½ teaspoon baking soda

½ teaspoon salt

1¼ cups low-fat buttermilk

⅓ cup canola oil

Grated zest of 1 orange

¼ cup orange juice

1 large egg

1 large egg white

½ cup mixed dried fruit, such as apricots, plums, pears, and apples, coarsely chopped

12 pecan halves

1 Preheat oven to 350°F. Spray 5 x 9-inch loaf pan with nonstick spray.

2 Combine flour, sugar, cornmeal, baking powder, baking soda, and salt in large zip-close plastic bag. Seal bag and shake until mixed well. Whisk together buttermilk, oil, orange zest and juice, egg, and egg white in large bowl until blended. Add flour mixture to buttermilk mixture and stir just until blended; stir in dried fruit.

3 Spoon batter into prepared pan. Arrange pecan halves in two lengthwise rows on top of batter.

4 Bake until toothpick inserted into center of bread comes out with moist crumbs clinging, about 1 hour 10 minutes. Cool in pan on wire rack 10 minutes. Remove bread from pan and let cool completely on rack.

PER SERVING (1 slice): 179 Cal, 6 g Total Fat, 1 g Sat Fat, 0 g Trans Fat, 14 mg Chol, 147 mg Sod, 28 g Carb, 9 g Sugar, 3 g Fib, 4 g Prot, 29 mg Calc.

FYI You can use dried cranberries, strawberries, blueberries or a mixture of dried fruit, such as dried cherries, cranberries, and golden raisins instead of the mixed dried fruit if you like.

Double Raspberry-Walnut Streusel Bars

serves
16

2 cups white whole wheat flour

½ cup packed light brown sugar

½ teaspoon ground cinnamon

½ teaspoon baking soda

¼ teaspoon salt

¼ cup finely chopped walnuts

1 large egg

¼ cup canola oil

½ cup fresh raspberries

1 (10-ounce) jar raspberry fruit spread

¼ cup quick-cooking (not instant) oats

1   Preheat oven to 350°F. Spray 9-inch square baking pan with nonstick spray.

2   Whisk together flour, brown sugar, cinnamon, baking soda, and salt in medium bowl; stir in walnuts. Beat egg and oil in 1-cup glass measure. Add egg mixture to flour mixture, stirring until blended well. With your fingers, stir mixture until moist crumbs form; reserve ½ cup.

3   Transfer remaining crumb mixture to prepared pan; press to form even layer. Bake until set and lightly browned along edges, about 10 minutes.

4   Coarsely mash raspberries in small bowl; stir in fruit spread. Spread evenly over hot crust. Mix oats with remaining ½ cup crumb mixture on sheet of wax paper; crumble over fruit spread.

5   Bake until fruit is bubbly at edges and topping is browned, 15–20 minutes. Let cool completely in pan on wire rack. Cut into 16 squares.

PER SERVING (1 square): 183 Cal, 5 g Total Fat, 0 g Sat Fat, 0 g Trans Fat, 13 mg Chol, 82 mg Sod, 31 g Carb, 16 g Sugar, 3 g Fib, 3 g Prot, 11 mg Calc.

FYI   You can easily change up the fruit in these bars. Try it with blueberry fruit spread and fresh blueberries or strawberry spread and fresh strawberries.

Double Raspberry-Walnut
Streusel Bars

Frosted Chocolate-Zucchini Mini Cupcakes

3 PointsPlus value PER SERVING

serves
24

CUPCAKES

2 cups white whole wheat flour

¾ cup granulated sugar

¼ cup unsweetened cocoa

2 teaspoons baking powder

½ teaspoon salt

¾ cup fat-free milk

¼ cup canola oil

1 large egg

1 large egg white

1 cup shredded zucchini, squeezed dry (about 1 small zucchini)

¼ cup mini semisweet chocolate chips

FROSTING

1 cup light cream cheese (Neufchâtel), softened

½ cup confectioners' sugar

1   Preheat oven to 400°F. Spray 24-cup mini-muffin pan with nonstick spray.

2   To make cupcakes, combine flour, granulated sugar, cocoa, baking powder, and salt in large zip-close plastic bag. Seal bag and shake until ingredients are mixed well. Whisk together milk, oil, egg, and egg white in large bowl. Add flour mixture to milk mixture and stir just until blended. Stir in zucchini and chocolate chips. Fill muffin cups evenly with batter.

3   Bake until tops of cupcakes spring back when lightly pressed, 10–15 minutes. Let cool in pan on wire rack 10 minutes. Remove cupcakes from pan and let cool completely on rack.

4   Meanwhile, to make frosting, with electric mixer on high speed, beat cream cheese and confectioners' sugar in medium bowl until smooth, about 1 minute. With small metal spatula, spread frosting over tops of cooled cupcakes.

PER SERVING (1 cupcake): 124 Cal, 5 g Total Fat, 2 g Sat Fat, 0 g Trans Fat, 15 mg Chol, 150 mg Sod, 18 g Carb, 9 g Sugar, 2 g Fib, 3 g Prot, 36 mg Calc.

FYI   Squeezing the excess liquid from the grated zucchini ensures that the cupcakes will not be soggy. Wrap the zucchini in a clean kitchen towel and twist the towel until the zucchini liquid is released. This is also a great technique to use when cooking zucchini for a side dish, as it prevents the cooked zucchini from becoming watery.

Food Processor Chocolate Chip–Oatmeal Cookies

½ cup quick-cooking
(not instant) oats

1 cup all-purpose flour

½ teaspoon baking soda

½ teaspoon salt

4 tablespoons unsalted butter,
cut into 4 pieces

¾ cup packed brown sugar

1 large egg

1 teaspoon vanilla extract

½ cup semisweet chocolate chips

¼ cup shredded unsweetened
coconut

1 Place oven racks in upper and lower thirds of oven. Preheat oven to 350°F. Spray 2 large baking sheets with nonstick spray.

2 Put oats in food processor and process until finely ground. Add flour, baking soda, and salt; pulse until blended. Turn mixture out onto sheet of wax paper. Put butter and brown sugar in food processor; process until blended well, scraping bowl down once. Add egg and vanilla; process until creamy. Add flour mixture and pulse just until combined. Add chocolate chips and coconut; pulse until mixed.

3 Drop dough by level tablespoonfuls, about 2 inches apart, on prepared baking sheets, making total of 24 cookies.

4 Bake until cookies are lightly browned along edges, 12–15 minutes, rotating baking sheets after 6 minutes. Let cool on baking sheets on wire racks 1 minute. With spatula, transfer cookies to racks and let cool completely.

PER SERVING (1 cookie): 103 Cal, 4 g Total Fat, 3 g Sat Fat, 0 g Trans Fat, 14 mg Chol, 80 mg Sod, 15 g Carb, 10 g Sugar, 1 g Fib, 1 g Prot, 9 mg Calc.

FYI Shredded unsweetened coconut can be found in health food stores and some grocery stores. The shreds are finer than flaked sweetened coconut.

Chewy Ginger Cookies

makes
24

1½ cups all-purpose flour

½ teaspoon baking soda

½ teaspoon salt

4 tablespoons butter, softened

⅔ cup packed brown sugar

2 tablespoons light or
dark molasses

1 large egg

1 teaspoon vanilla extract

¼ cup chopped crystallized ginger

2 tablespoons granulated sugar

1   Place racks in upper and lower thirds of oven. Preheat oven to 350°F. Spray 2 large baking sheets with nonstick spray.

2   Combine flour, baking soda, and salt in large zip-close plastic bag. Seal bag and shake until mixed well. With electric mixer on low speed, beat butter, brown sugar, molasses, egg, and vanilla in large bowl until mixed well. Add flour mixture and beat just until blended. Stir in ginger.

3   Roll slightly rounded tablespoonfuls of dough into balls, making total of 24 balls. Spread granulated sugar on sheet of wax paper. Dip tops of balls in sugar and place, sugar side up, about 2 inches apart, on prepared baking sheets.

4   Bake until cookies are cracked, soft in center, and firm along edges, 10–12 minutes, rotating baking sheets after 6 minutes. Let cool on baking sheets on wire racks 2 minutes. With spatula, transfer cookies to racks and let cool completely.

PER SERVING (1 cookie): 84 Cal, 2 g Total Fat, 1 g Sat Fat, 0 g Trans Fat, 14 mg Chol, 94 mg Sod, 15 g Carb, 8 g Sugar, 0 g Fib, 1 g Prot, 13 mg Calc.

FYI   You can use light or dark molasses in these cookies. Light molasses comes from the first boiling of sugar syrup and has a mild flavor and light brown color. Dark molasses comes from the second boiling and is thicker, darker, and not as sweet. It is most often used in gingerbread, ginger cookies, and Indian pudding.

Maple & Butter Roasted Pears with Chocolate Drizzle

serves
4

2 tablespoons pure maple syrup

2 teaspoons butter

2 (½-pound) large firm-ripe Bosc or Bartlett pears, peeled, halved, and cored

¼ cup dark chocolate (60%) chips

1 Preheat oven to 425°F.

2 Combine maple syrup and butter in medium ovenproof skillet, such as cast iron, and set over medium-high heat. Cook until butter is melted, about 30 seconds. Add pears, cut side down, and cook until lightly browned, about 6 minutes; turn pears over.

3 Transfer skillet to oven and bake until pears are just tender when pierced with fork, about 10 minutes longer. Let cool in skillet 10 minutes.

4 Meanwhile, place chocolate chips in small microwavable bowl and microwave on High until melted and smooth, 30–45 seconds, stirring every 15 seconds. Place pear half on each of 4 plates and drizzle evenly with sauce.

PER SERVING (1 pear half with 1 tablespoon sauce): 180 Cal, 6 g Total Fat, 4 g Sat Fat, 0 g Trans Fat, 5 mg Chol, 16 mg Sod, 33 g Carb, 25 g Sugar, 4 g Fib, 1 g Prot, 18 mg Calc.

FYI There are several varieties of pears available, including Anjou, Bartlett, Bosc, Comice, Forelle, and Seckel. Anjou and Bosc pears are in season in the fall, winter, and spring, while the others varieties are available in the spring and summer. Look for firm, well-colored pears without any blemishes. Ripen them at room temperature until they are fragrant and yield to gentle pressure, then refrigerate for up to 3 days.

IN A

BOWL OR POT

CHAPTER 12
IN A BOWL OR POT

STIR IT SWEET: NO-FUSS PUDDINGS, SORBETS, COMPOTES & MORE

Merriam-Webster's defines the word *stir* as "to disturb the relative position of the particles, by a continued circular movement." Whether you are making cake batter, pudding, sorbet, or poached fruit, chances are the recipe will call for stirring. This action is a way to mix different ingredients together or to turn them into something new. When egg yolks, brown sugar, cornstarch, vanilla, milk, and butter are stirred over gentle heat, they evolve into something totally new and delectable: a silky smooth butterscotch pudding. That is the power of stirring.

There are several utensils made for stirring, including wooden spoons, rubber spatulas, and wire whisks. What you choose depends on the ingredients and the desired results: wooden spoons are good for most stirring needs, rubber spatulas are especially good at gently combining ingredients without deflating them (known as folding) and for mixing batters and doughs, while a whisk excels at aerating (beating egg whites, for example) and gently but thoroughly blending liquids to form a new mixture, as in a sauce or custard.

Wooden Spoons

Wooden spoons are a staple in any kitchen and can be used in any pot or pan. They will not scratch enamel cast iron or nonstick finishes. Wooden spoons don't get hot, and since they are made of a natural material, they are very comfortable to hold—even for a long time. They are made of olive wood, cherry wood, and beech wood, as well as bamboo. All are good choices. Wooden spoons come in a variety of shapes, including slotted, flat-ended, and flat. Wooden spoons should be washed in hot, soapy water (do not soak) using a sponge or nylon scrub pad. They are not dishwasher safe.

Spatulas and Spoonulas

Rubber spatulas have been a staple in kitchens for decades. Their only downside was not being heatproof. Then along came silicone spatulas, which are heatproof up to 800°F and ideal for nonstick cookware. They are available in a variety of sizes and in sets of two and three, which is often a better buy.

A spoonula is a silicone spatula that is a hybrid of rubber spatula and spoon. Its shallow cup shape makes it especially handy for stirring liquids and for scooping. The heads of silicone spatulas can be removed and washed by hand with hot, soapy water or in a dishwasher.

Whisks

A whisk is the ideal cooking utensil for blending, emulsifying, aerating, or whipping. Most consist of a metal handle with wire loops that are looped and joined at the handle. Whisks come in a variety of shapes, including narrow, balloon, ball, and flat.

A standard whisk, also called a French whisk, has loops that are rather narrow, making it well suited for getting into the corners of straight-sided saucepans and for making salad dressings and marinades.

Balloon whisks have bulbous-shaped wires, which makes them great for beating egg whites or cream. As with most other whisks, they are made of stainless steel.

Ball whisks consist of a group of straight wires that stick out from the handle with each wire tipped with a tiny metal ball. These whisks are good at reaching into the corners of pots and for beating liquids.

A flat whisk, also known as a sauce or roux whisk, is different from standard whisks. It consists of a set of thick wire loops of different lengths that are arranged in a U-shaped pattern. Its flat shape makes it ideal of mixing batters and for gravies.

Creamy Rice Pudding with Cherries & Almonds

serves 6

2 cups low-fat (1%) milk

1¼ cups water

½ cup long-grain white rice

½ teaspoon salt

½ cup sugar

½ cup dried sweet cherries

1 teaspoon vanilla extract

⅓ cup sliced almonds, toasted

1 Combine 1 cup of milk, the water, rice, and salt in medium saucepan; bring to boil over medium-high heat, stirring occasionally. Reduce heat and simmer, covered, until rice is tender, about 30 minutes.

2 Stir remaining 1 cup milk, the sugar, and cherries into rice mixture; return to simmer. Cover and cook, stirring occasionally, until mixture is creamy, about 20 minutes. Remove saucepan from heat; stir in vanilla. Let pudding stand until warm, about 15 minutes, stirring occasionally.

3 Divide pudding evenly among 6 dessert dishes and sprinkle evenly with almonds.

PER SERVING (½ cup pudding and scant 1 tablespoon almonds): 196 Cal, 3 g Total Fat, 1 g Sat Fat, 0 g Trans Fat, 4 mg Chol, 233 mg Sod, 38 g Carb, 22 g Sugar, 2 g Fib, 5 g Prot, 119 Calc.

FYI To accentuate the flavor of the almonds, stir ¼ teaspoon almond extract into the pudding along with the vanilla in step 2.

Silky Butterscotch Pudding

serves 8

2 large egg yolks

⅔ cup packed light brown sugar

¼ cup cornstarch

1 tablespoon vanilla extract

2½ cups low-fat (1%) milk

2 tablespoons unsalted butter, cut into pieces

1 Stir together egg yolks, brown sugar, cornstarch, and vanilla in large bowl until mixed well.

2 Bring milk just to simmer in large saucepan over medium heat. Slowly pour half of hot milk into egg mixture, whisking constantly. Whisk mixture back into saucepan. Bring to simmer over medium-low heat, whisking constantly. Cook, whisking, until pudding bubbles and thickens, about 2 minutes. Remove saucepan from heat; stir in butter until melted.

3 Divide pudding evenly among 8 custard cups or ramekins. Press piece of plastic wrap directly onto surface of each pudding to prevent skin from forming. Cover and refrigerate until thoroughly chilled, at least 3 hours or up to 1 day.

PER SERVING (½ cup): 161 Cal, 5 g Total Fat, 3 g Sat Fat, 0 g Trans Fat, 64 mg Chol, 42 mg Sod, 26 g Carb, 22 g Sugar, 0 g Fib, 3 g Prot, 113 Calc.

FYI Combining uncooked eggs with a hot liquid, such as milk or cream uses a technique called tempering. By slowly combining the eggs with the hot liquid, the eggs gradually warm up, which prevents them from curdling (scrambling).

Deep Dark Mocha Pudding

serves **6**

PER SERVING

½ cup packed dark brown sugar

2 tablespoons granulated sugar

¼ cup unsweetened cocoa

2 tablespoons cornstarch

1 teaspoon instant espresso powder

¼ teaspoon salt

2 cups low-fat (1%) milk

¾ cup mini semisweet chocolate chips

1 teaspoon vanilla extract

1 Stir together brown sugar, granulated sugar, cocoa, cornstarch, espresso powder, and salt in large heavy saucepan until mixture is blended well.

2 Stir 1 cup of milk and the chocolate chips into saucepan; set over medium heat. Cook, whisking frequently, until chocolate is melted and mixture is smooth, about 4 minutes.

3 Whisk remaining 1 cup milk into chocolate mixture and cook, whisking frequently, until large bubbles pop on surface and pudding is thickened and smooth, about 10 minutes. Remove saucepan from heat and whisk in vanilla. Spoon pudding into serving bowl or divide evenly among dessert dishes or wineglasses. Serve warm or refrigerate to serve chilled.

PER SERVING (⅓ cup): 239 Cal, 8 g Total Fat, 5 g Sat Fat, 0 g Trans Fat, 4 mg Chol, 141 mg Sod, 43 g Carb, 37 g Sugar, 3 g Fib, 5 g Prot, 124 Calc.

Healthy Extra Serve the pudding topped with fresh raspberries and sliced small strawberries.

Raspberry Fool

  serves **4** | 20 min

PER SERVING

1 (6-ounce) container fresh raspberries

1 (17.6-ounce) container plain fat-free Greek yogurt

6 tablespoons sugar

¼ teaspoon vanilla extract

Pinch salt

1 Process raspberries in food processor just until smooth. Pour puree through fine sieve set over medium bowl; discard seeds.

2 Whisk yogurt, sugar, vanilla, and salt into raspberry puree until no streaks of white remain. Divide evenly among 4 small glasses or dessert dishes. Cover and refrigerate until set, at least 3 hours or up to overnight.

PER SERVING (⅔ cup): 134 Cal, 0 g Total Fat, 0 g Sat Fat, 0 g Trans Fat, 0 mg Chol, 83 mg Sod, 24 g Carb, 20 g Sugar, 3 g Fib, 12 g Prot, 93 Calc.

FYI This classic English dessert has been enjoyed since the 16th century. Our version can also be prepared with 6 ounces of blueberries, strawberries, blackberries, or a combination instead of the raspberries.

Sabayon with Strawberries

 serves **6**

PER SERVING

3 large egg yolks

⅓ cup sugar

3 tablespoons orange liqueur, such as Grand Marnier or Cointreau

1 (1-pound) container fresh strawberries, hulled and halved or quartered if large

1 Combine egg yolks, sugar, and liqueur in top of double boiler (or bowl); beat with portable electric mixer until well combined. Fill bottom of double boiler (or medium saucepan) with 1½ inches of water; bring to simmer. Set top of double boiler (or bowl) over bottom of pan and cook, beating, until mixture is tripled in volume, about 10 minutes.

2 Divide strawberries evenly among 6 wineglasses. Top each with about one-sixth of sabayon. Serve at once.

PER SERVING (1 parfait): 110 Cal, 3 g Total Fat, 1 g Sat Fat, 0 g Trans Fat, 105 mg Chol, 5 mg Sod, 18 g Carb, 15 g Sugar, 2 g Fib, 2 g Prot, 26 Calc.

FYI Zabaglione (zah-bah-YOH-nay) is an Italian dessert made by whipping egg yolks, Marsala wine, and sugar over simmering water until a light and foamy custard is formed. Sabayon (sah-bah-YAWN) is the French version, which uses orange liqueur instead of Marsala. Both renditions are delectable.

Classic English Trifle

serves
16

PER SERVING

6 cups fresh strawberries, hulled and halved (about two 1-pound containers)

1 (6-ounce) container fresh raspberries

1 cup seedless green grapes, halved

¼ cup sugar

1 (10-ounce) fat-free angel food cake, cut into ½-inch wedges

1 cup orange preserves

1 (16-ounce) container frozen fat-free whipped topping, thawed

¼ cup sliced almonds, toasted

1 Gently toss together strawberries, raspberries, grapes, and sugar in large bowl; let stand 15 minutes.

2 Line bottom of 12-cup trifle dish or straight-sided glass bowl with one-third of cake wedges. Brush cake with ⅓ cup of preserves. Top with one-third of fruit mixture (about 2 cups) and one-third of whipped topping (about 2 cups). Repeat layering two more times.

3 Cover trifle bowl with piece of plastic wrap; refrigerate until fruit juices are absorbed by cake, at least 2 hours or up to 6 hours. Sprinkle with almonds just before serving.

PER SERVING (about ⅔ cup): 168 Cal, 1 g Total Fat, 0 g Sat Fat, 0 g Trans Fat, 0 mg Chol, 166 mg Sod, 39 g Carb, 21 g Sugar, 2 g Fib, 2 g Prot, 44 Calc.

FYI Toasting almonds brings out their flavor and also crisps them. Preheat the oven or toaster oven to 350°F. Spread the nuts in a single layer in a baking pan. Bake, stirring occasionally, until golden brown and fragrant, about 10 minutes. Transfer to a plate to cool. Alternatively, spread the nuts in a large skillet and cook over medium heat, stirring often, until golden brown, about 8 minutes. Transfer the nuts to a plate and let cool.

Real Raspberry Gelatin

3 PointsPlus® value
PER SERVING

serves
4

1½ teaspoons unflavored gelatin

¾ cup water

3 (6-ounce) containers fresh raspberries

¼ cup sugar

8 tablespoons fat-free sour cream or plain fat-free Greek yogurt

1 Sprinkle gelatin over ½ cup of water in small bowl; let stand until softened, about 5 minutes.

2 Combine 2 containers of raspberries, remaining ¼ cup water, and the sugar in food processor; process just until smooth. Pour raspberry mixture through fine sieve set over medium heavy saucepan; discard seeds.

3 Bring raspberry mixture to boil over medium-high heat. Remove saucepan from heat; add gelatin mixture, whisking until gelatin is dissolved. Pour mixture into loaf pan; let cool to room temperature.

4 Refrigerate gelatin mixture until set, at least 6 hours or up to overnight. Cut into 16 slices and divide evenly among 4 dessert bowls. Top each serving with 2 tablespoons sour cream and one-fourth of remaining raspberries.

PER SERVING (¼ of gelatin mixture, 1 tablespoon reduced-fat sour cream, and about 5 raspberries): 122 Cal, 1 g Total Fat, 0 g Sat Fat, 0 g Trans Fat, 3 mg Chol, 50 mg Sod, 29 g Carb, 15 g Sugar, 8 g Fib, 3 g Prot, 74 Calc.

FYI It is important that the softened gelatin is completely dissolved in the hot liquid to ensure that the resulting dessert is completely smooth. To check, dip your thumb and forefinger into the gelatin mixture and rub the fingers together. There should be no trace of graininess. If needed, continue to stir until the gelatin is completely dissolved.

Triple Chocolate Sorbet

serves
12

PER SERVING

2½ cups water

¾ cup packed light brown sugar

½ cup granulated sugar

⅔ cup unsweetened cocoa

Pinch salt

1¾ cups mini semisweet chocolate chips

2 teaspoons vanilla extract

1 Combine water, brown sugar, granulated sugar, cocoa, and salt in large heavy saucepan; bring to boil over medium-high heat, whisking until sugar is dissolved.

2 Remove saucepan from heat. Add ¾ cup of chocolate chips and whisk until chocolate is melted and mixture is smooth. Pour chocolate mixture through fine sieve set over large bowl. Let cool to room temperature; whisk in vanilla. Refrigerate, covered, until thoroughly chilled, about 3 hours.

3 Pour chocolate mixture into ice-cream maker and freeze according to manufacturer's instructions. Stir in remaining 1 cup chocolate chips. Transfer to freezer container and freeze until firm, at least 2 hours or up to overnight.

PER SERVING (⅓ cup): 150 Cal, 4 g Total Fat, 2 g Sat Fat, 0 g Trans Fat, 0 mg Chol, 20 mg Sod, 32 g Carb, 20 g Sugar, 2 g Fib, 1 g Prot, 20 Calc.

Healthy Extra Chocolate and fruit—just about any type—are the perfect marriage of flavors. Make this excellent sorbet even more delicious by topping each serving with in-season fruit. Consider a mix of berries, diced pears, peaches, and plums, or sliced mango, papaya, and kiwifruit. If you like, sprinkle the fruit with chopped fresh mint, which also partners well with chocolate.

Red Zinger Granita

serves
6

PER SERVING

3 cups water

½ cup sugar

Pinch salt

10 Red Zinger tea bags

1 Place 9 x 13-inch baking pan in freezer.

2 Combine water, sugar, and salt in medium saucepan; bring to boil over medium-high heat, stirring until sugar is dissolved. Add tea bags. Transfer to bowl; cover tightly with plastic wrap and let steep 1 hour. Discard tea bags.

3 Let tea cool to room temperature. Refrigerate until thoroughly chilled, about 3 hours or up to overnight.

4 Pour tea mixture into baking pan in freezer. Cover pan with sheet of foil; freeze until ice crystals form around edges of pan, about 1 hour. With fork, scrape ice at edges in toward center. Repeat every 30 minutes until granita is semifirm, about 2 hours.

5 To serve, with fork, scrape across surface of granita, transferring ice shards to 6 wineglasses. Serve at once.

PER SERVING (1 cup): 40 Cal, 0 g Total Fat, 0 g Sat Fat, 0 g Trans Fat, 0 mg Chol, 24 mg Sod, 12 g Carb, 12 g Sugar, 0 g Fib, 0 g Prot, 0 Calc.

FYI Red Zinger tea is an artful blend of tart Chinese hibiscus, fruity Thai hibiscus, a bit of peppermint, and a little wild cherry bark, which lends the tea an earthy quality. This tea's deep crimson color and bold flavor make for a spectacular granita.

Coconut-Lemongrass Sorbet

serves 6

PER SERVING

1½ cups water

½ cup packed light brown sugar

2 lemongrass stalks, thinly sliced

Pinch salt

1 (14-ounce) can light (reduced-fat) coconut milk

1 Combine water, brown sugar, lemongrass, and salt in medium heavy saucepan; bring to boil over medium-high heat. Remove saucepan from heat; cover and let steep 20 minutes. Pour mixture through fine sieve set over large bowl; discard solids. Let cool to room temperature.

2 Whisk coconut milk into lemongrass mixture. Cover bowl with piece of plastic wrap. Refrigerate until thoroughly chilled, about 4 hours or up to overnight.

3 Whisk lemongrass mixture; pour into ice-cream maker and freeze according to manufacturer's instructions. Transfer to freezer container and freeze until firm, at least 2 hours or up to 6 hours.

PER SERVING (⅔ cup sorbet): 115 Cal, 4 g Total Fat, 0 g Sat Fat, 0 g Trans Fat, 0 mg Chol, 32 mg Sod, 21 g Carb, 18 g Sugar, 0 g Fib, 0 g Prot, 17 Calc.

FYI When purchasing lemongrass, look for stalks that are firm and pale, an indication of freshness. Wash it thoroughly, then peel off the tough outer leaves and trim the ends. With a very sharp knife, slice or chop the bulbous heart of the stalk as directed.

Lemon–Chocolate Chip Ice Cream

serves
8

20
min

PER SERVING

2 pints fat-free vanilla
ice cream

1 cup mini semisweet
chocolate chips

2 teaspoons grated
lemon zest

Spoon ice cream into medium bowl; let stand at
room temperature until softened, about 5 minutes.
Stir in chocolate chips and lemon zest; cover and
freeze until firm, about 30 minutes.

PER SERVING (about ½ cup ice cream): 197 Cal, 8 g Total Fat,
5 g Sat Fat, 0 g Trans Fat, 5 mg Chol, 52 mg Sod, 35 g Carb, 26 g Sugar,
5 g Fib, 3 g Prot, 91 Calc.

FYI Turn this delectable ice cream into a terrine.
Line a small loaf pan (about 4 to 6 cups) with plastic
wrap, allowing the ends to extend over the rim of
the pan. Pack the ice cream into the pan and fold the
plastic wrap over the ice cream. Freeze until very
firm, at least 4 hours or up to overnight. To serve,
unmold the terrine onto a cutting board and cut
into 12 slices. Place 2 slices on each of 6 plates and
garnish each serving with fresh strawberries,
a lemon slice, and a fresh mint sprig.

Strawberry-Vanilla Sundaes with Summery Fruit

serves
6

20
min

PER SERVING

1 small mango, peeled,
seeded, and cut into
½-inch dice

1 cup fresh blueberries

½ cup fresh blackberries

½ cup fresh raspberries

1 tablespoon sugar

Pinch salt

1 pint strawberry sorbet

1 pint fat-free vanilla
ice cream

1 Gently toss together mango, blueberries,
blackberries, raspberries, sugar, and salt in medium
bowl. Let stand at room temperature until sugar is
dissolved and juices are released, about 10 minutes.

2 Place ⅓-cup scoop each of sorbet and ice cream
in each of 6 shallow bowls; top evenly with fruit
mixture and serve at once.

PER SERVING (⅓ cup sorbet, ⅓ cup ice cream, and about ½ cup fruit):
194 Cal, 1 g Total Fat, 1 g Sat Fat, 0 g Trans Fat, 4 mg Chol, 58 mg Sod,
48 g Carb, 34 g Sugar, 6 g Fib, 2 g Prot, 66 Calc.

Healthy Extra Add a classic sundae fruit—
banana—to this dessert. Slice a medium banana
and divide evenly among the sundaes.

Peaches Poached in Lemon Syrup

serves
4

PER SERVING

4 (6-ounce) peaches

4 cups water

½ cup sugar

6 (4-inch) strips lemon zest, removed with vegetable peeler

Pinch salt

2 tablespoons lemon juice

¼ teaspoon vanilla extract

1   Bring large saucepan of water to boil. Lower peaches, one at a time, into water and cook 30 seconds. With slotted spoon, transfer peaches to cutting board. Slip off skins or peel peaches with small sharp knife; cut peaches in half and remove pits. Pour off water from saucepan.

2   Combine 4 cups water, peaches, sugar, lemon zest, and salt in same saucepan; bring to boil over medium-high heat. Reduce heat and simmer, turning occasionally, until peaches are softened, about 7 minutes. With slotted spoon, transfer peaches to serving bowl.

3   Increase heat to high and boil syrup until reduced to 2 cups, about 15 minutes. Remove saucepan from heat and whisk in lemon juice and vanilla; let cool to room temperature. Pour syrup through fine sieve set over peaches in serving bowl; discard solids.

PER SERVING (2 peach halves and ½ cup syrup): 120 Cal, 0 g Total Fat, 0 g Sat Fat, 0 g Trans Fat, 0 mg Chol, 41 mg Sod, 33 g Carb, 30 g Sugar, 2 g Fib, 1 g Prot, 13 Calc.

FYI   This poaching technique works for other fruits too, including nectarines, plums, and pears. Nectarines and plums do not need to be peeled after being poached.

Strawberries in Orange-Flower Water

serves
4

20
min

PER SERVING

1 (1-pound) container fresh strawberries, hulled and sliced

1 large orange, peeled and sectioned

2 tablespoons orange juice

1 tablespoon confectioners' sugar

1½ teaspoons orange-flower water

Pinch salt

4 fresh mint sprigs

Combine all ingredients except mint sprigs in medium bowl and gently toss until mixed well. Divide fruit mixture evenly among 4 dessert dishes; garnish each with 1 mint sprig.

PER SERVING (1 cup): 69 Cal, 0 g Total Fat, 0 g Sat Fat, 0 g Trans Fat, 0 mg Chol, 38 mg Sod, 17 g Carb, 3 g Fib, 1 g Prot, 37 Calc.

FYI   Orange-flower water is an essential ingredient in Middle Eastern cooking, especially desserts and drinks. It is made from the distillation of fresh bitter-orange blossoms. A little orange-flower water turns lemonade into an exotic drink and is an important ingredient in the drink Ramos Gin Fizz. It can be found in specialty food stores and in Middle Eastern markets.

Silken Tofu with Ginger Syrup & Berries

5 PointsPlus® value
PER SERVING

serves 4

20 min

¼ cup pure maple syrup, preferably dark grade B

3 tablespoons minced crystallized ginger

¼ teaspoon grated lemon zest

Pinch salt

1 (16-ounce) package soft silken tofu, cut crosswise into 4 slices

2 cups fresh blueberries and blackberries

Stir together maple syrup, ginger, lemon zest, and salt in 1-cup glass measure. Arrange tofu on a small platter; drizzle with syrup mixture and surround with berries.

PER SERVING (1 slice tofu, scant 2 tablespoons sauce, and ½ cup berries): 173 Cal, 3 g Total Fat, 0 g Sat Fat, 0 g Trans Fat, 0 mg Chol, 48 mg Sod, 31 g Carb, 21 g Sugar, 2 g Fib, 6 g Prot, 74 Calc.

Healthy Extra Add a cup of sliced strawberries to the blueberries and blackberries.

**Warm Cherries with Goat
Cheese & Thyme**

Warm Cherries with Goat Cheese & Thyme

 serves **4**

PER SERVING

1 tablespoon canola oil

1 tablespoon packed dark brown sugar

1 tablespoon water

1 teaspoon balsamic vinegar

1 pound fresh sweet cherries, pitted

1 teaspoon fresh thyme leaves

Pinch salt

8 (¼-inch) slices soft goat cheese

1   Combine oil, brown sugar, water, and ½ teaspoon of vinegar in large nonstick skillet and set over medium heat. Cook, stirring constantly, until some liquid is evaporated, about 3 minutes. Stir in cherries, ½ teaspoon of thyme leaves, and salt; cook, stirring frequently, until cherries begin to soften, about 5 minutes. Stir in remaining ½ teaspoon vinegar.

2   Place 2 slices of goat cheese in each of 4 bowls; spoon cherry mixture around cheese and sprinkle with remaining ½ teaspoon thyme.

PER SERVING (½ cup cherries and 2 slices goat cheese): 166 Cal, 8 g Total Fat, 3 g Sat Fat, 0 g Trans Fat, 9 mg Chol, 107 mg Sod, 22 g Carb, 18 g Sugar, 2 g Fib, 5 g Prot, 42 Calc.

FYI   The easiest way to pit cherries is with a cherry pitter. There are two types: a pitter that resembles a single-hole punch that removes the pit from one cherry at a time and a pitter that is composed of a clear plastic container and a trigger. The cherries are dropped into a chute and the trigger is pressed to remove each pit. Single-pit cherry pitters also make quick work of removing olive pits.

Grand Marnier–Macerated Fruit with Toasted Pound Cake

 serves **4**   20 min

PER SERVING

2 tablespoons orange juice

2 cups fresh strawberries, hulled and thickly sliced

1 papaya, peeled, seeded, and diced

1 apple, unpeeled, cored, and diced

2 nectarines or peaches, halved, pitted, and cut into wedges

2 apricots, halved, pitted, and cut into wedges

2 tablespoons Grand Marnier or Cointreau

2 tablespoons sugar

2 teaspoons grated orange zest

4 (1-ounce) slices fat-free pound cake, toasted

1 tablespoon chopped fresh mint

1   Gently toss together all ingredients except pound cake and mint in large bowl. Cover bowl with piece of plastic wrap and refrigerate at least 1 hour or up to 4 hours.

2   Place 1 slice of pound cake on each of 4 plates. Top each slice of cake with 1 cup fruit salad and sprinkle evenly with mint.

PER SERVING (1 slice cake and 1 cup fruit with juice): 220 Cal, 1 g Total Fat, 0 g Sat Fat, 0 g Trans Fat, 0 mg Chol, 99 mg Sod, 49 g Carb, 32 g Sugar, 5 g Fib, 3 g Prot, 45 Calc.

FYI   Grilling the slices of pound cake in a panini maker will make this dessert even more enticing.

Lush No-Bake Lemon Cheesecakes

½ cup low-fat (1%) milk

1¼ teaspoons grated lemon zest

1 large egg yolk

½ cup sugar

1 envelope unflavored gelatin

Pinch salt

1 (15-ounce) container fat-free ricotta cheese

¼ cup fresh lemon juice

½ teaspoon vanilla extract

1 Combine milk and lemon zest in small glass measure; microwave on High until it boils, 1½–2 minutes. Cover and let stand 15 minutes. Pour through fine sieve into heatproof medium bowl; whisk in egg yolk.

2 Set bowl over medium saucepan of simmering water (make sure bowl is not touching simmering water); cook, whisking constantly, until very pale, about 5 minutes. Gradually whisk in sugar, gelatin, and salt; cook, whisking constantly, until mixture is slightly thickened, about 5 minutes longer. Wearing oven mitts, remove bowl from saucepan and let mixture cool to room temperature, whisking occasionally.

3 Puree ricotta in food processor. Whisk ricotta, lemon juice, and vanilla into cooled gelatin mixture. Pour into 4 dessert dishes or glasses, dividing evenly. Loosely cover each dish with piece of plastic wrap; refrigerate until set, at least 3 hours or up to overnight.

PER SERVING (1 cheesecake): 173 Cal, 1 g Total Fat, 1 g Sat Fat, 0 g Trans Fat, 62 mg Chol, 188 mg Sod, 26 g Carb, 23 g Sugar, 0 g Fib, 17 g Prot, 377 Calc.

FYI Steeping the lemon zest in the hot milk infuses the milk with a delicate and enticing fresh lemon flavor and aroma.

Lush No-Bake Lemon Cheesecakes

Recipes by *Points Plus*⊕ value

Strawberry-Vanilla Sundaes with
   Summery Fruit, 353
Succulent Braised Pork Loin Asian-Style,
   133
Sweet Chili–Glazed Chicken Breasts with
   Pineapple & Cilantro, 273
Tabbouleh-Style Barley Salad, 21
Tandoori-Style Kebabs with Zucchini-
   Tomato Salad, 280
Tea-Smoked Salmon with Bok Choy &
   Radishes, 284
Tex-Mex Turkey Salad with Cilantro-Lime
   Dressing, 8
Thyme-Scented Halibut with Roasted
   Mixed Mushrooms, 190
Tortilla Casserole with Tomatillo Salsa, 219
Triple-Berry Bread Pudding, 309
Tropical Papaya-Shrimp Salad, 17
Turkey, Chutney & Cheddar Paninis, 301
Turkey Sausage Fajitas with Mushrooms &
   Peppers, 283
Tuscan Pork with Cremini Mushrooms &
   Rosemary, 171
Tuscan White Beans with Tomatoes, Basil
   & Shrimp, 245
Vegetable Sandwiches with Lemon-Basil
   Goat Cheese, 291
Warm Cherries with Goat Cheese &
   Thyme, 357
Wild Blueberry–Cornmeal Waffles, 298
Zesty Arugula & Tomato Salad–Topped
   Turkey Cutlets, 51

PointsPlus value: 6

BBQ-Sauced Turkey & Slaw Salad, 8
Beef & Root Vegetable Stew, 306
Bittersweet Chocolate–Orange Fondue, 312
Bulgur Salad with Citrus & Mint, 21
Chicken & Mixed Mushroom Tetrazzini,
   206
Creamy Chicken & Cantaloupe Salad, 5
Crisp Cod Cakes with Tomato-Peach Salad,
   57
Dried Fruit & Oat Porridge, 98
Easy & Delicious Chicken Mole, 147
Eggs in Purgatory, 39
French Country-Style Chicken Stew, 240
Grand Marnier–Macerated Fruit with
   Toasted Pound Cake, 357
Grilled Colombian-Style Flank Steak &
   Okra with Creamy Avocado, 263
Heavenly Hots, 37
Indian-Spiced Chicken with Apple &
   Onion, 185

Lemon–Chocolate Chip Ice Cream, 353
Lemony Arctic Char with Arugula-
   Cucumber Salad, 300
Lots of Whole Grains & Honey Waffles, 297
Maine-Style Crab Rolls, 27
Mixed Seafood Stew with Fennel & Orange,
   151
Moo Shu Chicken, 80
Moroccan Fish with Potatoes & Tomatoes,
   194
Olive Oil–Cornmeal Cake with
   Strawberries, 320
Open-Face Gruyère–Vegetable Melts, 39
Orange-Brined Turkey Breast with Fresh
   Cranberry Sauce, 188
Pasta, Bacon & Roasted Pepper Frittata,
   246
Pumpkin Belgian Waffles, 299
Red Curry Tofu-Noodle Bowl, 40
Shrimp & Sausage Gumbo, 243
Shrimp in Coconut Curry Sauce, 86
Split Pea & Spinach Soup, 109
Strawberry, Mozzarella & Thyme Paninis,
   304
Striped Bass Fillets with Fresh Artichokes
   & Cherry Tomatoes, 192
Three-Cheese Polenta Lasagna, 216
Turkey-Parmesan Meatball & Escarole
   Soup, 249
Turkey Sausage with Sun-Dried Tomato
   Couscous, 55
Weekend Roast Beef with Crusty Potatoes,
   163
Wild Salmon with Strawberry-Avocado
   Salsa, 191

PointsPlus value: 7

All-Tossed-Together Cobb Salad, 5
Beef & Asparagus Stir-Fry, 70
Beef Tenderloin with Port Wine Pan Sauce,
   165
Cajun Shrimp & Chile–Corn Bread
   Casserole, 214
Cape Cod Shrimp & Corn Chowder, 103
Cauliflower, Zucchini & Chickpea Biryani,
   220
Cheese, Beef & Noodle Casserole, 200
Chicken in White Wine, 139
Chicken Strips with Bok Choy & Udon
   Noodles, 80
Chicken-Tomatillo Chili with Cilantro &
   Sour Cream, 143
Chicken-Tortilla Soup with Corn &
   Avocado, 100

Chili-Rubbed Tenderloin with Spanish
   Peppers & Potatoes, 166
Chock-Full-of-Vegetables Split Pea Soup,
   109
Chunky Beef & Bean Chili, 233
Chunky Lobster & Cantaloupe Salad, 17
Cincinnati Four-Way Chili, 131
Deep Dark Mocha Pudding, 347
Easy Tomato, Rice & Corn Casserole, 217
Feta-Topped Pasta, Tomato & Pea Salad,
   19
Garlicky Chicken-Scallion Stir-Fry, 78
Greek-Style Pasta Salad, 20
Kofta Kebabs over Blueberry-Mint
   Couscous, 269
Korean-Style Soft Tacos, 276
Lamb-Bulgur Meatballs in Quick Tomato
   Sauce, 48
Leg of Lamb with Aleppo Pepper &
   Lemony Couscous Salad, 268
Lemon-Infused Scallops with Snow Peas,
   90
Lemony Brown Rice & Spinach Salad,
   20
Low-Country Gumbo, 101
Margarita Chicken with Charred Corn,
   275
Mexican Gazpacho Chicken Salad, 7
Milk Chocolate Fondue, 310
Mojo Pork Chops with Grilled Plantains,
   267
No-Fuss French-Style Beef Stew, 129
No-Fuss Meatless Skillet Lasagna, 60
Open-Face Chicken Paninis Vietnamese-
   Style, 301
Pepper-Rubbed Filets Mignons with Hobo-
   Pack Potatoes, 262
Picadillo-Style Shepherd's Pie with
   Chipotle Mashed Potatoes, 199
Pork Chops with Cabbage, Apple &
   Caraway, 134
Pot-Roasted Lamb with Tomatoes &
   Garlic, 136
Pork Tenderloin with Thyme-Scented
   Root Vegetables, 174
Roast Beef Salad with Grapefruit, Basil &
   Shallots, 4
Roast Chicken with Rustic Bread Stuffing,
   180
Sausage & Pepper Bread Pudding, 210
Smoked Paprika–Rubbed Cornish Hens
   with Caraway Onions, 282
Spinach & Provolone–Stuffed Chicken, 54
Sunday Supper Braciole, 43
Thai Vegetable & Tofu Stir-Fry, 93

PointsPlus value: 8

Asian Flavors Shrimp Salad Sandwiches, 25

Beef with Tomatoes & Green Beans in Black Bean Sauce, 68

Beef & Vegetable Sukiyaki, 69

Bibimbap, 73

Charred Beef Salad with Noodles & Mixed Greens, 44

Chicken & Dumplings, 145

Chunky Pork & Tomato Coconut Green Curry, 135

Classic Black Bean Soup, 108

Classic Pasta with Ragu, 130

Coconut Curry, Chicken & Rice Casserole, 209

Cuban-Style Picadillo, 45

Dilled Salmon Salad with Lemon-Buttermilk Dressing, 10

Edamame, Asparagus & Tomatoes with Thin Spaghetti, 117

Filet Mignon & Mushroom Stroganoff, 42

French Peasant-Style Fish Soup, 102

Fresh Tomato–Red Onion Sauce with Penne, 119

Garlic Roast Chicken with Crisp Potatoes & Mushrooms, 178

Honey Chicken with Cashews, 79

Italian Pot Roast, 232

Lamb, Eggplant & Orzo Casserole, 203

Lemon-Oregano Drumsticks with Artichokes & Potatoes, 186

Lemongrass & Shrimp Fried Rice, 87

Linguine with Turkey Bolognese, 116

Lobster Mac 'n' Cheese, 61

Panko-Topped Chicken & Sausage Cassoulet, 207

Penne with Feta, Roasted Zucchini & Fennel, 194

Perfect Summer Lobster Salad, 18

Pizza-Style Baked Pasta, 211

Porcini-Crusted Beef with Lemony Potatoes, 168

Pork Tenderloin in Sour Cream–Paprika Sauce, 46

Posole with Cheddar, Scallions & Cilantro, 150

Provençal Lamb with Tomatoes, Onions & Olives, 177

Pulled Pork & Cabbage Sandwiches, 234

Rustic Beef Short Ribs with Mustard Sauce, 231

Saigon Shrimp & Cellophane Noodle Salad, 14

Scallop Fried Rice, 88

Shredded Chicken Ragu with Pasta, 241

Shrimp, Avocado & Greens Paninis, 302

Spicy Beef Salad with Chipotle-Lime Dressing, 4

Stir-Fried Beef, Corn & Peppers Tex Mex–Style, 71

Stir-Fried Chicken Greek-Style, 79

Stracotto with Lemon Gremolata, 125

Street Fair Sausage, Potatoes & Peppers, 56

Summer Vegetable Risotto, 245

Szechuan Chicken with Noodles, 76

Tomato & Basil–Topped Halibut with Golden Onions, 191

Turkey–Mango Chutney Sandwiches, 24

Two-Bean Vegetarian Chili, 154

Vegetable & Chickpea Couscous, 157

Yogurt Pancakes with Any Berry Sauce, 36

PointsPlus value: 9

Barley Risotto with Mushrooms, Sausage & Tomato, 113

Butterflied Quail with Fresh Raspberry Sauce, 187

Crispy Chicken Parmesan Casserole, 206

Fragrant Indian-Spiced Lamb Stew, 47

Fresh Corn & Blueberry Pancakes, 35

Halibut Seviche with Corn & Avocado, 12

Lamb Burgers with Charred Onions & Feta, 270

Leg of Lamb with Eggplant, Zucchini & Tomato, 174

Mixed Mushroom–Tempeh Chili, 155

Moroccan Lamb Stew with Prunes & Cinnamon, 137

Mustard & Thyme–Rubbed Lamb Roast with Flageolets, 175

Saffron Clam Sauce with Capellini, 117

Sauerbraten, 126

Sausage & Bean Chili, 242

Shrimp & Kielbasa Jambalaya, 111

Singapore Noodles, 82

Smoky Chicken-Seafood Paella, 50

Spaghetti Carbonara with Broccoli & Bacon, 60

Spiced Chicken with Spinach-Almond Couscous, 144

Winter Squash & Sage Risotto, 114

Wok-Seared Wild Salmon with Asparagus, 85

PointsPlus value: 10

Beef Stew Burgundy-Style, 233

Bolognese Sauce with Bacon & Fennel, 45

Bombay Pork with Basmati Rice, 75

Chicken & Tomatillo Enchilada Casserole, 204

Chicken with Saffron Rice, 112

Chicken with Shiitake Mushrooms & Thyme, 142

Cowboy Stew, 127

Irish Stew with Potatoes, Pearl Onions & Carrots, 238

Pork Chop & Bean Cassoulet, 236

Provençal Chicken & Mussel Pot, 140

Risotto with Shrimp, Peas & Parmesan, 244

Szechuan Orange-Ginger Beef, 66

Thai Seafood Pot, 105

Turkey Salad with Chutney, Cashews & Cranberries, 9

TVP Bolognese & Pasta Casserole, 225

Weeknight Skillet Chicken & Rice, 51

Yankee Pot Roast, 124

PointsPlus value: 11

Chicken Pot au Feu, 241

Lamb & Apricot Tagine, 237

Scandinavian-Style Beef, 129

Tomato-Mushroom Bolognese with Whole Grain Linguine, 246

PointsPlus value: 12

Rabbit in Sour Cream Sauce with Cherry Tomatoes & Noodles, 148

Index

Page numbers in italics indicate illustrations.